Human Rights Controver

The Impact of Legal Form

Many countries confront similar human rights controversies, but despite the claimed universality of human rights values, they are not always resolved in the same way. Why?

What role do local legal conditions play? More specifically, does the domestic 'legal form' of human rights have a significant impact on the processes and outcomes of policy debates, law reform and decision-making on controversial issues? Is human rights discourse a more potent force in a country where rights are expressly recognised than they are in a country where there is a tradition of respect for underlying values, but where no bill of rights has been enacted? If bills of rights are influential, is a constitutionally entrenched model more effective than statutory models when it comes to the effective injection of human rights considerations into public discourse?

In this book, comparative socio-legal examination of three recent controversies – double jeopardy reform, recognition of same-sex relationships and the operation of hate speech laws – in four countries – Australia, Canada, New Zealand and the United Kingdom – provides a foundation for offering answers to these questions. Examination of these controversies suggests that differences in the design of domestic legal institutions and procedures for the injection of human rights values into legal decision-making processes can have a powerful effect on the manner in which human rights issues are constructed, handled and resolved.

Luke McNamara is an Associate Professor in the Faculty of Law, University of Wollongong, Australia.

Human Rights Controversies

The Impact of Legal Form

Luke McNamara

a GlassHouse book

First published 2007
by Routledge-Cavendish
2 Park Square, Milton Park, Abingdon, Oxon OX14 4RN, UK

Simultaneously published in the USA and Canada
by Routledge-Cavendish
270 Madison Ave, New York, NY 10016

A GlassHouse book

Routledge-Cavendish is an imprint of the Taylor & Francis Group, an informa business

© 2007 Luke McNamara

Typeset in Times and Gill Sans by
RefineCatch Limited, Bungay, Suffolk
Printed and bound in Great Britain by
Antony Rowe Ltd, Chippenham, Wiltshire

All rights reserved. No part of this book may be reprinted or reproduced or utilised in any form or by any electronic, mechanical, or other means, now known or hereafter invented, including photocopying and recording, or in any information storage or retrieval system, without permission in writing from the publishers.

British Library Cataloging in Publication Data
A catalogue record for this book is available from the British Library

Library of Congress Cataloging-in-Publication Data
McNamara, Luke.
  Human rights controversies : the impact of legal form /
Luke McNamara.
    p. cm.
  ISBN-13: 978–1–904385–32–5 (hbk.)
  ISBN-13: 978–0–415–42038–9 (pbk.)
 1. Human rights.   I. Title.
  K3240.M388   2007
  341.4′8—dc22
                                                    2006022254

ISBN10: 1–904385–32–X (hbk)
ISBN10: 0–415–42038–5 (pbk)
ISBN10: 0–203–94514–X (ebk)

ISBN13: 978–1–904385–32–5 (hbk)
ISBN13: 978–0–415–42038–9 (pbk)
ISBN13: 978–0–203–94514–8 (ebk)

Contents

Acknowledgments vii
Table of cases ix
Table of statutes xv

1 Introduction: Universal human rights in a world of localities 1

Introduction 1
The present study 5
Rationale for case study selection 6
Rationale for comparative analysis 8
Rationale for country selection 10
Approaching the correlation between form and quality 11
Legal form 13
Legal culture 15
Measuring the effect of legal form 18
Common [law] traditions and contemporary differences 19
Overview of chapters 36

2 Rolling back an established human right: 'Reforming' the rule against double jeopardy 37

Introduction 37
The merits of double jeopardy protection under scrutiny 43
United Kingdom 47
New Zealand 60
Canada 74
Australia 78
Conclusions 92

3   **Pushing the boundaries of human rights protection: Equality and the recognition of same-sex relationships**   99

*Introduction 99
Same-sex marriage: the demand for recognition 102
Legal responses and the impact of human rights discourse 104
Canada 105
United Kingdom 119
New Zealand 129
Australia 142
Conclusions 154*

4   **Balancing 'competing' human rights: Drawing the free speech/hate speech line**   159

*Introduction 159
International law obligations 164
United Kingdom 167
Canada 187
New Zealand 208
Australia 225
Conclusions 246*

5   **Conclusion: Does legal form matter?**   251

*Canada 252
United Kingdom 255
New Zealand 257
Australia 259
How legal form matters 262*

Bibliography   265
Index   295

Acknowledgments

A contemporary multi-country study of this sort is really only possible with the encouragement, support and assistance of many people. Whether they took the form of a quick email, a more substantial conversation, or regular exchanges, my communications with the following people were invaluable: Robin Allen, Kate Beattie, Calum Bennachie, Stuart Beresford, Aaron Berg, Christine Boyle, Gillian Calder, Paul Chartrand, Nigel Christie, Brenda Cossman, Gareth Crossman, Joris de Bres, Douglas Elliot, David Farrier, Alex Frame, Martin Friedland, Ryan Goodman, Leslie Green, Robert Hallowell, Rodney Harrison, Simon Healy, Janet Hiebert, Ran Hirschl, Rebecca Johnson, Dean Knight, Dino Kritsiotis, Kathleen Lahey, Alison Laurie, Nicole LaViolette, Juris Lavrikovs, Cameron Law, Hester Lessard, Sheila McIntyre, Eric Metcalfe, Gay Morgan, Peter Noorlander, Scott Optican, Jeremy Patrick, Wes Pue, David Rayside, Paul Rishworth, Kent Roach, Paul Roberts, Anthony Robinson, Bruce Ryder, David Schneiderman, Nan Seuffert, Anne Smith, Miriam Smith, Sarah Spencer, Alex Steel, Patrick Stevens, Lee Stuesser, Seamus Taylor, Micheal Vonn, Jeremy Webber, Lorraine Weinrib, Leah Whiu, Robert Wintemute, Bruce Ziff.

This book came to life during a sabbatical year at the Irish Centre for Human Rights (ICHR), National University of Ireland, Galway in 2004. I would like to thank Bill Schabas and the staff and students of the ICHR for providing an ideal environment for turning an idea into a research project. I am also grateful for the continuing support and encouragement of my colleagues at the University of Wollongong.

I acknowledge the financial support of the University of Wollongong, including a University Research Committee Small Grant in 2003 and a Study Leave Assistance Grant in 2004, and the Canadian Government, in the form of a Canadian Studies Faculty Research Award in 2005. This book also draws on research undertaken in Canada in 2002 with the support of grants from the Law Society of NSW Legal Scholarship Support Fund and the Legal Research Institute, Faculty of Law, University of Manitoba.

Thanks to Beverley Brown, the original Commissioning Editor for this book, and to Colin Perrin, Madeleine Langford and the staff at Routledge–Cavendish.

To Karen, Josie and Grace, thank you for tolerating the times that I have been 'away' while working on this book (overseas, in my office, in my study, in another world!).

The chapters in this book have benefited from the presentation of earlier versions at the following conferences and seminars: *Workshop: Free Speech, Hate Speech and Human Rights in Australia*, National Europe Centre, Australian National University, 8–9 September 2006; School of Law, University of Waikato, 24 August 2005; *Law's Empire: A Critically Engaged Socio-Legal Conference*, Harrison Hot Springs, Canada, 25–30 June 2005; School of Law, University of Nottingham, 22 October 2004; Irish Centre for Human Rights, NUI Galway, 15 April 2004; School of Law, University of Newcastle, 17 October 2003; Socio-Legal Studies Association Annual Conference, Nottingham Law School, 14–16 April 2003; *Converging Futures? Australia and Canada in a New Millennium*, Biennial Conference of the Association for Canadian Studies in Australia and New Zealand, Canberra, 12–14 September 2002.

Parts of chapter 4 have previously been published in *Regulating Racism: Racial Vilification Laws in Australia*, Sydney Institute of Criminology Monograph Series No 16 (2002); and 'Negotiating the Contours of Unlawful Hate Speech: Regulation Under Provincial Human Rights Laws in Canada', 2005, 38(1), *University of British Columbia Law Review*, pp 1–82.

Luke McNamara
Wollongong

Table of cases

Abrams v North Shore Free Press Ltd and Collins (1999) 33 CHRR D/435 (British Columbia Human Rights Tribunal) 207
Alberta Report v Alberta Human Rights and Citizenship Commission, 2002 ABQB 1081 (Alberta Court of Queen's Bench) 207
Attorney-General v Guardian Newspapers (No 2) [1990] 1 AC 109 (England and Wales Court of Appeal) 20
Australian Capital Television v Commonwealth of Australia (1992) 177 CLR 106 (High Court of Australia) 232

Barbeau v British Columbia (Attorney General) (2003) 13 BCLR (4th) 1 (British Columbia Court of Appeal) 106, 107, 114, 132
Bellinger v Bellinger [2003] 2 AC 467 (House of Lords) 123
Bissett v Peters [2004] NZHRRT 33 (10 August 2004) (New Zealand Human Rights Review Tribunal) 221
Bropho v Human Rights and Equal Opportunity Commission and West Australian Newspapers Ltd [2002] FCA 1510 (Federal Court of Australia); [2004] FCAFC 16 (Full Court of the Federal Court of Australia) 242
Brutus v Cozens [1973] AC 854 (House of Lords) 179
Bryl v Melbourne Theatre Company [1999] HREOCA 11 (Human Rights and Equal Opportunity Commission) 240, 241

Canadian Human Rights Commission v Taylor [1990] 3 SCR 892 (Supreme Court of Canada) 160, 195, 196–7, 198, 199, 201, 204, 207, 222, 223
Canadian Jewish Congress v North Shore Free Press Ltd and Collins (1997) 30 CHRR D/5 (British Columbia Human Rights Tribunal) 204–5, 207
Catholic Civil Rights League v Hendricks, 2004 CanLII 20538 (Quebec Court of Appeal) 106
Citron and Toronto Mayor's Committee v Zundel, 2002 CanLII 23557 (Canadian Human Rights Tribunal) 190
Clark v R [2005] NZSC 23 (Supreme Court of New Zealand) 76
Coleman v Power [2004] HCA 39 (High Court of Australia) 231, 232–3, 236
Connelly v DPP [1964] AC 1254 (House of Lords) 48
Corunna v West Australian Newspapers Ltd (2001) EOC 93–146 (Human Rights and Equal Opportunity Commission) 238–43

Daniels v Thompson [1998] 3 NZLR 22 (New Zealand Court of Appeal) 60
Derbyshire County Council v Times Newspapers Ltd [1993] AC 535 (House of Lords) 174

DPP v Humphreys [1977] 1 AC 1 (House of Lords) 48

Egan v Canada [1995] 2 SCR 513 (Supreme Court of Canada) 105

Fairfax (John) Publications Ltd v Kazak [2002] NSWADTAP 35 (NSW
  Administrative Decisions Tribunal - Appeal Panel) 236, 237–8
Fardon v Attorney General of Queensland [2004] HCA 46 (High Court of
  Australia) 35
Fitzpatrick v Sterling Housing Association [1999] 4 All ER 795 (House of
  Lords) 122

Garaudy v France, no 65831/01, ECHR 2003-IX (European Court of Human
  Rights) 181
Ghaidan v Godin-Mendoza [2002] 4 All ER 1162 (England and Wales Court of
  Appeal); [2004] 3 All ER 411 (House of Lords) 29, 30, 122–3, 132
Gifford v Strang Patrick Stevedoring Pty Ltd [2003] HCA 33 (High Court of
  Australia) 233
Glimmerveen & Hagenbeek v The Netherlands, Nos 8348/78 & 8406/78
  18 DR 187, (11 October 1979) (European Commission for
  Human Rights) 181
Grdic v R [1985] 1 SCR 810 (Supreme Court of Canada) 76
Green v United States 355 US 184 (1957) (United States Supreme Court) 37
Gushue v R [1980] 1 SCR 798 (Supreme Court of Canada) 76

Hagan v Australia Communication No. 26/2002: Australia (14/04/2003)
  CERD/C/62/D/26/2002 (UN Committee on the Elimination of Racial
  Discrimination) 244
Hagan v Trustees of Toowoomba Sports Ground Trust [2000] FCA 1615
  (Federal Court of Australia); [2001] FCA 123 (Full Court of the Federal
  Court of Australia) 243
Halpern v Canada (Attorney General) (2003) 65 OR (3d) 161 (Ontario Court of
  Appeal) 106, 107, 114
Hammond v DPP [2004] EWHC 69 (Admin) (England and Wales High
  Court) 182
Handyside v United Kingdom (1979–80) 1 EHRR 737 (European Court of
  Human Rights) 174
Hellquist v Owens and Sterling Newspapers Co (2001) 40 CHRR D/197
  (Saskatchewan Board of Inquiry); 2002 SKQB 506 (Saskatchewan Court of
  Queen's Bench) 208
Hobart Hebrew Congregation & Jones v Scully (unreported 21 September 2000)
  (Australia Human Rights and Equal Opportunity Commission) 235

Islamic Council of Victoria v Catch the Fire Ministries Inc [2004] VCAT 2510
  (Victorian Civil and Administrative Tribunal); [2005] VCAT 1159 (Victorian
  Civil and Administrative Tribunal) 162

Jacobs v Fardig (1999) EOC 93–016 (Human Rights and Equal Opportunities
  Commission) 238
Jeffrey v Police [1994] 11 CRNZ 507 (High Court of New Zealand) 214
Jersild v Denmark (1994) 19 EHRR 1 (European Court of Human
  Rights) 176, 181, 182, 185
Jones v Scully [2002] FCA 1080 (Federal Court of Australia) 235

Joslin v New Zealand (2002) Communication No 902/1999: New Zealand
(30 July 2002 2003) CCPR/C/75/D/902/1999 (UN Human Rights
Committee).. 129, 133, 149

Kane and Jewish Defence League of Canada v Alberta Report et al (unreported,
Alberta Human Rights and Citizenship Commission Panel, 30 April 2002)...... 206
Kane v Alberta Report 2001 ABQB 570 (Alberta Court of Queen's
Bench).. 203–6, 208
Karner v Austria [2003] ECHR 395 (European Court of Human Rights)...... 104, 120
Kazak v John Fairfax Publications Ltd [2000] NSWADT 77 (NSW
Administrative Decisions Tribunal (Equal Opportunity Division))................ 235–6
King-Ansell v Police (1979) 2 NZLR 531 (New Zealand Court of
Appeal) 209, 216

Lange v Australian Broadcasting Corporation (1997) 189 CLR 520 (High Court
of Australia).. 232, 235
Layland v Ontario (1993) 14 OR(3d) 658 (Ontario Divisional Court).................. 115
Leeth v Commonwealth (1992) 174 CLR 455 (High Court of Australia) 233
Lehideux & Isorni v France [1998] ECHR 90 (European Court of Human
Rights) 181, 185
Levy v Victoria (1997) 189 CLR 579 (High Court of Australia) 232
Living Word Distributors Ltd v Human Rights Action Group [2000] NZCA
179 (New Zealand Court of Appeal)... 212, 215, 220

M v H [1999] 2 SCR 3 (Supreme Court of Canada) 106, 118, 132
McGlade v Human Rights and Equal Opportunity Commission [2000] FCA
1477 (Federal Court of Australia)... 238
McGlade v Lightfoot [1999] HREOCA 1 (Human Rights and Equal Opportunity
Commission); [2002] FCA 1457 (Federal Court of Australia).......................... 238
Moonen v Film and Literature Board of Review [2000] 2 NZLR 9 (New Zealand
Court of Appeal)... 27, 213, 220, 223

Nationwide News Pty Ltd v Wills (1992) 177 CLR 1 (High Court of
Australia)... 232
Neal v Sunday News Auckland Newspaper Publications Ltd [1985] 5 NZAR
234 (New Zealand equal Opportunity Tribunal).. 210
Nealy v Johnston (1989) 10 CHRR D/6450 (Canadian Human Rights
Tribunal).. 197
New Zealand Human Rights Commission Proceedings Commissioner v Archer
[1996] 3 HRNZ 123 (New Zealand Human Rights Tribunal) 218, 219, 220
Nilsen and Johnsen v Norway (1999) 30 EHRR 878 (European Court of Human
Rights)... 184
Norwood v DPP [2003] EWHC 1564 (Admin) (England and Wales High Court
(Administrative Court)).. 178, 180–1
Norwood v United Kingdom (2004) 40 EHRR SE 111 (European Court of
Human Rights)... 180

Owens v Saskatchewan Human Rights Commission 2006 SKCA 41 (Saskatchewan
Court of Appeal) 208

Percy v DPP [2001] EWHC Admin 1125 (England and Wales High Court
(Administrative Court)) 181–2

Procurator Fiscal v Brown (Scotland) [2000] UKPC D3 (Privy Council) 176

Quilter v Attorney-General [1998] 1 NZLR 523 (New Zealand
Court of Appeal).. 123, 129, 130–4, 139, 215

R v Ahenakew 2005 SKPC 76 (Provincial Court of Saskatchewan) 199–200
R v Andrews [1990] 3 SCR 870 (Supreme Court of Canada)... 195, 196, 198, 199, 207
R v Biniaris (2000) 143 CCC (3d) 1 (Supreme Court of Canada) 76
R v Budai, Gill & Kim (2001) 154 CCC (3d) 289 (British Columbia Court of
Appeal).. 74, 77
R v Buzzanga (1979) 49 CCC (2d) 369 (Ontario Court of Appeal)....................... 194
R v Carroll [2002] HCA 55 (High Court of
Australia)... 39, 47, 76, 78, 79–80, 90, 91, 92, 96
R v Central Independent TV [1994] 3 All ER 641 (England and Wales Court of
Appeal).. 174
R v Degnan [2001] 1 NZLR 280 (New Zealand Court of Appeal) 60
R v Dunlop [2000] EWJ No 6400 (Teesside Crown Court) 46, 93
R v Elms, 2005 CanLII 24759 (Ontario Superior Court).. 200
R v Harding (2001) 57 OR (3d) 333 (Ontario Court of Appeal) 199
R v Keegstra [1991] 2 WWR 1 (Supreme Court of
Canada)..................................... 160, 194–5, 196, 197, 198, 199, 201, 204, 207, 222
R v Krymowski [2005] 1 SCR 101 (Supreme Court of Canada)..................... 199, 200
R v Oakes [1986] 1 SCR 103 (Supreme Court of Canada)...................................... 204
R v Safadi (1993) 108 NFld & PEIR 66 (Prince Edward Island Supreme Court);
(1994) CanLII 3378 (Prince Edward Island Supreme Court - Appeal
Division)... 199
R v Z [2000] 2 AC 483 (House of Lords) 48, 60
Radio 2UE Sydney Pty Ltd v Burns [2005] NSWADTAP 69 (NSW Administrative
Decisions Tribunal - Appeal Panel) 236
Ross v New Brunswick School District No 15 (1996) 133 DLR (4th) 1 (Supreme
Court of Canada) 206

Sambasivam v Public Prosecutor Federation of Malaya [1950] AC 458 (Privy
Council) 48
Saskatchewan Human Rights Commission v Bell (1994) 114 DLR (4th) 370
(Saskatchewan Court of Appeal) 160, 199, 208
Schnell v Machiavelli and Associates Emprize Inc & Micka, 2002 Can LII 1887
(Canadian Human Rights Tribunal)... 201

Taylor v Canada (1983) Communication No 104/1981: Canada (6 April 1983)
CCPR/C/18/D/104/1981 (UN Human Rights Committee) 195
Thomas v News Group Newspapers Ltd [2001] EWCA Civ 1233 (England
and Wales Court of Appeal)... 160, 173, 183–5
Thorne v BBC [1967] 1 WLR 1104 (England and Wales Court of Appeal) 168
Toben v Jones [2003] FCAFC 137 (Full Court of the Federal Court of
Australia)... 242

Veloskey v Karagiannakis [2002] NSWADTAP 18 (NSW Administrative
Decisions Tribunal - Appeal Panel) 237
Vriend v Alberta [1998] 1 SCR 493 (Supreme Court of Canada)........................... 106

Warman v Kulbashian, 2006 CHRT 11 (Canadian Human Rights Tribunal)........ 201

Wilkinson v Kitzinger [2006] EWHC 2022 (Fam) (England and Wales
  High Court of Justice (Family Division)).. 128
Wilson v Procurator Fiscal [2005] ScotHC HCJAC_97 (Scottish High Court)...... 186

Young v Australia (2003) Communication No 941/2000: Australia (18 September
  2003) CCPR/C/78/D/941/2000 (UN Human Rights Committee) 104, 149

Zdrahal v Wellington City Council [1995] 1 NZLR 700 (High Court of
  New Zealand) 220

Table of statutes

Australian legislation
Anti-Discrimination Act 1977
 (NSW) 234, 236, 238
 s 20C(1) 237
 s 20C(2) 238
 s 20C(2)(c) 237
Anti-Discrimination Act 1991(Qld)
 s 124A.. 244
Charter of Human Rights and
 Responsibilities Act 2006
 (Victoria) 3, 33
 s 8(3).. 7
 s 15.. 7, 231
 s 26 42
Civil Unions Act 2006 (ACT) 144
Constitution 12
 s 51(21) 143
 s 51(xxi) 154
Crimes Act 1914 (Aust) 227, 228
Crimes (Appeal and Review) Act 2001
 (NSW) 260
 s 100–s 101 97
Crimes (Appeal and Review)
 Amendment (Double Jeopardy) Act
 2006 (NSW) 97, 260
Criminal Code 1913 (WA) 230
Criminal Procedure Act 1986 (NSW)
 s 156... 42, 79
Human Rights Act 2004
 (ACT)................................. 3, 32, 145
 s 8(3).. 7
 s 16 7
 s 16(2) 231
 s 24 42
 s 37 33
Legislation Review Act 1987 (NSW)
 s 8A(1).. 34
 s 8A(1)(b)(i) 84

Marriage Act 1961 .... 100, 146, 152
 s 5.. 100, 143
 s 88EA 151
Marriage Amendment Act 2004 100,
  114, 143, 144, 147, 148, 152, 153, 261
Racial and Religious Tolerance Act
 2001 (Victoria)............................. 162
Racial Discrimination Act 1975
 (Aust) 33, 161, 226, 227, 228, 234,
                235, 238, 239, 241, 246
 s 9 234
 s 18B 229
 s 18C............... 238, 239, 240, 241, 243
 s 18C(1) 228–9, 235
 s 18C(2) (3) 229
 s 18D 229, 235, 238, 239, 240,
                241, 242, 243, 246
 s 18D(a)–(b) 239, 241
Racial Hatred Act 1995 (Aust) 163,
                230, 238, 243, 245
Racial Vilification Act 1996 (SA)
 s 4 231
Relationships Act 2003 (Tasmania) .. 144
Sex Discrimination Act 1984 (Aust) ... 33
Superannuation Industry (Supervision)
 Act 1993 (Aust)
 s 10–s 10A..................................... 144
Superannuation Legislation Amendment
 (Choice of Superannuation Funds)
 Act 2004 (Aust)............................ 144
Vagrants, Gaming and Other Offences
 Act 1931 (Qld) 236

Canadian legislation
Anti-terrorism Act, SC 2001, c 41
 s 88 190
Canadian Bill of Rights, SC 1960,
 c 44 19

Canadian Charter of Rights and
Freedoms, Part 1 of the Constitution
Act 1982, being Schedule B of the
Canada Act 1982 (UK), 1982,
c 11 .... 9, 10, 15, 17, 21, 22,
24, 42, 62, 63, 69, 83, 105, 108,
111, 113, 115, 116, 117, 136, 139,
160, 163, 193, 194, 231, 251,
253, 254–5, 262, 263
s 1 .... 21, 24, 105, 106, 192, 196
s 2(b) 160, 192, 193, 195,
196, 198, 201, 204,
222, 224, 247, 254
s 11 71
s 11(h) 41, 48, 75, 76,
77, 78, 79, 93, 253
s 15 .... 105, 106, 108, 114,
115, 116, 118, 120, 124, 132,
143, 151, 157, 193, 197, 198,
233, 247, 253, 255
s 15(1) 105, 108, 192
s 27 .... 192, 193, 197, 198, 247
s 33 .... 17, 21, 22, 31, 76, 111,
112, 113, 119, 192, 253
s 33(1)–(4) 22
s 52(1) 21
Canadian Human Rights Act, RSC
1985, c H-6 .... 106, 190, 222
s 13 .... 190, 191, 194, 195, 196,
197, 198, 199, 201, 222
s 13(1) 196
Civil Rights Protection Act, RSBC
1996, c 49 192
Constitution Act, 1867 (UK), 30 & 31
Victoria, c 3
s 91(27) 188
Constitution Act 1982, being
Schedule B of the Canada Act 1982
(UK), 1982, c 11 .... 10, 21, 160
Criminal Code, RSC 1985, c C-46 76,
161, 187, 188, 191, 194
s 318(1)–(2) 189
s 318(4) 189
s 319 .... 161, 191, 195, 222
s 319(1) 189
s 319(2) 189, 194, 196, 197,
198, 199, 200, 201
s 319(3) 189
s 319(6) 190
s 676 77
s 676(1)(a) 76
s 686(4)(b) 76

Defamation Act, RSM 1987, c D20.. 187
s 19 192
Department of Justice Act, RSC 1985,
c J-2
s 4.1 .... 23, 25
s 4.1(1) 23
Family Law Act, RSO 1990, c F3 106
Human Rights, Citizenship and
Multiculturalism Act, RSA 2000,
c H-14
s 2 203
s 2(1) 203, 204, 206
s 2(1)(a)–(b) 206
s 2(2) 203, 204
s 3 .... 191–2, 203
Human Rights Code, RSBC 1996,
c 210
s 7 205
Marriage for Civil Purposes Act, SC
2005, c 33 .. 99, 105, 108, 113, 114, 139
s 2 99
Saskatchewan Human Rights Code, SS
1979, c S-24.1
s 14 208
Supreme Court Act, RSC 1985,
c 5–26 22

EU legislation
Charter of Fundamental Rights of the
European Union [2000] OJ C3641
Art 11 173
Art 21 120
Art 50 40
Directive 2000/78 (Framework Directive
on equal treatment) 120, 121, 125
Treaty of Amsterdam [1997] OJ
C340/1 120

International treaties and conventions
European Convention for the
Protection of Human Rights and
Fundamental Freedoms 10, 28, 30,
32, 34, 40, 41, 43, 48,
51, 52, 53, 55, 56, 57,
60, 62, 68, 69, 70, 89,
94, 97, 121, 122, 125, 126,
156, 186, 255, 256, 257, 263
Art 10 .... 160, 173, 174, 176,
180, 181, 182, 184,
186, 248, 256, 257
Art 10(1) 175, 180
Art 10(2) 174, 175, 180, 184

Art 14 .... 104, 119, 120, 122, 125, 126, 143, 151, 156, 174, 175, 180, 181, 233, 256
Art 17 .... 174, 175, 180, 181
Protocol 7 .... 68, 69
Art 4 .... 40, 41, 50, 51, 52, 53, 55, 57, 70, 71, 73, 86, 90, 92, 94, 95, 96, 256
Art 4(1) 40
Art 4(2) 40, 52, 56, 68
Protocol 12 104
International Convention on the Elimination of All Forms of Racial Discrimination 101, 144, 159, 161, 164, 165, 166, 168, 187, 196, 208, 226
Art 4 .... 161, 164–5, 166, 167, 175, 188, 194, 225, 230, 242, 247
Art 5 .... 164, 165, 167
Art 14 144
International Convention on the Elimination of Discrimination Against Women 101
International Covenant on Civil and Political Rights 10, 20, 33, 35, 53, 55, 56, 57, 60, 61, 62, 68, 69, 73, 87, 88, 89, 92, 96, 140, 149, 196
Art 2 .... 133, 149
Art 6 149
Art 14 40–1
Art 14(7) 37, 40, 41, 51, 53, 54, 55, 56, 57, 61, 63, 68, 85, 86, 87, 88, 90, 95
Art 19 ...... 161, 165, 166, 167, 195, 242
Art 20 ...... 165, 166, 167, 175, 195, 210
Art 21–Art 22 166
Art 23 133
Art 26 .... 104, 129, 133, 134, 143, 161, 165
Universal Declaration of Human Rights 140, 164

New Zealand legislation
Bill of Rights Act 1990 .... 10, 15, 21, 24, 26, 27, 28, 29, 30, 43, 61, 62, 65, 66, 67, 68, 69, 71, 72, 73, 83, 95, 96, 97, 130, 131, 132, 134, 135, 136, 139, 140, 156, 163, 214, 215, 216, 217, 222, 224, 257, 258
s 4 .... 24, 26, 30, 96
s 5 .... 24, 27, 61, 63, 67, 137, 213, 214, 219

s 6 .... 26–7, 30, 123, 130, 131, 132, 133
s 7 .... 25, 26, 31, 63, 65, 66, 142, 219
s 14 .... 160, 212, 213, 214, 215, 219, 220, 222, 223, 224, 249
s 19 .... 27, 123, 129, 130, 131, 132, 135, 136, 142, 143, 151, 156, 215, 220, 233, 258
s 19(1) 129, 213
s 26 61
s 26(2) 41, 43, 48, 60, 61, 63, 64, 65, 66, 67, 68, 69, 71, 72, 73, 95, 96, 258
s 26(3) 63
Civil Union Act 2004 .... 100, 129, 156, 157, 258
Crimes Act 1961 .... 38, 64
s 357–s 359 60
Films, Videos and Publications Classification Act 1993 .... 212, 215
Human Rights Act 1993 .... 134, 135, 136, 137, 139, 140, 156, 161, 210, 212, 215, 216, 219, 221, 224, 249, 258
s 3 212
s 5 135
s 21(1)(m) 129
s 61 .... 211–12, 214, 216, 217, 219, 220, 221, 222, 223, 224, 249
s 92J 27
s 92K(2) 27–8
s 131 .... 211, 216, 219, 223, 224
Human Rights Amendment Act 2001 .... 27, 135
Human Rights Commission Act 1977 210
Marriage Act 1955 .... 123, 129, 130, 131, 133, 134, 141, 142
Property (Relationship) Amendment Act 2001 135
Race Relations Act 1971 .... 208, 209, 210, 212
s 9A 209, 210, 216
s 9A(1) 209
s 25 .... 208–9, 210, 216
Relationships (Statutory References) Act 2005 138
Resource Management Act 1991 220

United Kingdom legislation
Civil Partnership Act 2004 .... 100, 120, 127, 156, 256, 257

Crime and Disorder Act 1998........... 171
   s 28.. 171, 178
   s 31.. 171, 178
Criminal Justice Act 2003 ...... 38, 41, 43,
   45, 49, 50, 51, 56, 57, 64, 67, 69, 70,
   76, 81, 82, 86, 88, 93, 96, 255, 257
Criminal Procedure and Investigations
   Act 1996 81
   s 54.. 46, 48
Employment Equality (Sexual
   Orientation) Regulations 2003 121
Human Rights Act 1998 .... 10, 15, 21,
   27, 28, 29, 31, 41, 43, 48,
   49, 50, 51, 59, 62, 69, 71,
   83, 89, 91, 94, 121, 122, 123,
   125, 126, 156, 157, 160, 163, 173,
   174, 184, 186, 187, 251, 255, 256
   s 2 29
   s 3. 29, 30, 122, 123, 132, 133, 182, 256
   s 3(1)... 29
   s 3(2)(b) 29
   s 4 .... 29, 31
   s 12(4).. 184
   s 19 31–2
   s 19(1).. 32
Penalties for Disorderly Behaviour
   (Amount of Penalty) (Amendment
   No 2) Order 2004......................... 177
Prevention of Incitement to Hatred Act
   (Northern Ireland) 1970 171
Protection from Harassment Act
   1997 .... 183, 184, 185
   s 1 .... 172–3, 183

s 2 173
s 3 173
s 3(2)... 183
s 7 173
Public Order Act 1936...................... 168
   s 5 .... 169–70, 177
   s 5A 169, 170, 177
Public Order Act 1986............. 161, 162,
   171, 172, 177, 186
   s 3(4) 171–2
   s 5.......................... 170, 171, 172, 177,
   178, 180, 181, 182
   s 5(1) 170–1
   s 5(3) 171, 180
   s 6(4)... 171
   s 18 .... 170, 171, 176, 177, 178, 180
   s 18(1)... 170
   s 19 186
   s 29B 171
   s 29B(5)..................................... 171–2
   s 29J.. 172
Public Order (Northern Ireland) Order
   1987 171
Race Relations Act 1965................... 167
   s 6 .... 168, 169, 177
   s 6(1)... 168
Racial and Religious Hatred Act
   2006 .... 162, 171, 172
Rent Act 1977 .... 30, 122, 132, 133

United States legislation
United States Constitution, 1787...... 231
   First Amendment, 1791 ..... 197–8, 224

Chapter 1

Introduction: Universal human rights in a world of localities

Introduction

This book is a comparative study of the local resolution of controversies about the scope and significance of 'universal' human rights. It is motivated by three observations about the practices of, and scholarship surrounding, contemporary law and politics – all of which prompt further inquiry about the way in which law is implicated in the resolution of human rights controversies.

First, the discourse of human rights is an undeniable feature of political and legal debates around social justice and law reform at the global level of international law and relations, and within the domestic law and policy development and implementation processes ('local legal cultures') of many countries throughout the world. As Hiebert has observed, human rights are increasingly portrayed as 'critical standards for evaluating the merits of state actions . . .'.[1] Whatever reservations may be expressed about the usefulness of 'rights' as a category of legal analysis, or the desirability of rights assertions as vehicles for pursuing particular goals,[2] even the most sceptical of rights sceptics would have to agree that human rights discourse occupies a prominent position on the stage of policy debate and law reform in relation to a broad range of issues.[3]

Such is the ubiquity of rights discourse, political claims are often articulated as rights assertions even in contexts where the domestic legal infrastructure may appear to provide only a very weak foundation for such claims. Gearty has observed that 'few phrases are more often used or abused than "human rights"'.[4] Feinberg has referred to the practice of 'propositional claiming': asserting a right that is not generally recognised 'to make sure people listen'.[5]

---

1 Hiebert, 2002, p 200.
2 See, e.g., Glendon, 1991; Bakan, 1997.
3 Schmidt and Halliday, 2004; Ignatieff, 2000.
4 Gearty, 1993, p 93. See also Darrow and Alston, 1999; Schmidt and Halliday, 2004.
5 Feinberg, cited in Gunther, 1999, p 136.

To assert a human right as a justification for law reform, against law reform, or for a particular interpretation of law is essentially a political claim. Pursuing the claim using the discourse of human rights is usually designed to enhance the success prospects of the claim – by investing the claim with greater legitimacy or greater weight or purchase in the processes of policy-making, law reform or adjudication – including making it more likely that the claim will trump competing interests or values[6] (which, of course, may also be articulated as human rights claims). Beverley McLachlin (currently the Chief Justice of the Supreme Court of Canada) has referred to constitutional bills of rights like the Canadian Charter of Rights and Freedoms 1982 as providing 'an incontestable foundation for the assertion of individual and minority rights . . .'.[7]

The impetus for express domestic *legalisation*[8] or *constitutionalisation*[9] of human rights is undoubtedly strongly based in the idea/assumption that this creates a legal/political environment (legal culture) in which human rights are more likely to be respected and specific human rights claims are more likely to succeed, by rendering particular outcomes as legal imperatives rather than policy choices. The aim is to embed the trumping capacity of human rights discourse within the legal/political culture.

Of course, just because rights-claiming has become commonplace is no reason to assume that it is necessarily an effective political strategy. On the contrary, its very prevalence may be considered to raise questions about whether its currency is necessarily devalued. For example, Hastrup has suggested that 'For all the positive connotations, the constant appeal to "rights" might even entail a remarkable inflation.'[10]

Whether or not this is so, it is axiomatic that bills of rights do not guarantee progressive outcomes.[11] Sometimes rights claims 'work', and sometimes they don't.[12] This book aims to shed some light on when and why particular instances of rights-claiming work. What are the variables? In particular, what difference (if any) does legal form make?

Second, a related debate that has also exercised minds over the years is whether a bill of rights – that is, a formal legislative codification or constitutional entrenchment of human rights[13] – is a necessary component of the

---

6 See Stychin, 1998, p 137.
7 McLachlin, 1996, p 21.
8 See Meckled-Garcia and Cali, 2006.
9 See Hirschl, 2004.
10 Hastrup, 2001b, p 13.
11 Tushnet, 1996, p 5; Stychin, 1998, p 17.
12 Banakar, 2004.
13 The majority of domestic bills of rights are modelled, to a lesser or greater extent, on the rights contained in the International Covenant on Civil and Political Rights, to which, as of May 2006, there were 156 states parties: Office of the United Nations High Commissioner for Human Rights, 2006a.

legal infrastructure of a rights-respecting legal culture. If this answer is given in the affirmative, is a constitutionally entrenched bill of rights a 'better' rights protector than a statutory bill of rights? – the latter often being characterised as a compromise instrument; the compromise struck with an eye to respecting the democratic principle of legislative supremacy. As most countries have, over the years, adopted one or another model for the domestic legal recognition of human rights, the debate over the relative merits of different institutional set-ups has tended to fade. However, in some countries, including my own, the debate remains a live one, although one that has usually been conducted, in recent times, at the margins of mainstream policy-making and law reform processes.

The Australian experience is emblematic. Despite a series of failed attempts to have a national bill of rights adopted,[14] advocates continue to make the case,[15] buoyed in recent years by the Australian Capital Territory legislature's enactment of the Human Rights Act 2004 (ACT),[16] and the introduction of a Charter of Human Rights and Responsibilities in Victoria in 2006.[17]

Frequently, the argument in favour of a bill of rights is advanced on the basis of the inherent superiority or strength of a legislative or constitutional recognition model.[18] At the same time, arguments against a bill of rights also tend to rely on assumptions about the negative impacts of the legislative or constitutional codification of human rights, which are not necessarily grounded in practical operation and experience.[19] On both sides of the debate there is limited 'hard' evidence on whether it matters one way or the other – in liberal democratic political systems which purport to endorse general principles of human dignity, freedom, equality and non-discrimination – whether such values are reflected in common law principles, legislative provisions or constitutional articles.[20]

Third, international human rights institutions and advocates are increasingly emphasising the need for effective domestic implementation of

14 O'Neill *et al*, 2004, pp 89–93.
15 Alston, 1994; Charlesworth, 2002a; Williams, 2004; Thampapillai, 2005; Griffith, 2006. See also, New Matilda's Human Rights Bill 2006, produced as part of a campaign for a national bill of rights: www.humanrightsact.com.au
16 Papers from the conference 'Assessing the First Year of the ACT Human Rights Act, Australian National University Canberra, 29 June 2005, are available at http://cigj.anu.edu.au/events/ACTBill05.php
17 Charter of Human Rights and Responsibilities Act 2006 (Vic). The introduction of the Charter followed recommendations from a Victorian Department of Justice working party (see Victoria, Human Rights Consultation Committee 2005).
18 Charlesworth, 2002; Australian Capital Territory Bill of Rights Consultative Committee, 2003; Behrendt, 2003; Williams, 2004.
19 Carr, 2001; Loughlin, 2001; Williams, 2003.
20 It is appropriate to concede that a focus on which *form of law* provides the optimal infrastructure for the realisation of human rights goals tends to presuppose the value of law in some form, and leave unchallenged the hegemony of law when it comes to human rights. See Evans, 2005.

'universal' standards at the level of local political/legal systems. Heyns and Viljoen have suggested that:

> At the beginning of the new millennium, it is clear that the concept of human rights is widely accepted as the 'idea of our time'. The conceptual battle is over, and the focus has shifted to the implementation of human rights.[21]

There is now a substantial body of literature examining the gap between international human rights law and domestic laws, and the issue of variations in interpretation of 'universal' norms at the domestic level. Some scholars have focused on the role of international institutions within the United Nations system,[22] or have attempted to measure the impact of international human rights treaties.[23] Others have addressed and compared the policy preferences and interpretive choices of domestic legislatures and courts.[24] Others still have addressed the implications of cultural diversity and globalisation for domestic compliance with universal international human rights norms.[25]

This research has shown that notwithstanding the claimed 'universality' of the values embodied in international human rights instruments, there is significant variation in the legal 'shape' of these so-called universal human rights values in different countries, and that there is a qualitative difference in the extent to which, in practice, individuals and groups in different states enjoy the human rights in question, and/or are able to use human rights law as a vehicle for achieving particular social justice goals.[26]

In this context, empirical research in the field of human rights implementation and enforcement has yet to adequately explore the question: whether the *legal form* in which human rights are recognised in domestic systems has any significant impact on the extent to which human rights are enjoyed,[27] or the extent to which human rights law can be successfully mobilised in pursuit of particular social justice goals. In addition, relatively little attention has been devoted to detailed examination of the impact of local legal cultures[28] as a mediating influence on the domestic implementation of international norms in the human rights field.[29] Yet, as Offord has observed:

---

21 Heyns and Viljoen, 2001, p 483. See also, Heyns and Viljoen, 2002.
22 Alston and Crawford, 2000; Bayefsky, 2001; Symonides, 2003.
23 Harland, 2000; Hathaway, 2002; Heyns and Viljoen, 2002; Goodman and Jinks, 2003.
24 Bailey, 1999; Kirby, 1999; Harland, 2000; Orlin *et al*, 2000; Tomlinson, 2001; Cram, 2002; Huscroft and Rishworth, 2002; Jayawickrama, 2002.
25 Falk, 2000; Patman, 2000; Cowan *et al*, 2001; Bell *et al*, 2000; Brysk, 2002; Donnelly, 2002.
26 Harland, 2000; Heyns and Viljoen, 2002; Jayawickrama, 2002; Niemi, 2003.
27 Goodman, 2004.
28 Nelken, 1997; Nelken and Feest, 2001. See also, Laquer in Ignatieff, 2001, p 131.
29 Hastrup, 2001a.

... global thought does not reproduce itself with consistency; it follows the contours of the local, is re-interpreted, and re-positioned in order to have meaning and purpose. Human rights nomenclature is one element of human rights consciousness, which is a modified, local event feeding from global language and thought.[30]

The present study

The question which this book aims to answer is located at the intersection of these three overlapping lines of inquiry: Does law, and the specifics of legal form, matter in the handling and resolution of political controversies where the discourse of human rights is mobilised on one or more sides of the debate?

This is not the sort of question that can be answered for all purposes, for all places, for all time. As Stychin has observed, it is not enough to recognise that 'the power of rights discourse is culturally specific' (with significant variation across even ostensibly similar 'western cultures'); it is also important to appreciate that 'the function of rights can shift over time within cultures'.[31]

It follows that this book does not set out to offer a general theory of the relationship between legal form and the quality of human rights enjoyment, but it does embark on the task of beginning to build an evidentiary base, which may allow for a degree of generalisation about where legal form sits in relation to the range of variables that moderate outcomes in particular instances. This approach has the potential to offer insights about 'optimal' legal mechanisms for promoting the enjoyment of human rights that are grounded in the tangible experiences of specific human rights controversies.

To these ends, this book is based on a comparative case-study approach. It examines the way in which three human rights controversies – reform of the rule against double jeopardy, legal recognition of same-sex relationships, and the operation of hate speech laws – have, in recent years, played out in four countries: Australia, Canada, New Zealand and the United Kingdom.

In each of the case studies, human rights discourse (norms, values and positive laws) has been mobilised in pursuit of particular human rights objectives – from protecting the rights of persons accused of criminal offences from the power of the state to subject them to prosecution and deprive them of liberty, to extending the principles of equality and non-discrimination to gay and lesbian relationships, to balancing the need to offer protection from hate speech with respect for free expression values – with varying degrees of success.

---

30 Offord, 2003, p 19. See also, Darrow and Alston, 1999.
31 Stychin, 1998, p 17.

Rationale for case study selection

The case studies have been chosen to illustrate three different ways in which law can be mobilised in the pursuit of particular human rights goals:

- Legislative redefinition (that is narrowing) of the scope of the protection against re-prosecution afforded by the principle of double jeopardy is an example of where an established legal right is threatened with express erosion or curtailment. In this context, human rights discourse can be expected to be deployed primarily in a *defensive* way – in an effort to dissuade proponents of the proposed erosion.
- Judicial and legislative response to demands for the formal legal recognition of same-sex relationships as equivalent to marriage is an example of where an attempt is made to push the parameters of recognised principles of human rights protection. In this context, human rights discourse is deployed to support an *extension* of the application of principles of equality and non-discrimination.
- Judicial and quasi-judicial assessment of the validity and operational scope of hate speech laws is an example of where there is a perceived clash between competing human rights: the human dignity and anti-discrimination rights not to be subjected to the harms associated with hate speech and the right to free speech. In this context, human rights discourse is mobilised on both sides of the dispute, and is brought to bear on the task of *balancing* the competing claims.

These different contexts may also be understood in terms of what is *expected* of human rights laws.

First, there may be said to be an expectation that human rights laws will provide individuals with a degree of insulation from the potentially negative effects of governmental actions, by constituting a constraint on the range of permissible policy options. How well have human rights laws and values provided insulation or protection with respect to criminal procedure reforms that erode the principle of double jeopardy?

Second, we may expect human rights laws to facilitate just policy-making in response to 'new' human rights challenges posed by equality-seeking groups and individuals. How well have human rights laws and values played this role with respect to demands for formal recognition of the equivalent legitimacy of heterosexual and homosexual relationships?

Third, there is an expectation that human rights laws should provide a framework for weighing up and balancing competing interests and rights. How well have human rights laws and values played this role with respect to the perceived tension between the right to freedom of expression and the rights protected by legislative restrictions on hate speech?

Expressed in this way, the three case studies all involve situations where authoritative political-legal judgments or decisions are made in settings where human rights claims are prominent and, to a lesser or greater extent, contested. The aim is to reveal whether the *legal form* of human rights values is an influential variable in the processes and outcomes of these decision-making events, whether they take place in executive, legislative, or judicial settings.

Of course, the categories of *defence, assertion* and *balance* are by no means exhaustive of the types of contexts in which human rights discourse can be mobilised, but they do illustrate that the selected case studies have the potential to yield valuable insights beyond the specifics of the particular controversy – including insights about the relationship between human rights discourse, legal form, legal culture and the practical fulfilment of human rights objectives.

Even when explained in this way, my choice of human rights controversies might strike some readers as idiosyncratic. Certainly, I make no claim that these examples represent the only possible vehicles for exploring the underlying questions with which this book is concerned. By way of explanation it is reasonable to concede that there is a degree of parochialism in their selection. Each of the three controversies has resonated loudly in Australia in recent years, partly because they have highlighted an apparent gap in the legal infrastructure for human rights protection, in the absence of a domestic bill of rights. In Australia there is no 'superior law' reference point for the protections associated with the rule against double jeopardy; the 'legal right', such as it is, not to be re-prosecuted for the same crime after acquittal is sourced in the common law and reflected in various ways in criminal statutes. The status of the general principle of equality before the law and non-discrimination is even more precarious: the Australian Capital Territory and Victoria are the only Australian jurisdictions where there is an express legislative guarantee of equality before the law;[32] at the national level, there is no general prohibition on discrimination on the basis of sexual orientation.[33] Outside of the ACT and Victoria,[34] the 'right' to freedom of expression, which is at the heart of the controversy surrounding hate speech laws, receives no explicit legislative or constitutional endorsement in Australia; it is supported primarily by the common law, augmented by a limited implied constitutional immunity.[35]

---

32 Section 8(3) of the ACT Human Rights Act 2004 provides that 'Everyone is equal before the law and is entitled to the equal protection of the law without discrimination. In particular, everyone has the right to equal and effective protection against discrimination on any ground.' See also s 8(3) of the Charter of Human Rights and Responsibilities Act 2006 (Vic).
33 Sexual orientation is a recognised ground of unlawful discrimination in all states and territories: Ronalds and Pepper, 2004.
34 See Human Rights Act 2004 (ACT), s 16; Charter of Human Rights and Responsibilities Act 2006 (Vic), s 15.
35 Chesterman, 2000; Gelber, 2002a; Blackshield and Williams, 2006.

In this context, my awareness of the *absences* in Australia's human rights legal infrastructure almost inevitably prompted inquiry about whether similar and contemporaneous controversies could be observed elsewhere, and if so whether the *presence* of explicit legal recognition, in one form or another, of the human rights in issue, had influenced the terms of debate or yielded different outcomes.

It might also be observed that the selected case studies are limited to the domain of civil and political rights, and do not touch any of the serious questions which remain about the capacity of human rights law and rights discourse to take seriously the reality of economic and social disadvantage and inequality.[36] This is a valid observation about the scope of the present study, but it is a limitation that is invoked by design, rather than neglect. The focus on selected civil and political rights claims is consistent with this book's primary objective: to interrogate the significance of legal form in relation to human rights, which at least at the level of political values and fundamental principles, are regarded as part and parcel of the prevailing liberal democratic paradigm in the four countries under investigation.

Rationale for comparative analysis

This objective demands a comparative approach. No meaningful conclusions about the impact of local legal form on the resolution of human rights controversies could be reached on the basis of a single jurisdiction study. Laying the experiences of a number of countries side by side in the form of four stories around a common human rights controversy has the potential to illuminate similarities and differences, in terms of both processes and outcomes. As Landman has observed,

> ... comparing across a range of countries ... provides a 'quasi-experimental' situation of control test rival hypotheses. ... [T]he generalizations that result from comparing countries help predict likely outcomes in other countries not included in the original comparison, or outcomes in the future, given the presence of certain antecedent factors.[37]

The variable factor that is the primary focus of the current study is the legal form in which various human rights are recognised.

In addition to meeting the particular needs of the present research project, the adoption of a comparative case-study approach is also a response to calls for a more rigorously comparative approach to constitutionalism

---

36 Leckie, 1998; Scott, 1999; Hirschl, 2000; Otto and Wiseman, 2001; Steiner and Alston, 2001, ch 4; Robinson, 2004; Roth, 2004; Rubenstein, 2004.
37 Landman, 2002, p 892.

and human rights. For example, Hirschl has commented that despite evidence of growing 'intellectual interest in the field of comparative constitutionalism and judicial politics', there has been relatively little 'genuinely comparative, problem-driven or theme-oriented scholarship'.[38] In a similar vein, Woodiwiss has emphasised the need to recognise and value 'the diversity of local human rights discourses'.[39] In the Canadian context, Herman has observed:

> My own view is that the Charter's potential depends on who is claiming what and why. . . . What is needed is a comparative analysis – one that examines what different groups have achieved or not, and why. Contrasting the struggles of these groups with those of similar movements in countries which lack constitutional rights would also be helpful.[40]

Although Herman was referring specifically to assessments of the capacity of the Canadian Charter of Rights and Freedoms to 'make a difference', her comments apply with equal force to the range of legal forms adopted in other countries.

Researchers and authors are increasingly recognising the value of comparative study of human rights laws.[41] To date, however, the focus of legal scholarship has tended to be on doctrine and the judiciary. Schmidt and Halliday have made the case for complementary applied socio-legal research on the domestic impact of human rights laws:

> The dominant force of established research on human rights combines, we believe, to leave a gap in need of redress. That gap is in seeking focused empirical study of human rights implementation at the domestic level of developed nations, where that includes an interest in institutional and individual behaviour deeper than legislatures and constitutional courts. Research on human rights, reflecting in part the concerns of international lawyers, has been slow to probe deeply into national systems to acquire empirical evidence about the dynamics of compliance with human rights norms. . . . [S]cholars of international law in particular have not generally employed a methodological apparatus that moves significantly beyond the structural elements of the judicial system or the legal decision-making of judges.[42]

---

38 Hirschl, 2004, p 222.
39 Woodiwiss, 2003, p 11.
40 Herman, 1997, p 213.
41 Alston, 1999; Harland, 2000; McCrudden, 2000; Orlin, Rosas and Scheinin, 2000; Heyns and Viljoen, 2002; Huscroft and Rishworth, 2002; Jayawickrama, 2002; Niemi, 2003; Hirschl, 2004.
42 Schmidt and Halliday, 2004, p 3. See also, Harvey, 2005; Meckled-Garcia and Cali, 2006; Campbell *et al*, 2006.

This book takes up the challenge posed by Schmidt and Halliday by adopting both a comparative approach and a socio-legal orientation.

Rationale for country selection

The four countries selected for examination in this study have, in relevant respects, a good deal in common. For example, they: share an Anglo common law tradition; are parties to the major international human rights instruments – including the International Covenant on Civil and Political Rights (ICCPR) – and are generally regarded in the international community as relatively 'good citizens' when it comes to human rights.[43] Ostensibly, the states under examination appear to have a common commitment to respecting human rights values and associated universal standards. However, to this end they currently employ significantly different institutional mechanisms in their domestic legal arrangements – what I refer to as 'legal form':

- Australia: is the only one of the four countries not to have adopted a national bill of rights of some sort. It still relies significantly on the common law, along with very limited constitutional protections, and federal, state and territory statutory recognition of selected human rights, primarily in relation to nondiscrimination;
- New Zealand: has codified core civil and political rights, based on the ICCPR, in a 'regular' statute – the Bill of Rights Act 1990 (BORA);
- The UK: has been a party to the European Convention for the Protection of Human Rights and Fundamental Freedoms (ECHR) since the 1950s, and in 1998 moved to incorporate the Convention into domestic law when it enacted the Human Rights Act 1998 (HRA);
- Canada: is the only one of the four countries to have constitutionally entrenched core civil and political rights (as well as some Aboriginal and minority rights) – in the form of the Canadian Charter of Rights and Freedoms (Charter) contained within the Constitution Act 1982.

A comparative case-study approach across four countries that represent four different models of legal infrastructure for the protection of core civil and political rights provides an opportunity to illuminate the relationship between legal form and the potency of human rights discourse under conditions of controversy.

Of course, it would be naive to assume that *legal form* can be neatly isolated

---

43 For what it is worth, all four countries received the highest rating in the 2005 'Freedom in the World Country ratings' published by the US-based NGO Freedom House: www.freedomhouse.org/ratings/index.htm. The rating is based on an assessment of the status of political rights and civil liberties.

from the range of other legal and non-legal variables that have influenced the handling and resolution of the human rights controversies upon which this book focuses. As Hirschl has observed, 'disentangling the contribution of constitutionalization [or legalization] from that of other societal and institutional factors is an almost impossible task'.[44] However, by choosing, for the purposes of comparison, four western countries with shared British common law traditions,[45] and similar systems of government, and where the prevailing legal form of human rights culture has not been the product of dramatic national political transformation (as in, for example, South Africa),[46] an attempt has been made to provide as common a 'base line' as possible against which to illuminate the impact of legal form. The selection of four developed 'western' democracies is also designed to ensure that the specific objectives of this comparative analysis are not confounded at the initial hurdle of the important ongoing debate about the legitimacy of international human rights law's universal aspirations in the face of fundamental cultural differences in countries across the globe.[47] One of my objectives in interrogating the universality claim from a different perspective, is to recognise that scrutiny of the limits of universality is important, not just which reference to familiar east/west or north/south debates regarding cultural relativism and fundamental difference in values, but also as it applies within countries that ostensibly share similar vales with respect to human rights. The focus is the distance between universal aspirations and local legal/political realities.[48]

Approaching the correlation between form and quality

The legal forms for the protection of human rights associated with the four subject countries are commonly represented by human rights advocates and scholars as located on a spectrum from the 'weakest' form of human rights protection – the Australian 'common law' model – to the 'strongest' form of human rights protection – the Canadian 'constitutional rights model'. The statutory bill of rights model (or what is sometimes referred to as the 'Commonwealth' model[49]) – versions of which operate in New Zealand and the UK – tends to be portrayed as a compromise or 'stepping stone' middle ground between these two extremes. For example, the public position of the

---

44 Hirschl, 2004, p 151.
45 It is important to acknowledge the existence of Indigenous legal traditions in Australia, New Zealand and Canada, as well as Canada's French civil law tradition.
46 Hirschl, 2004; Schmidt and Halliday, 2004.
47 Patman, 2000; Cowan *et al*, 2001; Bell *et al*, 2002; Donnelly, 2002.
48 I am not specifically concerned with the normative question of which human rights *should* be regarded as universal: see Talbott, 2005.
49 Gardbaum, 2001; Hiebert, 2006a.

NSW Council for Civil Liberties is that: the current situation with respect to the legal recognition of human rights in Australia is inadequate; the ultimate goal is a constitutional bill of rights; and that an acceptable middle ground or developmental stage is a statutory bill of rights.[50]

I am not inherently hostile to the idea of a qualitative hierarchy of legal forms for the protection of human rights, but I think it needs to be approached as a proposition to be tested rather than an article of faith to be blindly accepted. Although I do not necessarily share Campbell's anxiety about the dangers of an enhanced judicial role in the interpretation and application of human rights values,[51] I do agree with him that:

> In the constitutional debate we have passed the stage where it is simply assumed that to be supportive of the human rights movement it is necessary to advocate a United States-style constitution with an entrenched Bill of Rights and a judicial override of legislative enactments.[52]

I am also motivated by counter-intuitive examples and what they can tell us about the relationship between legal form and the practical enjoyment of human rights. For example, consider the following account, from an opinion editorial in a Sydney newspaper written by Michael Kirby (currently a judge of the High Court of Australia):

> I remember the first time I heard of the High Court of Australia. When I was a boy my grandmother remarried. Her new husband was a communist. A finer man I never met. In 1949 the Menzies Government promised to outlaw communism. The law was challenged in the High Court. On the day the court struck the law down as unconstitutional, a great burden of fear lifted from our family. I was 11. It was a curious feeling. Far away judges, without any help from a bill of rights, had held that the law on communists was incompatible with the Australian constitution. At virtually the same time in the United States, the Supreme Court, by majority, had upheld similar legislation as valid.[53]

What this relatively simple anecdote suggests is that if we want to take the human rights 'temperature' of a country, on a given issue, at a given time – we need to have reasonably sophisticated measuring equipment. If our measuring devices only pick up whether or not a particular human right (for example, freedom of association) is expressly recognised in a domestic

---

50 NSW Council for Civil Liberties, 2005. See also, Australian Law Reform Commission 1994; cf Campbell, 1999; Charlesworth, 2002a.
51 Campbell, 1999.
52 Campbell, 1999, p 8.
53 Kirby, 2003a, p 71.

constitutional document, bill of rights, or other statute, we risk making some fairly serious errors of judgment about the human rights environment we are trying to diagnose.

Most of the world's states have 'voted with their feet', but in a very small number of states, including Australia, the debate continues as to whether a bill of rights should be adopted.[54] It may be that constitutional entrenchment of human rights (as in Canada) necessarily translates into optimal protection for human rights, and that conversely, a hybrid common law-subject specific statute-based approach with no 'superior' legislative reference point for civil and political rights (as in Australia) is relatively ineffective as a way of respecting human rights. Ultimately, however, if the conventional wisdom of bill of rights proponents regarding the hierarchy is sound, then it should be possible to substantiate the pecking order (more or less) 'empirically'.

In this book, therefore, I set out to test as a proposition, rather than accept as a given,[55] that explicit legal incorporation of human rights at the domestic level – for example, in the form of a constitutional charter or bill of rights – necessarily produces the best outcomes in terms of the quality of the human rights protection which is afforded in practice.

Legal form

So far I have been using the term 'legal form' as if it is a term of art with an unambiguous meaning. Of course, this is not the case. But the term is simply a shorthand phrase for referring to the key features of the legal infrastructure and institutional design of domestic legal regimes for the protection of human rights.

McCrudden has observed that:

> ... The growth in human rights thinking has been a significantly *legal* phenomenon. The form in which states have chosen to develop their commitment to human rights has as often been 'legal' as 'political'. This is not to say that the motivation for human rights developments, whether at international or national levels, has not been political, only that it has developed primarily in legal forms.[56]

It is not just that there has been an emphasis on law, but that '... the development of human rights protections within national legal systems ... has taken many different forms'.[57] Campbell has emphasised 'the choice of mechanisms available to a country with a strong tradition of parliamentary

---

54 Griffith, 2000.
55 Hirschl, 2004.
56 McCrudden, 2000, p 29; see also, Campbell, 1999.
57 McCrudden, 2000, p 29; also, Orlin and Scheinin, 2000.

democracy',[58] a designation that can reasonably be applied to each of the subject countries of the present study.

The varied features of domestic regimes for the recognition and protection of human rights that are intended to be conveyed by the term 'legal form' include both substantive components – that is, the content of positive laws – and procedural components. The latter include: the respective roles of the legislature and the judiciary in the articulation of authoritative interpretations and applications of human rights norms (parliamentary or judicial supremacy?); the presence and nature (or absence) of pre-enactment processes for assessing the human rights implications of new statutes; the status of primary human rights statutes with respect to other domestic legal instruments (superior or parallel?); and the justiciability of international human rights law standards in domestic courts.

In their study of the domestic implementation of international human rights norms, Heyns and Viljoen stressed the importance of ensuring that norms are 'internalized in the domestic legal and cultural system'.[59] Goodman and Jinks have emphasised the processes of 'acculturalisation' in human rights compliance, whereby states come to adopt the 'beliefs and behavioural patterns of the surrounding [international human rights] culture'.[60] Whichever terminology is used,[61] the point is that effective implementation is not automatically achieved merely by the domestic enactment of human rights laws – irrespective of which legal form is adopted. As Williams has noted:

> ... any scheme that is designed to improve the protection of civil liberties must be judged according to its scope not only to change the text of the law but also to improve the culture of rights protection.[62]

In this book I am less concerned with the reasons why particular design choices have been made in different countries, than I am with the consequences of the choice of legal form with respect to the potency of human rights discourse and the quality of human rights enjoyment and protection. Is it possible to support the contention that particular legal forms are qualitatively better at translating universal human rights standards into domestic practice?[63] Is there a correlation between the adoption of particular legal forms and achievement of the goal of 'embedding human rights guarantees' in the governmental structures and practices of a state?[64] In particular,

---

58 Campbell, 1999, p 7.
59 Heyns and Viljoen, 2001, p 488.
60 Goodman and Jinks, 2004, p 638.
61 See also, Risse *et al*, 1999.
62 Williams, 2004, p 79.
63 See Galligan and Sandler, 2004.
64 Justice, 2001, p 5.

where a particular issue evokes significant controversy and polarisation in the local setting, is the capacity of 'rights talk' to cut across or 'trump' competing policy options enhanced or diminished, depending on the prevailing legal form?

Proponents of a constitutional bill of rights argue that this particular legal form is best equipped to ensure that international human rights standards prevail in the resolution of local disputes: this approach 'would put rights above politics'.[65] The central objection of opponents of the constitutional entrenchment of human rights is that this model hands the task of authoritative decision-making in relation to controversial policy issues over to an unelected judiciary and that this is fundamentally undemocratic and incompatible with the principle of parliamentary supremacy. Others have taken a more measured approach, emphasising the merits of a statutory bill of rights approach, which avoids the democratic distortions of constitutional entrenchment. For example, Webber has argued that in countries with a relatively strong tradition of respect for human rights (as in the four countries that are the subject of the present study), 'entrenched bills of rights are rarely appropriate' and a statutory bill of rights is preferable.[66] Yet another perspective on the significance of legal form is illustrated by the current position of the Australian government that neither a constitutional nor a statutory bill of rights is necessary for the effective protection of human rights,[67] and that codification of human rights values can actually do more harm than good.[68]

Current arrangements in each of the four countries – centred around the Charter of Rights and Freedoms 1982 in Canada, the Bill of Rights 1990 in New Zealand, the Human Rights Act 1998 in the UK and the continuing absence of a national bill of rights in Australia – represents the ascendancy of a particular normative position on the significance and implications of legal form when it comes to the goal of creating a domestic political and legal environment – what I will refer to as a local legal culture – in which respect for human rights is embedded. In fact, the concept of legal form comes into sharper relief when put alongside the concept of 'legal culture'.

Legal culture

The term 'legal culture' will be more familiar to readers, courtesy of its regular deployment by sociologists of law, comparative lawyers and

---

65 Stott Despoja, 2000.
66 Webber, 2006, p 264, n 7.
67 Williams, 2003; Commonwealth of Australia, 2005.
68 Howard, 2004.

socio-legal scholars.[69] Although it will be more familiar than the term 'legal form', its precise meaning is harder to pin down because it is used in a variety of ways and for a variety of purposes.[70] Some commentators have questioned its validity and utility on the basis that it is imprecise and conceptually vague.[71] Proponents have countered that despite its flaws, legal culture remains a 'useful concept'.[72]

At least for present purposes, very broad conceptions of the concept of legal culture, such as are reflected in Dorf's reference to 'the legal culture of the common law countries ...',[73] are not particularly helpful; nor are very narrow definitions which treat legal culture as little more than the practices and attitudes of legal professionals.[74] Although it is too court-focused, the following definition offered by Banakar is a good starting point:

> Legal culture consists, partly, of the taken-for-granted values and behavioural patterns of the judiciary, and partly, of ordinary men and women's knowledge of laws, but also of their attitude towards, and perception of, the judicial order in general and laws in particular. In that sense, legal culture is an integral part of the mainstream custom and tradition of a group of people.[75]

I would add to this definition: the values and practices of, and attitudes towards, the executive and legislative arms of government, particularly with reference to their law-making activities. In addition, the term legal culture encompasses the conventions and protocols that dictate the interplay between the different arms of government with respect to the resolution of policy controversies which have significant human rights implications – alongside the procedural dictates that can be attributed more directly to the prevailing legal form.

Although sceptical about the explanatory capacity of the concept of legal culture, Cotterrell has emphasised the need to recognise the force of localisation (as well as globalisation).[76] This is particularly important in relation to human rights where there is a high expectation of local adherence to a

---

69 Friedman, 1975; Watson, 1982; Varga, 1992; Kritzer and Zemens, 1993; Bierbrauer, 1994; Friedman, 1994; Sullivan *et al*, 1994; Gessner *et al*, 1996; Nelken, 1997, 1995; Blankenberg, 1998; Casanovas, 1999; Legrand, 1999; Potter, 2000; Dalberg-Larsen, 2001; Nelken and Feest, 2001; Ogus, 2002; Glenn, 2003; Koch, 2003; Friedman and Perez-Perdomo, 2003.
70 Friedman, 1997.
71 E.g., Cotterell, 1997, 2002, 2004.
72 Friedman, 1997.
73 Dorf, 2004, p 843.
74 Klare, 1998; Hunt, 1999.
75 Banakar, 2004, p 165.
76 Cotterrell, 2002.

common universal standard: '... the drive for legal uniformity is very strong given that the universality of the values to be represented in human rights law is powerfully championed.'[77] Cotterrell points out that:

> ... human rights as legal ideas ... can have very different practical meanings in different contexts and be subject to controversial interpretation. It is not difficult for them to be subordinated or adapted to the regulatory requirements of instrumental community.[78]

The point is that it is likely that it is not just the local legal form that is influential in any given instance, but also those aspects of the local legal culture that cannot be reduced to the formal legal infrastructure.

Canada's resolution of the controversy over same-sex marriage is illustrative. The adoption of a fully inclusive, equality-based redefinition of civil marriage illustrates the need to understand the prevailing distribution of supreme decision-making authority on human rights matters in Canada, not simply in terms of the express constitutional arrangements, which reserve to legislatures the power to override judicial findings of Charter incompatibility[79] (legal form), but with reference to the existence in Canada of a tradition of deference to judicial interpretations of the nature and scope of Charter rights, and a strong convention that the legislative override power should not be exercised.

This example serves as a reminder that it will often be very difficult to extract legal form from the web of influences that determine outcomes in particular instances of controversy and political choices where human rights claims feature prominently. Hirschl has referred to '... the question of multiple causality: disentangling the contribution of constitutionalisation from that of other societal and institutional factors is an almost impossible task'.[80] In a similar vein, Tushnet has noted that it is often impossible to disentangle a bill of rights from the political mobilisation of which it is a part, so that it may not be possible to conclude with great certainty that the particular outcome or result is a result of the bill of rights or the political mobilisation.[81]

Ultimately, the central argument advanced in this book is that legal form *does* matter in the resolution of human rights controversies, though not necessarily in the neat or predictable way imagined by adherents of the conventional wisdom regarding the claimed constitutional entrenchment-to-common law hierarchy. Legal form can only be fully appreciated as a

---

77 Cotterrell, 2002, p 45; also, Douzinas, 1996, 2000.
78 Cotterrell, 2002, p 48.
79 See Canadian Charter of Rights and Freedoms 1982, s 33.
80 Hirschl, 2004, p 151.
81 Tushnet, 1996, p 16.

component of the broader local legal culture in which human rights controversies are conceived and outcomes determined. But legal form (or the absence of law) is not just *any* component of legal culture. The examples addressed in this book suggest that it may be both a key constitutive element of local legal culture and a competing source of normative authority.

Measuring the effect of legal form

As noted above, if the 'conventional wisdom' hierarchy of legal models for human rights protection is sound, then it should be possible to substantiate the pecking order more and less 'empirically'. I use the latter term somewhat loosely, particularly in light of the inherent and widely acknowledged difficulties associated with attempts to measure the 'enjoyment' of human rights.[82] In order to 'test' the hierarchy hypothesis, the book will, in relation to each of the three controversies, examine the way in which human rights claims have been deployed in public and official discourse,[83] how they have been received by relevant legal and political authorities and institutions, and the nature of their impact (or 'non-impact') on the terms of the resolution of the controversy.

Consequently, I have not set out to offer a quantitative evaluation of the status of the human rights examined, let alone a ranking of the four countries. Rather, I will lay side by side the stories of how controversies surrounding double jeopardy roll-back, same-sex relationship recognition and the free speech/hate speech line have played out in Australia, the UK, New Zealand and Canada, respectively. Attention will be focused not only on the terms of resolution or *outcomes*, but on the processes of rights-claiming and counter-claiming. Specifically, I will be looking for evidence of any significant difference in the nature and potency of rights discourse, across the four jurisdictions and the legal form models that they represent. Particular attention will be paid to the following questions:

- How have political preferences been articulated in public discourse as human rights claims? How have they been received? What impact does legal form have on the terms of articulation?
- What is the relationship between the legal form of human rights and the influence of the 'human rights dynamic' on legal decision-making processes?
- How consistently and how prominently were the human rights implications of reform proposals considered by key individuals and agencies involved in law-making processes (including law reform bodies, govern-

---

82 Green, 2001; Goodman and Jinks, 2003.
83 Burton and Carlen, 1979.

ment departments, parliamentary committees, public submitters and legislators), and with what effect?
- To what extent and in what ways did legal form influence the strategies and arguments employed by litigants, and the approach adopted, and the decisions reached by judicial and quasi-judicial adjudicators?
- What impact has the prevailing legal form had on the strategies employed by human rights advocates and interest groups (successfully or unsuccessfully)?[84]
- Relatively speaking, has legal form had an observable effect on the outcomes achieved in the resolution of particular controversies, in terms of the option chosen from a range of more or less human rights-respecting possibilities?

Before turning to the case studies of three human rights controversies that constitute the body of this book, I will provide an outline of the key differences in the contemporary legal regimes for the protection of human rights in Australia, New Zealand, the UK and Canada.

Common [law] traditions and contemporary differences

In 2004, the authors of a leading Australian textbook on human rights law in Australia observed:

> Australia is now in a unique position in relation to human rights. It is the only 'western' nation that has neither a constitutionally entrenched Bill of Rights nor a Bill of Rights as part of its ordinary legislation. Even the world's newest nation, the Democratic Republic of East Timor, which Australia helped to create, has a constitutionally entrenched Bill of Rights.[85]

Australia's unique status with respect to domestic legal arrangements for the protection of human rights is a fairly recent phenomenon, particularly in those countries that have inherited the British common law tradition. A similar survey conducted just 30 years ago would have identified Canada as the only country of the four which are the subject of the present study to have adopted a bill of rights (in the form of the Canadian Bill of Rights 1960). But the second half of the twentieth century saw the growth of international human rights law and the rise of constitutionalism.[86] The traditional common

---

84 See Maiman, 2004.
85 O'Neill *et al*, 2004, p 1. See also, Griffith, 2000; Bronitt and Jobling, 2005.
86 Hirschl, 2004; Epp, 1996.

law conception of rights and liberties was essentially 'negative' or 'residual' – frequently articulated in a version of the phrase adopted in 1990 by Lord Donaldson in *Attorney-General v Guardian Newspapers (No 2)*:[87] 'every citizen has a right to do what he likes, unless restrained by the common law or by statute.'[88] However, in the aftermath of the Second World War, as Hiebert has noted, 'Westminster-based parliamentary systems incurred growing international and domestic pressures to articulate rights for the purpose of constraining state action'.[89] The adequacy of primary reliance on the common law as the 'protector' of rights and liberties was increasingly challenged.

All four of the subject countries were relatively 'early adopters' of the ICCPR – which has been the primary touchstone for domestic bills of rights developed since the 1970s. The ICCPR opened for signature in 1966, came into force in 1976, and was ratified by the UK and Canada in 1976, New Zealand in 1978 and Australia in 1980.[90] Rishworth has noted that, although the United Nations Human Rights Committee has, on occasion, expressed a preference for constitutional entrenchment as the preferred method of domestic implementation (in a manner reminiscent of the conventional 'pecking order' described earlier in this chapter), international instruments such as the ICCPR are conceived and expressed in terms of human rights *outcomes*. No particular legal form or institutional arrangement is mandated.[91] Indeed, through the 1980s and 1990s, each of the four countries that are the subject of the present study pursued different paths in terms of making domestic legal arrangements for the fulfilment of international human rights obligations.

The brief country outlines that follow will not attempt to offer a detailed history or a comprehensive account of contemporary legal arrangements,[92] nor will variations in the substantive content of domestic human rights instruments be considered. (Where relevant, the latter will be addressed in the case study chapters.) The characterisation of each country's legal regime for the inclusion of human rights considerations in processes of law-making, interpretation and application will focus on relevant differences in the institutional arrangements and associated scrutiny procedures. Key variables include: the presence of pre-enactment vetting procedures for proposed new legislation; the nature and extent of judicial opportunities to interpret legislation in light of prevailing human rights standards; the capacity for the court to make statements and findings with respect to the compatibility of

---

87 *Attorney-General v Guardian Newspapers (No 2)* (1990).
88 Ibid, p 178. See Clements, 2000; Havers and English, 2000; Blackburn, 2001, p 948.
89 Hiebert, 2004, p 1964.
90 Office of the United Nations High Commissioner for Human Rights, 2006a.
91 Rishworth, 2003a, p 12; also, Huscroft, 2002, p 3.
92 For further details, see Rishworth *et al*, 2003 (New Zealand); Lester and Pannick, 2004 (United Kingdom); O'Neill *et al*, 2004 (Australia); Sharpe and Roach, 2005 (Canada).

common law and statutory provisions with prevailing human rights standards; and the question of supremacy, as between the judiciary and the legislature, with respect to authoritative determinations on the validity of existing legal rules and standards.[93]

Canada

At the heart of the human rights scrutiny mechanisms established by the Canadian Charter of Rights and Freedoms, which forms part of the Constitution Act 1982,[94] is the power of the judiciary to invalidate legislation or overturn common law rules considered to be unjustified infringements of the rights and freedoms protected by the Charter. Section 52(1) of the Constitution Act 1982 provides that 'any law that is inconsistent with the provisions of the Constitution [including the Charter] is, to the extent of the inconsistency, of no force or effect'.

Not all forms of legal interference with Charter rights will be regarded as constitutionally invalid. Section 1 of the Charter states:

> The *Canadian Charter of Rights and Freedoms* guarantees the rights and freedoms set out in it subject only to such reasonable limits prescribed by law as can be demonstrably justified in a free and democratic society.

Without doubt, this strong power of judicial review – which has no formal equivalent in the arrangements established by the New Zealand Bill of Rights Act 1990 or the UK's Human Rights Act 1998 – has meant that litigation has been a key strategy in the efforts of individuals to seek legal recognition of their rights or redress in various contexts, and that the courts have played a prominent role in the resolution of numerous human rights controversies. It would be a mistake, however, to characterise the Canadian model as one that *formally* vests in the judiciary supreme or sole authority when it comes to the recognition and protection of human rights. To do so would be to ignore the presence of s 33 in the Charter, and to marginalise the way in which the Charter, as a normative influence, has been incorporated into Canadian political discourse,[95] including the policy development and law creation processes in which executive and legislative arms of government actively participate.

---

93 As a preface to the country overviews that follow I would like to acknowledge the significant contribution that Janet Hiebert's excellent work on comparative bills of rights analysis (2002, 2003, 2004, 2005a, 2005b, 2006a, 2006b) has made to my understanding of the regimes that operate in each of the countries that are the subject of the present study.
94 Canadian Charter of Rights and Freedoms, Part 1 of the Constitution Act 1982, being Schedule B to the Canada Act 1982 (UK), 1982, c 11.
95 Smith, 1999, p 74.

Section 33 of the Charter creates a mechanism whereby legislatures can 'override' certain of the Charter's provisions:

(1) Parliament or the legislature of a province may expressly declare in an Act of Parliament or of the legislature, as the case may be, that the Act or a provision thereof shall operate notwithstanding a provision included in section 2 or sections 7 to 15 of this Charter.
(2) An Act or a provision of an Act in respect of which a declaration made under this section is in effect shall have such operation as it would have but for the provision of this Charter referred to in the declaration.

Declarations have a five-year shelf life (s 33(3)), but can be renewed (s 33(4)).

The s 33 override is a controversial feature of Canada's human rights infrastructure,[96] and has provided one of the playing fields for the enduring debate over parliamentary versus judicial supremacy when it comes to the application of human rights standards. Although Canada's is the most empowered judiciary of any of the four countries that are the subject of the present study, s 33's inclusion in the Charter reveals that the principle of parliamentary supremacy that has so heavily influenced the design of human rights protection arrangements in New Zealand and the UK, and, most strikingly, in Australia, was also influential in Canada. However, as will be discussed in Chapter 3, in the course of examining judicial and legislative responses to demands for the legal recognition of same-sex relationships, one of the features of Canada's legal culture with respect to human rights (as distinct from its legal form) is a strong reluctance on the part of Canadian legislatures to invoke their override power.[97] Huscroft argues that this convention has developed, in part, because 'there is a tendency to conflate the decisions of the Supreme Court of Canada with the Charter itself'.[98] This tendency is encouraged by another feature of the constitutional arrangements for ensuring compatibility between Canadian laws and the Charter: the facility for the Government of Canada to seek advisory opinions from the Supreme Court of Canada on whether proposed legislation is constitutionally valid.[99]

Canadian scholarship and media coverage on the operation of the Canadian Charter of Rights and Freedoms focuses heavily on *judicial* scrutiny. As Hiebert and Kelly have demonstrated, there is a tendency to discount mechanisms of *executive* scrutiny and *parliamentary* scrutiny.[100] Kelly argues that the former are well developed and that 'Charter vetting' has become insti-

---

96 Sharpe and Roach, 2005, pp 86–92.
97 Kahana, 2001; Huscroft, 2002; Billingsley, 2002; Grover, 2005.
98 Huscroft, 2002, p 13.
99 Supreme Court Act, RS, 1985, c S-26, s 53.
100 Hiebert, 2002; Kelly, 2005.

tutionalised in law-making processes at the federal level, with the Department of Justice playing a key role in creating 'a rights culture within the legislative process and the machinery of government'.[101] The formal procedural link between executive review and parliamentary assessment is the statutory obligation on the Minister of Justice under s 4.1 of the Department of Justice Act:[102]

> 4.1 (1) ... [T]he Minister shall ... examine ... every Bill introduced in or presented to the House of Commons by a minister of the Crown, in order to ascertain whether any of the provisions thereof are inconsistent with the purposes and provisions of the Canadian Charter of Rights and Freedoms and the Minister shall report any such inconsistency to the House of Commons at the first convenient opportunity.

The problem, Kelly argues, is that well-developed executive scrutiny processes has supplanted, rather than supplemented, opportunities for meaningful parliamentary scrutiny of the human rights implications of proposed legislation. Hiebert reports that:

> The Canadian Justice Minister has never made a report of inconsistency. The absence of reports does not mean a lack of meaningful rights review before legislation is introduced ... The absence of reports is explained by a bureaucratic and political practice that requires necessary amendments to be made to a bill so that the minister of justice is satisfied that the legislation has a credible chance of surviving a Charter challenge. The prevailing assumption is that the government should not pursue legislation that is considered to be so patently inconsistent with the Charter that it would require the justice minister to report to parliament. Before reaching this stage, the bill should be either amended or withdrawn.[103]

It is worth noting, in the context of this book's broader concerns with the relationship between legal form and legal culture, that the Charter scrutiny procedures that currently operate in Canada are not a direct product of the former. On the contrary, as Hiebert has pointed out, 'the idea behind creating a statutory reporting obligation for the justice minister was to foster an enhanced parliamentary role to evaluate the rights dimension of legislation'.[104] In practice, active Charter scrutiny at the executive/Cabinet level has meant that the parliamentary select committees with responsibility

---

101 Kelly, 2005, p 222.
102 RS 1985, c J-2.
103 Hiebert, 2005a, p 248; see also, Hiebert, 2002, pp 7–19.
104 Hiebert, 2005a, p 249.

for scrutinising the Charter implications of proposed bills – currently the House of Commons Standing Committee on Justice and Human Rights, and the Senate Standing Committee on Legal and Constitutional Affairs – have tended to operate at the margins of the public debate surrounding human rights controversies.

New Zealand

The Bill of Rights Act 1990 (NZ) (BORA) was drafted with a close eye on the institutional arrangements that had been put in place in Canada by the Charter of Rights and Freedoms,[105] and reflects what has been described as 'a peculiarly New Zealand solution'[106] to the dilemma of where supreme authority should lie.[107] The final version of the BORA reflected a conscious decision to expressly retain for the Parliament supreme authority over the implications of the BORA for New Zealand law and policy. Section 4 states:

> No court shall, in relation to any enactment (whether passed or made before or after the commencement of this Bill of Rights),—
>
> (a) Hold any provision of the enactment to be impliedly repealed or revoked, or to be in any way invalid or ineffective; or
> (b) Decline to apply any provision of this enactment—
>
> by reason only that the provision is inconsistent with any provision of this Bill of Rights.

Section 5 of the BORA sets a standard for legitimate infringements of BORA rights that borrows heavily from s 1 of the Canadian Charter of Rights and Freedoms. Section 5 states:

> Subject to section 4 of this Bill of Rights, the rights and freedoms contained in this Bill of Rights may be subject only to such reasonable limits prescribed by law as can be demonstrably justified in a free and democratic society.

Consistent with the emphasis on *legislative* (rather than judicial) responsibility for ensuring compliance with and respect for human rights standards, the BORA requires the Attorney General to report to the Parliament if s/he

---

105 Thomas, 2004, p 26.
106 Dame Silvia Cartwright, Governor General of New Zealand (Cartwright, 2001).
107 Some commentators have argued that New Zealand should follow Canada's lead more closely: see Butler, 1997; Butler, 2000; Leane, 2004.

believes that proposed legislation will represent an unjustifiable infringement of rights protected by the BORA. Section 7 states:

> Where any Bill is introduced into the House of Representatives, the Attorney-General shall, –
>
> (a) In the case of a Government Bill, on the introduction of that Bill; or
> (b) In any other case, as soon as practicable after the introduction of the Bill, –
>
> bring to the attention of the House of Representatives any provision in the Bill that appears to be inconsistent with any of the rights and freedoms contained in this Bill of Rights.

In stark contrast to the manner in which successive Canadian Justice Ministers have exercised the parliamentary function under s 4.1 of the Department of Justice Act, New Zealand Attorneys General have not been shy about making s 7 reports. Between 1990 and 2005, Attorneys General made s 7 reports advising Parliament of an unjustified BORA infringement in relation to a total of 35 bills – 18 Government bills and 17 private member's bills.[108]

But what is the impact of s 7 reports? Are they an effective brake on the law-making process? The available evidence suggests that, in practice, even a formal declaration by the Attorney General that a bill will unjustifiably limit BORA rights by no means guarantees that the relevant legislation will be amended or abandoned. Research by Huscroft[109] and Hiebert[110] suggests that a s 7 inconsistency report from the Attorney General may have little affect on the Parliament's willingness to enact the legislation in question. Of the government bills that have been the subject of a s 7 report, very few were amended in response to the rights infringements identified by the Attorney General. Hiebert observes that:

> Despite the frequency of section 7 reports, they have seldom led to amendments to redress the perceived inconsistencies. In some cases, the relevant [parliamentary select] committee explicitly challenged the conclusion that the reported rights infringement was indeed unreasonable or unjustified.[111]

Hiebert argues that the preparedness of the New Zealand Government to introduce and pursue bills that the Attorney General deemed to be an

---

108 Huscroft, 2003a; Hiebert, 2005b; Hiebert, 2006b.
109 Huscroft, 2003a.
110 Hiebert, 2005b.
111 Hiebert, 2005b, p 79.

unjustified infringement on rights protected by the BORA, raises questions about the practical realities of New Zealand's model for injecting human rights considerations into the law-making process. She asks:

> How influential is the New Zealand Attorney General in Cabinet in terms of constraining choices that clearly contradict with protected rights? How much of a constraint do ministers believe that the New Zealand Bill of Rights Act 1990 should have to effect policy decisions?

This question is especially relevant in a context where mechanisms for facilitating *legislative* BORA-scrutiny of bills (as opposed to *executive* scrutiny) are limited.[112] The unicameral New Zealand Parliament does not have a specialist BORA or human rights standing committee.[113] Bills are routinely referred to one of a number of select committees (depending on the subject matter of the bill). Bills that raise potential BORA compatibility are commonly, though not routinely, referred to the Justice and Electoral Committee. While it is common for select committees to address the implications of proposed legislation for BORA rights and freedoms in the fulfilment of their review function,[114] examination of select committee reports suggests that the rigour of BORA scrutiny and the weight attached to such matters in the committee's overall assessment of the bill's merits are variable.[115]

As in Canada, human rights scrutiny of proposed new laws is built into New Zealand's bureaucratic procedures – including mandatory BORA compatibility assessment by the Ministry of Justice (or by the Crown Law Office for bills generated by the Ministry of Justice) – and procedures for Cabinet deliberation.[116] Although law-makers in New Zealand do not face the risk of judicial invalidation that motivates their equivalents in Canada, Huscroft suggests that s 7 of the BORA provides 'considerable incentive to formulate policy in such a manner as to avoid a report from the Attorney-General'.[117] He argues that this is 'the main significance of the reporting duty: it has formalised the place of the Bill of Rights in the policy development process . . .'[118]

On its face the BORA limits the judicial role to an interpretive obligation, constrained by the express reservation of parliamentary supremacy in s 4. Section 6 states:

---

112 Hiebert, 2005a, p 248.
113 See Hiebert, 2005a, pp 245–6.
114 See New Zealand House of Representatives 2005, Standing Orders 285–90.
115 See, e.g., New Zealand House of Representatives, Law and Order Committee 2005; discussed in Chapter 2.
116 Hiebert, 2005b, pp 73–4.
117 Huscroft, 2003d, p 196.
118 Ibid, p 196. See also, Richardson, 2004.

Wherever an enactment can be given a meaning that is consistent with the rights and freedoms contained in this Bill of Rights, that meaning shall be preferred to any other meaning.

The BORA did not empower the New Zealand judiciary to invalidate legislation in the way that the Charter empowers Canadian courts, nor did it provide for the issuance of 'declarations of incompatibility' of the type that the Human Rights Act 1998 (UK) empowers the courts to make. However, in 1999 the New Zealand Court of Appeal held that, implicit in the BORA, was a judicial power to declare legislation to be inconsistent with the BORA.[119] In *Moonen* the Court held that the purpose behind the inclusion of s 5:

> ... necessarily involves the Court having the power, and on occasions the duty, to indicate that although a statutory provision must be enforced according to its proper meaning, it is inconsistent with the Bill of Rights, in that it constitutes an unreasonable limitation on the relevant right or freedom which cannot be demonstrably justified in a free and democratic society.... In the light of the presence of s 5 in the Bill of Rights, New Zealand society as a whole can rightly expect that on appropriate occasions the Courts will indicate whether a particular legislative provision is or is not justified thereunder.[120]

The Government is under no statutory obligation to respond to such a declaration or to remedy the court-determined unjustified infringement, although it is clearly the Court of Appeal's intention that the Government should 'take notice' of such declarations. In *Moonen* the Court suggested that a judicial declaration of incompatibility 'will be of value should the matter come to be examined by the Human Rights Committee [under the ICCPR]. It may also be of assistance to Parliament if the subject arises in that forum'.[121]

Unsurprisingly, the Court of Appeal's move in *Moonen* attracted some criticism,[122] but it did not prompt a hostile reaction from the Government.[123] In fact, in 2001[124] the New Zealand Parliament introduced an express power to make declarations of invalidity, but only in relation to an enactment deemed to be inconsistent with the right to freedom from discrimination embodied in s 19 of the BORA.[125] Under s 92K(2) of the Human Rights Act

---

119 *Moonen v Film and Literature Board of Review* (2000).
120 Ibid, para 20.
121 Ibid.
122 See, e.g., Allan, 2001.
123 See, Thomas, 2004.
124 Human Rights Amendment Act 2001 (NZ).
125 Human Rights Act 1993 (NZ) s 92J. Rishworth, 2003c, p 35; Huscroft, 2003b; Butler, 2004, pp 351–2.

1993 (NZ) the responsible Minister is to obliged to make a formal response to the Parliament.

Rishworth has argued that the relative modesty of the legal form of New Zealand's primary domestic human rights law may belie its real significance as a mechanism for injecting human rights considerations into policy debates and legal decision-making processes. Notwithstanding its 'ordinary statute' status, Rishworth suggests that the BORA has effectively become part of New Zealand's 'constitutional canon',[126] and that while it may not take the legal form of a 'supreme law', it enjoys 'practical sanctity'.[127] Huscroft finds further reason to look beyond form in the Court of Appeal's articulation of a judicial responsibility to make declarations of incompatibility in appropriate cases. He concludes:

> If it turns out that governments invariably legislate in accordance with the declarations of the courts, the preservation of Parliamentary sovereignty in New Zealand ... will prove meaningless – a matter of form rather than substance.[128]

A number of commentators have suggested that, at least to date, Huscroft's fear that the intended allocation of interpretive authority under the BORA could be subverted by a convention of deference to judicial rulings, has not been realised. Generally, New Zealand courts have tended to adopt a cautious and deferential approach to BORA-based scrutiny of legislation duly enacted by Parliament[129] – in contrast to the relatively 'active' approach of the courts of the UK since the coming into force of the Human Rights Act 1998 (UK).[130] In any event, for present purposes, what is important about Huscroft's analysis is that it emphasises that legal form does not necessarily proscribe the limits of the capacity of human rights sensitivity to operate as a significant influence within the broader legal culture.

United Kingdom

Although the specific motivation for the UK's enactment of the Human Rights Act 1998 – domestic incorporation of the European Convention on Human Rights, which the UK had ratified in 1951 – reflected its European identity rather than its Commonwealth identify, the latter was a significant influence on the particular *form* in which the UK adopted its version of a bill

---

126 Rishworth, 2003a, p 3.
127 Sir Robin Cooke, quoted in Rishworth 2003a, p 4. See also, Joseph, 1999, p 317; Starrenburg, 2004, p 115.
128 Huscroft, 2002, p 15. See also, McLean, 2001.
129 Hiebert, 2006b.
130 Butler, 2004.

of rights.[131] The Human Rights Act 1998 (UK) (HRA), which came into force in October 2000, resembles the New Zealand model. Like the BORA, the HRA imposes an interpretive obligation on the courts, and does not extend to the judiciary the power to invalidate legislation. Section 3 of the HRA states:

(1) So far as it is possible to do so, primary legislation and subordinate legislation must be read and given effect in a way which is compatible with the Convention rights.
(2) This section – ...
   (b) does not affect the validity, continuing operation or enforcement of any incompatible primary legislation ...

Section 2 requires courts to take into account the jurisprudence of the European Court of Human Rights (and the former European Commission of Human Rights). This is a feature of the UK's domestic regime for human rights protection that has no direct equivalent in Canada, New Zealand, or Australia. Although there is the potential for the jurisprudence of the United Nations Human Rights Committee under the ICCPR to influence judicial decision-making in all four countries, only in the UK is local decision-making directly and strongly influenced by an 'external' normative standard and a 'supranational court'.[132]

Section 3's direction to read and give effect to legislation in a way that is compatible with the ECHR has been described as 'deeply obscure'.[133] Certainly, once the HRA came into force, it was not long before controversy arose about the legitimate scope of the judiciary to 'interpret' legislation so as to render it Convention-compatible. Section 3 became a touchstone for the perennial debate over judicial activism and the difference between *interpreting* and *legislating*,[134] and in practice, early decisions revealed a range of judicial approaches 'from the highly cautious and deferential, to the highly innovative and activist'.[135] In the House of Lords 2004 decision in *Ghaidan v Godin-Mendoza*,[136] Lord Nicholls observed that '[t]he courts, including your Lordships' House, are still cautiously feeling their way forward as experience in the application of section 3 gradually accumulates'. Nonetheless, Lord Nicholls went on to characterise s 3 of the HRA as a powerful tool that

---

131 See Lester, 2002; Klug, 2004; Richardson, 2004.
132 Arden, 2000; Blackburn, 2001.
133 Marshall, 2002, p 112. See also, *Ghaidan v Godin-Mendoza* (2004), para 27 per Lord Nicholls.
134 Kavanagh, 2004.
135 Ibid, p 285. See also, Klug 2004.
136 *Ghaidan v Godin-Mendoza* (2004).

made it legitimate for the courts to effectively 're-write' legislation that was found to be incompatible with the ECHR:

> ... [T]he interpretative obligation decreed by section 3 is of an unusual and far-reaching character. Section 3 may require a court to depart from the unambiguous meaning the legislation would otherwise bear. In the ordinary course the interpretation of legislation involves seeking the intention reasonably to be attributed to Parliament in using the language in question. Section 3 may require the court to depart from this legislative intention, that is, depart from the intention of the Parliament which enacted the legislation. ... [T]he conclusion which seems inescapable is that the mere fact the language under consideration is inconsistent with a Convention-compliant meaning does not of itself make a Convention-compliant interpretation under section 3 impossible. Section 3 enables language to be interpreted restrictively or expansively. But section 3 goes further than this. It is also apt to require a court to read in words which change the meaning of the enacted legislation, so as to make it Convention-compliant. In other words, the intention of Parliament in enacting section 3 was that, to an extent bounded only by what is 'possible', a court can modify the meaning, and hence the effect, of primary and secondary legislation.[137]

The House of Lords went on to endorse the Court of Appeal's s 3-inspired interpretation of provisions in the Rent Act 1977 that defined a spouse in heterosexual terms ('a person who was living with the original tenant as his or her wife or husband') – in such a manner as to include same-sex couples ('as *if they were* his or her wife or husband').[138] (This decision is discussed further in Chapter 3.)

The House of Lords decision in *Ghaidan v Godin-Mendoza* is consistent with Butler's observation that the interpretive obligation in s 3 of the HRA 'has been used more adventurously'[139] by courts in the UK than s 6 of the BORA has been used by judges in New Zealand. That is, they have been less constrained in their willingness to fashion a compatible interpretation of legislative provisions that are ostensibly inconsistent with the prevailing human rights standard.

Unlike the New Zealand BORA, the HRA expressly authorises the courts to issue declarations of incompatibility in relation to legislative provisions that are found to be incompatible with a Convention right (s 4). Blackburn has described s 4 declarations as 'of a non-legal character',[140]

---

137 *Ghaidan v Godin-Mendoza* (2004), paras 29–32.
138 Ibid, para 35.
139 Butler, 2004, p 358.
140 Blackburn, 2001, p 963.

to emphasise that they do not render the impugned legislative provision invalid, and there is no mandatory obligation on the Government to remedy the incompatibility:

> In many respects the declaration is analogous in its domestic effect to an adverse judgment being made against the UK by the European Court of Human Rights whose decisions are not binding or directly enforceable with the UK, depending instead for their effect on positive action being taken by the UK Government to bring forward legislation to amend its domestic law so as to bring it in to conformity with the Strasbourg ruling. So too, following a declaration of incompatibility by a UK court under the Human Rights Act, the government will be morally obliged to respond by considering what changes are necessary to render UK law consistent with the judicial ruling.[141]

Klug reports that '[u]nlike the Canadian "notwithstanding clause" [ie s 33 of the Charter], the Declaration of Incompatibility provision is being used'.[142] In 2004, Lord Steyn reported that in the first four years of operation of the HRA, the courts made 15 declarations of incompatibility under s 4,[143] a number of which led to the 'incompatible' statutory provision being amended by Parliament.[144]

Consistent with having formally rejected the option of vesting supreme authority over the interpretation and application of the HRA in the judiciary, in the name of respecting parliamentary sovereignty,[145] the UK model contains relatively strong mechanisms for executive and legislative scrutiny of the human rights implications of existing proposed new laws. Hiebert describes the aim as the creation of an environment in which:

> ... [g]overning would be influenced by self-imposed and external evaluations of rights as a dimension of legislative decision making. The goal was to facilitate a rights culture that constrains inappropriate decisions from occurring in the first place.[146]

The equivalent of the Attorney General's reporting duty under s 7 of the BORA is the broader responsibility articulated in 19 of the HRA:

---

141 Blackburn, 2001, p 963. See also, Debeljak, 2003b.
142 Klug, 2004, p 6.
143 *Ghaidan v Godin-Mendoza* (2004), para 39 per Lord Steyn.
144 United Kingdom, Department for Constitutional Affairs, 2003.
145 Debeljak, 2003a.
146 Hiebert, 2006a, pp 3–4.

(1) A Minister of the Crown in charge of a Bill in either House of Parliament must, before Second Reading of the Bill –

    (a) make a statement to the effect that in his view the provisions of the Bill are compatible with the Convention rights ('a statement of compatibility'); or

    (b) make a statement to the effect that although he is unable to make a statement of compatibility the government nevertheless wishes the House to proceed with the Bill.

The breadth of the ministerial responsibility to make an ECHR compatibility report on each and every government bill necessarily required the adoption of procedures for routine executive scrutiny of the human rights implications of policy proposals and draft bills.[147]

Another of the distinctive features of the UK model is the creation of a specialist parliamentary committee with responsibility for scrutinising all bills for the ECHR compatibility. The Joint Committee on Human Rights (JCHR) has been described by Lord Lester (a member of the Committee) as a 'parliamentary watchdog and bloodhound',[148] whose work 'has given section 19 [of the HRA] its potency'.[149] Lord Lester's early (2002) assessment was that the inclusion of the JCHR in the UK's scrutiny processes was 'successful in increasing the impact of the HRA and the Convention, and of international human rights law generally, on Ministers, civil servants, and Parliamentarians'.[150] Hiebert's more recent and impartial assessment is also positive,[151] although Parliament does not always head its concerns and implement its recommendations. Hiebert concludes that in a broader policy development and law-making context where '[c]oncentration of power in the executive, short-term objectives, and electoral calculations may combine to produce bills that unduly compromise rights, even where a government's general commitment to respect rights is genuine', the JCHR has provided an 'important critical counterpoint'.[152]

Australia

Within the Commonwealth of Australia, the only jurisdictions to have adopted a bill of rights are the Australian Capital Territory[153] and the state of

---

147 See Lester, 2002, pp 4–5.
148 Lester, 2002, p 2. See also, Feldman, 2002; Hiebert, 2005a.
149 Lester, 2002, p 7.
150 Lester, 2002, p 28.
151 Hiebert, 2006a.
152 Ibid, pp 36–7. Hiebert adds that 'interest-group pressures and public opinion more generally, as well as the judiciary, provide others': p 37.
153 Human Rights Act 2004 (ACT).

Victoria.[154] In the rest of the country, Australia's legal 'regime' for the protection of human rights consists of a selection of common law principles, narrow constitutional rights and freedoms (both express and implied), and specific statutory rights, primarily in the form of anti-discrimination provisions.[155]

Proposals for a national Bill of Rights, based on the ICCPR, have emerged on the Australian political and law reform agenda periodically since the early 1970s, although it has been more than almost two decades since either of the major political parties has seriously entertained the idea.[156] The view that has prevailed over this period is reflected in the following public comment made by the then Australian Attorney General, Daryl Williams, at a Bill of Rights Conference in 2002:

> I am proud to be the First Law Officer of a free and democratic country where human rights protection is first class. I am a proud supporter of the system that has given us stability and security and has fostered a community where tolerance, fairness and equality are valued, respected and protected. And I am convinced that there is no need for a Bill of Rights in Australia. Those who advocate a Bill of Rights undervalue the strengths of the arrangements that have served us so well and that are such an important part of our social fabric. Australia has a unique combination of strong democratic institutions and constitutional, common law and statutory protections for human rights. These protections are the envy of many countries throughout the world.[157]

In the absence of a primary domestic human rights instrument along the lines of Canada's Charter, New Zealand's BORA, or the UK's HRA, formal institutional mechanisms for injecting human rights sensitivity into Australian law-making and adjudication processes are very limited. Apart from the Australian Capital Territory[158] and Victoria[159] no jurisdiction has an equivalent of any of the Justice Minister/Attorney General human rights compatibility reporting procedures that operate in the other three countries.

A degree of legislative scrutiny is provided by the work of parliamentary select committees with responsibility to comment, *inter alia* on the 'rights and liberties' implications of bills. For example, since 2003, the NSW Parliament's Legislation Review Committee[160] has had a mandate:

---

154 Charter of Human Rights and Responsibilities Act 2006 (Vic).
155 E.g., Racial Discrimination Act 1975 (Aust); Sex Discrimination Act 1984 (Aust).
156 See O'Neill *et al*, 2004, pp 88–93.
157 Williams, 2003, p 1.
158 Human Rights Act 2004 (ACT), s 37; Evans, 2004, pp 297–300.
159 Charter of Human Rights and Responsibilities Act 2006 (Vic), s 28.
160 Since 2003 the author has been a legal adviser to the Committee.

(a) to consider any Bill introduced into Parliament, and
(b) to report to both Houses of Parliament as to whether any such Bill, by express words or otherwise:
  (i) trespasses unduly on personal rights and liberties, or
  (ii) makes rights, liberties or obligations unduly dependent upon insufficiently defined administrative powers, or
  (iii) makes rights, liberties or obligations unduly dependent upon non-reviewable decisions, or
  (iv) inappropriately delegates legislative powers, or
  (v) insufficiently subjects the exercise of legislative power to parliamentary scrutiny.[161]

The Committee's stated aims are not only to 'better enable the Parliament to determine when a bill might trespass unduly on rights and liberties', but also 'to influence sponsoring Ministers and their departments and the legislative drafters to consider the human rights impact of legislation at the policy formulation and drafting stages'.[162]

One of the curious features of the New South Wales Legislation Review Committee's review process – and the same is true of the Australian Parliament's Senate Scrutiny of Bills Committee[163] and the comparable committees which operate in other states[164] – is that there is no identified instrumental reference point for assessing the rights implications of bills. Where, for example, the UK's JCHR has a specific mandate and primary focus on the compatibility of bills with the ECHR, roughly analogous Australian parliamentary select committees are required to assess proposed legislation with reference to 'personal rights or liberties' – a generic phrase that does not directly relate to any particular set of substantive rules (whether domestic or international). It might be argued that this gives Australian parliamentary committees greater flexibility to draw on a range of *sources* of human rights laws and principles. However, the reality is that there can be no guarantee that such norms will have any purchase in debate surrounding the human rights implications of proposed laws. In practice, the pronouncements of parliamentary scrutiny committees generally have a low profile in Australian public discourse on human rights and law reform. While it is possible to identify occasions on which Parliament has amended legislation in response to scrutiny

---

161 Legislation Review Act 1987 (NSW), s 8A(1).
162 New South Wales Parliament, Legislation Review Committee 2005, p 23.
163 Australian Parliament, Senate 2006, Order 24.
164 See the jurisdiction overviews presented at the the Ninth Australasian and Pacific Conference on Delegated Legislation and Sixth Australasian and Pacific Conference on the Scrutiny of Bills, Canberra, 2–4 March 2005 www.parliament.act.gov.au/conferences/scrutiny/scrutiny.htm (accessed 25 May 2006).

committee recommendations,[165] there are numerous counter-examples – where Parliament has enacted legislation notwithstanding scrutiny committee advice that it 'trespasses on rights and liberties'.[166]

In the absence of domestic human rights instruments, opportunities for judicial scrutiny of the human rights legitimacy of exiting laws are limited.[167] In addition to the application of the provisions of anti-discrimination legislation in appropriate cases, judges sometimes draw on common law rights and constitutional guarantees in exercising their adjudication function. Resort to international human rights law when interpreting Australian common law or statutes, though not unknown,[168] remains relatively rare and uneven.[169] On the current High Court of Australia, only Kirby J has demonstrated a consistent preparedness to actively employ international human rights standards, including those embodied in the ICCPR, as a reference point for interpreting and assessing the legitimacy of Australian laws.[170]

At the federal *executive* level, Australia has relatively well-developed arrangements for the inclusion of human rights considerations in processes of policy development and law-making. In 1994, the then Labour Government adopted a National Action Plan on Human Rights, an initiative that was renewed and revised by the current Liberal-National (Conservative) Government in 2005.[171] Although the government has diminished its status and 'clout' in recent years,[172] the Australian Human Rights and Equal Opportunity Commission remains a prominent participant in public debates over human rights policy and law reform.[173]

This overview reveals that, to a large extent, it is the form*lessness* of Australian law with respect to the protection of human rights that currently constitutes its most distinctive attribute when compared with Canada, New Zealand and the UK. As between these latter three countries it is possible to discern subtle and not so subtle differences in the style or *form* of the primary legal regime for the injection of human rights sensitivity into policy development, law-making and adjudication processes. But in terms of its formal arrangements, Australia undeniably stands apart; distinguished by the *absence* of any form of statutory or constitutional bill of rights, and associated scrutiny and vetting mechanisms.

165 New South Wales Parliament, Legislation Review Committee 2005, pp 20–1.
166 See, generally, Kinley, 1999, p 169f; O'Neill, 2004, pp 186.
167 See Taylor, 2004.
168 See Mathew, 1995; Doyle and Wells, 1999; Kinley, 1998; Bailey, 1999.
169 O'Neill *et al*, 2004, pp 47–9, 186–8, 206–9.
170 Kirby, 1999. For a recent example, see *Fardon v Attorney General of Queensland* (2004), paras 181–6.
171 Commonwealth of Australia, 2005.
172 See Boniface, 2003.
173 Australia, Human Rights and Equal Opportunity Commission, 2005.

Proactivity and legal form

As will be obvious from these country overviews, formal institutional arrangements for human rights protection tends to primarily conceive of human rights scrutiny as a quality control mechanism for new laws, which may directly or incidentally, impact adversely on human rights. But human rights discourse can also be an important driver of policy directions and associated legislative initiatives. It might be anticipated that, to a large extent, the effectiveness of human rights discourse as a proactive normative influence on policy adoption and law reform will depend on the ideological commitment of the government of the day, or the degree of convergence between human rights-based imperatives and the policy preferences of governments. But it is also appropriate to consider the extent to which the legal form in which particular human rights are recognised (or not) renders human rights discourse a more or less potent influence on the policy formation and agenda setting practices of law-makers. This is a question that is of particular relevance in the context of controversies over the inadequacy of *existing* legal rules (as opposed to potentially rights-infringing *new* laws) and the desirability of their reform so as to better reflect human rights values – such as the controversy over the legal recognition of same-sex relationships, to be considered in Chapter 3.

Overview of chapters

The first of the comparative case studies – erosion of the double jeopardy protection – is presented in Chapter 2. Chapter 3 considers recent attempts to extend the principles of equality and non-discrimination to same-sex relationships. In Chapter 4 recent developments in the enduring controversy surrounding the operation of hate speech laws are examined. Finally, in Chapter 5, I reflect on what has been revealed by the 12 'stories' of human rights controversy told in chapters 2, 3 and 4, about the significance of the local legal form of human rights. At the end of the day: does it matter?[174]

---

174 I acknowledge the many scholars who have previously posed this question, or versions of it. For example: Epp, 1996 ('Do Bills of Rights Matter? The Canadian Charter of Rights and Freedoms'); Keith, 1997 ('A Bill of Rights: Does it Matter? A Comment'); Hathaway, 2002 ('Do Human Rights Treaties Make a Difference?'); Banakar, 2004 ('When Do Rights Matter? A Case Study of the Right to Equal Treatment in Sweden'); Arthurs and Arnold, 2005 ('Does the Charter Matter?').

Chapter 2

Rolling back an established human right: 'Reforming' the rule against double jeopardy

> 'The underlying idea, one that is deeply ingrained in at least the Anglo-American system of jurisprudence, is that the State with all its resources and power should not be allowed to make repeated attempts to convict an individual for an alleged offense, thereby subjecting him to embarrassment, expense and ordeal and compelling him to live in a continuing state of anxiety and insecurity, as well as enhancing the possibility that even though innocent he may be found guilty.'
> *Green v United States*, 355 US 184, 187–188 (1957) per Black J

Introduction

The immunity from re-prosecution after acquittal – known colloquially as the rule against double jeopardy – was, until very recently, regarded as one of the bedrock human rights underpinning the fair administration of criminal justice.[1] In his seminal work on the subject, Friedland observed that 'no other procedural doctrine is more fundamental or all-pervasive'.[2] O'Neill *et al*, in a leading Australian human rights law text, have observed:

> The idea that no one shall be liable to be tried or punished again for an offence for which they have already either been finally acquitted or convicted is well established in Anglo-Australian law.[3]

While there is some academic disagreement about whether the immunity against re-prosecution after acquittal underpinned by the rule against double jeopardy constitutes a 'human right',[4] for present purposes, its inclusion in Art 14(7) of the International Covenant on Civil and Political Rights (ICCPR), and the practical significance that it has long held and the status

---

1 See Vincent, 2003.
2 Friedland, 1969, p 3. See also, Sigler, 1969; Hunter, 1985.
3 O'Neill *et al*, 2004, p 236.
4 See, e.g., Bagaric and Neal, 2005, p 89.

that it has long enjoyed in the common-law tradition (as Prakash has noted, 'Implicitly, it acts as a limit on State power by preventing prosecution as an instrument of oppression'[5]), are regarded as sufficient to justify the 'right' designation. The New Zealand Law Commission has stated that what is 'known as "the rule against double jeopardy" . . . is a basic safeguard of civil liberties in every legal system comparable with our own'.[6]

An adjective commonly used to convey both the age and the importance of the rule against double jeopardy is 'ancient'.[7] But in recent years the antiquity of the rule against double jeopardy has taken on a new significance. In three of the four states that are the subject of the present comparative study, legislators have moved to 'roll back' the protection extended by the rule against double jeopardy principle so as to allow for the re-prosecution of a person who has been acquitted in certain circumstances. In 2003 the United Kingdom (UK) Parliament enacted the Criminal Justice Act 2003. Part 10 of this Act, which came into force on 4 April 2005, introduced a 'new and compelling evidence' exception to the rule against double jeopardy.[8] In the same year, Australia's Standing Committee of Attorneys General considered the matter, with the New South Wales Government proceeding to circulate a consultation draft – Criminal Appeal Amendment (Double Jeopardy) Bill 2003 (NSW). Three years later, attempts to develop a uniform national approach modelled on the UK's approach were at an impasse. In 2004, the New Zealand Government introduced into the Parliament a Criminal Procedure Bill that will, *inter alia*, amend the Crimes Act 1961 (NZ) to add a 'tainted acquittal' and a 'new and compelling evidence' exception to the rule against double jeopardy. Although the progress of this omnibus bill has been slow, at the time of writing it had passed through second reading and in 2007 the New Zealand Parliament is expected to pass it. Canada is the only one of the four countries where the issue of double jeopardy reform has not found its way on to the legislative reform agenda.

Opponents of the introduction of statutory exceptions to the double jeopardy rule have attempted to bolster their position by emphasising the dangers of tampering with a human right with an ancient pedigree. For example, in the House of Lords debate on the double jeopardy provisions of the Criminal Justice Act 2003 (UK), Lord Brittan of Spennithorne noted:

> It is worth remembering that these ancient protections have not existed accidentally and have not survived for so long as to be ancient protections for no good reason. They have survived for so long precisely because they

---

5 Prakash, 2002–2003, pp 270–1.
6 New Zealand Law Commission, 2001, p vii.
7 See, e.g., Roberts, 2002a, p 206; Kirby, 2003b, p 231–2.
8 Rozenberg, 2005.

have stood the test of time and been a hallmark of a civilized society which is not moved by populist concerns to do what seems cheap and easy and popular because of particular cases which have come to notoriety.[9]

However, the 'ancient' motif has been employed just as frequently by advocates of legislative roll-back. From this side of the debate, 'antiquity' is a pejorative term – carrying the connotation that the traditional scope of the immunity extended by the rule against double jeopardy is outdated, anachronistic and in need of reform. In response to an observation by Lord Neill, in the course of debate in the House of Lords, that he was 'surprised at the meekness with which the Committee is accepting the situation, where a centuries' old rule against double jeopardy is being jettisoned',[10] the Attorney General, Lord Goldsmith, stated: 'The noble lord, Lord Neill of Bladen, said that it is a centuries-old rule. Yes, it is. . . . [T]hat does not necessarily mean that it is right for all time.'[11] Roberts has observed that the double jeopardy rule was 'squarely in the [UK] government's legislative sights, targeted as an anachronistic legal fetter on the delivery of justice ripe for a dose of Blairite modernization'.[12] In the Australian debate, the rule against double jeopardy has been characterised as akin to a perishable food item that has reached its 'use-by' (expiration) date.[13] Following the High Court of Australia's 2002 decision that the rule against double jeopardy prevented the Crown from prosecuting the alleged killer of a 17-month-old girl for perjury, after he had previously been acquitted of murder,[14] the victim's mother, stated:

> It's an 800-year-old law. In every other way of life we move ahead with the times, but we seem to run the treadmill with the 800-year law of double jeopardy. Why can't we change it? Why can't it be changed?[15]

The rule against double jeopardy, as it has traditionally been understood in the UK, Canada, Australia and New Zealand – that is, as allowing for a person who has been charged with a crime to plead *autrefois convict* or *autrefois acquit* – has its origins in British common law. However, a version of the rule, which draws also on the analogous (though not necessarily identical[16]) civil law principle of *ne bis in idem* forms part of international human rights law.

---

9 United Kingdom Parliament, Hansard (House of Lords), 17 July 2003, 1067.
10 Ibid, 1059.
11 Ibid, 1071.
12 Roberts, 2002, p 199.
13 Hinch, 2003.
14 *R v Carroll* (2002).
15 Faye Kennedy, quoted in Australian Broadcasting Corporation, Radio National, 2005.
16 See Emmerson and Ashworth, 2001, pp 304–7.

Article 14(7) of the International Covenant on Civil and Political Rights states:

> No one shall be liable to be tried or punished again for an offence for which he has already been finally convicted or acquitted in accordance with the law and penal procedure of each country.

This provision is mirrored in Art 50 of the Charter of Fundamental Rights of the European Union:

> No one shall be liable to be tried or punished again in criminal proceedings for an offence for which he or she has already been finally acquitted or convicted within the Union in accordance with the law.

However, one of the things that has hindered the emergence of an international consensus on the precise nature and scope of the immunity against re-prosecution after acquittal is that the more significant European Convention on Human Rights (ECHR) appears to define the 'right' in narrower terms, leaving more scope for re-prosecution. The principle was not included in the Convention proper, but is now expressed in Art 4 of Protocol 7 to the Convention:

> (1) No one shall be liable to be tried or punished again in criminal proceedings under the jurisdiction of the same State for an offence for which he has already been finally acquitted or convicted in accordance with the law and penal procedure of that State.
> (2) The provisions of the preceding paragraph shall not prevent the reopening of the case in accordance with the law and penal procedure of the State concerned, if there is evidence of new or newly discovered facts, or if there has been a fundamental defect in the previous proceedings, which could affect the outcome of the case.[17]

Unlike the traditional common-law formulation (and arguably, the formulation in Art 14(7) of the ICCPR[18]) Art 4(2) of Protocol 7 to the European Convention expressly allows for re-prosecution after acquittal in the case of new evidence of 'fundamental defect'.

In April 1984, a few months before Protocol 7 was opened for signature by Council of Europe member states, the United Nations Human Rights Committee released a General Comment on Art 14, in which it attempted to

---

17 Paragraph (3) provides that 'No derogation from this Article shall be made under Article 15 of the Convention'.
18 On the ICCPR standard, see Joseph, Schultz and Castan, 2004, pp 460–1.

bridge the apparent gap between the ICCPR standard and the prevailing European civil law standard (*ne bis in idem*), which is expressed in Art 4 of Protocol 7. The Committee observed that:

> In considering State reports differing views have often been expressed as to the scope of paragraph 7 of article 14. Some States parties have even felt the need to make reservations in relation to procedures for the resumption of criminal cases. It seems to the Committee that most States parties make a clear distinction between a resumption of a trial justified by exceptional circumstances and a re-trial prohibited pursuant to the principle of ne bis in idem as contained in paragraph 7. This understanding of the meaning of ne bis in idem may encourage States parties to reconsider their reservations to article 14, paragraph 7.[19]

Despite the Committee's attempts to reassure state parties that the restrictions imposed on them by Art 14(7) of the ICCPR on them are not as great as they might have imagined, a degree of uncertainty and of jurisdiction-to-jurisdiction variability remains. As Emmerson and Ashworth have observed, the lack of consensus 'has inhibited the adoption of a uniform double jeopardy principle in international human rights law'.[20]

Nonetheless, at least in the four countries which are the subject of the present study, there was, until recently, a relatively common standard that dictated that where a person had been acquitted and all conventional appeal options had been exhausted, re-prosecution of the same person for the same crime was impermissible. Specifically, neither a subsequent finding that the original acquittal was tainted by misconduct by the accused or another person (for example, perjury or jury tampering), nor the subsequent revelation of new evidence that suggested guilt, justified exposure of a person to re-prosecution for a crime of which they had previously been acquitted.

At the domestic level, the right is expressly recognised in s 11(h) of the Canadian Charter of Rights and Freedoms, s 26(2) of the New Zealand Bill of Rights Act 1990, and Protocol 7 to the ECHR (Art 4). (Although the UK has not formally ratified this protocol, it was widely treated, in the public discourse leading up to the enactment of the Criminal Justice Act 2003, as the primary human rights reference point, by virtue of the domestic implementation of the ECHR via the Human Rights Act 1998, and the Government's intention (still unrealised) to ratify Protocol 7.) In Australia, the rule against double jeopardy finds statutory expression as a human right only in

---

19 United Nations, Human Rights Committee, 1984.
20 Emmerson and Ashworth, 2001, p 304. See also, Fletcher, 2003.

the Australian Capital Territory[21] and Victoria.[22] In all other parts of the country, the 'right' is supported only by the common law and procedural provisions in criminal law statutes.[23]

And yet, despite the common ground that has traditionally existed, notwithstanding these differences in legal form, in 2006, across the four subject countries, there is now considerable variation in the scope of the human right underpinned by the rule against double jeopardy. In the UK the right is now curtailed by two legislative exceptions to the rule against double jeopardy, which allow for re-prosecution where the original acquittal was 'tainted' or where new and compelling evidence becomes available. Assuming the passage of the Criminal Procedure Bill that is currently before the New Zealand Parliament, New Zealand will soon follow suit. In Canada, and in Australia (at least for the time being, pending the resolution of the NSW Government's intentions), the right retains its traditional scope.

In this chapter I will consider the origins and trajectory of the move to curtail the human right not to be exposed to prosecution for a crime after having been acquitted of that crime. Consistent with the broader aims of this book I will focus on the way in which the processes and outcomes of mooted legislative reform in relation to the rule against double jeopardy have been shaped and influenced by the prevailing legal framework for the protection of human rights in each jurisdiction. This case study provides an opportunity to assess the impact of human rights sensitivity in relation to the resilience of an established human right 'under siege'[24] or 'under threat'[25] – that is, faced with a concerted curtailment campaign, in furtherance of competing policy objectives relating to 'law and order' and the interests of victims of crimes and their families.[26]

The manner in which the story of double jeopardy reform has played out in recent years does not fit neatly into the conventional hierarchy of legal models for the protection of human rights outlined in Chapter 1. Certainly, some parts of the story follow the script: there can be little doubt that the entrenchment of the rule against double jeopardy in the Charter of Rights and Freedoms – and its consequent 'off limits' status in Canadian political discourse and legal culture – is a large part of the explanation as to why the calls for the introduction of statutory exceptions which have resonated in the UK, New Zealand and Australia have not emerged in Canada. On the other

---

21 Section 24 of the Human Rights Act 2004 (ACT) states: 'No-one may be tried or punished again for an offence for which he or she has already been finally convicted or acquitted in accordance with law.'
22 Charter of Human Rights and Responsibilities Act 2006 (Vic), s 26.
23 See, e.g., Criminal Procedure Act 1986 (NSW), s 156.
24 Prakash, 2002–2003, p 267.
25 Bagaric and Neal, 2005, p 88.
26 Hogg and Brown, 1998; Roach, 1999; Garland, 2001; Weatherburn, 2004.

hand, the rule against double jeopardy has proved to be surprisingly resilient in Australia, belying the assumed fragility and susceptibility to legislative override of a right sourced in the common law. In the UK and New Zealand express legislative recognition of the human right underpinned by the rule against double jeopardy, via the Human Rights Act 1998 and the Bill of Rights Act 1990, respectively, has not prevented the legislative erosion of the traditional parameters of the right. In fact, as will be argued below, the emergence of the ECHR as the primary human rights reference point in the UK's twenty-first-century legal culture actually operated as a facilitative mechanism rather than a point of resistance in the debate surrounding Part 10 of the Criminal Justice Act 2003.

The New Zealand story is also counter-intuitive from the point of view of the assumed value of the legal codification of human rights and associated scrutiny procedures. The New Zealand Parliament's determination to include provisions in the Criminal Procedure Bill, currently before Parliament, which will introduce tainted acquittal and new and compelling evidence exceptions to the immunity against re-prosecution created by the rule against double jeopardy for all offences punishable by 14 years imprisonment, notwithstanding a report from the Attorney General that this was an unjustified infringement of s 26(2) of the Bill of Rights Act 1990, reveals a surprising feature of New Zealand's legal culture with respect to the impact of human rights sensitivity on the policy-making and law-reform process: rights impairment worn as an electorally appealing 'badge of honour' – as evidence of just how far the Government is willing to go in pursuit of its preferred (and the electorate's favoured) policy outcomes. A government's determination to pursue a policy of *curtailing* human rights can have considerable appeal, particularly where the rights in question are perceived as benefiting only undeserving 'criminals'.

The merits of double jeopardy protection under scrutiny

At first glance, the rule against double jeopardy seems an unlikely target for a campaign to 'reign in' human rights. It has operated for centuries as something of a 'given' in the criminal justice system. Why then did it emerge in the late 1990s and early 2000s as a subject of considerable controversy? In recent years, legislatures in the UK, New Zealand and Australia (specifically, the state of New South Wales) have considered bills for the legislative erosion of the human rights associated with the rule against double jeopardy. In each case the move has been motivated by media/popular outcry over a specific case in which persons accused of a serious criminal offence (murder) were widely considered to have been the beneficiaries of an 'unmeritorious acquittal'. They were characterised as criminals who 'got away with it'. Of course, such reactions to the outcome of a criminal trial are not new. Controversy over 'wrongful' acquittals has at least as long a history as controversy over wrongful convictions and miscarriages of justice.

The convergence of at least two developments helps to explain why political and law reform attention turned, at the turn of the twenty-first century, to the question of the integrity of the traditional immunity from re-prosecution of an acquitted person. The first is the growth of the victim's rights movement, with an emphasis on correcting a perceived imbalance between the criminal justice system's (over-)concern for the interests and rights of offenders and its (under-)concern for the interests and rights of victims of crime.[27] The second is the forensic implications of the growth of DNA technology. When he announced that the NSW Government planned to introduce exceptions to the rule against double jeopardy, the then Premier, Bob Carr, stated: 'The law has to keep pace with science. Just as DNA evidence can expose wrongful convictions, it should also be available to convict the guilty.'[28] This is a deceptively simplistic take on the relationship between available evidence-gathering technologies and the task of protecting the interests of persons suspected of having committed crimes. The mere fact that new technology makes possible something that was previously regarded as 'impossible' (although, even this is a mis-characterisation of the impact of DNA testing – it has always been possible to attempt to gather 'new evidence' after a person has been acquitted – the difference is that DNA testing is perceived as 'easy' and 'foolproof') does not itself make that something desirable. (Witness the debate around human cloning.[29]) Nonetheless, the 'DNA argument' has been a powerful component of the case advanced by proponents of rolling back the immunity against re-prosecution after acquittal.[30]

As a number of commentators have noted, the aftermath of a high profile, controversial acquittal is hardly the ideal environment for sound law reform judgment. In the UK, Roberts observes:

> The reaction to a particular case can be vocal, powerful and immediate. In a highly charged atmosphere which might understandably arise it may be all too easy to discount the reassurance gained by reflecting, in less emotive circumstances, on long-standing traditional bulwarks of individual liberty.[31]

Similar sentiments were expressed, more bluntly, by a participant in an online

---

27 See Roach, 1999; Cape, 2004; Rock, 2004; Strang, 2004.
28 New South Wales, Office of the Premier, 2003. See Johns, 2003, pp 35–48; also, *New Zealand Herald*, 2004.
29 Healey, 2003; Klotzko, 2004; McGee and Caplan, 2004.
30 England and Wales Law Commission, 1999, p 43.
31 Roberts, 2002a, p 206.

discussion following the screening of an ABC Television documentary on the Deidre Kennedy/Carroll case in April 2003:

> I am not happy about this program. Vox pop law reform is a very ugly and formerly un-Australian thing. Social and law reform from the middle pages of the Daily Telegraph [a Sydney tabloid newspaper] is cheap.[32]

'Vox pop law reform' is an undeniable feature of the political processes in many countries where elected governments are sensitive to the electoral mood. Nowhere is this more evident than in relation to issues surrounding crime and 'law and order'. The emergence of double jeopardy reform as a subject of serious reform attention must be understood within the broader 'law and order' discourse that is a powerful influence on government policies in relation to criminal law and criminal justice administration. The decision of governments in the UK, New Zealand and Australia (specifically, New South Wales) to embrace the idea of rolling back double jeopardy protection is just one specific manifestation of a broader tendency towards 'talking and acting tough' on crime.[33] In an editorial during the debate over double jeopardy reform in the UK, *The Daily Telegraph* observed:

> Whenever this Government finds itself under pressure over crime, its instinctive reaction is to propose the abolition or curtailment of one or another ancient civil liberty.[34]

After the enactment of the Criminal Justice Act 2003, Ashworth observed that the double jeopardy roll-back provisions in Pt 10:

> ... suggest that the Act was based, not on a determination to ensure that fundamental rights were respected, but rather on a policy of going as far as possible to minimise or otherwise avoid those rights.[35]

In a similar vein, an Australian commentator observed that the NSW Government's announcement in early 2003 that it planned to introduce legislation to roll back the rule against double jeopardy was part of a pre-election 'to-and-fro' between the Premier and the Opposition leader, who 'spent the past two months promising new repressive measures, each accusing the other of stealing law-and-order policies'.[36] In New Zealand, the Government's

---

32 Australian Broadcasting Corporation, ABC TV, 2003.
33 Hogg and Brown, 1998.
34 'Danger of double jeopardy', *The Daily Telegraph*, 20 June 2002, cited in Broadbridge, 2002, p 26.
35 Ashworth, 2004, p 527.
36 Skeers, 2003; see also, Haesler, 2003.

announcement that it intended to introduce legislation to reform the rule against double jeopardy was characterised by critics as 'a pre-electioneering stunt'.[37] Criminologist, Trevor Bradley, was reported as having described the proposal as 'an opening bid in "a law and order auction"' before the next election.[38]

In the UK, the issue of double jeopardy reform was placed on the mainstream political agenda following the failed private prosecution of the alleged killers of Stephen Lawrence, and the subsequent recommendation in the Macpherson Report: 'That consideration should be given to the Court of Appeal being given power to permit prosecution after acquittal where fresh and viable evidence is presented.'[39] In the same year, Billy Dunlop admitted having murdered a young woman named Julie Hogg 10 years previously. He had been tried for murder in 1991, but was acquitted. After he confessed to Hogg's murder, Dunlop was charged with perjury, convicted and sentenced to six years' imprisonment.[40] The fact that he could not be re-prosecuted for murder prompted Julie Hogg's mother, Ann Ming, to campaign for reform of the rule against double jeopardy.[41]

In New Zealand the issue of double jeopardy reform was put on the agenda by the case of Kevin Moore. Moore was tried for murder in 1992 and acquitted.[42] It emerged that Moore had arranged for a friend to supply untrue alibi evidence at the trial, and in 1999, Moore was convicted of conspiracy to pervert the course of justice. He was sentenced to the maximum sentence of seven years imprisonment, but it was clear that the sentencing judge felt that that was inadequate, given that it was 'substantially less' than the sentence Moore would have received had he been convicted of murder.[43]

In Australia, the issue was placed on the agenda by the case of Raymond Carroll. In 1985, Carroll was tried for the murder of a 17-month-old girl in 1973. He was convicted at first instance, but appealed successfully to the Queensland Court of Criminal Appeal, which ordered that a verdict of acquittal be entered. In 1999, Carroll was charged with perjury, the essence of the prosecution's case being that he had give false evidence at his original trial when he denied having killed Deidre Kennedy. Carroll was convicted of perjury. However, his conviction was overturned by the Queensland Court of Criminal Appeal, a decision which was confirmed when the Crown appealed

---

37 Henzel, 2004.
38 Ibid; see also, Kennedy, 2004.
39 Macpherson, 1999, Recommendation 38. The double jeopardy rule had already been 'relaxed' in relation to 'tainted acquittals': Criminal Procedure and Investigations Act 1996, s 54, following a recommendation by the United Kingdom, Royal Commission on Criminal Justice, 1993.
40 *R v Dunlop* (2000).
41 Gyllenspertz, 2002.
42 Gregory, 2001.
43 See New Zealand Law Commission, 2000.

unsuccessfully to the High Court of Australia. The High Court ruled that the prosecution of Carroll for perjury was an abuse of process because it was, effectively, an attempt to retry Carroll for the murder of Deidre Kennedy – in that the essence of the Crown's case was that he had, in fact, killed the girl, thereby establishing that he had lied when he denied having done so at the 1985 murder trial.[44] Adopting a broader interpretation of the immunity against re-prosecution underpinned by the common-law rule against double jeopardy than their counterparts in the UK, Canada and New Zealand, the High Court ruled that the bringing of a perjury charge against Carroll in these circumstances was an abuse of process.

In Canada, controversial acquittals in recent years (discussed below) have not generated the same sort of heat around the rule against double jeopardy as in the UK, New Zealand and Australia. Dissatisfaction with particular outcomes has not led to calls for the introduction of either tainted acquittal or new evidence exceptions to the traditional (and in Canada's case, constitutionally entrenched) immunity against re-prosecution after acquittal.

The remainder of this chapter will be devoted to a review of the double jeopardy reform debate as it has played out in the UK, New Zealand and Australian in recent years. A brief discussion of the status of the rule against double jeopardy in Canada will be included, in order to explain why the issue has not been on the law reform agenda. Following the country-by-country review, the final section of this chapter will offer comparative reflections on the impact that the local legal form of human rights protection, and the associated public discourse around human rights, have had on moves to roll back the traditional common-law immunity against re-prosecution after acquittal.

United Kingdom

> Lord Neill: 'I am surprised at the meekness with which the Committee is accepting the situation, where a centuries' old rule against double jeopardy is being jettisoned.'

> The Attorney General, Lord Goldsmith: 'The noble lord, Lord Neill of Bladen, said that it is a centuries-old rule. Yes, it is. . . . [T]hat does not necessarily mean that it is right for all time.'
> During debate on the double jeopardy reform provisions of the Criminal Justice Bill, House of Lords, 17 July 2003[45]

The traditional common-law right not to be re-prosecuted after acquittal

---
44 *R v Carroll* (2002).
45 United Kingdom Parliament, Hansard (House of Lords), 17 July 2003, 1059, 1071.

has been codified in many jurisdictions, including Canada (in s 11(h) of the Charter of Rights and Freedoms 1982) and New Zealand (in s 26(2) of the Bill of Rights Act 1990). In the UK, no such codification has taken place, and the right remains sourced in the common law.[46] Although a range of human rights drawn from the ECHR were incorporated into domestic law by the Human Rights Act 1998 (UK), they did not include a formulation of the right. Despite being firmly established in the European civil law tradition, the principle of *ne bis in idem* was not expressly articulated in the original European Convention. Subsequently, it was expressed in the 7th Protocol to the Convention, but this Protocol has not yet been ratified by the UK.

In addition to providing for the pleas of *autrefois acquit* and *autrefois convict* where a person is charged with the same offence, the common law also provides that a court may stay a prosecution as an abuse of process if a person is charged with a different offence on the same facts.[47] In *R v Z*, the House of Lords ruled that the immunity against re-prosecution did not extend so far as to prevent the prosecution, at a subsequent trial for a different offence, from adducing evidence that the defendant was in fact guilty of an offence of which s/he had previously been acquitted.[48] However, where the subsequent charge is perjury, based on an allegation that the accused lied under oath when s/he denied having committed the offence with which s/he was originally charged, there must be 'additional evidence which the Crown could not have had available using reasonable diligence at the time of the first trial'.[49]

In 1996, the UK Parliament introduced a statutory exception to the common-law rule against double jeopardy. Under s 54 of the Criminal Procedure and Investigations Act 1996 (UK), the prosecution may make an application to the High Court to quash an acquittal (paving the way for a retrial) where the person acquitted 'has been convicted of an administration of justice offence involving interference with or intimidation of a juror or a witness (or potential witness) in any proceedings which led to the acquittal', and where 'there is a real possibility that, but for the interference or intimidation, the acquitted person would not have been acquitted . . .'[50]

From the Stephen Lawrence Inquiry to the Criminal Justice Act 2003[51]

Prompted by the Macpherson Report's recommendation (noted above), on July 1999, the status of the rule against double jeopardy was referred by the

---

46 *Connelly v DPP* (1964); *R v Z* (2000).
47 *Connelly v DPP* (1964).
48 *R v Z* (2000). *Sambasivam* (1950) was overruled.
49 *DPP v Humphreys* (1977), pp 40–1. See New Zealand Law Commission, 2001, 12.
50 England and Wales Law Commission, 2001, pp 10–12.
51 For an overview, see Broadbridge, 2002.

Home Secretary to the Law Commission. In addition to taking into account Recommendation 38, the Commission was asked to take into account 'the powers of the prosecution to re-instate criminal proceedings; and also the UK's international obligations'.[52] The issue was also considered by the Home Affairs Select Committee,[53] and the Auld Report.[54]

Each of these inquiries recommended a 'relaxation' of the rule against double jeopardy, in the form of a 'new evidence' exception. The only significant area of disagreement was over the crimes for which the option of re-prosecution after acquittal should be available. The Law Commission ultimately concluded that the exception should only apply to 'murder, genocide consisting in the killing of any person, or ... reckless killing'.[55] The Home Affairs Committee thought that the revised double jeopardy rule should only apply to crimes that carried a maximum sentence of life imprisonment.[56] Lord Justice Auld recommended that the exception 'should extend to ... grave offences punishable with life and/or long terms of imprisonment as Parliament might specify'.[57]

In 2002, the Government produced a White Paper on criminal justice reform, in which, *inter alia*, it outlined its plans to introduce a 'new evidence' exception along the lines recommended by the Law Commission, but available not only in relation to murder, but also in relation 'to a number of other very serious offences such as rape, manslaughter and armed robbery'.[58]

The Criminal Justice Bill, which included provisions to this effect, was introduced into the Parliament on 21 November 2002. The Bill was eventually passed by the House of Lords in November 2003 and the Criminal Justice Act 2003, including Pt 10 on 'Retrial for Serious Offences', received Royal Assent on 20 November 2003. Part 10 came into force on 4 April 2005.[59]

Given the nature and pedigree of the rule against double jeopardy and in light of the institutional pre-enactment scrutiny arrangements that have been put in place since the introduction of the Human Rights Act 1998, it should come as no surprise that 'human rights sensitivity' was a highly visible feature of the official discourse and public debate over double jeopardy reform in the UK. What is more surprising is that human rights discourse did not constitute a normative or technical hurdle that proponents of change had to

---

52 England and Wales Law Commission, 1999.
53 United Kingdom Parliament, House of Commons Select Committee on Home Affairs, 2000.
54 Auld, 2001.
55 England and Wales Law Commission, 2001, para 4.30.
56 United Kingdom Parliament, House of Commons Select Committee on Home Affairs, 2000, para 24.
57 Auld, 2001, Chapter 12, paras 61–2.
58 United Kingdom Government, 2002. See Fitzpatrick, 2002.
59 The Criminal Justice Act (Commencement No 8 and Transitional and Saving Provisions) Order 2005, Statutory Instrument 2005 No 950 (C 42).

overcome. Rather, human rights discourse was powerfully and effectively invoked to legitimate and facilitate erosion of the rule against double jeopardy.

The human rights associated with the rule against double jeopardy was recognised at *common law* in the UK for some 800 years, prior to their recent legislative configuration. However, what very quickly became clear in the debates leading up to the enactment of Pt 10 of the Criminal Justice Act 2003 was that the common law was no longer the primary reference point for the form and content of civil rights associated with the administration of criminal justice. Instead, all roads led to the ECHR, specifically Art 4 of Protocol 7 to the Convention (see above).

Article 4 was the dominant (and sometimes only) reference point for human rights scrutiny of the proposal to 'relax' the rule against double jeopardy even though, at the time, the UK had yet to ratify the Protocol – such was the magnitude of the paradigm shift that had occurred with the coming into force of the Human Rights Act 1998.

The shape and impact of human rights discourse: facilitator of change rather than barrier to reform

One of the features of the UK debate double jeopardy reform, which is immediately apparent from an examination of the public discourse, is that concern for the human rights implications of the proposed changes was highly visible. For example, as Roberts has observed, one of the features of the Law Commission's Consultation Paper was that it 'had a keen eye to Convention-compliance in the post-Human Rights Act 1998 era'.[60] Given the issues at stake and the timing of the proposals, coming just a few years after human rights had been 'brought home' in the UK, this high visibility is hardly surprising. In any event, as discussed in Chapter 1, the Human Rights Act 1998 now requires that all law reform proposals be scrutinised for their human rights impact and compatibility with prevailing standards, and the example of the lead-up to the enactment of the Criminal Justice Act 2003 shows just how firmly this form of human rights sensitivity has been embedded in the UK's law reform processes.

But does it follow that the high visibility of human rights sensitivity will necessarily set a high hurdle for those who advocate erosion of an existing human rights standard?

The answer, of course, is no. There is no necessary correlation between the visibility of human rights sensitivity and the extent to which the rights in question are protected from proposed erosion. High visibility does not, by definition, mean strong protection. Much depends on how human rights

---

60 Roberts, 2002b, p 395. For other academic commentary and analysis, see Dennis, 2000; Dingwall, 2000; James, Taylor and Walker, 2000; Fitzpatrick, 2002; Roberts, 2002a.

sensitivity is manifested. In the UK debates over double jeopardy reform, the dominant manifestation of human rights sensitivity was the need to ensure that the amended rules were compatible with the standard set by the European Convention on the Protection of Human Rights and Fundamental Freedoms – specifically Art 4 of Protocol 7 (quoted above). This manifestation was obviously a direct product of the prevailing model of human rights protection that came into operation in 2000 – based on domestic implementation of the ECHR via the Human Rights Act 1998.

There are two related points here regarding how human rights sensitivity was manifested in the UK double jeopardy reform discourse. First, there is the adoption of the ECHR as the primary reference point, to the exclusion of other possible reference points (notably, the standard set by Art 14(7) of the ICCPR, and the standard of protection set by English common law, pre-2003). Second, there is the emphasis on assessing 'compatibility' with a specific international/European human rights standard, which largely takes the form of a technical and legalistic exercise in scrutiny, based on a close reading of the wording of the article in question (in this case, Art 4 of Protocol 7 to the ECHR). An illustration of this tendency is the inclusion in key reports of a 'checklist' or accounting 'line item' subheading on 'The Implications of Human Rights Law'[61] or 'Human Rights Considerations'.[62]

These examples illustrate the way in which consideration of human rights implications in the UK's double jeopardy reform debate tended to be reduced to a 'lowest common denominator' approach, focused almost exclusively on the very narrow question of whether the proposed reforms deserved the 'ECHR tick of approval', rather than engaging in a broader examination of whether the proposed changes were legitimate in light of other relevant human rights standards as well as underlying principles and values. The central question of the human rights legitimacy of rolling back the rule against double jeopardy could be constructed as a very simple 'open and shut' case – asked and answered (in the affirmative) with relative ease. Of course, the apparent 'simplicity' of the human rights assessment exercise in the case of Pt 10 of the Criminal Justice Act 2003 was presumably influenced by the fact that, on this occasion, the 'trump' reference point – Art 4 of Protocol 7 to the ECHR – actually imposed a lower standard than the human rights standards embedded in the (then) prevailing common-law rule.[63] This left plenty of room for 'relaxation' of the rule against double

---

61 England and Wales Law Commission, 2001, Pt III.
62 United Kingdom Parliament, House of Commons Select Committee on Home Affairs, 2000, paras 56–7. The Home Affairs Committee's treatment of the issue is little more than a statement of agreement with the Law Commission that the proposed changes were compliant with ECHR obligations.
63 See Emmerson and Ashworth, 2001, pp 308–12.

jeopardy, while still ensuring that the relevant domestic laws of the UK stayed above (or on) the line ruled by the ECHR.

The following contribution to the media debate, from David Pannick QC, is illustrative:

> An absolute double jeopardy rule is not required by fundamental human rights. Article 4 of the Seventh Protocol to the European Convention on Human Rights allows for a person to be tried for an offence for which he or she was previously acquitted 'if there is evidence of new or newly discovered facts, or if there has been a fundamental defect in the previous proceedings which could affect the outcome of the case'.[64]

It was particularly interesting (and a little curious) that Art 4 of Protocol 7 to the ECHR was routinely adopted and regarded as the primary reference point in the public discourse on the double jeopardy reform proposals despite the fact that the UK Government had not at the time ratified the Protocol, and so was not bound by it.[65] There was, one assumes, a certain pragmatism in this strategy. It is unlikely that Protocol 7 would have been elevated to the status that it was if it had not been widely regarded as 'in sync' with the Government's proposed changes.

Pannick's comment (above), illustrates the way in which, contrary to the manner in which international human rights law standards are commonly invoked in domestic law reform debates, the ECHR standard was deployed in the UK double jeopardy reform debate as a facilitating device that positively permitted, rather than merely tolerated, the proposed erosion of the common-law rule. The ECHR was not so much a hurdle to be overcome, but an exhibit that could be introduced into evidence in support of the changes.

The most extreme version of this strategy was in the Government's *Justice for All* White Paper, where the ECHR was portrayed as not merely *permitting* the proposed roll-back of the rule against double jeopardy, but almost *encouraging* it: 'The European Convention on Human Rights (Article 4(2) of Protocol 7) explicitly recognises the *importance of being able* to reopen cases where new evidence comes to light.'[66] In this account, the ECHR is portrayed as 'on-side' with the government's agenda to rebalance a criminal justice system weighted too much in favour of criminals and too much against the prosecution, victims and the wider community.[67]

The theme of the ECHR as facilitative was also evident in the reports of the

---

64 Pannick, 2000.
65 At the time of writing, the United Kingdom Government had not ratified Protocol 7 despite public assertions since at least July 2004 that it planned to do so.
66 United Kingdom Government, 2002, para 4.63 (emphasis added).
67 Ibid, Foreword.

Law Commission[68] and the Home Affairs Committee,[69] and the contributions of academic proponents of double jeopardy reform.[70]

A corollary of the prominence of the ECHR in the UK public discourse on the human rights legitimacy of the proposed changes to the rule against double jeopardy, was that the ICCPR, notwithstanding its claimed universality and the fact that the UK was legally bound by its terms (in a way in which the UK was not formally bound by Art 4 to Protocol 7 to the ECHR – not having yet ratified the Protocol) was marginalised. The standard set by Art 14(7) of the ICCPR was either ignored or assumed to be 'virtually identical'[71] to the standard set by the Art 4 of Protocol 7 to the ECHR.

The Law Commission explicitly recognised that 'The UK is bound under international law to ensure that its domestic practice complies with the obligations which it has undertaken under both the ... ICCPR ... and the ... ECHR.'[72] The Commission also acknowledged that 'Both treaties contain provisions which have a direct bearing on issues considered in this report.'[73] However, the bulk of its treatment of 'The Implications of Human Rights Law'[74] is devoted to a discussion of Art 4 of Protocol 7 to the ECHR, including the manner in which the European Court of Human Rights has interpreted it.[75] After its brief examination of Art 14(7) of the ICCPR,[76] the Commission's implicit conclusion is that Art 14(7), when read in conjunction with the UN Human Rights Committee's General Recommendation 13,[77] should be regarded as setting a standard equivalent to the standard set by the Art 4 of Protocol 7 to ECHR.

The Home Affairs Committee report contains no mention of the ICCPR at all, let alone any consideration of whether Art 14(7) might impose a higher standard than Art 4 of Protocol 7 to the ECHR.[78]

The accuracy of the conflation of the terms of the two instruments on the issue of the scope of the protection against double jeopardy is, at least, debatable, as the '11th hour' change of heart of the Joint Committee on Human Rights suggests.

The only time when the ICCPR 'came to life' in the UK double jeopardy

---

68 See England and Wales Law Commission, 2001, pp 29–34.
69 United Kingdom Parliament, House of Commons Select Committee on Home Affairs, 2000, paras 56–7.
70 See, e.g., Dennis, 2000, p 938.
71 Ibid, p 935.
72 See England and Wales Law Commission, 2001, para 3.1.
73 Ibid.
74 Ibid, Part III.
75 Ibid, paras 3.11–3.20.
76 Ibid, 3.4–3.6.
77 United Nations, Human Rights Committee, 1984.
78 United Kingdom Parliament, House of Commons Select Committee on Home Affairs, 2000, see 'Human Rights Considerations', paras 56–7.

debates was in the second of two reports by the Joint Committee on Human Rights on the proposed double jeopardy reforms. After previously having given the Criminal Justice Bill provisions an unequivocal 'tick' in terms of international human rights compatibility (after what, it must be said, was a rather cursory examination),[79] the Committee was prompted to have a second look when it realised that in the House of Commons the bill's definition of 'new and compelling evidence' had been significantly broadened (by removing the requirement that the evidence must not have been available at the time of the first trial).

The Committee expressed serious concern at this amendment and felt that it dramatically changed the relationship between the proposed double jeopardy roll-back and international human rights standards:

> We have reconsidered the human rights implications of Part 10 of the Bill in the light of these amendments. It seems to us that, as amended, the provisions appear likely to be incompatible with ICCPR Article 14.7, which provides: 'No one shall be liable to be tried or punished again for an offence for which he has already been finally convicted or acquitted in accordance with the law and penal procedure of each country.' This Article binds the UK in international law. It has not been introduced to national law in the UK. There was no need to do so: the rule against double jeopardy is currently entirely compatible with it. The Bill's provisions could be incompatible with the obligation in international law. The UN Human Rights Committee has accepted that the reopening or resumption of a criminal trial in exceptional circumstances might be acceptable, but would not sanction a straightforward retrial. In our Second Report, we accepted that newly available and compelling new evidence might fall within the former category. If the evidence in question is not new, this is very doubtful.[80]

The Committee suggested that its last minute concerns about the human rights credentials of the proposed legislation were a direct product of amendments introduced in the Parliament after the Committee had first considered the bill. This may have triggered or justified the reconsideration, but a close side-by-side reading of the two Joint Committee on Human Rights reports gives the impression that second time round a much keener eye was being passed over the bill in terms of human rights sensitivity. It is not obvious why the distinction between a (permissible) 'resumption of a trial justified by exceptional circumstances'[81] or 'straightforward retrial' (whatever this

---

79 United Kingdom Parliament, Joint Committee on Human Rights, 2003a.
80 United Kingdom Parliament, Joint Committee on Human Rights, 2003b, p 15.
81 United Nations, Human Rights Committee, 1984, para 19.

phrase means) should come down to a distinction between whether the 'new evidence' was unavailable at the first trial, or 'available but not used'.

It was perhaps after pondering this issue (without commenting upon it) that the Committee saw fit to belatedly point out (this part had not changed from the original bill) that 'the title of Part 10 of the Bill is "Retrial for serious offences", and the word "retried" is used in the body of the clauses'.[82]

Rather than following this insight through to the conclusion that the whole Pt 10 procedure for post acquittal proceedings was inconsistent with Art 14(7), the Committee recommended some cosmetic surgery to the Bill:

> In order to avoid the risk that the United Kingdom might unnecessarily appear to the international community to be indifferent to the requirements of international human rights law, we recommend that the title of Part 10 should be changed to 'Reopening trials after acquittal of serious offences', and that 'retried' and similar terms should similarly be replaced wherever they occur.[83]

Of course, if the Committee's substantive objection was well founded, then the 'appearance' of indifference would not be 'unnecessary' at all – it would be entirely accurate. No amount of cosmetic amendment would save the legislation from inconsistency with Art 14(7) of the ICCPR.

For present purposes, what is even more interesting than the Committee's substantive shift on the merits of the bill, is the shift in its preferred reference point for human rights scrutiny of the bill. Atypically, in the UK discourse, the ICCPR was adopted as the primary reference point, in preference to the ECHR.

Second time round, the Committee emphasised that 'The terms of P7/4 [of the ECHR] allow greater leeway to the state than the ICCPR appears to do'.[84] While this was noted in the Committee's first report, the Committee there concluded, after considering the UN Human Rights Committee's General Comment 13,[85] that '[t]he difference between the requirements of the two instruments may therefore be less than appears at first sight'.[86] Certainly, the Committee's conclusion in its first report – that the 'the Bill's proposal relating to double jeopardy . . . would not be incompatible with human rights, although we recognize that the proposals are highly controversial in terms of

---

82 United Kingdom Parliament, Joint Committee on Human Rights, 2003b, p 15.
83 Ibid, p 18.
84 Ibid, pp 15–16.
85 United Nations, Human Rights Committee, 1984.
86 United Kingdom Parliament, Joint Committee on Human Rights, 2003a, para 49.

policy'[87] – was explicitly adduced from an application of 'the principle set out in P7/4.2';[88] that is, the ECHR standard.

In addition to emphasising, with greater conviction, that Art 14(7) of the ICCPR imposed a higher standard than Art 4 of Protocol 7 to the ECHR, the Committee also emphasised, in a stronger way than it had done in its original report, that '. . . P7/4 does not bind the UK, and the more restrictive terms of ICCPR Article 14.7 do . . .'[89]

The Committee explicitly conceded that in its first report it had been willing to go with the prevailing view that the two standards were likely to be interpreted as equivalent and acknowledged that this was the interpretation that was 'most favourable to the Government'.[90] It is not clear what motivated the Committee to shift position on the relationship between the standards set by the relevant provisions of the ECHR and the ICCPR. The new-found differential cannot logically have been 'caused' by the amendments to the definition of 'new and compelling evidence'. Perhaps the (re)discovery of the higher and binding ICCPR standard was a convenient, pragmatic and purposive strategy. The Committee may have been genuinely concerned by, and opposed to, the broadened 'new evidence' definition and so 'went looking' for a human rights law hook on which its concerns could be hung.

Whatever the Committee's precise motivation or strategy, its conclusion was unequivocal: 'We therefore consider that the Bill as currently drafted gives rise to a significant threat to the right under ICCPR Article 14.7, which binds the UK in international law.'[91]

Neither the Committee's substantive comments on the new evidence definition, nor its cosmetic suggestions regarding references to 'retrial' were reflected in the final form of Pt 10 of the Criminal Justice Act 2003.

It remains to be seen whether the UN Human Rights Committee shares the concerns of the UK Joint Committee on Human Rights, when next it considers a periodic report from the UK Government on its compliance with the ICCPR.[92]

The double jeopardy roll-back provisions of the Criminal Justice Bill 2002 were opposed by several civil liberties and lawyers groups, including Liberty, Legal Action Group, the Bar Council and the Criminal Bar Association.[93] However, contributions to the public debate by these groups did not adopt the

---

87 United Kingdom Parliament, Joint Committee on Human Rights, 2003a, para 52.
88 Ibid.
89 United Kingdom Parliament, Joint Committee on Human Rights, 2003b, p 16.
90 Ibid, p 17.
91 Ibid. See also, Ashworth, 2004, p 527.
92 The United Kingdom's next periodic report to the Human Rights Committee is due on 1 November 2006.
93 Liberty, Legal Action Group, Bar Council, Criminal Bar Association, 2002.

reasonably familiar strategy of asserting incompatibility with international human rights standards – presumably on the basis that such arguments would not carry any weight, given the prevalence of the view that the legislation was compatible with the ECHR. In fact, such a strategy would likely have been, at least in the atypical case of double jeopardy (where the consensus was that the English common-law status quo offered a higher standard of protection than international/European standards), not only ineffective, but counterproductive.

Justice was one of the only organisations to even refer publicly to international (as well as some comparative domestic) human rights standards. However, the ICCPR and the ECHR are mentioned in terms that effectively concede that neither represented an impediment to proposed new exceptions to the rule against double jeopardy, and that the two standards were equivalent.[94] For example, Justice observed that 'In international law, article 14(7) of the International Covenant on Civil and Political Rights *does not prevent* the re-opening of the case in accordance with the law and penal procedure of the state concerned if there is evidence of new or newly discovered facts, or if there has been a fundamental defect in the previous proceedings which could effect the outcome of the case'.[95] Note that the standard said to be set by ICCPR is articulated in language taken from Art 4 of Protocol 7 to the ECHR. Interestingly, Justice suggested that the ECHR standard allowed for retrial based on new evidence 'provided the evidence was not available at the time of the trial . . .',[96] which is not a requirement under the final form of Pt 10 of the Criminal Justice Act 2003.

That assertions of incompatibility were not part of the strategy employed by opponents of the proposed changes was noted by the Home Affairs Committee, when it observed that the view that the changes were consistent with the ECHR:

> . . . is not generally contested by the legal and civil liberties bodies which are opposed to a relaxation of the double jeopardy rule. The Criminal Bar Association, Criminal Law Committee of the Law Society, the Society of Labour Lawyers, Liberty, Justice and British Irish Rights Watch all base their criticism of the proposals on the principles and practice of English law.[97]

Rather, the main reference points in the submissions of civil liberties and lawyers groups were general principles of fairness, and the emphasis was on

---

94 See also, Justice, 2002.
95 Justice, 2003 (emphasis added).
96 Ibid.
97 United Kingdom Parliament, House of Commons Select Committee on Home Affairs 2000, para 57. Cf Ashworth, 2004, p 527.

highlighting practical problems associated with the proposed new procedures.[98] In particular, Liberty emphasised the unlikelihood that a subsequent trial would be fair where jury members were likely to know that the Court of Appeal had decided that the 'new and compelling evidence' constituted strong evidence of guilt.[99] Some contributions focused on attempting to limit the scope of the 'relaxation' of the rule against double jeopardy to a small number of serious offences. The Law Society's Criminal Law Committee initially opposed the proposed reforms, but eventually gave cautious and qualified approval to the exceptions to the rule against double jeopardy:

> The Committee has consistently opposed the relaxation of the role of double jeopardy, as we were unconvinced that the safeguards proposed were adequate. It is accepted that the tighter safeguards . . . [described in the Government's *Justice For All* White Paper] overcome our objections in respects of certain cases.[100]

The Committee recommended that 'the offences should be limited to murder and manslaughter, and possibly rape'.[101]

In a briefing document designed to inform House of Lords consideration of the bill, Liberty noted:

> We are left with the impression that the government has decided on a list of defendants who, in their opinion, should have their case retried and produced a list of offences to accommodate them. The list is far more extensive than the one originally suggested in *Justice for All* . . . Although Liberty opposes the removal of double jeopardy protection in principle, if retrials for serious offences are to be permitted, we would wish to see a much more restricted listed limited to murder and rape.[102]

There was some modest success on this issue. In the House of Lords the Government did agree to a minor reduction in the number of offences to which the option of retrial after acquittal would be available.[103] In the House of Lords the Attorney General noted:

> The Government has listened carefully to the criticisms leveled at Schedule 4 [now Schedule 5] in both Houses. What comprises the most serious offences remains a matter of judgment, but I believe that the

---

98 See Broadbridge, 2002, pp 32–6.
99 Liberty, 2002a; Liberty, 2002b; Liberty, 2003.
100 Law Society of England and Wales (2002), para 19.
101 Ibid, para 21; see also, Justice, 2002, para 73.
102 Liberty, 2003, pp 42–3.
103 See Criminal Justice Act 2003 (UK), Sched 5.

retrial procedure should apply to offences other than murder, soliciting murder and genocide alone, as was proposed by the Opposition. Having said that and having looked again at this matter, we believe there is scope to reduce the number of offences that should qualify for the retrial provisions. Therefore, we are proposing a number of amendments which will help to focus the list on the gravest offences and remove those which are not of the highest order of seriousness but are relatively high-volume offences – for example, causing grievous bodily harm.[104]

Parliamentary opponents of the new evidence exception in the Criminal Justice Bill adopted similar strategies to those employed by groups such as Liberty and Justice. In addition, there was also emphasis on the fact that the proposed changes would leave the UK out of step with established practice throughout the world. For example, in the House of Lords, Baroness Kennedy observed:

> We are talking about a rule of constitutional importance which is recognized throughout the common law world and even beyond. It is applied in virtually all developed legal systems. . . . We are running in the face of a principle that is accepted around the world. . . . Interfering with . . . [the rule against double jeopardy] is a shocking step away from the principles on which our system is based.[105]

This line of objection represents an interesting attempt to construct an international standard based on state practice, rather than by reference to the terms of international human rights law. On the whole, however, Weinberg is right when he says of the parliamentary debate:

> Resistance in Parliament to repeal of the venerable double jeopardy guarantee was surprisingly limited. The argument that repeal advanced the protection of victims' rights carried the day, overcoming civil liberties concerns that had underlain the guarantee as a fundamental right of Englishmen for eight centuries.[106]

In the broader context of the UK's post-Human Rights Act 1998 environment (see Chapter 1), and the specific environment surrounding human rights scrutiny of the double jeopardy reform proposals described above, it is not surprising that opponents of the proposed legislation did not, on the whole, articulate their arguments with reference to international human rights

---

104 United Kingdom Parliament, Hansard (House of Lords), 4 November 2003, 691–2.
105 United Kingdom Parliament, Hansard (House of Lords), 17 July 2003, 1061, 1063. See also, Lord Thomas of Gresford, ibid, 1066.
106 Weinberg, 2004.

instruments. However, it is somewhat surprising that the groups in question did not attempt to make the case that the ICCPR imposed a higher standard than the ECHR, and that the consistency of the double jeopardy provisions of the Criminal Justice Bill with the standard imposed by the former might be open to question. That such a strategy was not pursued is indicative of the dominance of the ECHR as the primary reference point for the exercise of human right scrutiny in the UK.

New Zealand

> No case has been established in New Zealand for a 'new evidence' exception to the rule against double jeopardy . . . [W]e think it highly improbable that such a course could be justified in New Zealand.
> New Zealand Law Commission, *Acquittal Following Perversion of the Course of Justice* (Report 70, March 2001), pp viii, 1

Section 26(2) of the Bill of Rights Act 1990 states: 'No one who has been finally acquitted or convicted of, or pardoned for, an offence shall be tried or punished for it again.' Section 26(2) is not regarded as in independent source of the right not to be re-prosecuted after acquittal (or conviction): according to the New Zealand Law Commission, it 'does no more than restate in an abridged form sections 357–359 of the Crimes Act 1961'.[107] These provisions are in turn, based on the traditional common-law formulations of the *autrefois convict* or *autrefois acquit* pleas.[108] Consistent with the position adopted by the House of Lords in *R v Z*,[109] the New Zealand Court of Appeal has held that the immunity against re-prosecution after acquittal underpinned by the rule against double jeopardy is not so broad as to prevent the prosecution, in a subsequent prosecution on a different charge, from asserting that the accused was in fact guilty of a crime of which s/he had previously been acquitted. In *R v Degnan* the Court held that 'Evidence . . . is not rendered inadmissible at law by reason of the fact that a previous trial based on that evidence has resulted in an acquittal or a stay of proceedings'.[110]

As a result of the controversy surrounding Kevin Moore's avoidance of a murder conviction (above), the Minister of Justice asked the New Zealand Law Commission to consider the issue of whether the rule of double jeopardy should be relaxed so as to allow an accused such as Moore to be retried for the substantive offence of which he had been acquitted at a 'tainted' trial.[111]

---

107 New Zealand Law Commission, 2001, p 3; see also, Optican, 2003, p 745; Mahoney, 1990.
108 See *Daniels v Thompson* (1998).
109 *R v Z* (2000).
110 *R v Degnan* (2001), para 37 per Tipping J.
111 New Zealand Law Commission, 2000 (discussion paper); New Zealand Law Commission, 2001 (final report).

The Law Commission recommended the introduction of a tainted acquittal exception to the rule against double jeopardy, so that, for example, a person like Kevin Moore who had secured a murder acquittal by committing an administration of justice offence could be re-prosecuted for murder. The Commission gave close consideration to relevant domestic and international reference points for human rights scrutiny – namely, s 26(2) of the BORA and Art 14(7) of the ICCPR. Drawing on the England and Wales Law Commission's analysis of the scope of Art 14(7),[112] the New Zealand Law Commission concluded that 'the retrial of a defective proceeding would not offend against Article 14(7) or section 26 [of the BORA]'.[113] In its final report the Commission framed a 'carefully restricted limitation . . . upon the Bill of Rights prohibition against double jeopardy' which, in its view, conformed with the requirement under s 5 of the BORA that any limits on the rights protected by the Bill of Rights must be 'reasonable' and 'demonstrably justified in a free and democratic society'.[114]

In its analysis of proposals for reform of the rule against double jeopardy, the Law Commission drew a clear distinction between what it regarded as a justifiable (that is, BORA- and ICCPR-compliant) exception to the prohibition on re-prosecution after acquittal – in the case of a tainted acquittal – and an unjustifiable exception – in the case of new and compelling evidence. The Commission noted that 'No case has been established in New Zealand for a "new evidence" exception to the rule against double jeopardy',[115] and added that 'we think it highly improbable that such a course could be justified in New Zealand'.[116]

It came as something of a surprise then when the Government announced in May 2004 that it planned to introduce both a 'tainted acquittal' exception and a 'new evidence' exception to the rule against double jeopardy.[117] The immediate response of the New Zealand Law Society's Criminal Law Committee was that the proposal for a new evidence exception was 'rather more controversial' than the proposal for a tainted acquittal exception, and had 'not been the subject of the same scrutiny and debate'.[118]

One of the strategies employed by the New Zealand Government to defend its own policy preference for a new evidence exception in addition to a tainted acquittal exception was to point to the fact that this step had already been taken by the UK Parliament (as well as being on the agenda in Australia).[119]

---

112 England and Wales Law Commission, 1999.
113 New Zealand Law Commission, 2000, p 11; also, New Zealand Law Commission, 2001, p 4.
114 New Zealand Law Commission, 2001, p 13.
115 Ibid, p viii.
116 Ibid, p 1.
117 New Zealand Minister of Justice, 2004a.
118 New Zealand Law Society, 2004a.
119 New Zealand Minister of Justice, 2004b.

The Justice Minister, Phil Goff, stated publicly that introducing a new evidence exception would:

> ... bring New Zealand in with like-minded countries. The UK Government has moved to change the law along similar lines, while the European Convention on Human Rights provides that a case may be reopened if there is evidence of new or newly discovered facts.[120]

The Justice Minister's reference to the ECHR was curious, given that New Zealand is not a party to the ECHR – especially when no reference was made to the ICCPR, to which New Zealand is a party. In fact, this public statement by the Justice Minister was emblematic of the case-making approach of proponents of double jeopardy reform in New Zealand as reflected in the public discourse: a tendency to marginalise or under-emphasise those normative human rights reference points that loomed as potential barriers to the introduction of exceptions to the immunity against re-prosecution after acquittal (like the BORA and the ICCPR) and to rely heavily on the 'UK precedent' and the ECHR reference point which was pivotal in making the UK case (it allowed proponents of a new evidence exception to defend their policy preference as entirely consistent with the prevailing European human rights standard), even though the latter has no direct formal relevance in New Zealand. This example suggests a fluidity in New Zealand's public discourse on human rights: the BORA does not necessarily dominate in the way in which the Charter of Rights and Freedoms has long done in Canada, and the Human Rights Act/ECHR has in the UK in more recent times. At least in the case of double jeopardy reform there was a certain opportunism about the Government's strategy of drawing attention to the 'reform friendly' reference point of the ECHR and the UK precedent rather the more obviously relevant, but not so 'helpful' BORA and ICCPR.

When the Criminal Procedure Bill was first introduced into the New Zealand Parliament in June 2004, the Green Party's Justice spokesperson, Nandor Tanczos, questioned why the Government was introducing a new evidence exception when:

> ... there is no evidence that this is a compelling problem. Where is the evidence that peoples are being acquitted on the basis of these things and that we have such a problem with it that a law needs to be passed that contravenes the longstanding principle against double jeopardy?[121]

---

120 New Zealand Minister of Justice, 2004a.
121 New Zealand House of Representatives, Hansard, 29 June 2004, p 14219.

Introducing the bill, the Associate Minister of Justice, Rick Barker, indicated that the Government wanted to be proactive:

> There have been cases overseas where conclusive evidence of guilt has surfaced, post-acquittal. It is my view that most New Zealanders would be outraged if that situation occurred here and our justice system was unable to bring the offenders to justice.[122]

Mr Baker emphasised that the creation of two exceptions to the double jeopardy rule was 'consistent with the law in the UK, and with reforms proposed in Australia'.[123] Notably, there was no reference to Canada – the only one of the four traditional Commonwealth/common-law comparator countries not to have gone down the double jeopardy reform road – despite the significant extent to which New Zealand borrowed from Canada's experience with the Charter of Rights and Freedoms in framing the BORA.

In fact, human rights discourse was almost completely absent from the Minister's first reading speech. There was no explicit reference to human rights, and no mention of s 26(2) of the BORA or Art 14(7) of the ICCPR. The Minister described the right that the bill would curtail in euphemistic terms, noting that the proposed new evidence exception would be a departure from 'the criminal justice tradition of only one trial'.[124]

During the first reading debate on 29 June 2004, the National Party expressed serious reservations about the proposed new evidence exception. National Party spokesperson on justice, Richard Worth, noted that while the move 'may, perhaps, be justified on a populist basis',[125] it was 'highly controversial' and indicated that Parliament was 'in danger of pursuing criminal adventures for all the wrong reasons'.[126] Reservations about the new evidence were also expressed by MPs from New Zealand First, the Greens and the United Future Party.[127] The bill was referred to a parliamentary committee – the Law and Order Committee.

On 22 June 2004, the Attorney General, Margaret Wilson, completed a report on the Criminal Procedure Bill under s 7 of the New Zealand Bill of Rights Act 1990.[128] The Attorney General concluded that the proposed tainted acquittal exception was a justifiable infringement of the right protected by s 26(2). She observed that an acquittal, which was 'only

---

122 New Zealand House of Representatives, Hansard, 29 June 2004, p 14213.
123 Ibid.
124 Ibid.
125 Ibid, p 14215.
126 Ibid.
127 Ibid, pp 14217–23.
128 The s 7 reporting procedure is explained in Chapter 1.

obtained by an orchestrated perversion of the trial ... is not a legitimate acquittal and is not deserving of the basic protection'.[129]

The Attorney General characterised the new and compelling evidence exception as 'qualitatively different'[130] from the tainted acquittal exception. It was much harder to justify because it 'goes to the core of the purposes informing s 26(2)'.[131] She concluded that the relevant amendments to the Crimes Act 1961 were 'inconsistent with the "double jeopardy" right contained in s 26(2) of the *Bill of Rights Act* ... [and] do not appear to be justifiable in terms of s 5 of the *Bill of Rights Act*'.[132] The Attorney General's chief objection to the proposed new and compelling evidence exception was that the option of applying for permission to retry a person after acquittal was not limited only to the most serious of offences, but would be available in the case of all crimes (more than 40 at the time of the Attorney General's report) that carry a maximum penalty of 14 years or more. She concluded:

> I consider that a specific and limited schedule of offences must be regarded as a minimum requirement of any scheme that makes an exception to double jeopardy for fresh and compelling evidence cases. ... [I]t may have been possible to achieve a reasonable limitation of the double jeopardy right by reference to a specific and narrow list of offences, where the predominant nature of the captured offending is serious enough to warrant the erosion of this fundamental right.[133]

The Attorney General expressly disagreed with the view expressed by the UK Parliament's Joint Committee on Human Rights that the range of offences to which the exception applied was 'a matter for political judgment, not a matter of human rights'.[134] In her view the potential breadth of the erosion of the right against double jeopardy was central to an assessment of the justifiability of the human rights infringements.

In expressing a preference for specific and enumerated serious offences to which the new and compelling evidence exception would apply, the Attorney General relied on the 'precedent' set by Pt 10 of the UK's Criminal Justice Act 2003, and the approach recommended in Australia by the Model Criminal Code Officers Committee (see below).[135]

This was an interesting variation on the common phenomenon of cross-

---

129 New Zealand, Attorney General, 2004, para 14.
130 Ibid, para 16.
131 Ibid.
132 Ibid, para 1.
133 Ibid, paras 25, 26.
134 United Kingdom Parliament, Joint Committee on Human Rights, 2003a, para 46.
135 Australia, MCCOC, 2003.

referencing proposed law reforms to steps taken or under consideration in traditional comparator countries, actively employed by the New Zealand Government in relation to their proposed amendments to the rule against double jeopardy. On this occasion, equivalent legislative reforms in the UK and equivalent reform proposals in Australia were invoked by the New Zealand Attorney General not merely to render politically and legally 'conceivable' the erosion of double jeopardy protections, but also for the more specific 'counter-purpose' of establishing parameters for the justifiable scope of limits on the right associated with the double jeopardy principle and recognised by s 26(2) of the BORA.

The availability of a procedure whereby the Attorney General can formally advise the New Zealand Parliament, in advance of enactment, that proposed legislation is, in his/her opinion, an unjustified limit on human rights protected by the BORA, suggests that the BORA has the potential to be a significant and relatively autonomous influence on the law-making process in New Zealand. This impression would appear to be reinforced by evidence that the s 7 report procedure is regularly employed, but is undermined by evidence that the New Zealand Parliament frequently enacts legislation, notwithstanding advice from the Attorney General that it unjustifiably limits BORA rights (see Chapter 1).

Hiebert's assessment that s 7 reports are a modest hurdle in the face of a Government committed to pursuing a particular policy agenda (see Chapter 1) has been echoed in relation to the specific issue of double jeopardy reform. In the wake of the Attorney General's s 7 report on the double jeopardy reform provisions of the Criminal Procedure Bill 2004, Optican observed that '... there's never been a s 7 report in history that has stopped a Bill getting passed if Parliament wanted it passed'.[136] Hiebert observes:

> It is particularly striking that despite the Attorney-General's suggestion that the unreasonable nature of the rights infringement in the [double jeopardy reform provisions of the] Criminal Procedure Bill 2004 could be addressed by adopting a 'specific and limited schedule of offences', as is the case in the United Kingdom, this suggestion did not influence the scope of the Bill.[137]

Some commentators have suggested that rather than give parliamentarians pause, a s 7 report – that the bill in question would effect an unjustifiable infringement of rights protected by the BORA – might, on some occasions, be conscripted by government (or other supporters of the bill) as a 'badge of honour'; along the lines of: 'we are so committed to the policy behind this

---

136 Quoted in Milner, 2005.
137 Hiebert, 2005b, p 89.

legislation, and are so convinced that it is what New Zealanders want, that we are even prepared to wear the criticism that the legislation infringes rights protected by the BORA'.[138] Of course, this sort of strategy is only feasible in an environment – informed by elements of both legal form and legal culture – where the standards set by a primary human rights legal instrument are regarded as within the parameters of legitimate political disagreement, rather than absolute limits, and where Parliament is the ultimate arbiter of the extent to which human rights standards should constrain legislative action. The prospects of such a strategy being adopted in a particular instance have also been exacerbated in the New Zealand context by the overuse of s 7 reports by Attorneys General – what Rishworth has described as the 'cry wolf' factor.[139] Huscroft concurs: 'The main consequence of over-reporting is that the seriousness of a report is diminished . . .'.[140] The story of the passage of the Criminal Procedure Bill is illustrative.

On 29 July 2005, the Law and Order Committee released its report on the Criminal Procedure Bill. The Committee acknowledged that 'The rule against double jeopardy is a fundamental principle of law . . . [that] stems from the Magna Carta and is codified under section 26(2) of the Bill of Rights Act . . .'.[141] However, by majority,[142] the Committee recommended that the Criminal Procedure Bill be passed, without any substantive amendments to the provisions dealing with the rule against double jeopardy. In the face of the Attorney General's opinion that the new evidence exception was an unjustifiable breach of s 26(2), the Committee reached a different conclusion: 'the new and compelling evidence proposal represents . . . a principled balancing of the two competing interests of finality and justice in the criminal justice system.'[143] Retrial of a person acquitted of a serious offence was 'in the interests of justice . . . [w]here new evidence emerges after an acquittal undermining its legitimacy from a factual perspective . . .'.[144] Unlike the Attorney General, the Committee was satisfied that the inclusion of all offences for which the maximum penalty is 14 years imprisonment or more was appropriate.

One of the most striking features of the Law and Order Committee's report on the double jeopardy reform provisions is how little time was devoted to the issue of BORA compatibility – despite the best efforts of

---

138 Paul Rishworth, personal communication, 18 August 2005; Scott Optican, personal communication, 18 August 2005.
139 Paul Rishworth, personal communication, 18 August 2005.
140 Huscroft, 2003a, p 215. See also, Hiebert, 2005b, p 77.
141 New Zealand House of Representatives, Law and Order Committee, 2005, pp 5–6.
142 National Party and United Future members of the Law and Order Committee did not support the proposed exceptions.
143 New Zealand House of Representatives, Law and Order Committee, 2005, p 11.
144 Ibid.

submitters like the New Zealand Law Society[145] and the New Zealand Human Rights Commission[146] to place s 26(2) at the front and centre of the Committee's deliberations. For example, the New Zealand Law Society argued that both the tainted acquittal and new evidence exceptions were unjustified infringements of BORA. In relation to the new and compelling evidence exception, the Law Society argued:

> The provision infringes section 26(2) of the NZ Bill of Rights Act. It is submitted that the proposed provisions are not justified in accordance with section 5 of the Act as they are not necessary in light of:
> (a) The extremely limited number of cases to which the section would apply in any event.
> (b) The clear alternative which would maintain both the common law rule and the rule as stated in section 26(2) against double jeopardy.[147]

The Committee made no serious attempt, in its published report, to engage with the substance of the BORA-based objections of the Attorney General to the proposed new evidence exception advanced by the Attorney General (as well as by submitters like the New Zealand Human Rights Commission and the New Zealand Law Society), preferring instead to simply reach a different conclusion. This illustration may be seen to confirm the fears of those commentators who have expressed concern about the 'cry wolf' effect of the overuse of s 7 reports, but it also invites more general speculation about the place and style of human rights assessments in the process of bill scrutiny in which the New Zealand Parliament's select committees participate. Human rights considerations are clearly in the frame, but, at least in the case of the Criminal Procedure Bill, BORA rights were not regarded as a primary touchstone for legitimacy, but as simply part of the mix of political factors and values to be taken into account.

It is interesting to compare the approach taken by the New Zealand Parliament's Law and Order Committee in relation to the double jeopardy reform provisions of the Criminal Procedure Bill and the approach of the UK Parliament's Joint Committee on Human Rights to the equivalent provisions of the Criminal Justice Act 2003 (UK). While it must be acknowledged that the latter has a more explicit and specific mandate – for conducting pre-enactment human rights impact assessments of proposed legislation – the New Zealand select committees are relied upon to play an equivalent role, albeit as part of a wider assessment of the merits of proposed legislation.

---

145 New Zealand Law Society, 2004b. See also, New Zealand Press Association, 2004a (discussing a submission by Donald Stevens QC).
146 New Zealand Human Rights Commission, 2004a.
147 New Zealand Law Society, 2004b, p 11.

Although it did not wake up to the full implications of the proposed new evidence exception until the eleventh hour (see discussion above), the UK Joint Committee eventually engaged in a close and critical analysis of the compatibility of the exception with the human rights protected by both the ECHR and the ICCPR. In contrast, the New Zealand Law and Order Committee barely grappled with the implications of s 26(2) of the BORA and ignored Art 14(7) of the ICCPR completely when it addressed the new evidence exception to the prohibition on retrial after acquittal. Reinforcing the impression that there is a degree of pragmatic selectivity in New Zealand's pre-enactment human rights scrutiny practices, the only time that the ICCPR was mentioned was when it was deployed in support of the relatively uncontroversial tainted acquittal exception. The Committee observed that Art 14(7), as interpreted by the United Nations Human Rights Committee,[148] allowed the 're-opening [of] criminal acquittals (as distinct from retrial) ... where there has been a fundamental flaw in the proceedings'.[149] Curiously, the Human Rights Committee's General Comment No. 13 is not the source of the concept of 'fundamental flaw' as the rationale for the legitimate 'resumption of a trial'[150] after acquittal. Rather, the language used by the New Zealand Law and Order appears to have its origins in Art 4(2) of Protocol 7 to the ECHR, which expressly permits the 'reopening' of a case where 'there has been a fundamental defect in the previous proceedings, which could affect the outcome of the case'. In any event, the direct reference to the ICCPR (and the indirect reference to ECHR Protocol 7) in the context of its discussion of the tainted acquittal exception, but not in its discussion of the new evidence exception, reveals a selectivity about the Committee's invocation of international human rights standards in its determination to endorse the thrust of the Government's double jeopardy reform agenda.

As this discussion of the Law and Order Committee's report on the Criminal Procedure Bill reveals, it is an illuminating exercise to identify and compare the dominant normative reference point for 'human rights impact' assessment of the proposed statutory exceptions to the rule against double jeopardy at various points in the law reform process. For the New Zealand Law Commission the primary reference points were the BORA and the ICCPR. For the Attorney General, the BORA was the primary reference. Both of these findings were anticipated – as a direct result of the particular legal form operative in New Zealand since 1990. More surprising was the New Zealand Government's tendency, demonstrated both in the parliamentary debates as

---

148 United Nations, Human Rights Committee, 1984.
149 New Zealand House of Representatives, Law and Order Committee, 2005.
150 United Nations, Human Rights Committee, 1984, para 19.

well as statements made outside the legislature, to downplay the ICCPR (to which New Zealand is a party) and the BORA, and to draw attention to the combined effect of the standard set by the ECHR regime (notwithstanding that New Zealand is not a party to the European Convention or the 7th Protocol), and the precedent set by the UK Parliament's enactment of Pt 10 of the Criminal Justice Act 2003.

There is an obvious logic to this emphasis – the Government prioritised those normative reference points that were most sympathetic to its preferred policy outcome – but it is an approach which is hard to reconcile with the existence and formal legal status of the BORA, which was enacted in 1990 to serve as the primary domestic reference for assessing the human rights legitimacy of both existing laws and proposed new laws. This example reinforces the impression that New Zealand's BORA has not achieved the standing in the policy-formation and law-making process that has been achieved by Canada's Charter of Rights and Freedoms 1982 and the UK's Human Rights Act 1998. Whether this is considered desirable or undesirable will likely depend on one's point of view. On the one hand, the successful introduction of statutory exceptions to the right not to be re-prosecuted after acquittal in New Zealand may be considered a 'victory' for the principle of parliamentary supremacy – proof that the enactment of a statutory bill of rights need not involve a weakening of the legislature's control of the political reigns.[151] On the other hand, the fact that proponents of double jeopardy reform were able, with relative ease, to marginalise s 26(2) of the BORA in the public discourse surrounding the Criminal Procedure Bill suggests that aspirations for the transformation of local legal culture, frequently associated with the domestic adoption of a primary human rights law, may have been imperfectly realised in New Zealand.

One of the opposition strategies, employed (unsuccessfully) by the New Zealand Human Rights Commission in its submission to the Law and Order Committee, was to question the adequacy of the 'UK precedent' argument advanced by Government proponents of curtailment of the right not to be re-prosecuted after final acquittal.

> While there might be a trend amongst some governments of 'like-minded' jurisdictions to introduce a new evidence exception to the double jeopardy rule the HRC is not persuaded that such a trend provides a sound basis for erosion of this fundamental right.
> It is clear that the origins of the changes made in the UK largely flow from an inadequate investigation by the police into the murder of Stephen Lawrence. While it is always appropriate to have regard to changes in the law in other jurisdictions there is a need to have regard

---

151 See Hiebert, 2004, 2006a.

to the context in which the change originated. When a proposed change in the law involves a derogation of a fundamental, longstanding right there is a need to pause and reflect before deciding to make a similar change to New Zealand law. The HRC is not convinced that the factors which led to the changes in the UK warrant the New Zealand Parliament making what would be a more extensive inroad into the right than that made in the UK.[152]

The New Zealand Law Society extended this line of analysis further, suggesting that it was dubious for the New Zealand Government to attempt to invoke indirectly the (relatively permissive) normative human rights standard constituted by Art 4 of Protocol 7 to the ECHR by pointing to the 'UK precedent', given that the UK was not even a party to the relevant protocol at the time of its legislature's enactment of Pt 10 of the Criminal Justice Act 2003 (UK):

> In support of this exception in New Zealand the Minister of Justice has argued that the United Kingdom legislation has not been challenged in terms of the European Convention on Human Rights, and that this therefore accords it a certain legitimacy. However, it appears the United Kingdom is not a party to the relevant part of that convention [Protocol 7] whereby that provision could be challenged.[153]

The practice of intra-Commonwealth law reform 'borrowing' has a strong tradition in New Zealand (as well as in Australia, Canada and the UK).[154] However, in relation to the issue of double jeopardy reform, the strategy was employed in a somewhat unconventional, and opportunistic manner. Westminster was a valuable reference point on this occasion, not for reasons of shared common-law tradition. On the contrary, on this occasion, the UK was a valuable reference point for proponents of curtailment of the rule against double jeopardy precisely because it had recently made a significant change to the scope of a traditional common-law human right. Moreover, this was not a case of the natural evolution and transformation that is a hallmark of common-law jurisdictions. The introduction of a statutory new and compelling evidence exception to the traditional prohibition on re-prosecution after acquittal was facilitated – as evidenced by the public discourse surrounding Pt 10 of the Criminal Justice Act 2003 (UK) – by the European standard embodied in the ECHR and its protocols (specifically, Art 4 of Protocol 7). By drawing the legislative precedent set by the Parliament of the

---

152 New Zealand Human Rights Commission, 2004a, paras 13.1–13.2.
153 New Zealand Law Society, 2004b, p 15.
154 See Hurlburt, 1986; Opeskin and Weisbrot, 2005; Sayers, 2005.

UK into a position of prominence within New Zealand's public debate over the Criminal Procedure Bill, the Government was also drawing in an otherwise inaccessible normative reference point for human rights scrutiny: the European standard set by Art 4 of Protocol 7 to the ECHR. The New Zealand Government might have been expected to engage prominently and directly in a defence of its proposed double jeopardy reforms against claims that the new evidence exception was incompatible with New Zealand's primary domestic reference point for human rights scrutiny – the BORA, and s 26(2) in particular – an argument advanced by, among others, the Attorney General of New Zealand, the New Zealand Human Rights Commission, and, implicitly, by the New Zealand Law Commission. Instead, the New Zealand Government fashioned an alternative UK-Europe inspired human rights standard which was, unsurprisingly, more sympathetic to the legislative reform path which the Government wanted to steer.

For present purposes, what is particularly important about this part of the story of double jeopardy reform in New Zealand is what it reveals about the degree to which the BORA is embedded as the primary human rights reference point in New Zealand's policy development, public debate and lawmaking processes. The answer would appear to be, at least on this occasion, relatively lightly. The point is not simply that the terms of the BORA do not necessarily dictate the terms of resolution of specific human rights controversies. As explained in Chapter 1, given the nature of the New Zealand 'model' established by Parliament when it enacted the BORA, New Zealand's post-1990 human rights scrutiny mechanisms were never expected to operate in this way. However, it is reasonable to assume that after 1990 the BORA would be the primary reference point for human rights analyses of the legitimacy of existing laws and proposed new laws. And in many instances over the course of the last decade and a half, the BORA has played this role – in both legislative and judicial contexts. But that it could be effectively marginalised by proponents of statutory exceptions to the immunity against re-prosecution after acquittal supported by s 26(2) of the BORA, in preference to normative human rights reference points that offered endorsement rather than resistance, is a distinctive product of New Zealand's local legal culture with respect to human rights. It is hard to imagine a serious debate over double jeopardy reform ever developing in Canada (discussed below), but if it did, there can be no doubt that s 11 of the Charter of Rights and Freedoms would be at the very centre of the public discourse – whether conducted in the courts, the legislature, the party room or the media. Similarly, though perhaps not (yet) to the same extent, since the enactment of the Human Rights Act 1998 (UK), the ECHR has consistently occupied a prominent position in debates over the human rights implications of government policies and legal measures. The story of the double jeopardy reform provisions of New Zealand's Criminal Procedure Bill suggests that the BORA does not enjoy the same status as equivalent legal instruments in Canada and the UK. This difference is explained in part by the particular legal form of human rights protection, including the fact that of the three countries to have adopted a bill of rights, New Zealand is the place where the authoritative involvement of the judiciary has been most heavily constrained (see Chapter 1).

The progress of the Criminal Procedure Bill was slowed in the second half of 2005 when a general election was called. After Labor, under Helen Clark, was returned (as a minority government) in September 2005, the bill was reintroduced into the New Zealand Parliament. When debate on the bill resumed in May 2006, the Government reiterated its determination to amend the rules with respect to the scope of the double jeopardy protection, s 26(2) of the BORA notwithstanding. In his second reading speech, the Minister for Courts, Rick Barker, stated that 'Despite the Attorney General's view that ... [the new evidence exception] was not justified under the New Zealand Bill of Rights, the [Law and Order select] committee concluded, as did the Government, that the proposal is a principled balancing of the competing interests of finality and justice'.[155]

When the New Zealand Government announced in May 2004 that it planned to introduce statutory exceptions to the prohibition on retrial after acquittal, Nigel Hampton QC observed that the proposal 'seems to ignore the entrenchment of ... [the rule against double jeopardy] in the Bill of Rights'.[156] In fact, this observation could be said to apply not just to the original proposal, but also the public debate on the merits of the proposed change that has subsequently taken place over an extended period, as the Criminal Procedure Bill has moved slowly through the New Zealand Parliament. Section 26(2) of the BORA has not been completely absent from the public discourse. Groups such as the New Zealand Human Rights Commission and the New Zealand Law Society have attempted to push it to the centre of the debate, but with minimal success. The movement towards the introduction of tainted acquittal and new and compelling evidence exceptions to the rule against double jeopardy in New Zealand is also the story of the vulnerability of the human rights protected by the BORA; vulnerability to marginalisation in the context

---

155 New Zealand House of Representatives, Hansard, 9 May 2006, p 2868. The National Party (Opposition) voted in support of the Bill's second reading, but noted that it had reservations about the double jeopardy reform provisions of the Bill: see Kate Wilkinson, New Zealand House of Representatives, Hansard, 9 May 2006, p 2880. The Criminal Procedure Bill did not proceed to the Committee stage of debate before Parliament rose for 2006. In August 2006 the National Party foreshadowed that when debate resumed it would propose amendments to the Criminal Procedure Bill that would remove the tainted acquittal exception and limit the new and compelling evidence exception to cases in which the relevant evidence was DNA evidence (New Zealand Parliamentary Library, 2006).
156 Quoted in Henzell, 2004. See also, Kennedy, 2004.

of a policy debate and law reform process in the face of competing 'law and order' imperatives.

If, by characterising the right not to be re-prosecuted after acquittal as a human right that is 'entrenched', Hampton meant to convey that this right was insulated from the prevailing political climate and the dictates of competing influences on policy formation and law reform, then subsequent events in New Zealand showed this to be a mis-characterisation. On the contrary, the discourse surrounding the double jeopardy reform provisions of the Criminal Procedure Bill suggests that the human right underpinned by the rule against double jeopardy, notwithstanding its express articulation in the BORA, does not enjoy the sort of superior status or immunity usually conveyed by references to entrenched rights. Although s 26(2) of the BORA did not serve to *facilitate* the introduction of statutory exceptions to the rule against double jeopardy – as Art 4 of Protocol 7 to the ECHR did in the UK – it proved to be ineffective in fortifying the traditional common-law prohibition on re-prosecution after acquittal against legislative erosion.

The story of the BORA's modest potency in the debate over double jeopardy reform in New Zealand is, in large part, a product of legal form. One of the defining characteristics of the particular bill of rights model adopted by New Zealand in 1990 is that the statutory expression of certain rights does not necessarily elevate them out of the 'political mix' of values and considerations that impact on the law reform process. But consideration must also be given to the influence of New Zealand's legal culture with respect to human rights. One of the features of the post-1990 environment revealed by the example of double jeopardy reform is that human rights sensitivity has achieved only a modest degree of penetration into the conventions and practices which inform the process of policy debate and law formation in New Zealand. Resort to the normative authority of human rights discourse by proponents of legislative change can be selective and pragmatic, depending on the degree of synergy between the preferred policy outcome and the values or preferences reflected in statements of human rights principles like the BORA. An additional, and perhaps more surprising, lesson to emerge from the story of double jeopardy reform in New Zealand is that it is not merely the prominence of normative human rights standards that is variable and selective, but the source of those standards. The New Zealand Government's effective deployment of the 'UK precedent', and indirectly, the more sympathetic human rights standard represented by Art 4 of Protocol 7 to the ECHR (to the exclusion of the relevant provisions of the ICCPR, to which New Zealand is a party), is a further illustration that the BORA has not necessarily achieved the status of primary touchstone for human rights scrutiny that is commonly associated with a domestic bill of rights.

Canada

> The Canadian government should resist following the United Kingdom's lead. In any event, it is likely that the Supreme Court of Canada would strike down such legislation as being contrary to the double jeopardy clause in the Charter.[157]
>
> Martin Friedland, *Criminal Law Quarterly* (2004)

The story of double jeopardy reform in Canada is a short one: statutory exceptions of the type introduced in the UK and New Zealand in recent years have never been on the Canadian law reform agenda. The only formal examination of the topic by a law reform agency – a working paper produced by the Law Reform Commission of Canada in 1991 – recommended that the protections that are afforded to persons accused of crime, based on the rule against double jeopardy, should be strengthened rather than weakened.[158]

The 'non-emergence' of calls for erosion of the immunity against reprosecution after acquittal, underpinned by the rule against double jeopardy, is noteworthy, given that Canadian policy-making and law reform have been subject to the same sorts of influences that have seen the issue rise to prominence in each of the other three countries that are the subjects of the present study – including the victim's rights movement,[159] advances in DNA technology,[160] and controversial acquittals. For example, in 1995, Peter Gill (and his five co-accused) were acquitted of murder after a jury trial in the Supreme Court of British Columbia. It was later revealed that during the trial Gill had been engaged in a sexual relationship with one of the jurors, Gillian Guess, and that she had played a part in persuading her fellow jurors to find Gill (and his five co-accused) not guilty. In 2002, Gill was convicted of obstructing justice and sentenced to six years imprisonment. In the context of a 2001 Crown appeal against the original murder acquittal (discussed below), Ryan JA, in the British Columbia Court of Appeal, observed:

> ... I recognize that the phenomenon of 'tainted acquittals' presents a serious problem for modern society. The notion that a person can successfully escape conviction for a crime by tampering with a witness or a juror undermines the trust of the public in the proper administration of justice.[161]

After noting the legislative reform proposals that were then on the table in the

---

157 Friedland, 2004, p 431.
158 Law Reform Commision of Canada, 1991.
159 Roach, 1999.
160 Gerlach, 2004.
161 *R v Budai, Gill and Kim* (2001), para 139.

UK and New Zealand, Ryan JA concluded: 'If this complex problem is to be addressed in Canada, it is for Parliament to take the initiative.'[162] While there was considerable disquiet in Canada that Gill had received a substantially lesser penalty than he would have received if he had been convicted of murder,[163] no serious momentum for legislative reform developed.

More recently, in 2005, families of the victims of the 1985 Air India bombing[164] in which 329 people on a flight out of Vancouver airport were killed, expressed profound disappointment when two men charged with conspiracy and murder in relation to the bombing were acquitted in March 2005.[165] However, most public responses took the form of calls for a public inquiry into the bombing and its investigation, rather than calls for the two men to be re-tried.[166] In May 2005, the Canadian Government asked former Ontario Premier, Bob Rae, to complete a report on the matter,[167] and in November 2005, Ray recommended that a public inquiry be held.[168] The newly elected Conservative Party Prime Minister, Stephen Harper, announced a Commission of Inquiry on 1 May 2006.[169]

It is tempting to explain Canada's relatively unique experience as a simple and direct product of the constitutional status enjoyed by the human right based on the rule against double jeopardy. Section 11(h) of the Charter of Rights and Freedoms states:

> Any person charged with an offence has the right . . . if finally acquitted of the offence, not be tried for it again and, if finally found guilty and punished for the offence, not be tried or punished for it again.

Certainly, this is an important part of the explanation: Charter rights, including the right not to be re-prosecuted after acquittal, are so firmly embedded in Canada's legal culture that there is no space in Canadian public discourse for the idea of an express statutory assault on the rule against double jeopardy. Friedland's reponse to developments in the UK (quoted above) is illustrative: his advice to the Canadian Government that it resist the temptation to follow the UK's lead is both a statement of policy preference (that is, no diminution of the rule against double jeopardy) and a statement

---

162 *R v Budai, Gill and Kim* (2001), para 142. See Friedland, 2004, p 431.
163 See, e.g., Knight, 2002.
164 Thanks to Micheal Vonn, Policy Director of the BC Civil Liberties Association, for drawing my attention to the example of the Air India bombing acquittals: personal communication, 31 May 2005.
165 Canadian Broadcasting Corporation, CBC News, 2005a.
166 See Canadian Broadcasting Corporation, CBC News, 2005b; Saunders, 2005.
167 Rae, 2005.
168 Canada, Department of Public Safety and Emergency Preparedness, 2005.
169 Canada, Office of the Prime Minister, 2006.

of constitutional reality – that subject to the 'dormant' s 33 of the Charter (see Chapter 1), the Canadian courts have the last word on the Charter/human rights compatibility of legislation, and any move to replicate Pt 10 of the Criminal Justice Act 2003 (UK) would not survive judicial scrutiny.

But an explanation based exclusively on observing that the Charter places the rule against double jeopardy 'off limits' would be incomplete. Factors other than the particular legal form of human rights protection in Canada need also to be considered. Explanations for the absence of any sort of groundswell for double jeopardy roll-back in Canada need also to take account of the manner in which the Canadian courts have interpreted the scope of the traditional common-law right, recognised in legislation,[170] and protected since 1982 by s 11(h) of the Charter as a constitutional right.[171]

First, there is no prohibition on the prosecution of a person for perjury where the basis for the charge is that the accused had lied under oath at a previous trial when s/he denied having committed a criminal offence after which s/he was acquitted.[172] The subsequent perjury charge may legitimately be based on the contention that the accused had, in fact, been guilty of the original crime – so long as the Crown adduces evidence at the perjury trial that was not reasonably available at the original trial.[173] (In Australia, the High Court's counter-conclusion – that a perjury charge in such circumstances was an abuse of process, no matter how compelling the new evidence[174] – was the decision which thrust the issue of double jeopardy reform into the media spotlight, and onto the political agenda.)

Second, in Canada the Crown enjoys more extensive appeal rights than their equivalents in the UK, New Zealand and Australia, where the prosecution's rights of appeal do not generally include the right to appeal an acquittal and expose the defendant to a retrial.[175] Under Pt XXI of the Canadian 'Criminal Code', the Crown may appeal 'against a judgment or verdict of acquittal . . . of a trial court in proceedings by indictment on any ground of appeal that involves a question of law alone'.[176] Where the appeal is upheld the appellate court may order a new trial or, if the original was not a jury trial, enter a verdict of acquittal.[177]

170 Criminal Code, RSC 1985, c C-46.
171 Friedland, 1969; Freeman, 1988; Law Reform Commission of Canada, 1991.
172 *Gushue v R* (1980); *Grdic v R* (1985).
173 See, generally, Friedland and Roach, 1994, pp 866–78; and Law Reform Commission of Canada 1991, pp 13–14.
174 *R v Carroll* (2002).
175 See England and Wales Law Commission 2001, pp 17–27; *Clark v R* (2005) (Supreme Court of NZ). In Australia, limited Crown rights of appeal against an acquittal on indictment have been introduced in only Western Australia and Tasmania: NSW Law Reform Commission, 1995, para 2.1; Corns, 2003, pp 88–9; Johns, 2003, pp 20–2.
176 Criminal Code, s 676(1)(a). See *R v Biniaris* (2000).
177 Criminal Code, s 686(4)(b). See Law Reform Commission of Canada, 1991, p 4.

In the case of Peter Gill (discussed above), the Crown appealed against Gill's acquittal, under s 676 of the Criminal Code, on the basis that the trial judge had erred in law by failing to dismiss Gillian Guess from the jury, or at least conduct a proper inquiry into whether she should be dismissed, when he was advised by court staff that there had been improper contact and communication between Gill (one of the accused) and Guess (a juror). In May 2001, the British Columbia Court of Appeal upheld the appeal, set aside the verdicts of acquittal, and ordered that Gill and two of his co-accused be re-tried.[178] Mackenzie JA observed:

> I accept that inevitably there will be prejudice to the respondents if their acquittals are set aside and the case is retried. . . . In my opinion, where the integrity of the judicial process is fundamentally involved, the prejudice occasioned by a new trial is outweighed by the necessity of granting the remedy to maintain public respect and confidence in the system.[179]

In February 2002, Gill, Budai and Kim applied for leave to appeal to the Supreme Court of Canada, but their applications were dismissed. The Crown did not proceed to retrial, electing to pursue an obstruction of justice charge against Gill. He was convicted in the British Columbia Supreme Court in May 2002 and sentenced to six years' imprisonment.

The (non)story of double jeopardy reform in Canada is consistent with the conventional wisdom 'pecking order' regarding the relative weight of constitutionalised human rights. Regard also needs to be had to the particular contours of the rule against double jeopardy in Canada: the prosecution enjoys relatively wide rights to appeal after a conviction (which may lead to retrial), and prosecutions for perjury based on denial of guilt at a trial which resulted in acquittal have been ruled by the Supreme Court of Canada to be compatible with s 11(h) of the Charter. But when placed alongside the stories of legislative curtailment of the human rights supported by the rule against double jeopardy in the UK and New Zealand, it is plain that the legal form of human rights protection in Canada, as well as the legal culture regarding the primacy and immunity of Charter rights, which has developed over more than two decades, are key explanations as to why, even when faced with similar 'law and order' and 'victims' rights' pressures as its national equivalents in the UK, New Zealand and state equivalents in Australia, the Canadian Government has not seen fit to move to curtail the traditional prohibition on retrial for the same crime after acquittal. Perhaps even more importantly, from the point of view of illustrating the extent to which Charter-based

---

178 *R v Budai, Gill and Kim* (2001).
179 Ibid, para 106.

human rights sensitivity has permeated into Canadian legal culture and political consciousness, demands for reform of the rule against double jeopardy have simply not featured among the claims made, and strategies employed, by victims of crime dissatisfied with the operation of the Canadian criminal justice system. Section 11(h) of the Charter, and the judiciary's unchallenged interpretive authority in relation to its scope and implications, has not simply served as an effective defender of the traditional common-law immunity against calls for constitutionally entrenched status of the human right underpinned by the rule against double jeopardy. Rather, the constitutionalisation of the rule against double jeopardy has effectively prevented such claims from ever materialising in Canada's public discourse regarding the criminal justice system's offender/victim and finality/accuracy balances.

Australia

> It looks likely that the rule will be reformed and probably overturned by at least some state parliaments sometime later this year.
>
> Tim Carmody SC
> *Australian Story* Online Forum, 7 April 2003[180]

When the High Court's decision in *Carroll*[181] attracted the attention of the Australian media and politicians across the country in late 2002 and early 2003, the prospects of the common-law rule against double jeopardy being allowed to stand in its traditional form – including as a bar against re-prosecution after acquittal even where strong new evidence is discovered – seemed slim. In 2003, Deidre Kennedy's mother, Faye Kennedy, in conjunction with a Queensland member of the Australian Parliament, Peter Dutton, initiated a petition seeking reform of the rule against double jeopardy so as to allow the re-prosecution of Carroll for murder.[182] The national newspaper, *The Australian*, became actively involved in the campaign,[183] announcing that it would pay for legal advice from barrister, Tim Carmody SC, as to the feasibility of Faye Kennedy bringing a civil action against Carroll.[184] A number of political leaders publicly backed calls for a legislative reduction in the

---

180 Australian Broadcasting Corporation, ABC TV, 2003.
181 *R v Carroll* (2002).
182 Hele, 2003; Marshall, 2005.
183 *The Australian*, 11 December 2002, p 1; *The Weekend Australian*, 14–15 December 2002, pp 2, 20; discussed in Australia, MCCOC, 2003, p 27.
184 Walker, 2003. After Tim Carmody was appointed to the bench of the Family Court of Australia in mid-2003, the option of a civil action funded by *The Australian* was put on hold, with Editor-in-Chief Chris Mitchell reportedly 'taking a wait-and-see approach', pending the outcome of the push for legislative reform of the rule against double jeopardy: Marshall, 2005, pp 337–8.

scope of the immunity against re-prosecution, with support also coming from some prominent former judges.[185]

Given the ostensible vulnerability of the double jeopardy rule in Australia – although articulated in legislation governing the procedure of criminal trials and pleas,[186] the rule is otherwise a 'mere' common-law principle without any explicit recognition in Australian constitutional law or human rights legislation,[187] and therefore subject to the constitutional reality of parliamentary supremacy – and given the propensity of Australian legislatures in recent years to enact 'tough' legislation in response to perceived inadequacies in the protection afforded by the criminal law to victims of crime, it was hard to argue with Tim Carmody's April 2003 prediction that by the end of the year, the scope of the immunity underpinned by the rule against double jeopardy would have been reduced by legislative measures.

And yet, in mid-2006, more than three years later, no Australian jurisdiction had introduced legislative exceptions to the rule against double jeopardy. In spite of its relatively modest legal form, the Australian version of the right not to be re-prosecuted after acquittal had proven to be surprisingly resistant in the face of a concerted roll-back campaign, centred around the Carroll/ Kennedy case.[188] Notwithstanding the absence of anything resembling s 11(h) of the Canadian Charter of Rights and Freedoms, the Australian human right/immunity underpinned by the common-law rule against double jeopardy stood as a significant constraint on the power of the state to prosecute and punish. In fact, following the High Court's decision in *Carroll*,[189] the Australian common-law version of the immunity was broader than in the UK, New Zealand, or Canada.

Australia is now the only one of the four countries which is the subject of the present study where the rule against double jeopardy prohibits not only re-prosecution for the same crime, but subsequent prosecution for perjury where the essence of the allegation is that the accused was in fact guilty of the crime originally charged and lied under oath when s/he denied committing the offence at the original trial.[190] Departing from its counterparts in the House of Lords, the New Zealand Court of Appeal and the Supreme Court of Canada, in *Carroll* the High Court of Australia ruled that a perjury prosecution in such circumstances was unacceptable, irrespective of the quality of the new evidence on which the prosecution planned to rely. Gleeson CJ and Hayne J stated:

---

185 Nason and Emerson, 2002.
186 See, e.g., Criminal Procedure Act 1986, s 156.
187 See, generally, Australia, MCCOC, 2003; and Johns, 2003.
188 Kirby, 2003b, pp 238–40.
189 *R v Carroll* (2002).
190 For a critique of the breadth of the immunity endorsed by the High Court in *Carroll*, see Vasta, 2006.

The [Queensland] Court of Appeal concluded that the further evidence adduced at the perjury trial was deficient and unsatisfactory, and that it added little to the original evidence, but it considered that examining the strength and cogency of the new evidence was crucial to the exercise of the discretion to stay the proceeding. In that respect, the reasoning of the Court of Appeal was unduly favourable to the prosecution. The inconsistency between the charge of perjury and the acquittal of murder was direct and plain. The laying of the charge of perjury, solely on the basis of the respondent's sworn denial of guilt, for the evident purpose of establishing his guilt of murder, was an abuse of process regardless of the cogency and weight of the further evidence that was said to be available.[191]

From Carroll to ... the Status Quo?

Following the High Court's decision in *Carroll*, the adequacy of the rule against double jeopardy became a prominent topic of political and media debate. As described above, after the decision was handed down, Deidre Kennedy's mother, Faye Kennedy, embarked on a campaign to persuade the Queensland Government to introduce legislative exceptions to the rule against double jeopardy, with high profile support from Peter Dutton, a Liberal Party MP in the Australian Parliament and Chris Mitchell, the Editor-in-Chief of *The Australian* newspaper.[192]

In February 2003, clearly motivated by the *Carroll* case and controversy surrounding the failure to secure the conviction of Deidre Kennedy's killer, the Premier of NSW announced that his Government would pass legislation introducing an exception to the rule against double jeopardy. In some respects, it is curious that the NSW Government was the first to move on this issue given that the Kennedy/Carroll case was from a different state – Queensland – and that it was the Queensland Government that was the primary focus of the campaign for legislative curtailment of the rule against double jeopardy by Faye Kennedy and her supporters. As noted above, an impending state election in NSW, and the opportunity to 'outdo' the Conservative Opposition on tough law and order policy, are likely to have been motivating factors.[193]

The Queensland Government took the position that it would only introduce state legislation as part of a uniform national approach. In April 2003, the Queensland Attorney General referred the question of double jeopardy reform to the Standing Committee of Attorneys General (SCAG). SCAG

---

191 *R v Carroll* (2002), para 44. See also, McHugh J at para 118; and discussion in Prakash, 2002–2003, pp 269–70; and Johns, 2003, pp 7–8.
192 Australia, MCCOC, 2003, p 27; Kirby, 2003b, pp 238–40.
193 Skeers, 2003.

then referred the matter to its Criminal Code Officers' Committee (MCCOC). MCCOC is a national criminal law reform body, which for more than a decade has been making recommendations for the updating and national standardisation of criminal laws in Australia – criminal law being primarily a matter of state jurisdiction under Australia's federal constitutional structure.[194]

In September 2003, the NSW Government introduced a draft bill – the Criminal Appeal Amendment (Double Jeopardy) Bill 2003 (NSW) – and invited public comment. The Bill proposed two exceptions to the rule against double jeopardy:

- a 'tainted acquittal' exception similar to the provisions contained in the Criminal Procedure and Investigations Act 1996 (UK);
- a 'new evidence' exception modelled closely on the relevant provisions of the Criminal Justice Bill 2002 (UK) (now Pt 10 of the Criminal Justice Act 2003 (UK)).

In November 2003, MCCOC released a discussion paper,[195] which proposed that criminal laws across Australia be modified so as to allow for retrial after acquittal in cases of 'tainted acquittals' and 'new evidence'. In February 2004, MCCOC made recommendations to this effect to the SCAG.[196]

In March 2004, SCAG did not reach agreement on the proposal for a uniform new evidence exception to the rule against double jeopardy, and directed MCCOC to develop further the proposal for a tainted acquittal exception. Almost as quickly as it had arrived on the national criminal law reform agenda, the push for major double jeopardy reform appeared to have stalled.[197] At the time of writing, MCCOC had not produced a final report 'follow-up' to its 2003 discussion paper, although the federal Justice Minister has recently reiterated his determination to keep the issue on SCAG's agenda.[198]

Double jeopardy remained, however, on the agenda of the NSW Government. In November 2004, the Criminal Appeal Amendment (Double Jeopardy) Bill 2003 was discussed in the NSW Labor Party caucus, where, as one journalist put it, the proposal 'hit resistance'.[199] Concern was expressed that a November 2003 report on the bill on the adequacy of the 'safeguards' in the proposed bill, completed by Justice Jane Mathews[200] at the Attorney

---

194 Commonwealth of Australia Constitution Act 1900 (63 and 64 Vict c 12), ss 51, 107.
195 Australia, MCCOC, 2003.
196 Australia, MCCOC, 2004.
197 See Australia, Minister of Justice and Customs, 2004; and Australian Broadcasting Corporation, ABC Radio, 2006.
198 Australian Broadcasting Corporation, ABC Radio, 2006.
199 Davies, 2004.
200 Mathews, 2003.

General's request, had not been made available to caucus members, or to the public. The report was duly released, a year after its completion.

In May 2005, the Queensland Attorney General confirmed that the Government was no longer pursuing the option of double jeopardy reform. The issue 'had slipped off the Government's agenda because there was no national agreement on how the ancient rule should be reformed'.[201] In August 2005, the NSW Attorney General, Bob Debus, publicly restated his Government's commitment to introduce statutory exceptions to the double jeopardy rule.[202]

The profile and impact of human rights discourse

Any attempt to reach firm conclusions about the role that human rights sensitivity had played in the story of double jeopardy reform in Australia is rendered difficult by the fact that there has been relatively little sustained public examination of proposed statutory exceptions to the common-law-based immunity against re-prosecution after acquittal. Equivalent proposals in the UK and New Zealand were the subject of close examination by law reform agencies[203] and parliamentary select committees,[204] with explicit consideration of the human rights implications of the proposed reforms. The record of parliamentary debates surrounding the Criminal Justice Act 2003 (UK) and the Criminal Procedure Bill (NZ) represent another component of the official discourse surrounding double jeopardy, and an important source for assessing the impact of human rights sensitivity in the law-making process.

By contrast, in Australia, the record of public and official discourse on proposals for the introduction of statutory exceptions to the immunity against re-prosecution underpinned by the rule against double jeopardy is relatively slim. No Australian government has referred the matter to a law reform commission. In NSW, the Government chose to circulate a draft bill for comment in 2003 without any prior research or recommendations from the NSW Law Reform Commission (or any equivalent body). After public comment on the bill had been sought, the Attorney General commissioned only a very narrow report (by Justice Mathews) on the adequacy of the proposed 'safeguards', rather than a comprehensive review of the merits of legislative curtailment of the rule against double jeopardy. Justice Mathews

---

201 Cole, 2005.
202 Roberts, 2005.
203 England and Wales Law Commission, 1999; England and Wales Law Commission, 2001; New Zealand Law Commission, 2000; New Zealand Law Commission, 2001.
204 United Kingdom Parliament, Joint Committee on Human Rights, 2003a; United Kingdom Parliament, Joint Committee on Human Rights, 2003b; New Zealand House of Representatives, Law and Order Committee, 2005; also New Zealand Attorney General, 2004.

prefaced her report by drawing attention to the very limited terms of reference for her review:

> The Attorney General's letter makes it clear that my advice is to be restricted to the adequacy of the safeguards contained in the draft Bill. In particular, my brief does not extend to advising the Attorney upon the desirability of abolishing the double jeopardy rule in the first place. This is a policy matter upon which, it seems, a decision has already been taken by the Government. Accordingly, I do not propose to discuss the merits or otherwise of introducing the proposed legislation, although it should be noted that a number of submitters voiced strong objection, as a matter of principle, to the making of any inroads into the rule against double jeopardy.[205]

The only other reports to have been completed on the issue of double jeopardy reform is the November 2003 report by MCCOC on *Issue Estoppel, Double Jeopardy and Prosecution Appeals Against Acquittals*,[206] and a short report on the NSW Government's consultation draft bill – the Criminal Appeal Amendment (Double Jeopardy) Bill 2003 – produced by the NSW Parliament's Legislation Review Committee, as part of its statutory scrutiny responsibilities.[207] A number of civil liberties and lawyers groups made public comments on the proposed changes to the rule against double jeopardy – primarily in response to the 2003 MCCOC report and the NSW Consultation Draft Bill. There was considerable media reporting and comment, and a small body of academic commentary emerged around the issue.[208]

It is worth noting, before moving on to make a number of observations about the profile of human rights sensitivity in the Australian debate on double jeopardy reform, that the modest volume of official and public discourse is partly explained by the particular legal form in which human rights are protected in Australia. One of the deniable consequences of the adoption of primary legal reference points for human rights in Canada, New Zealand and the UK – in the form of the Charter of Rights and Freedoms 1982, the Bill of Rights Act 1990, and the Human Rights Act 1998, respectively – is that human rights scrutiny has been institutionalised as part of the policy formation and law creation process. Of course, this does not mean the dictates of

---

205 Mathews, 2003, pp 3–4. Justice Mathews encouraged the NSW Government to await MCCOC's final report on double jeopardy before introducing legislation into the NSW Parliament.
206 Australia, MCCOC, 2003.
207 See Chapter 1. The author is a legal adviser to the NSW Legislation Review Committee and provided advice on the Criminal Appeal Amendment (Double Jeopardy) Bill 2003.
208 See, e.g. Prakash, 2002–2003; Corns, 2003; Parkinson, 2003; Kirby, 2003b; and Bargaric and Neal, 2005.

these human rights documents always trump competing policy goals, but it does mean that opportunities for explicit consideration of the human rights implications of proposed legal changes are 'built-in' to the processes of policy formation and legislative enactment. Given the absence of a bill of rights, nationally and in the majority of states/territories,[209] opportunities for mandatory explicit human rights analysis of proposed legislation in Australia are limited. In the New South Wales Parliament, the terms of reference of the Legislation Review Committee include consideration of whether proposed legislation 'trespasses unduly on personal rights and liberties',[210] but to date, the available evidence does not suggest that the Committee's views and recommendations consistently exert a strong influence on the law-making process.[211] In addition, in Australia there is very little scope for post-enactment human rights-inspired judicial scrutiny of the validity or preferred interpretation of legislation.[212]

Three related observations can be made about the impact of human rights sensitivity on the public discourse surrounding proposals for legislative curtailment of the rule against double jeopardy in Australia.

First, the visibility of human rights sensitivity in the public discourse has been relatively low when compared to the equivalent debates in the UK and New Zealand, but this has not been consistent across the spectrum of contributions to the debate. The degree of attention paid to such matters has varied. Proponents of legislative curtailment have largely ignored relevant human rights reference points in their merits assessments, while opponents of legislative reform have actively attempted to draw the normative force of human rights standards into the debate.

The 2003 MCCOC discussion paper is illustrative of the former. The report opens in an encouraging manner, emphasising that scrutiny of proposed changes to double jeopardy rules 'requires a fundamental reconsideration of why we have these rules at all. There is no point in debating the existence of a rule unless we know (really) why we have it'.[213] However, all that follows is a rather unfocused and derivative treatment of 'four moral and legal justifications for maintaining the existing double jeopardy laws' previously identified by the England and Wales Law Commission,[214] along with a later underdeveloped critique of the notion that there is necessarily tension between the

---

209 See Chapter 1.
210 Legislation Review Act 1987 (NSW), s 8A(1)(b)(i) (discussed in Chapter 1).
211 See New South Wales Parliament, Legislation Review Committee, 2005; and discussion in Chapter 1.
212 See Chapter 1.
213 Australia, MCCOC, 2003, p 55.
214 Ibid.

'rights of the accused' and 'victim's rights'.[215] Confusingly, the report quotes at some length from the work of English academic, Paul Roberts,[216] with implicit approval before concluding, '[t]he reader can (and should) gauge the worth of these arguments for himself or herself',[217] and then going ahead to endorse reform equivalents to those proposed by the England Wales Law Commission (of which Roberts was an incisive critic).

The Committee did note that 'the rule against double jeopardy has a long history in the common law',[218] and acknowledged that the principles have been internationally recognised in Art 14(7) of the ICCPR.[219] However, the Committee appears to have attached very little significance to the latter international human rights law standard, observing that Art 14(7) is a 'command [which] leaves a great deal to interpretation'.[220] The Committee suggests, rather flippantly, that the inclusion of the word 'finally' in the ICCPR formulation means that the debate over double jeopardy reform can really be boiled down to an argument over the definition or re-definition of 'finally'.[221]

One might have expected a little more from an established and respected law reform body. On the other hand, MCCOC's primary mission – to achieve national codification of criminal laws in Australia – may explain why detailed engagement with human rights consideration appears to have been considered beyond the scope of its mandate.[222] This, in itself, is telling with respect to the sometimes peripheral status of human rights considerations in Australian law reform debates.

But as noted above, the Australian picture is not one of consistent invisibility. In the recent public discourse on double jeopardy reform, civil liberties and lawyers groups such as the NSW Council for Civil Liberties (NSWCCL) and Australian Lawyers for Human Rights have largely provided the counterweight. In one respect, this is to be expected, given the mandate of such groups. But the point is not that there are different and competing *arguments* on either side of the debate, including competing interpretations of prevailing human rights standards. This, of course, is to be expected. The point is that in Australia there have been different (and 'competing') *reference points* for the injection of human rights discourse into (or its exclusion from) the debate. In the absence of a primary normative framework, such as might be established by the adoption of a domestic bill of rights, there has been no underlying

---

215 Australia, MCCOC, 2003, p 70.
216 Roberts, 2002a, 2002b.
217 Australia, MCCOC, 2003, p 58.
218 Ibid, p 1.
219 Ibid.
220 Ibid.
221 Ibid.
222 It is probable that human rights considerations would have been considered more fully had the matter been the subject of a reference to the Australian Law Reform Commission (or state equivalents).

consensus about *which* human rights standards are relevant, let alone how they should be interpreted and applied. By contrast, in the UK, the public discourse surrounding proposals for double jeopardy reform was characterised by near unanimity that the primary human standard was the one embodied in Art 4 of Protocol 7 to the ECHR – to the point of marginalising the equally, perhaps more, relevant standard embodied in Art 14(7) of the ICCPR, and even though the UK had not yet ratified the protocol in question.

The second observation is that, as in New Zealand, the case for legislative reform in Australia has relied heavily on the 'precedent' set by Pt 10 of the UK's Criminal Justice Act 2003. Proponents of double jeopardy reform in Australia may not have had direct access to an equivalent of Art 4 of Protocol 7 to the ECHR – to facilitate, or provide a normative justification for, legislative roll-back of the rule against double jeopardy – but they have had access to a reference point which, at least in the Australian law reform context, has the potential to be just as effective: a Commonwealth comparative justification. References to the 'UK precedent' – set by Pt 10 of the Criminal Justice Act 2003 – have been a prominent feature of the public discourse in Australia. For example, in September 2003, the NSW Government identified as one of the objectives of its Criminal Appeal Amendment (Double Jeopardy) Bill 2003, 'to enable a person acquitted of an offence to be retried (in the case of a very serious offences) if there is fresh and compelling evidence of guilt (*in line with proposed legislation before the UK Parliament*)'.[223] The rationale for such references is that the case in favour of changing a common-law rule of long-standing – in this case, the rule against double jeopardy – can be strengthened significantly if the change is not unprecedented, particularly if the precedent is provided by a jurisdiction that still maintains considerable status in Australia as a comparative reference point. What is particularly interesting about the invocation, on this occasion, of the familiar Commonwealth comparative justification, is that the precedent set by Pt 10 of the Criminal Justice Act 2003 was, in important respects, the product of a geopolitical environment (Europe) and an associated normative legal standard (Art 4 of Protocol 7 to the ECHR) – forces which define the *differences* rather than the similarities between the UK and its Commonwealth peers. As in New Zealand (discussed above), Australian proponents of legislative curtailment of the immunity against re-prosecution after acquittal underpinned by the rule against double jeopardy attempted to create a normative justification for their preferred policy outcome out of the combined effect of a traditional colonial connection and a European standard which, on its own, would have minimal purchase in Australian legal and political discourse.

The third observation about the public discourse surrounding double

---

223 New South Wales Government, 2003 (emphasis added). See also, Australia, MCCOC, 2003, pp 44–51.

jeopardy reform proposals in Australia is that, to the extent that international human rights standards, specifically, Art 14(7) of the ICCPR, have been explicitly invoked, this has resulted primarily from the contributions of civil liberties and lawyers groups which have opposed relaxation of the rule against double jeopardy. Proponents of legislative reform have apparently felt little compulsion to defend their preferences in terms of their compatibility with international human rights treaties to which Australia is a party (such as the ICCPR). This points to the relative impotence of international human rights law in Australia's legal culture, a feature that has been exacerbated in the last decade by the Liberal/National (Conservative) Government's apparent defiance in the face of adverse findings and associated recommendations from United Nations treaty monitoring bodies, such as the Human Rights Committee.[224]

A number of the arguments advanced by groups that opposed legislative curtailment in Australia were based on general principles of fairness, mirroring the approach adopted by their counterparts in the UK. For example, the Queensland Legal Aid Commission expressed 'serious concerns about the so-called protections' in MCCOC's proposals:

> Even with laws preventing publication of the appeal court's decision to quash an acquittal, it can be expected that the public (that is, the jury) will be aware a case is a retrial and that the highest court in the State has considered there is a strong case against the accused and a public interest in another trial.[225]

However, a significant point of distinction between the public comments of Australia and UK civil liberties organisations and lawyers' groups is that the former tended to place much greater emphasis on the claim that erosion of the rule against double jeopardy would be inconsistent with Australia's international human rights law obligations. For example, the NSWCCL did not merely voice its opposition to the MCOCC proposals in terms of general principles and values, but suggested that the legislation based on the proposals would violate international human rights standards and therefore place Australian in breach of its obligations under the ICCPR.[226] In the NSWCCL's

---

224 Kinslor, 2002; Hovell, 2003; Niarchos, 2004; Charlesworth *et al*, 2006.
225 Legal Aid Queensland 2004, p 9. See also, Farrar, 2003 (President, Law Society of the ACT); and Law Institute of Victoria, 2004.
226 New South Wales Council for Civil Liberties and the UNSW Council for Civil Liberties, 2004, pp 8–9. The NSWCCL also speculated that legislation based on the MCCOC proposals may be invalid and struck down by the High Court of Australia as inconsistent with an implied constitutional right to a fair trial in the Australian Constitution, and as inconsistent with a 'fundamental common law immunity' (i.e. the rule against double jeopardy (pp 6–9)). See also, Pentony and Rice, 2004.

construction of the human rights normative framework in which proposals for the legislative curtailment of the rule against double jeopardy should be evaluated, the ICCPR is not only 'front and centre', but is characterised as a significant *barrier* to erosion of the rule against double jeopardy (and as largely requiring the maintenance of the status quo). The NSWCCL acknowledged that the 'The principle in international law affords less protection than existing Australian law',[227] but for the Council it did not necessarily follow that 'relaxation' of the rule against double jeopardy would be compatible with Art 14(7). On the contrary, the NSWCCL concluded that:

> If the changes to double jeopardy proposed by the MCCOC are introduced, it is highly likely that they would be in violation of Australia's international human rights commitments.... It is worrying that any Australian Parliament in the 21st Century would consider any legislation that so blatantly violates international human rights standards.[228]

The NSWCCL's position on the implications of Art 14(7) diverges radically from the view that was widely accepted in the UK debates (by proponents and opponents alike): the standard set by Art 14(7) left room for both tainted acquittal and new evidence exceptions to the general immunity against re-prosecution after acquittal. The Council drew attention to the fact that the MCCOC proposal (in this respect, identical to the procedure subsequently established in the UK by Pt 10 of the Criminal Justice Act 2003) provided for a *retrial* and argued that this could not be considered a (permissible) 'resumption' of the original case. It interpreted the Human Rights Committee's General Comment 13 as confirming that 'the retrial of a criminal is strictly prohibited'.[229] Michael Kirby, a member of the High Court of Australia, advanced a similar argument.[230] He argued that legislation allowing for 'a fresh hearing of a charge concerning the crime in respect of which an acquittal was earlier entered ... [would] on the face of things, ... constitute a breach of Australia's international human rights obligations'.[231]

In the course of her report on the adequacy of the proposed safeguards in the NSW Government's 2003 Consultation Draft Bill, Justice Mathews observed that 'The double jeopardy rule protects fundamentally important individual liberties. It is an internationally recognised human right, enshrined in the International Covenant on Civil and Political Rights (ICCPR)'.[232] In its examination of the same bill, the NSW Parliament's Legislation

227 NSWCCL, p 8.
228 Ibid, p 9.
229 Ibid, p 8. See also, University of NSW Council for Civil Liberties, 2003; and Haesler, 2003.
230 Kirby, 2003b. Justice Kirby did not participate in the 2002 *Carroll* decision.
231 Kirby, 2003b, p 244.
232 Mathews, 2003, p 5.

Review Committee noted, 'the importance of the double jeopardy rule within both the common law tradition and as an internationally recognised human right'.[233]

In contrast to the almost nonexistent profile of the ICCPR in the UK's debates,[234] and its modest profile in New Zealand's debates (see above), these examples of contributions to the Australian debate over curtailment of the rule against double jeopardy reveal, on their face, that the ICCPR has real currency in Australia's legal culture, and the capacity to operate as an effective brake on proposed incursions into an established human right. Rhetorical flourish? Strategic hyperbole? Maybe, but irrespective of the 'correctness' of such contributions, it is significant that they have been a relatively prominent part of the Australian public discourse on double jeopardy reform.

The obvious question is: Why? What explains the divergence across three countries in terms of the significance attached to an international human right standard, in terms of its capacity to serve as a 'brake' on proposals for the erosion of an established human right?

Part of the explanation, it would appear, can be found in the peculiarity of Australia's contemporary legal framework for the protection of human rights. In the absence of a primary domestic human rights instrument, like the UK's Human Rights Act 1998, or a dominant regional human rights standard, like the ECHR, the ICCPR can assume an elevated prominence – at least for opponents of the proposed double jeopardy reforms in search of normative reference points to bolster their position. There is a certain irony in attempts to 'talk up' the ICCPR as a barrier to double jeopardy reform, because although it may, from a distance, seem to offer a significant degree of protection against re-prosecution after retrial, those who have attempted to invoke ICCPR or other international human rights standards in other contexts will know that it has very little purchase in the current Australian political climate. This is especially apparent in the tendency of the Conservative Federal Government, during the past decade, to ignore or deflect criticism from United Nations treaty-monitoring bodies.[235] While observing that 'Hitherto it has been regarded as a serious thing for Australia to find itself in breach of its obligations under international law, including the ICCPR',[236] Kirby concedes that 'Perhaps this is changing'.[237] As noted above, one of the demonstrable points of distinction between the Liberal-National Government under John Howard, compared to its Labor Party predecessor under Paul Keating, is that the current Australian Government has, on a number of occasions, explicitly

---

233 NSW Parliament, Legislation Review Committee, 2003, p 6.
234 The only comparable contribution to the United Kingdom public discourse came, belatedly, from the Joint Committee on Human Rights (see above).
235 Pentony and Rice, 2004.
236 Kirby, 2003b, p 244.
237 Ibid.

declined to be moved by the findings and recommendations of treaty monitoring bodies such as the Human Rights Committee, the Committee Against Torture, and the Committee on the Elimination of Racial Discrimination, and has characterised the interventions of such bodies as an assault on Australian sovereignty.[238]

While the reference points may differ, and while the goals may be diametrically opposed, the strategy of Australian opponents of double jeopardy, in drawing in Art 14(7) of the ICCPR shares much with the strategy of the UK Government (and indirectly, the New Zealand Government) in drawing in Art 4 of Protocol 7 to the ECHR: the aim is to trump competing arguments and policy options by offering up an authoritative barometer with which to determine whether the proposed legislative reforms measure up to the standards required of a human rights-respecting society. A key difference is that the particular legal form(lessness) of human rights protection in Australia affords greater latitude to participants on public discourse over controversial law reforms – to embrace (or ignore) potentially applicable normative reference points, such as the provisions of an international human rights treaty.

It is unlikely that the last chapter of the story of double jeopardy reform in Australia has been told. But to date, one of the most surprising aspects of the story is that despite the occurrence of a high-profile 'law and order' campaign in favour of legislative reform, analogous to that which has occurred in the UK and New Zealand in recent years, the Australian version of the immunity from re-prosecution enjoyed by all persons who have been acquitted of a crime is, for the time being at least, unqualified by the new and compelling evidence and tainted acquittal exceptions of the type that have been introduced in the UK and New Zealand. The ostensibly slender common-law foundations of the rule against double jeopardy in Australia have not made it more vulnerable to curtailment, according to the dictates of law and order politics. On the contrary, the rule against double jeopardy has proven, so far, to be more resilient in Australia than it was in the UK and New Zealand. Despite some initial enthusiasm in the wake of the High Court's decision in *Carroll*, all Australian state/territory jurisdictions, except NSW, appear to have come down in favour of the status quo – at least for the time being. Attempts to develop a uniform national approach, via MCCOC and SCAG, appear to have stalled. Despite a 30,000-signature petition organised by Faye Kennedy and Peter Dutton MP,[239] the Queensland Government has declined to introduce a bill into the state legislature. In NSW, the Government has formally maintained the position that it supports the introduction of tainted

---

238 Hovell, 2003; Kinslor, 2002.
239 Roberts, 2005; Marshall, 2005, p 294.

acquittal and new and compelling evidence statutory exceptions to the prohibition on re-prosecution after acquittal, and that it intends to introduce legislation to this effect.[240] However, by mid-2006, in the more than three years since the then Premier, Bob Carr, prompted by the High Court's decision in *Carroll*, announced in February 2003 that the NSW Government would follow the UK's lead, no bill had been introduced into the NSW Parliament.

What role has human rights sensitivity played in making Australian lawmakers more hesitant than their counterparts in the UK and New Zealand to roll back an established human right? Certainly, some proponents of reform have attempted to lay the blame for government inaction at the feet of those who advanced human rights-based counter-arguments. On the Queensland Government's decision not to introduce legislative exceptions to the rule against double jeopardy, Peter Dutton MP expressed the view that 'It seems they've been listening to a narrow civil libertarian argument and have gone to water unfortunately'.[241] This assessment almost certainly overstates the influence exerted by groups such as the Queensland Council for Civil Liberties, and the Australian Council for Civil Liberties, which have strongly opposed calls for statutory curtailment,[242] but it does not seem too speculative to suggest that unease about the implications of eroding one of Australia's relatively few firmly embedded traditional (common-law) human rights may have been one of the factors that has led most Australian governments to dismiss calls for the introduction of legislative exceptions to the rule against double jeopardy, and the NSW Government to hesitate.

One of the consequences of the particular legal model of human rights protection that prevails in Australia is that there is a 'fuzziness' that surrounds public debates on the human rights implications of law reform proposals. It might be assumed that this renders the rights in question relatively vulnerable, easily outweighed by competing political considerations with no capacity for the former to legally 'trump' the latter. On some occasions, this may be so. However, the example of the double jeopardy debate in Australia suggests that the lack of 'hard edges' to human rights discourse – such as is provided by an unequivocally dominant normative reference point such as the European standard incorporated into UK law by the Human Rights Act 1998 – can actually work the other way. That is, it can serve to encourage an enhanced cautiousness about curtailment of those human rights which *do exist* in the Australian legal system, even if only at common law. This wariness may also be associated with a tendency to 'talk up' the status of external legal

---

240 Roberts, 2005.
241 Quoted in Roberts, 2005, p 7.
242 See, e.g., O'Gorman, 2002 (Terry O'Gorman is the Vice President of the QCCL and President of the ACCL).

standards that might be considered to have any sort of currency in the Australian political/legal environment – like the ICCPR.

It is important to recognise that while these tendencies towards cautiousness and elevation of the ICCPR's standing can be observed in contributions to the Australian public discourse, they have not been consistently adopted. However, the point is that even in the absence of a 'common page' when it comes to the identification of normative reference points, human rights sensitivity has still featured in the public discourse and exerted an influence on the outcomes. In fact, the Australian experience to date with double jeopardy reform suggests that the absence of an authoritative reference point that can support 'open and shut' answers to questions regarding human rights compatibility – such as Art 4 of Protocol 7 to the ECHR in the equivalent UK debate – can actually leave space and create greater freedom in which debate participants can advance opinions and argument about the state and contents of (arguably) relevant human rights principles. In Australia it has been more difficult to draw neat lines or delineate hard edges around the rule against double jeopardy. Consequently, opponents of double jeopardy rollback in Australia have been relatively successful (so far) in generating disquiet about the implications of such a move. Human rights sensitivity has achieved a significant amount of purchase in the public discourse over double jeopardy reform, post-*Carroll*, despite the fact (and to some extent, because of the fact) that the traditional immunity against re-prosecution has only relatively slender formal legal foundations: the largely unadorned common-law rule against double jeopardy.

That, by mid-2006, no Australian legislature had yet moved to overturn the High Court's 2002 decision in *Carroll*, or followed the lead of the Parliaments of the UK and New Zealand in introducing statutory exceptions to the rule against double jeopardy, may simply be a product of political pragmatism. The timing of 'law and order' inspired legislative reform is notoriously opportunistic, nowhere more so than in New South Wales, where the current Labor Government faces a state election in early 2007.[243] However, at a minimum, the Australian story of the controversy over double jeopardy reform serves as a reminder about the need to consider not only the legal form of human rights under siege, but the extent to which they are embedded in the wider legal culture.

Conclusions

In arguing against the introduction of a new evidence exception to the rule against double jeopardy in Australia, Parkinson has suggested that any such change 'would be more important for its symbolic significance (that the

---

243 See Hogg and Brown, 1998; Brown *et al*, 2006, pp 803–5; Clennell and Norrie, 2006.

criminal law will not allow acquitted persons to escape justice where new evidence of guilt emerges) than for its practical impact'.[244] The general point is well made, but curtailment of the human right underpinning the rule against double jeopardy is unlikely to be a *purely* symbolic gesture. When Pt 10 of the Criminal Justice Act 2003 (UK) came into operation in April 2005, the Home Office's National Crime Faculty estimated that acquittals in relation to more than 30 murders might be reviewed.[245] In November 2005, England's Director of Public Prosecutions gave approval for the first application under Pt 10 of the Criminal Justice Act 2003 (UK): an application to the Court of Appeal seeking permission for the re-prosecution of Billy Dunlop in relation to the 1989 murder of Julie Hogg.[246] In September 2006, Dunlop pleaded guilty to a charge of murder and was subsequently sentenced to life imprisonment.[247]

What do the four stories told in this chapter reveal about the significance of legal form for the resilience of the right underpinned by the rule against double jeopardy – that is, the immunity against re-prosecution after acquittal? Do they challenge or bolster the conventional hierarchy of rights regimes? The answer is – they do a bit of both.

The Canadian 'non-story' of double jeopardy reform serves to reinforce the view that where rights are constitutionally entrenched – as the rule against double jeopardy is in s 11(h) of the Charter – and where the judiciary is, in effect, the supreme arbiter of the Charter's implications, there is little prospect of head-on legislative challenges to those rights. The relatively broad appeal rights of the prosecution in Canada need also to be taken into account, to the extent that they offer a pressure-valve mechanism for dealing with allegedly 'unmeritorious acquittals', which are largely unavailable in the other three countries.

Pentony and Rice have suggested that the fact that double jeopardy reform has been on the agenda in Australia in recent times illustrates the vulnerability of human rights that are only protected by the common law, rather than supported by a domestic bill of rights. They observe that 'the common law is always subject to the will of parliament. Legislation can modify or negate any right or protection provided by the common law'.[248] The implication is that express recognition in a bill of rights can be expected to fortify the traditional common-law immunity against re-prosecution after acquittal. While the basic point about parliamentary supremacy is undoubtedly correct, the argument advanced by Pentony and Rice tends to overstate

---

244 Parkinson, 2003, p 621.
245 British Broadcasting Corporation, BBC News, 2005.
246 Cowan, 2005.
247 England and Wales, Crown Prosecution Service, 2006.
248 Pentony and Rice, 2004.

both the security that can reasonably be expected to flow from legislative codification in the form of a bill of rights, and the ease with which common-law human rights can be eroded – at least in a legal culture where the challenged values are firmly embedded.

The UK's experience of double jeopardy reform illustrates that an explicit and authoritative human rights standard is not necessarily a 'stronger' mechanism of protection. Clearly, much depends on the content of the standard in question, and the status of the standard in the wider legal environment. In the UK, codification of the right not to be re-prosecuted after acquittal – based on the ECHR, and the relatively low threshold set by Art 4 of Protocol 7 – did not offer an anchor for resistance by opponents of legislative curtailment of the rule against double jeopardy. On the contrary, explanations of the relative ease with which the debate over double jeopardy reform was won by proponents of change must be understood with reference to key elements of the UK's post-Human Rights Act legal infrastructure and legal culture: namely, a technical 'checklist' approach to assessing human rights compatibility, where the primary criterion (Art 4 of Protocol 7) expressed a double jeopardy standard, based on the European civil law *ne bis in idem* principle, that affords less protection to acquitted persons than the traditional common-law formulation. Unlike their peers in New Zealand and Australia, proponents of legislative reform in the UK had access to a supranational human rights benchmark, which provided a strong justification for lowering the traditional common-law threshold of protection to the 'European standard' embodied in Art 4 of Protocol 7 to the ECHR.

Legal form did not determine the outcome of the debate over double jeopardy in the UK, but it made a significant contribution. The UK's 1998 move to embed respect for human rights in its domestic legal culture served, at least on this occasion (and paradoxically, from the point of view of the conventional 'pecking order'), to render an established right more vulnerable to erosion than it had been previously.

In the post-Human Rights Act 1998 environment, human rights sensitivity as a modality for scrutinising the legitimacy of the reform proposals took a particular form – highly visible, neat, clean, legalistic, open and shut – mandated by the terms of a single supranational legal standard: Art 4 of Protocol 7 of the European Convention on Human Rights. The pre-eminence of the ECHR as a reference point served to simplify the task of assessing the human rights credentials of the roll-back proposals, in a way which offers a stark contrast with the 'messiness' and uncertainty that can characterise equivalent assessment tasks in the absence of such a dominant and unequivocally accepted reference point. Not only did the ECHR *not* stand as a barrier to the erosion of the rule against double jeopardy, it was mobilised by proponents of change to offer its imprimatur to the new rules on immunity from prosecution after acquittal – a clean bill of human rights health. Proponents of change did not have to work very hard at all to defend the reforms. On this occasion, human rights sensitivity – distilled down to the essence of Art 4 of Protocol 7 – was on their side. In the UK's post-1998 legal and political environment the prevailing reference point for human rights served to 'pave the way' for the diminution of a long-standing civil right – a function not commonly associated with international or regional human rights instruments.

If proponents of legislative roll-back in the UK played up what was widely regarded as the authoritative human rights standard (Art 4 of Protocol 7 to the ECHR), their equivalents in New Zealand took the opposite approach: they played *down* the significance of the human rights standards embodied in s 26(2) of the BORA and Art 14(7) of the ICCPR. These strategies of over-emphasis and underemphasis, respectively, were deployed in pursuit of the same objective: to legitimate the introduction of statutory exceptions to the immunity against re-prosecution after acquittal supported by the rule against double jeopardy.

When it announced its intention to introduce a bill that would, *inter alia*, create tainted acquittal and new evidence exceptions to the rule against double jeopardy, the New Zealand Government did not have the luxury of a human rights legal standard with which it could authorise the change – as had occurred in the UK. On the contrary, New Zealand's primary domestic human rights reference point – s 26(2) of the BORA – loomed as a potential barrier rather than a facilitator, given that it is generally assumed to be a codification of the traditional (and relatively wide) common-law parameters of the immunity against re-prosecution.

In practice, during the course of New Zealand's public discourse on double jeopardy reform over a period of years, the BORA achieved little prominence and even less purchase. This was most evident in the Government's pursuit of a new evidence exception in the face of assessments by both the New Zealand Law Commission and the New Zealand Attorney General that legislation based on such a policy would be an unjustifiable infringement of s 26(2) of the BORA. That the Government and, it would seem, the Parliament, are willing and able to proceed to make legislative inroads into the rule against double jeopardy in the face of such advice, suggests that human rights sensitivity has exerted only a weak influence on the policy-development and law-making process. Notwithstanding the express 'legalisation' of the human rights values embodied in the rule against double jeopardy with the enactment of the BORA in 1990, the executive and legislative arms of government have exercised a relatively high degree of control over the terms in which human rights considerations are permitted to impact on policy development and law reform processes.

To a considerable extent, this observation can be explained with reference to the *form* of New Zealand's particular model for recognising and protecting human rights. Parliament is the ultimate arbiter of the dictates of the BORA. It can and does make its own assessment of the extent to which it is acceptable for BORA rights to be infringed in the pursuit of competing policy agendas. But the story of double jeopardy reform in New Zealand must also consider the extent to which the BORA has embedded human rights sensitivity into New Zealand's legal *culture*, including the discourses of law-making. What is surprising is not so much that the Cabinet reached a different conclusion to the Attorney General about whether the new evidence exception contained in the Criminal Procedure Bill was a 'reasonable limit' that could 'be demonstrably justified in a free and democratic society' (as per s 4 of the BORA), or that the parliament looks set to follow suit, but that supporters of the legislative curtailment were not compelled to offer much in the way of a sustained argument in support of this conclusion. BORA (and to an even greater extent, ICCPR) considerations were marginalised. The extent to which the New Zealand Government has managed both the style and the intensity of human rights sensitivity in debates surrounding the Criminal Procedure Bill was highlighted by the ministerial tendency to overlook the domestic (though potentially unhelpful) reference point constituted by s 26(2) of the BORA, in favour of the 'UK precedent' and thereby indirectly, the more 'reform friendly' reference point of Art 4 of Protocol 7 to the ECHR.

When compared with governments in all three of the other countries that are the subjects of this study, governments in Australia would appear to enjoy the highest degree of freedom when it comes to rendering in law their preferred policies, including with respect to the rules that should govern the operation of the criminal justice system. Consequently, when the NSW Government announced in the wake of the High Court of Australia's decision in *Carroll* that it would introduce statutory exceptions to the rule against double jeopardy, modelled on Pt 10 of the *Criminal Justice Act* 2003 (UK) – an announcement that quickly prompted movement towards a uniform national response along the same lines – there were few obvious obstacles on the path from policy choice to legislative enactment. More than three years on, no Australian legislature had introduced a bill for the legislative curtailment of the common-law-based immunity against re-prosecution after acquittal. It would be premature to conclude that defenders of the traditional rule against double jeopardy have won the battle, but it is fair to say that the common-law human right not to be exposed to re-prosecution after acquittal has proved to be surprisingly resilient. It is not possible to be definitive, based on an examination of the public discourse, about what motivates Cabinet decisions – such as the decision of the NSW Government to delay the introduction of a double jeopardy reform bill. In any event, guessing correctly on the 'will they/won't they?' question has not been the goal of the stories told, and the analysis offered, in this chapter.

What *is* revealed by the story of the debate surrounding double jeopardy reform in Australia is that even in the absence of an express provision in a bill of rights or equivalent legislative instrument, and even in the absence of formal human rights scrutiny mechanisms, such as those that operate in each of the other three countries that are the subject of the present study, opponents of double jeopardy have managed to inject human rights sensitivity into the public discourse, with some effect. The relative 'formlessness' of Australia's version of the human right reflected in the rule against double jeopardy has, to some extent, strengthened, rather than weakened, the position of those who have opposed the reform push. Absent the undeniable trumping capacity of the ECHR in the UK, or the paradoxical nature of New Zealand's institutional design for the recognition of human rights (which can result in the BORA appearing at the centre, or at the margins, of the law-making process – depending on the Government's preferences and strategic approach), Australia's public discourse on double jeopardy reform has been distinguished by a surprisingly high amount of contestation. The absence of universally accepted normative parameters – such as might be provided by a national bill of rights regime – has helped to strengthen the discursive position of opponents of double jeopardy roll-back and has, to some extent, contributed to a cautiousness on the part of government proponents. This cautiousness may yet be abandoned, but however the Australian story of double jeopardy reform ends, the events of the last few years encourage a different sort of admonition: about too readily accepting the 'common-sense' hierarchy of legal regimes for the protection of human rights.

Postscript

In October 2006, the New South Wales Parliament became the first Australian legislature to enact statutory exceptions to the rule against double jeopardy when it enacted the Crimes (Appeal and Review) Amendment (Double Jeopardy) Act 2006 (NSW). The NSW Director of Public Prosecutions may now apply to the NSW Court of Criminal Appeal for permission to retry an acquitted person if there is 'fresh and compelling' evidence (Crimes (Appeal and Review) Act 2001 (NSW), s 100) or where the original acquittal was 'tainted' (s 101).

Chapter 3

Pushing the boundaries of human rights protection: Equality and the recognition of same-sex relationships

Introduction

In June 2005, shortly after the Canadian Parliament's House of Commons passed legislation that defined marriage so as to include same-sex couples, New Democratic Party Leader Jack Layton expressed the view that 'Canada is now sending out a signal that it is possible to really provide full equality to people with different sexual orientation and to celebrate those differences. . . . I think it will sound a real clarion call around the world . . .'.[1]

How many countries ultimately move to follow Canada's lead remains to be seen, but in the United Kingdom (UK), New Zealand and Australia, national legislatures had already, during the course of 2004, made their own responses (for the time being at least) to the claim that same-sex couples should be able to access the legal institution of marriage. Canadian judicial and legislative developments leading up to the enactment of the Civil Marriage Act 2005 may well have been influential, but none of these three countries reached the conclusion that a commitment to fundamental principles of equality and non-discrimination demanded the adoption of a new sexual orientation-neutral definition of marriage. Instead, the legislatures of the UK and New Zealand enacted legislation that created a new 'marriage-like' status – of civil partnership and civil union respectively – to which same-sex couples would have access, while preserving the legal category of marriage for heterosexual couples. The contrast with Australia is even more stark: the federal parliament not only declined to enact an inclusive definition of marriage, but refused to create a parallel institution for same-sex couples *and* passed legislation that confirmed the traditional common-law opposite-sex definition of marriage.

Ironically, if one takes the Australian Government at its word, the latter move was prompted by Canadian developments and the need to guard against the prospect of Australian same-sex couples marrying in Canada

---

1 Curry and Galloway, 2005, p A1.

and then returning to Australia to seek recognition of their marriage. The clarion call that was received in Australia was rather different to the one contemplated by Jack Layton.

Legislation dealing with the legal status of same-sex relationships, enacted in all four countries during the course of 2004–2005 can be plotted along a rough spectrum from recognition to non-recognition. At one end of the spectrum, the Canadian Civil Marriage Act 2005 reformulated the legal definition of marriage as 'the lawful union of two persons to the exclusion of all others'.[2] At the other end of the spectrum, the Australian Marriage Amendment Act 2004, expressly added the traditional common-law formulation of the definition of marriage to the Marriage Act 1961 (Aust): 'the union of a man and a woman to the exclusion of all others, voluntarily entered into for life.'[3] In between these two extremes of full equality-based recognition and non-recognition, are the partial 'separate but (almost) equal' recognition approaches of the UK and New Zealand. The Civil Partnership Act 2004 (UK)[4] and the Civil Union Act 2004 (NZ)[5] both provide for the legal recognition of a new 'marriage-like' relationship. In the UK it is available only to same-sex couples; in New Zealand it is available to both same-sex couples and opposite-sex couples.

For four countries that have followed reasonably similar law reform paths in the context of their fight against discrimination on the basis of sexual orientation – from decriminalisation of homosexual sex, to the prohibition of discrimination in employment, education and the provision of public services, and so on – the diversity of their respective responses to what is commonly (though not uncontroversially) regarded as the 'last stage'[6] in the achievement of formal legal equality for gay men and lesbians might be seen as something of a surprise.

Of course, the formal legal status of relationships is only a part (and, for some, a relatively minor part) of the wider struggle for gay and lesbian relationship equality. Resolution of the 'marriage issue' is not necessarily representative of the way in which other issues of relationship benefits and responsibilities for same-sex couples have been addressed in the four countries. This is particularly so in the Australian context where there has been a stark contrast between the responses of federal and state/territorial governments to same-sex equality demands.[7] But the diversity of recent

2   Civil Marriage Act 2005 (Canada), s 2.
3   Marriage Act 1961 (Aust), s 5.
4   The Civil Partnership Act 2004 (UK) came into force 5 December 2005, and the first civil partnerships were registered on 21 December 2005.
5   The Civil Union Act 2004 (NZ) came into force on 26 April 2005.
6   See Waaldijk's, 2001, ' "standard sequences" in "legislative recognition of homosexuality" ': Wintemute, 2004a, p 1148.
7   ALSO Foundation, 2004; Gay and Lesbian Rights Lobby, 2004.

national-level responses to the issue of relationship 'status' is worthy of investigation in its own right. It invites closer consideration of the way in which the controversy over the legal status of same-sex relationships has played out in each of the countries in recent years, and examination of the factors that might explain the diversity of approaches. Consistent with my primary concern in this book with the significance of legal form for the enjoyment of human rights, in this chapter I will consider the ways in which the different legal frameworks for the protection of equality rights in Canada, the UK, New Zealand and Australia, respectively, have shaped the contours of the debate and influenced the legislative outcomes.

It is important to observe at the outset of this chapter that the controversy over the legal status of same-sex relationships is different in nature to the controversies considered in Chapters 2 and 4, in at least two important respects.

First, recognition of same-sex relationships is not an issue in relation to which states are being pushed to comply with an explicit and unequivocal existing human rights standard. As noted in Chapter 1, this is a controversy that emanates from attempts to push the parameters of established principles of equality and non-discrimination.[8] International human rights law with respect to sexual orientation is relatively undeveloped – when compared, for example, with equality and non-discrimination rights with respect to gender (International Convention in the Elimination of Discrimination Against Women (CEDAW)), and race/ethnicity (International Convention on the Elimination of All Forms of Racial Discrimination (ICERD)).[9] Nonetheless, the push for formal legal recognition of same-sex relationships is clearly underpinned by the notion that the equality and non-discrimination principles that are at the heart of CEDAW and ICERD should apply with equal force to gays and lesbians. Therefore, the key variable as between the four countries that are the subject of the current comparative study is the state of their domestic laws with respect to equality rights generally, as well as sexual orientation rights specifically. The same-sex marriage controversy offers a unique opportunity to examine the relative dynamism of different legal models for human rights protection when it comes to dealing with 'new' human rights claims. Does 'legal form' impact on the receptiveness of local legal/political cultures to demands that 'push the limits' of the existing human rights framework?

This feature of the case study also makes it a good vehicle for countering the tendency, particularly among human rights lawyers, to adopt a hierarchical, top-down approach to the emergence of new human rights standards – as originating with the creation of international standards and followed by

---

8   Bourassa and Varnell, 2002.
9   Tahmindjis, 2005. See also, LaViolette and Whitworth, 1994; Sanders, 1996; Offord, 2003; Stychin, 2004.

domestic implementation of those standards. Obviously, this overly neat schema misrepresents the nature of the human rights movement and the dynamic relationship between domestic developments and international activities. In the area of sexual orientation human rights developments have been occurring at the local level in each of the four countries (and elsewhere), notwithstanding the absence of an explicit universal human rights standard with respect to sexual orientation.

Second, whereas the controversy surrounding double jeopardy reform arises out of an attack on the right not to be subjected to retrial after acquittal, and a responsive attempt to *defend an established right*, and the controversy over hate-speech laws emerges out of the tension associated with *balancing competing rights*, at the heart of the controversy over the legal status of same-sex relationships is an attempt to *extend the parameters* of the principle of equality. In this particular context, the following question is addressed in this chapter: Does legal form make any difference when human rights-asserting individuals or groups seek to push the limits of existing legal rules and political values with respect to human rights – in this case, non-discrimination/equality for gay men and lesbians? Particular attention will be focused on the way in which the human rights implications of the proposed mechanisms of recognition (or non-recognition) have been constructed and portrayed, and how what I termed in Chapter 1 the 'human rights dynamic' has impacted on the nature of the debates and the outcomes of the respective law reform processes.

Same-sex marriage: the demand for recognition

The push for gay and lesbian access to the institution of marriage, or the achievement of equivalent legal recognition, has emerged over the course of the last decade or so as a prominent component of the gay and lesbian human rights movement – at least in those parts of the world where other significant milestones (such as decriminalisation of homosexual sex, prohibition of workplace discrimination) have been reached.[10] For some it is regarded as the 'last step' in the achievement of full formal legal equality. For example, in the second reading speech on the Civil Union Bill, New Zealand's Associate Minister of Justice, David Benson-Pope, observed:

> The passage of this bill, together with the Relationships (Statutory References) Bill, will mark the culmination of a long march, marked by the passage of the Human Rights Act in 1993 and, even before that, the Homosexual Law Reform Act in 1984. This journey has taken us beyond a situation in which homosexual activity was criminalized, through what

10 See Waaldijk, 2001; Eskridge, 2002; Wintemute, 2004b.

has at times been only a grudging tolerance of same-sex couples, through the point where same-sex couples will finally be accorded genuinely equal respect and recognition.[11]

In Canada, Svend Robinson, prominent gay activist and former NDP MP in the Canadian Parliament, described the effect of the Civil Marriage Act 2005, in the following terms: '... the final barrier to full equality for gays and lesbian people in Canada was eliminated'.[12]

However, assigning this sort of 'pinnacle' status to marriage is controversial. As Murphy notes, 'For some . . . the idea of same-sex marriage is just as repugnant as heterosexual marriage'.[13]

At the time of writing, gay men and lesbians can marry in the Netherlands, Belgium, Canada, Spain and the state of Massachusetts in the USA. In addition, a larger number of countries have enacted laws that give same-sex couples access to a formal 'marriage-like' relationship status (for example, civil partnership). One of the interesting features of these developments is that they have taken place in the absence of explicit recognition of gay and lesbian human rights at the level of international law.[14] There has been a strong push for such recognition in recent years, led by organisations such as the International Lesbian and Gay Law Association. In 2003, Brazil tabled a motion at the UN Commission on Human Rights, calling for discrimination on the basis of sexual orientation to be expressly prohibited under international human rights law.[15] In 2004, New Zealand and Canada made a joint statement calling on the Commission to address the issue of discrimination against gays and lesbians:

> Discrimination against people on the grounds of their sexual orientation takes place in all too many countries. This is a reality. We cannot ignore it. And we cannot pretend it does not exist. . . . The United Nations has been silent on sexual orientation for far too long. It is time to break that silence. The issue should be on the agenda and the Commission should respond. A failure to speak out can only be interpreted as condoning discrimination and prejudice. We recognise that this is a difficult and complex issue but we are not prepared to compromise on the equality in dignity and rights of all people. It is time to start talking. We hope this Commission will not remain silent for much longer.[16]

---

11 New Zealand House of Representatives, Hansard, 2 December 2004, p 17388.
12 Robinson, 2005, p A13.
13 Murphy, 2004, p 543; see also, Auchmuty, 2004; and Ettelbrick, 2004; cf Calhoun, 2000.
14 See Tahmindjis, 2005.
15 International Lesbian and Gay Association, 2003.
16 International Lesbian and Gay Association, 2004.

The matter was again postponed and was not on the formal agenda of the Commission on Human Rights at its 2005 meeting. However New Zealand made another statement, on behalf of 32 countries including Canada and the UK (but not Australia). The statement expressed deep regret that the Commission was 'still not ready to address the original Brazilian resolution'.[17] The resolution was not on the agenda of the Commission on Human Rights at its final session in March 2006. It remains to be seen whether the new United Nations Human Rights Council, which replaced the Commission on Human Rights in June 2006, will provide a forum for addressing the silence surrounding sexual orientation in international human rights instruments.

Although there remains no specific international human rights law protections for gays and lesbians, existing equality standards contained in Art 26 of the International Covenant on Civil and Political Rights[18] and Art 14 of the European Convention on Human Rights (ECHR)[19] have been mobilised to some extent to partially fill the void in existing international human rights law.[20]

Legal responses and the impact of human rights discourse

The following examination of recent developments in Canada, the UK, New Zealand and Australia with respect to the legal recognition of same-sex relationships will focus on the culmination (or most recent key event) in the push for equality-based human rights protection. In all cases, with the exception of Australia, this stage has been preceded by attempts to deploy litigation as a strategy for achieving the goal of equal recognition of same-sex relationships, drawing on existing human rights laws in the respective countries. For each country a brief overview of these 'lead-up' events will be provided, along with

---

17 International Lesbian and Gay Association, 2005.
18 Article 26 of the ICCPR: 'All persons are equal before the law and are entitled without any discrimination to the equal protection of the law. In this respect, the law shall prohibit any discrimination and guarantee to all persons equal and effective protection against discrimination on any ground such as race, colour, sex, language, religion, political or other opinion, national or social origin, property, birth or other status.' The Human Rights Committee has interpreted this non-exhaustive list as including sexual orientation: see *Young v Australia* (2003).
19 Article 14: 'The enjoyment of the rights and freedoms set forth in [the] Convention shall be secured without discrimination on any ground such as sex, race, colour, language, religion, political or other opinion, national or social origin, association with a national minority, property, birth or other status.' The European Court of Human Rights has interpreted Art 14 as including sexual orientation: *Karner v Austria* (2003). A 'free standing' right to non-discrimination is contained in Protocol 12 to the ECHR, which came into force in April 2005. The United Kingdom has not yet ratified Protocol 12 (see United Kingdom Parliament, Joint Committee on Human Rights, 2005).
20 See Charlesworth, 2002b.

a brief account of prevailing relevant human rights legal standards in each country. Against this backdrop, the public discourse surrounding significant recent legislative enactments in each of the four countries will be examined.

Canada

At the centre of the Canadian story of the achievement of same-sex marriage, culminating in the passage of the Civil Marriage Act 2005, is the equality guarantee contained in s 15 of the Canadian Charter of Rights and Freedoms. But, of course, when it comes to capturing the legal form of human rights in Canada it is necessary to go beyond the mere words of the Charter and recognise other key design features – most notably, the justiciability of Charter rights and the capacity of the courts to invalidate legislation (and redefine the common law) on the basis of Charter incompatibility. Even this is not the end of the story. As will be demonstrated below, the ultimate success of the full marriage equality push by Canadian gay and lesbian activists cannot be fully explained unless we look beyond legal form and recognise the impact of Canada's broader legal culture with respect to human rights.

The legal environment and the lead-up to the Civil Marriage Act 2005

Section 15 of the Charter states:

> (1) Every individual is equal before and under the law and has the right to the equal protection and equal benefit of the law without discrimination and, in particular, without discrimination based on race, national or ethnic origin, colour, religion, sex, age or mental or physical disability.

Momentum towards the formal statutory redefinition of marriage in 2005 began a decade earlier when the Supreme Court of Canada held in *Egan* that sexual orientation was an 'analogous ground' to those expressly listed in s 15.[21] It followed that any law that discriminated on the basis of sexual orientation was potentially constitutionally invalid unless saved by s 1 of the Charter.[22] In a series of cases over the next few years, the courts spelt out the implications of the inclusion of sexual orientation as a Charter equality ground.

Even before the decision in *Egan*, sexual orientation had been added to

---

21 *Egan v Canada* (1995).
22 Section 1 states that: 'The Canadian Charter of Rights and Freedoms guarantees the rights and freedoms set out in it subject only to such reasonable limits prescribed by law as can be demonstrably justified in a free and democratic society.' See Chapter 1.

anti-discrimination legislation in the majority of jurisdictions in Canada.[23] In 1996, sexual orientation was added to the Canadian Human Rights Act 1977 and in 1998 the Supreme Court of Canada ruled that s 15 of the Charter required that a similar step should be taken in those provinces and territories that had not already done so.[24]

In 1999, in a case involving the breakdown of a lesbian couple's relationship, and the definition of 'spouse' in the Ontario Family Law Act, the Supreme Court of Canada ruled that s 15 of the Charter demanded that unmarried same-sex couples should be treated in the same way as unmarried opposite-sex couples.[25] In the specific circumstances of this case this meant that M was entitled to apply for spousal maintenance from H. In the wake of this decision 'the rights and obligations of unmarried same-sex and opposite sex couples ... [were] equalized in hundreds of federal, provincial, and territorial statutes'.[26]

Such a brief summary[27] of landmark legal decisions and events obviously overstates the ease with which Canada addressed the discrimination faced by gay and lesbian Canadians with respect to the practical benefits and responsibilities of relationships. In particular it understates the extent of the hostility and resistance in some quarters,[28] and the perseverance of activists, litigants and advocates.[29] However, it does serve to convey a sense of the inevitability of the reform trajectory, which developed rapidly, once the equality guarantee in s 15 of the Charter was formally regarded as extending to gays and lesbians. By 2000, formal relationship status or marriage was one of the few outstanding issues in the struggle for full formal legal equality.

The specific issue of the access of same-sex couples to the civil institution of marriage was forced onto the national law reform agenda by a series of provincial trial court decisions in 2001–2002.[30] Between May 2003 and February 2004 key appellate court decisions were handed down in British Columbia, Ontario and Quebec. In each of these three cases, the court ruled that the traditional opposite-sex definition of marriage as a union of 'one man and one woman' was unconstitutional because it was inconsistent with the equality guarantee in s 15 of the Charter of Rights and Freedoms, and could not be justified under s 1.[31]

Significantly, the courts held that only one remedy would be adequate to

---

23 Wintemute, 2004a, p 1150.
24 *Vriend v Alberta* (1998).
25 *M v H* (1999).
26 Wintemute, 2004a, p 1156.
27 See, further, Manfredi, 2004, pp 82–90; Wintemute, 2004a; Hurley, 2005.
28 Hiebert, 2002; Cossman, 2002.
29 Hiebert, 2002.
30 See Lahey and Alderson, 2004.
31 *Barbeau v British Columbia* (2003), para 7 per Prowse JA. See also, *Halpern v Canada* (2003), and *Catholic Civil Rights League v Hendricks* (2004).

satisfy the demands of the Charter's equality guarantee: the redefinition of marriage as 'the lawful union of two persons to the exclusion of all others'. In *Barbeau*, Prowse JA, British Columbia Court of Appeal, concluded that:

> ... redefinition of marriage to include same-sex couples ... is the only road to true equality for same-sex couples. Any other form of recognition of same-sex relationships, including the parallel institution of RDP's [ie civil union or civil partnership], falls short of true equality. This Court should not be asked to grant a remedy which makes same-sex couples 'almost equal', or to leave it to governments to choose amongst less-than-equal solutions.[32]

The federal government's initial reaction to the judicial developments had been to begin an examination of policy options with respect to the legal recognition of same-sex relationships,[33] including referral of the question to the House of Commons Standing Committee on Justice and Human Rights.[34] However, a week after the 10 June 2003 decision of the Ontario Court of Appeal in *Halpern*, Prime Minister Jean Chrétien announced that the federal government would enact legislation defining marriage as 'the lawful union of two persons to the exclusion of all others' – thereby confirming that the legal status of marriage would be available to both opposite-sex and same-sex couples across the country.

However, the Government elected to first submit the proposed amendments to the Supreme Court of Canada for constitutional scrutiny, with a view to receiving confirmation that the proposed redefinition was within the exclusive power of the Federal Parliament under Canada's federal system of government, and consistent with the Charter. New Prime Minister Paul Martin later added an additional question: Was the traditional opposite-sex requirement for marriage consistent with the Charter? In essence the Government was asking the Supreme Court of Canada to express an authoritative view on a question that had been answered in the negative by three provincial appellate courts, but never previously considered by the highest court in the country. From a political perspective it seems clear that the Government, in adopting the strategy of referring the amendments to the Supreme Court of Canada, wanted to be able to defend its proposed policy shift on the basis that it had *no choice*. That is, marriage would be legislatively redefined so as to ensure access for same-sex couples, not because this was necessarily the Government's favoured option or preferred interpretation of

---

32 *Barbeau v British Columbia* (2003), para 156. See also Lahey and Alderson, 2004, pp 29, 33, where Lahey characterises civil union-type regimes as 'segregated "non-marriage"', and as proof of 'just how deeply homophobic attitudes have invaded the legal imagination'.
33 Canada, Department of Justice, 2002.
34 Hurley, 2005, p 27.

s 15 of the Charter, but because the Supreme Court of Canada had formally declared that this should occur.

On the constitutionality of the proposed legislative redefinition of marriage, the Supreme Court gave the answers that the government wanted and that most observers expected.[35] A gender/sexual orientation-neutral legislative definition of marriage was within the authority of the Canadian Parliament and consistent with the Charter. However, the Government did not get the 'clincher' that it was looking for in posing the additional question. The Court declined to answer the late addition question on the constitutionality of the traditional common-law definition of marriage. On first glance the Court's 'no comment' position on whether the Charter *mandated* the redefinition of marriage suggested that there would still be room for the Government's proposal to be characterised as a political choice rather than a 'constitutional imperative'.[36] However, it is reasonably clear from the tenor of the Court's judgment that if it had answered the final question, the answer would have been: No – the traditional opposite-sex definition of marriage is not consistent with the equality guarantee in s 15 of the Charter. For example, the Court observed that:

> Section 1 of the proposed legislation is consistent with the Charter. The purpose of s. 1 is to extend the right to civil marriage to same-sex couples and, in substance, the provision embodies the government's policy stance in relation to the s. 15(1) equality concerns of same-sex couples. This, combined with the circumstances giving rise to the proposed legislation and with the preamble thereto, points unequivocally to a purpose which, far from violating the Charter, *flows from it*.[37]

The Civil Marriage Bill (Bill C-38) was introduced into the House of Commons of the Canadian Parliament on 1 February 2005. On 20 July 2005 it received royal assent, after having been passed by the House of Commons and the Senate.

Bill C-38 and the Charter Imperative

The Canadian story of the legal recognition of same-sex relationships is distinctive – not only because of the (full equality) terms in which it has resolved the issue of the legal recognition of same-sex relationships, but in the way in which the particular Charter-dominated nature of the human rights dynamic compelled reform in the direction of the redefinition of marriage,

---

35 *Reference re Same-Sex Marriage* (2004).
36 Egale Canada/Canadians for Equal Marriage 2005.
37 *Reference re Same-Sex Marriage* (2004), para 43 (emphasis added).

and made it very difficult for objectors to achieve any real purchase in the policy debates and law reform process.

The relative ease and speed with which marriage was redefined in Canada so as to be sexual orientation-inclusive should not be mistaken for a suggestion that it was the product of broad consensus. The issue was controversial; Bill C-38 was vigorously debated in the Canadian Parliament. The Conservative Party opposition and some members of the governing Liberal Party opposed it. (The support of the NDP was crucial to the passage of the Bill.)

Perhaps the most important explanation for the achievement of same-sex marriage in Canada is that it came to be seen as a 'constitutional imperative'. The Charter's equality guarantee demanded that the definition of marriage be updated, and by mid-2003 the Canadian Government had actively adopted the position that it had 'no choice' but to accept what the Charter demanded, and what the courts had already done. Bill C-38 was, therefore, not an affirmative step of extending equality to same-sex couples, but a statement of confirmation or acceptance that equality had already been extended.

During debate on Bill C-38 in the House of Commons, the Prime Minister, Paul Martin, observed:

> Understand that in seven provinces and one territory, the lawful union of two people of the same sex in civil marriage is already the law of the land. The debate here today is not about whether to change the definition of marriage – it's been changed. The debate comes down to whether we should override a right that is now in place.[38]

In response to the suggestion that a parallel civil union-type regime would be adequate to achieve legal recognition of same-sex relationships, the Prime Minister observed:

> ... the court have clearly and consistently ruled that this option would offend the equality provisions of the Charter. For instance, the British Columbia Court of Appeal stated that, and I quote: 'Marriage is the only road to true equality for same-sex couples. Any other form of recognition of same-sex relationships ... falls short of true equality.'[39]

In a joint submission to the Legislative Committee on Bill C-38, Egale and Canadians for Equal Marriage characterised full recognition of the right of same-sex couples to marry as 'a constitutional imperative': 'If C-38 doesn't

---

38 Canada Parliament, Hansard (House of Commons), 16 February 2005, 1530.
39 Canada Parliament, Hansard (House of Commons), 16 February 2005, 1530. Some commentators have argued that a relationship registration scheme might still be desirable as an alternative to marriage for those couples who do not want to marry. See, e.g. LaViolette, 2002; Law Commission of Canada, 2001.

pass, the equal marriage debate will continue. Constitutional imperatives do not go away.'[40] This characterisation effectively captures what is so distinctive about the Canadian story of the legal recognition of same-sex relationships when compared with the three other countries that are the subject of the present study. It is not just that Canada reached a different outcome – marriage rather than civil partnership, civil union or non-recognition – but that this outcome, and no other, came to be seen as *required* by the constitutional status of the right to equality in Canada. The human rights standard of formal legal equality embedded in the Charter meant that no other resolution of the controversy was possible. In contrast, as will be revealed below, governments in the UK, New Zealand and Australia, while influenced in varying degrees by the demands of human rights discourse, still had a degree of policy-making breathing space in which they could formulate alternative solutions to demands for same-sex relationship recognition, based on principles of equality and non-discrimination.

The respective roles played by the judicial and executive/legislative arms of Canadian Government in relation to this particular human rights controversy are significant, and revealing as to one of the distinctive features of the constitutional entrenchment model of human rights protection: the capacity for the judiciary to respond to human rights demands where the legislature may be reluctant to act for fear of suffering electoral damage.

Wintemute has observed:

> Both the courts and the legislatures in Canada ... were reluctant to 'press the button' and make marriage equality happen, fearing that the foundations of civilization might 'explode'. Someone had to be the first. Given the legal and political culture in Canada ... with regard to controversial human rights issues, an appellate court was in a better position to do so than a legislature.[41]

Moreover, once the 'first moves' had been made by the judiciary and advocates of full access of same-sex couples to marriage were able to defend their position, not simply in political/moral terms, but in legal/constitutional terms, legislators were prompted to follow the lead – some relatively quickly, presumably confident that the electoral repercussions were likely to be modest; others grudgingly and bitterly.[42] If the Charter demanded that full equality be extended to gay and lesbian couples, and if the overwhelming message from the judiciary was that anything less than marriage (for example, the UK or New Zealand models of civil partnership/union) was not full

---

40 Eagle Canada/Canadians for Equal Marriage, 2005.
41 Wintemute, 2004a, p 1166.
42 Cossman, 2002; Hiebert, 2002.

equality, then the redefinition of marriage to include both opposite-sex couples and same-sex couples was not merely a political choice about which individuals and political parties could reasonably differ, but an outcome which was inevitable.

Less than two years prior to the introduction of Bill C-38, Paul Martin had supported a parliamentary motion in support of the traditional opposite-sex definition of marriage.[43] In 2005, his position had changed.[44] So it was not the existence of a right to equality in the Charter *per se* which had been instrumental in shifting Martin's personal position and the broader policy landscape, but the way in which this legal right had been deployed by activists and adjudicated upon by judges in the interim. In 2003, there had been no authoritative legal ruling that the Charter *mandated* that same-sex couples should have access to marriage. By 2005, the government had conceded that such a mandate was now an undeniable feature of Canada's legal environment.

This example illustrates the way in which human rights laws in Canada, underpinned by the Charter, can be mobilised as a powerful dynamic to trump government opposition or recalcitrance. But it would be a mistake to explain the Canadian story of same-sex marriage as *simply* about the legal form of the right to equality, including the judiciary's interpretive supremacy over its substance. Section 33 of the Charter retains for the legislature the power to override a judicial ruling of constitutional invalidity (albeit, with a time limit). The construction of the s 33 override as a 'non-option' in the public discourse over Bill C-38 speaks to a feature of Canada's local legal/political culture which cannot be explained merely by reference to the text of the Charter or the content of Charter jurisprudence. That the use of the override to reassert the traditional opposite-sex definition of marriage was widely regarded as beyond contemplation in the realpolitik of Canadian debate about Bill C-38, underscores the need to look at legal form as well as the wider legal culture in order to develop a meaningful appreciation of the status of human rights considerations and the power of human rights discourse in any country.

The point is well illustrated by reactions to an attempt by the Conservative Party opposition to advance an alternative policy option – the passage of two statutes: one to reassert the traditional (heterosexual) definition of marriage and one to establish a 'parallel' civil union institution for same-sex couples. In

---

43 The motion, tabled in the House of Commons by the Canadian Alliance on 17 September 2003, stated: 'That, in the opinion of this House, it is necessary, in light of public debate around recent court decisions, to reaffirm that marriage is and should remain the union of one man and one woman to the exclusion of all others, and that Parliament take all necessary steps within the jurisdiction of the Parliament of Canada to preserve this definition of marriage in Canada.' The motion was defeated by a narrow margin (137 to 132): Canada Parliament, Hansard (House of Commons), 17 September 2003.
44 Canada Parliament, Hansard (House of Commons), 16 February 2005, 1530.

response, 134 law professors from across Canada signed an open letter to Conservative Party leader, Stephen Harper. It powerfully illustrates the extent to which the convention that the legislature should not invoke their power under s 33 of the Charter, despite its formal availability, is entrenched in Canada's wider legal culture:

> Even though the Supreme Court of Canada did not address this issue in the recent same-sex marriage reference, courts in British Columbia, Saskatchewan, Manitoba, Newfoundland, Ontario, Quebec, Nova Scotia and the Yukon are now unanimously of the view that a definition of marriage that excludes same-sex couples is unconstitutional. The consensus of constitutional experts is that these decisions are correct. You must explain to Canadians how your plan to entrench the traditional definition of marriage will pass constitutional muster. The truth is, there is only one way to accomplish your goal: invoke the notwithstanding clause. . . . You should either invoke the use of the notwithstanding clause, and justify this decision to Canadians, or concede that same-sex marriage is now part of Canada's legal landscape. If you intend to override Canadians' constitutional rights, you at least owe it to them to say this openly and directly.[45]

The adoption of a strategy of publicly 'daring' Harper to concede that his preferred option would only be possible with reliance on the notwithstanding clause – a step which was unprecedented at the national level – serves as a reminder as to how firmly entrenched the Charter is in Canadian political consciousness. (The letter was also strategically clever in that it was expressed as a definitive statement of Canadian constitutional law rather than a moral or philosophical case for same-sex marriage, which ensured that it received the support of law professors across the ideological spectrum, presumably including social conservatives who would not have supported the cause of gay and lesbian marriage.[46]) In terms of Canada's formal constitutional framework, there is no question that, 'technically', the notwithstanding clause could be invoked for the purposing of limiting marriage to opposite-sex couples. However, Charter (equality) consciousness is so embedded in Canada's legal culture that any move to invoke this law-making option would be highly controversial and electorally perilous.[47]

In Justice Minister Irwin Cotler's public articulation of the 'no choice' or

---

45 'Open Letter to The Hon. Stephen Harper from Law Professors Regarding Same-Sex Marriage' 25 January 2005, www.law.utoronto.ca/samesexletter.html (accessed 20 October 2005).
46 Rebecca Johnson, personal communication, 22 June 2005.
47 Webber, 2006. See discussion of s 33 of the Charter in Chapter 1.

'no other option' position it is possible to see quite clearly the combined influence of elements of legal form (the judiciary's interpretation of the demands of s 15) and legal culture (the extreme reluctance of the government to deploy the notwithstanding clause), even though the terms of the constitutional distribution of legal authority in Canada made this legally possible. The Justice Minister observed:

> There are before us two alternatives – we can move forward to provide uniformity of the laws in this area, by passing the Government's bill, or we can move backwards to overrule the court decisions and restore the traditional definition of marriage as the law in Canada, by using the notwithstanding clause. . . . But in order to do so, Parliament would first have to publicly acknowledge that they are prepared to deliberately discriminate against same-sex couples who wish the same degree of commitment as other married couples. That is how it works. Members who vote in favour of using the notwithstanding clause must realize that they are acknowledging publicly that the law is discriminatory but insisting that the law be proclaimed despite the effect on constitutionally protected minority rights. . . . The Government views use of the notwithstanding clause to overrule Charter rights of a minority as inconsistent with responsible leadership. It leaves open all minorities to the possibility of deliberate discrimination through legislation.[48]

As a product of both legal form and legal culture then, the Charter's equality guarantee was regarded as foreclosing all other options and leaving full access to marriage as the only legitimate response to demands for equality-based recognition of same-sex relationships. As will be revealed later in this chapter, to the extent that a human rights imperative is identifiable in the three other countries that are the subjects of the present study, it has had neither the potency nor the autonomy from the policy preferences of executive government that were demonstrated so powerfully in the lead-up to the enactment of the Civil Marriage Act 2005.

In indicating that his government would not rely on s 33 of the Charter to reassert the traditional opposite definition of marriage, the Prime Minister, Paul Martin, said:

> The notwithstanding clause is part of the Charter of Rights. But there's a reason that no prime minister has ever used it. For a prime minister to use the powers of his office to explicitly deny rather than affirm a right enshrined under the Charter would serve as signal to all minorities that no longer can they look to the nation's leader and to the nation's

48 Cotler, 2005.

Constitution for protection, for security, for the guarantee of their freedoms. We would risk becoming a country in which the defence of rights is weighed, calculated and debated based on electoral or other considerations.[49]

After a similar strategy had been employed to help defeat the 2003 parliamentary resolution affirming the traditional opposite definition of marriage, Manfredi observed:

> The successful transformation of a motion about the definition of marriage into a *de facto* referendum on the notwithstanding clause is indicative of a growing convention that it should never be invoked by any legislative body. The rapid decline in the clause's perceived legitimacy as an instrument of government is one of the key developments in the post-Charter era of rights talk.[50]

During parliamentary debate on the Australian Marriage Amendment Act 2004 (discussed below), which he opposed, Democrat Senator Brian Greig made reference to the 'Canadian experience' in a way that was clearly laudatory and designed to hold it up, as an example of what Australia should do. But he mis-characterised the forces that led, ultimately, to the passage of the Civil Marriage Act 2005 – giving too much credit to the legislative and executive branches of government. With reference to the increase in popular support for same-sex marriage, he said: 'That only happened because leadership was shown by their political parties. The political parties argued, in the face of controversy, to support same-sex marriages.'[51]

In fact, the hand of provincial and federal governments has been incrementally forced by a series of judicial decisions on the application of s 15 to sexual orientation discrimination and same-sex relationships. In fact, it was often a case of executive and legislative arms of government being 'dragged kicking and screaming' to comply with judicial rulings on what the Charter demanded with respect to the removal of discrimination against same-sex couples.[52]

Perhaps, on the specific issue of same-sex marriage, the federal government could have elected to resist gay and lesbian access to marriage more vigorously – by, for example, pursuing appeals in cases like *Barbeau* and *Halpern* – but it would be an overstatement to suggest that the Canadian government freely adopted a policy position in favour of same-sex marriage. It is a measure of the Charter's significance that executive and legislative arms of

49 Canada Parliament, Hansard (House of Commons), 16 February 2005, 1535.
50 Manfredi, 2003, p 21.
51 Australia Parliament, Hansard (Senate), 12 August 2004, p 26512.
52 Hiebert, 2002; Robinson, 2004.

government were persuaded to fall into line in support of full formal legal equality for same-sex relationships, even though this outcome was not an overwhelming demand of the Canadian electorate; was sometimes inconsistent with personal and party political preferences; and where a different political choice would likely have been made in the absence of the Charter.

Wintemute has commented on the speed with which Canada moved from having a discriminatory age of consent for homosexual sexual activity two decades ago to providing for same-sex marriage:

> Since 17 April 1985, progress towards achieving formal legal equality for LGB individuals and same-sex couples in Canada has been dramatic. . . . Although the Charter cannot take sole credit for this progress, it has served to crystallize as constitutional principle the anti-discrimination rules adopted voluntarily by legislatures in the late 1980s and early 1990s, which resulted from political campaigns made possible by increasing social acceptance of LGB individuals. Charter litigation has permitted LGB individuals and same-sex couples to focus this new constitutional principle on remaining areas of formal legal inequality and gradually to compel their removal by courts and legislatures.[53]

Without doubt, the Canadian story of the achievement of same-sex marriage is an illustration of the potential power of human rights in the legal form of judicially interpreted Charter guarantees – a point which resonates even more strongly when compared with the recent resolution of the same-sex relationship controversy in the UK, New Zealand and Australia. But it is also an illustration of the broader impact of the Charter on Canada's legal culture – as a powerful influence on the construction of political 'choices'.

The story of same-sex marriage in Canada is a tale *par excellence* of the 'discursive hegemony'[54] of the Charter in Canada's legal culture.[55] Section 15 cut a swathe through the divided ranks of elected politicians and their electorate to deliver the 'prize' which, to date, has been won by gay and lesbian activists in only a handful of countries. But it would be a mistake to explain the Charter's significance simply in terms of legal form. If the achievement of same-sex marriage was reducible to the mere positing of a human right to equality in Canadian law, the breakthrough would have come as soon as s 15 came into operation in 1985. In fact, when the Ontario Divisional Court was required to address the issue in 1993, it rejected the argument that the refusal of the Ottawa City Clerk's Office to issue a marriage licence to two men constituted unlawful discrimination.[56] It was almost

---

53 Wintemute, 2004a, pp 1179–80.
54 See Angenot, 2004.
55 Smith, 2005b.
56 *Layland v Ontario* (1993).

a decade later before the Charter imperative for same-sex marriage was fully formed.[57]

Certainly, the Charter provided the constitutional mandate for the courts to participate actively in the policy-making and law reform process, and s 15 provided the legal text out of which the courts, over the course of a decade or so of litigation, incrementally fashioned a conception of equality which eventually made the issue of gay and lesbian access to the institution of marriage a 'no brainer' – it flowed logically and inevitably from the Supreme Court's conception of the formal legal equality demanded by the Charter.[58] But the Charter's significance needs also to be understood in terms of its transformative effect on Canadian legal culture. Hiebert has observed that the application of s 15 of the Charter to gay and lesbian equality claims has:

> demonstrated the Charter's potential to transform legal culture in a way that critically examines the fairness and legitimacy of the dominant legal, social, and moral assumptions of legislative decisions. The Charter does not simply appear to coincide with this evolution. It has provided both the occasion and the foundation from which to reassess previous judicial assumptions and approaches.[59]

Another important part of the transformation effected by the Charter was the shift in strategies employed by gay and lesbian activists. Miriam Smith has observed that after 1985, when s 15 came into force, there was a 'changed political opportunity structure'.[60] The Charter 'encouraged the shift from gay liberation to rights talk as a form of equality seeking',[61] with an emphasis on 'legal and court-centred activism'.[62] The emergence of Egale as the most prominent national gay and lesbian activist group in the 1990s is illustrative.[63] Egale's methods, focusing on Charter litigation, and its goals, articulated in terms of formal legal equality, are an important part of the story of the success of the same-sex marriage movement. The Charter has been important not just as an instrument for the achievement of pre-established goals. It has shaped the goals of the gay and lesbian movement and encouraged the prioritisation of associated strategies, including 'legal mobilization'.[64] 'Success' came to be defined in terms that lined up with the liberal equality foundation

---

57 Rebecca Johnson, personal communication, 22 June 2005.
58 See Lahey and Alderson, 2004, pp 74–5.
59 Hiebert, 2002, p 212.
60 Smith, 1999, p 73.
61 Ibid, p 74.
62 Ibid, p 93.
63 Smith, 2005b, p 337.
64 Ibid, p 329.

on which the Canadian Charter of Rights and Freedoms is based.[65] Cossman has commented that the strategic prioritisation of formal equality-seeking litigation involved the pursuit of an 'unapologetically assimilationist agenda' and succumbing to the 'politics of sameness'.[66] For Boyd and Young:

> Given that many in the lesbian and gay community celebrate and value their differences from the normative model of the heterosexual couple, such an approach is problematic. This strategy is not 'the fault' of lesbians and gay men who make claims for spousal status ... Rather, equality discourse tends to force arguments in this comparative, conservative direction and thereby render the diversity of intimate relationships marginal or, indeed, invisible.[67]

Of course, not all gay and lesbian activists regard the Charter, the pursuit of formal legal equality, and access to marriage as unmitigated goods.[68] In particular, many object to the fact that pursuit of the Charter equality path to justice has involved adopting a sameness paradigm: homosexual relationships are no different to heterosexual relationships and, therefore, there is no basis for drawing a distinction between them in terms of legal status.[69] More radical goals and strategies have tended to be marginalised[70] by the Charter equality juggernaut. Herman has observed that:

> Since the 1980s, a liberal minority rights paradigm has been ascendant while radical sexual politics, *of both the left and the right*, are not as visible within public discourse on rights and sexuality.[71]

A related point is that the nature of Charter litigation as an activist strategy is such that individuals have been able to commence proceedings – with possible implications for gay men and lesbians generally – without necessarily having the support or input of broader social movements.[72] In this way, marriage became the assumed goal of the gay and lesbian community, even though many would not have put it at the top of the reform agenda of many individuals and organisations.[73] Moreover, when this cause met political resistance and prompted a homophobic backlash, individuals and organisations

---

65 Herman, 1994; Boyd and Young, 2003. See also, Eberts, 1999.
66 Cossman, 2002, p 236. For debate on the desirability of adopting legal strategies in pursuit of social justice goals, see Brown and Halley, 2002; and in response, Green, 2004.
67 Boyd and Young, 2003, pp 773–4.
68 Smith, 1999.
69 Boyd and Young, 2003.
70 Sheila McIntyre, personal communication, 4 July 2005.
71 Herman, 1994, p 5.
72 Nicole LaViolette, personal communication, 27 June 2005. See also, Smith, 2005b.
73 Boyd and Young, 2003.

that were not keen to pursue access to the existing institution of marriage were prompted to speak out in defence of those for whom marriage was the goal.

One final dimension of the story of the legal recognition of same-sex relationships in Canada should also be mentioned: the extent to which there was complementarity between the specific claims being advanced in s 15 Charter litigation and ascendant values in the wider Canadian political environment.[74] In particular, a number of commentators have emphasised the need to appreciate the ideological fit between the Supreme Court of Canada's pivotal decision in *M v H* and 'neo-liberalism's politics of privatization'.[75] Cossman has observed that in *M v H*:

> Same-sex couples won the right to sue each other when their relationships break down. This was not a case that involved the extension of government or employer benefits, but rather, it was the kind of equality case that fits perfectly with an agenda of fiscal responsibility. The result of the ruling was to expand the scope of spousal support obligations, and thereby reduce demands on the state.... The ruling is consistent with the politics of reprivatization—a process in which the costs of social reproduction are being shifted from the public to private spheres and the family is being reconstituted as the natural site of economic dependency.[76]

Subsequent judicial and legislative reforms with respect to the equal provision of state (public) benefits to individuals in same-sex relationships do not fit so squarely in a neoliberal paradigm,[77] but the insight that ideological fit played a role in the initial breakthrough remains important. In fact, these subsequent developments provide further evidence of the way in which the transformation of the terms of the debate about same-sex relationships from one dictated by ideological or political preferences to one determined by a constitutional imperative was a critical factor in the success of the same-sex marriage campaign.

Canada's same-sex marriage story may not be over just yet. In January 2006, Canadians elected a minority Conservative Party Government under Prime Minister Stephen Harper. The Conservative Party went into the election with the following commitment as part of their platform:

> A Conservative government will: Hold a truly free vote on the definition of marriage in the next session of Parliament. If the resolution is passed,

---

74 See Stychin, 1998, p 141.
75 Cossman, 2002, pp 236–7. See also Boyd, 1999; Boyd and Young, 2003.
76 Cossman, 2002, p 237.
77 Ibid.

the government will introduce legislation to restore the traditional definition of marriage while respecting existing same-sex marriages.[78]

Just prior to the January 2006 election, a group of 104 law professors repeated the strategy that had been employed a year earlier: issuing an open letter to Stephen Harper warning that any attempt to legislate for the 'restoration' of the traditional heterosexual definition of marriage, without relying on s 33 of the Charter, would be unconstitutional and struck down by the courts:

> You have stated that it would not be legally necessary to use the notwithstanding clause to protect a statutory definition of marriage that excludes same sex couples. As law professors, we strenuously disagree. . . .
>
> It appears to be your intention to pass a law that you know is almost certainly unconstitutional and then leave it to the courts to clean up the mess. This would be untenable and irresponsible and we call on you to take a more responsible approach, namely to first refer your proposed legislation to the Supreme Court of Canada.
>
> You have insisted that the Supreme Court would defer to Parliament's decision to adopt a discriminatory definition of marriage, despite the overwhelming weight of legal jurisprudence to the contrary. If you truly believe that, then you should have no hesitation in agreeing to a Supreme Court reference. . . .
>
> If your government proceeds to pass a law that is so clearly unconstitutional, the result will be legal confusion, a lack of uniformity, and unnecessary, protracted and costly litigation.[79]

At the time of writing, a motion in pursuit of this commitment had not yet been introduced into the Canadian Parliament.[80]

United Kingdom

The non-discrimination guarantee in s 14 of the ECHR, as incorporated into domestic law by the Human Rights Act 1998, may not have been the legal 'centre-piece' of the UK's recent debates on the recognition of same-sex relationships – in the way that s 15 of the Charter of Rights and Freedoms dominated the Canadian debate. Nonetheless, its impact was significant as part of what might be called the 'European imperative' – which was a major influence on the terms in which the UK resolved the controversy: the

---

78 Conservative Party of Canada, 2006, p 33.
79 See Egale Canada, 2006.
80 Canadians for Equal Marriage, 2006.

enactment of the Civil Partnership Act 2004, which created a parallel 'marriage-like' legal institution for same-sex couples.

The legal environment and the lead-up to the Civil Partnership Act 2004

Article 14 of the ECHR states:

> The enjoyment of the rights and freedoms set forth in this Convention shall be secured without discrimination on any ground such as sex, race, colour, language, religion, political or other opinion, national or social origin, association with a national minority, property, birth or other status.

Like s 15 of the Canadian Charter, Art 14 of the ECHR does not expressly identify sexual orientation as a prohibited ground of discrimination, but it is now firmly established in European Court of Human Rights ('Strasbourg') jurisprudence that the protection of Art 14 extends sexual orientation.[81] This development forms part of a broader momentum in Europe, as reflected in:

- the 1997 Treaty of Amsterdam, which authorised the European Council to 'take appropriate action to combat discrimination based on sex, racial or ethnic origin, religion or belief, disability, age or sexual orientation';[82]
- Art 21 of the Charter of Fundamental Rights of the European Union 2000, which prohibits discrimination on a range of grounds including sexual orientation;[83]
- a resolution passed by the European Parliament in March 2000 to the effect that European Union member states should 'guarantee one-parent families, unmarried couples and same-sex couples, rights equal to those enjoyed by traditional couples and families, particularly as regards tax laws, pecuniary rights and social rights';[84] and
- the European Union's 2000 'Framework Directive on equal treatment in employment prohibiting direct and indirect discrimination on the grounds of religion or belief, age, disability or *sexual orientation*'.[85]

The UK complied with this Directive in 2003 when it passed the Employment

---

81 *Karner v Austria* (2003).
82 Treaty of Amsterdam Amending the Treaty on European Union, the Treaties Establishing the European Communities and Related Acts, Official Journal C 340 of 10 November 1997.
83 Charter of Fundamental Rights of the European Union, Official Journal C 364 of 18 December 2000.
84 European Parliament, 2000; see Wilets, 2003.
85 EU Directive 2000/78/EC Nov 27, 2000 (emphasis added). See also European Parliament, 2006.

Equality (Sexual Orientation) Regulations 2003. This law is limited in scope and certainly did not mandate the legal recognition of same-sex relationships. However, the European Union Directive, on which it was based, and the other European policy developments mentioned, clearly formed part of the broader policy context out of which the UK Government's proposals for civil partnership legislation for same-sex couples emerged. Auchmuty has observed that 'once the UK incorporated the European Convention on Human Rights into domestic law in the Human Rights Act 1998, which came into force in October 2000, the rights culture flourished here too, transforming the legal terrain'.[86] She describes the creation of a civil partnership scheme as 'but one product of the new climate'.[87] Another feature of the emerging European standard was the growth in the number of states that had moved to create laws for the formal recognition of same-sex relationships, whether as marriage or a 'parallel' civil institution.[88]

Despite all of these developments, in 2003 when the UK Government formally adopted a policy of extending non-discrimination-based recognition to same-sex relationships, it was doing so in a context where no particular outcome was mandated. There was no equivalent of the Canadian constitutional imperative, which, at the very same time, was recognised as demanding the sexual orientation inclusive re-definition of marriage. The development of a formal European human rights law imperative on the recognition of same-sex relationships was nascent. In the 2000s the first tentative steps were being taken towards putting the articulation of specific European standards with respect to the recognition of same-sex relationships on the formal law reform agenda. In 2005, a resolution was introduced into the Parliamentary Assembly of the Council of Europe by members of the Socialist Group calling for the Parliamentary Assembly, 'to study the situation of legal recognition of same-sex partnerships in Europe from the perspective of the ECHR and the jurisprudence of the Court . . . and to make such recommendations as may be appropriate'.[89] In January 2006 the European Parliament passed a resolution calling on member states to 'ensure that same-sex partners enjoy the same respect, dignity and protection as the rest of society'.[90]

But by 2001, internal pressure was already being generated by gay and lesbian activists and human rights advocates,[91] following the introduction of private members' bills in the House of Commons in October 2001[92] and in the House of Lords in January 2002.[93] In response to the latter bill, which had

---

86 Auchmuty, 2004, p 107.
87 Ibid.
88 International Lesbian and Gay Association – Europe, 2005.
89 Parliamentary Assembly of the Council of Europe, 2005.
90 European Parliament, 2006.
91 Stychin, 1998, p 136.
92 The Relationship (Civil Registration) Bill 2001, introduced by Labour MP, Jane Griffiths.
93 The Civil Partnership Bill 2002.

been developed by Stonewall and the Odysseus Trust, and introduced by Lord Lester, the Government was moved to undertake to study the issue and formulate its policy position. Meanwhile, domestic litigation on the implications of the ECHR for laws affecting same-sex couples was also emerging as a significant influence on the shape of the Government's response.

Shortly after the Human Rights Act 1998 came into force, domestic courts were being called upon to address the implications of the UK's obligations under the ECHR with respect to same-sex couples. In 1999, in a case decided on the law as it stood prior to the domestic implementation of the ECHR into UK law, the House of Lords held that the term 'spouse' in the Rent Act 1977 did not include a same-sex partner.[94] Three years later, the Court of Appeal was called upon to consider essentially the same question, with one important difference – this time the definition of 'spouse' had to be interpreted in light of the ECHR, the HRA having come into force in October 2000.[95]

The Court of Appeal began by confirming that 'Sexual orientation is now clearly recognised as an impermissible ground of discrimination, on the same level as the examples, which is all that they are, specifically set out in the text of article 14'.[96] In accordance with its interpretive obligation under s 3 of the Human Rights Act 1998,[97] and in order to render the definition of 'spouse' in the Rent Act as compliant with the ECHR, and Art 14 in particular, the Court of Appeal interpreted 'the words "as his or her wife or husband" to mean "as *if they were* his or her wife or husband"'.[98] It followed that unmarried same-sex couples were included within the scope of the legislation.

Stonewall has described *Mendoza* as the UK's 'first major gay human rights case and the first case in which the Court of Appeal has used the Human Rights Act to rewrite previous legislation'.[99] It highlighted two important features of the post-Human Rights Act environment – one of which can be attributed directly to the particular legal form for the protection of human rights adopted in the UK in 1998; the other of which is a combined product of legal formal and legal culture. The first feature is the emergence of Art 14 of the ECHR as a primary and strong reference point for judicial decision-making on gay and lesbian equality claims. The second less predictable feature of the post-Human Rights Act environment demonstrated by *Mendoza* is the judiciary's demonstrated willingness to adopt a robust approach to the legislative obligation to interpret domestic laws in a manner consistent with the ECHR, wherever possible. The legal form of human rights protection in the UK (specifically s 3 of the Human Rights Act 1998) made *possible* the Court of Appeal's decision in *Mendoza* (subsequently

---

94 *Fitzpatrick v Sterling Housing Association* (1999).
95 *Ghaidan v Mendoza* (2002).
96 Ibid, para 32.
97 See Chapter 1.
98 *Ghaidan v Mendoza* (2002), para 35.
99 Stonewall, 2005.

endorsed by the House of Lords[100]), but it did not necessarily *mandate* the decision. In explaining the judiciary's willingness to 'rewrite' legislation, consideration also needs to be given to aspects of the local legal culture – including judges' attitudes towards the HRA and their role in the protection of fundamental human rights, as well as the reactions of executive and legislative arms of government. Such factors can effect a practical modification of the formal institutional design for the distribution of responsibilities for protecting human rights between the legislature and the judiciary.[101] Judges may adopt a dominant position with respect to working out the legal implications of human rights standards even where the legal form has been designed in such a way as to ensure legislative supremacy with respect to the influence of the human rights dynamic on the law-making process.[102]

That this phenomenon is a product of the combined effects of legal form and legal culture is illustrated by a comparison of how courts in the UK and New Zealand have applied their ostensibly equivalent interpretive obligation under s 3 of the HRA and s 6 of the Bill of Rights Act 1990, respectively.[103] Based on a comparative examination of selected cases, Butler has concluded that the New Zealand Court of Appeal is more reticent and less 'activist' than the House of Lords.[104] In relation to litigation pursued in support of legal recognition of same-sex relationships (*Quilter v Attorney General* (1998)), the New Zealand Court of Appeal explicitly and definitively deferred to the parliamentary intention behind the Marriage Act 1955 in assessing the compatibility of the traditional opposite-sex definition of marriage with the sexual orientation non-discrimination standard in s 19 of the BORA (discussed further below).[105] In contrast, in *Mendoza,* the House of Lords described the s 3 interpretive obligation as of 'an unusual and far-reaching character'.[106] Lord Nicholls observed that in order to achieve ECHR-compliance, a court may be required to 'depart from the unambiguous meaning the legislation would otherwise bear' and 'depart from the intention of the Parliament which enacted the legislation'.[107]

---

100 *Ghaidan v Godin-Mendoza* (2004).
101 Hiebert, 2004.
102 Young, 2002.
103 Rishworth, 2003b.
104 Butler, 2004.
105 See Butler, 2004, p 354.
106 *Ghaidan v Godin-Mendoza* (2004), para 30 per Lord Nicholls.
107 *Ghaidan v Godin-Mendoza* (2004), para 30. See Sedley, 2005. *Cf Bellinger v Bellinger* (2003), discussion in Butler, 2004 and Wintemute, 2005.

The Civil Union Bill: anticipating an emerging European imperative

In June 2003, the government released a paper outlining its proposed law reform response: Civil Partnership: A Framework for the Legal Recognition of Same-Sex Couples.[108] A legislative scheme for the registration of civil partnerships was characterised as:

> an important equality measure for same-sex couples in England and Wales who are unable to marry each other. It would provide for the legal recognition of same-sex partners and give legitimacy to those in, or wishing to enter into, interdependent, same-sex couple relationships that are intended to be permanent.[109]

Even at this early stage of consultation, the Government was at pains to draw a distinction between the relationship status that it proposed for same-sex couples and marriage: 'It is a matter of public record that the Government has no plans to introduce same-sex marriage. This consultation document is about a civil partnership registration scheme.'[110] The Government's explicit statements distinguishing (homosexual) civil partnership from (heterosexual) marriage can be explained in terms of its desire to placate social conservatives and those who might object on religious grounds to the offering of a marriage-like status to gay men and lesbians. But this positioning also draws attention to the relatively loose constraints under which the UK Government was operating in the formulation of policy with respect to same-sex relationships. Notwithstanding increasing expectations on European states to address existing areas of law in which same-sex relationships were discriminated against, and despite the pressure being generated by domestic judicial developments, the Government still had considerable room to move – particularly when compared with its Canadian counterpart. While a significant motivator, the emerging European human rights imperative in favour of same-sex equality did not dictate a particular outcome in the way that the constitutional imperative created by s 15 of the Charter of Rights and Freedoms did in Canada. There was still space for alternative conceptions of how the controversy surrounding the legal status of same-sex relationships might legitimately be resolved in accordance with general human rights values rather than specific and proscriptive human rights law imperatives. Relatively early engagement also offered the opportunity to influence the terms of the emerging European standard on the legal recognition of same-sex relationships. A passive 'wait and see' approach would have carried the risk of eventually

---

108 United Kingdom Government, Women and Equality Unit, 2003a.
109 Ibid, p 13.
110 Ibid. See Auchmuty, 2004, p 102.

being forced (for example, by the demands of Strasbourg jurisprudence) to comply with an imposed standard that the UK had played little part in shaping.[111]

In a November 2003 follow-up report,[112] which catalogued and commented on responses to the June 2003 consultation paper, the Government emphasised that its decision to introduce a system for registration of same-sex relationships in the form of civil partnerships had not been forced by 'European' legal obligations: 'There is no EU law that requires member states to create a legal status for same-sex couples.'[113] Rather, the Government had been moved to do so 'for reasons of general equality and social justice'.[114] The Government's position was that the UK had already complied with Council Directive 2000/78/EC of 27 November 2000: Establishing a General Framework For Equal Treatment in Employment and Occupation, which required EU members to prohibit discrimination based on sexual orientation (as well as religion or belief, disability and age)[115] and formal legal recognition of same-sex relationships was not required by the Directive.

It might be said that the Government was not forced to act by prevailing human rights law dictates (as in Canada, discussed above), but neither was it completely free *not to act* (as the Australian Government has been, see below). The various external and internal developments referred to above combined to create an environment in which there was considerable momentum towards meaningful recognition of same-sex relationships in accordance with principles of non-discrimination and equality. Even had it been minded to do so, the Government would have found it difficult to ignore demands for legislative reform. Instead, what the Government found was that there was strong electoral and party political support for the creation of a marriage-like status for same-sex couples, even before the adoption of such a policy became a European legal imperative.

In its report on the Civil Partnership Bill 2004, the Joint Committee on Human Rights characterised the creation of 'civil partnerships' as a human rights measure, which was consistent with, though not (yet) strictly required by the ECHR and the Human Rights Act 1998, in light of recent decisions of the European Court of Human Rights and the English courts.[116] The Committee noted that that the Strasbourg court had ruled that Art 14 of the Convention covers differential treatment on the basis of sexual orientation 'and that where sexual orientation is the ground for different treatment, there is a need for particularly convincing and weighty reasons to justify such

---

111 Robert Wintemute, personal communication, 12 November 2004.
112 United Kingdom Government, Women and Equality Unit, 2003b.
113 Ibid, p 16.
114 Ibid.
115 Employment Equality (Sexual Orientation) Regulations 2003 (UK).
116 United Kingdom Parliament, Joint Committee on Human Rights, 2004.

a difference of treatment'.[117] The Committee acknowledged that ECHR jurisprudence had not yet reached the point where Art 14 was regarded as mandating access of same-sex couples to marriage, but accepted as legitimate the Government's position that the reforms were designed to anticipate the demands that may be imposed upon the UK by emerging Strasbourg jurisprudence in the near future. The Committee concluded that it was:

> ... satisfied that the Bill removes some existing incompatibilities in the present law and is designed to avert future findings of incompatibility in light of recent trends in the development of the case-law under the ECHR and the Human Rights Act 1998.

The Joint Committee's analysis of the Civil Union Bill effectively captures the way in which the non-discrimination/equality standard set by the ECHR/HRA was mobilised in a proactive or anticipatory way to support the Government's preferred resolution of the human rights controversy surrounding the legal recognition of same-sex relationships. Evidently, this can be an effective strategy to harness support for, or at least mute opposition to, a policy preference. Significantly, however, because the government was moving in advance of an emerging legal imperative, rather than being pushed along by an existing one, it was in a position to impose its own version of the demands of equality when it came to same-sex relationships. On second reading in the House of Commons, the Deputy Minister for Women and Equality, Jacqui Smith, described the Civil Partnership Bill as 'an important equality Bill',[118] despite the fact that it maintained a distinction between (heterosexual) marriage and (homosexual) civil partnership.

Ironically, parliamentary opponents of the bill attempted to turn the 'separate but equal' institution of civil partnership back on the government. For example, Conservative Party MP, Ann Widdecombe asked:

> The Minister [Jacqui Smith] has several times used the word 'equality'. Will she be very specific? Is the equality that she seeks that whereby a homosexual relationship based on commitment is treated in future in exactly the same was as marriage in law.[119]

Another Conservative Party MP, Edward Leigh, suggested that 'It would surely be much fairer to Members on both sides of the House if the Government came clean and announced that they support gay marriage. Why will they not do so'?[120]

---

117 United Kingdom Parliament, Joint Committee on Human Rights, 2004, p 6.
118 United Kingdom Parliament, Hansard (House of Commons), 12 October 2004, 174.
119 Ibid, 176–7.
120 Ibid, 177.

Clearly, the Government had decided to advance the Civil Partnership Act 2004 (UK) as an equality-advancing measure, while continuing to deny gay and lesbian couples access to the institution of marriage. For many gay and lesbian activists the bill was nonetheless worth supporting. Throughout the public and parliamentary debates, the leading gay and lesbian rights organisation, Stonewall, strongly supported the Civil Partnership Act 2004. In response to criticism that it should have pushed for the sexual orientation inclusive re-definition of marriage, Stonewall stated its 'main focus was on the outcome in terms of rights and responsibilities, rather than the label. Civil partnership achieves parity with marriage in every respect'.[121]

The view that the 'separate but equal' compromise was acceptable was not unanimously held by activists. For example, Outrage! criticised the civil partnership model because it delivered something less than full equality:

> We believe that in the light of several European Union and Commonwealth countries already having pioneered the route [to same-sex marriage], it is cowardly and regressive of the UK government to not put this option on the table. The UK should demonstrate leadership, initiative and moral courage, not trail behind many of its EU partners and former colonies.[122]

But in the environment in which the Civil Partnership Act 2004 emerged, the UK Government was still in a position to exercise a degree of choice – and its preferred choice was to maintain a distinction, even if in name only, between (heterosexual) marriage and (homosexual) civil partnership. Same-sex marriage was not constitutionally mandated in the way that it came to be in Canada. In the UK, the emerging European equality imperative was an important influence on policy formulation and law reform, but there was still room for the Government to take into account competing political values and considerations of electoral pragmatism.

A recent decision of the High Court of Justice suggests that, for the time being at least, the UK's Civil Partnership Act 2004 is sufficient to meet the emerging European human rights imperative with respect to sexual orientation non-discrimination and equality. In 2005, two women, married in Canada in 2003, applied to have their marriage recognised in the UK. Celia Kitzinger and Sue Wilkinson stated publicly:

---

121 Stonewall, 2006.
122 Outrage!, 2003. See also, Gay and Lesbian Humanist Association, 2004; and Outrage!, 2005.

> This is fundamentally about equality. We want our marriage to be recognised as a marriage – just like any other marriage made in Canada. It is insulting and discriminatory to be offered a civil partnership instead. Civil partnerships are an important step forward for same-sex couples, but they are not enough. We want full equality in marriage.[123]

The barrister for the two women, Karon Monaghan, commented that part of the motivation behind the litigation (supported by Liberty) is 'that if it's successful, it will put pressure on the Government to consider whether or not civil partnership status affords true equality'.[124] The Odysseus Trust, while conceding that '[i]nternational human rights law does not yet require that the ban on same-sex marriages be lifted', suggested that it was 'strongly arguable that continuing to define marriage as a relationship "between man and wife" will soon be held to be in conflict with the Convention'.[125]

In July 2006, Sir Mark Potter ruled that there was no such conflict.[126] In rejecting the argument that the enactment of the Civil Partnership Act 2004 and the continued limitation of marriage to opposite-sex couples violated the non-discrimination principle embodied in Art 14 of the ECHR, Potter P concluded:

> Parliament has taken steps by enacting the CPA to accord to same-sex relationships effectively all the rights, responsibilities, benefits and advantages of civil marriage save the name, and thereby to remove the legal, social and economic disadvantages suffered by homosexuals who wish to join stable long-term relationships. To the extent that by reason of that distinction it discriminates against same-sex partners, such discrimination has a legitimate aim, is reasonable and proportionate, and falls within the margin of appreciation accorded to Convention States.[127]

For the foreseeable future, it seems the fact that the laws of England and Wales, Scotland and Northern Ireland provide for the legal recognition of a marriage-like parallel status for same-sex couples, and are non-discriminatory with respect to key relationship responsibilities and benefits, will be regarded as sufficient to meet the demands of the European equality imperative.

---

123 Liberty, 2005.
124 Harris, 2005.
125 The Odysseus Trust, 2005. Wintemute (2005, p 195) suggested that it is unlikely that the Strasbourg court will regard the traditional opposite sex definition of marriage to be a violation of the ECHR, 'given that civil marriage has so far been opened to same-sex partners in only . . . three of 46 Council of Europe Member States . . .'.
126 *Wilkinson v Kitzinger* (2006).
127 *Wilkinson v Kitzinger* (2006), para 122.

New Zealand

In terms of elements of legal form, the obvious reference point for the movement towards legal recognition of same-sex relationships in New Zealand is the non-discrimination principle expressed in s 19 of the Bill of Rights Act 1990 ('BORA'). Sexual orientation is one of the enumerated grounds. But the story of the creation of a legal institution of 'civil union' in 2004 is not one that can be explained in terms of the direct invocation of a legal imperative as occurred in Canada, or the pre-emptive move to anticipate an emerging European legal imperative, as occurred in the UK. In fact, the concerted movement for same-sex relationship recognition in New Zealand followed an unsuccessful attempt to mobilise s 19 in support of a challenge to the traditional definition of marriage in the Marriage Act 1955.[128] An attempt to mobilise s 26 of the ICCPR in support of the goal of achieving a sexual orientation neutral definition of marriage was also unsuccessful.[129] Yet, within a short period after these 'failures', a parallel institution for the recognition of same-sex relationships (which is also available to opposite-sex couples) was created by the Civil Union Act 2004. The story of the initial failures and the ultimate (albeit, arguably compromised) success of the fight for equality-based recognition of same-sex relationships offers valuable insights about the significance of the form in which human rights are protected in New Zealand.

The legal environment and the lead-up to the Civil Union Bill 2004

Section 19 of the BORA provides that '(1) Everyone has the right to freedom from discrimination on the grounds of discrimination in the Human Rights Act 1993'. Sexual orientation is a prohibited ground of discrimination.[130] Huscroft has suggested that the use of the language of non-discrimination in s 19 of the BORA, rather than the language of equality before the law, was a deliberate attempt by the New Zealand Parliament to contain the demands of the BORA and to avoid handing the judiciary a powerful tool for revamping New Zealand law in accordance with principles of equality.[131] However, fundamental human rights principles and values cannot necessarily be contained by the specifics of legislative text:

> The Government was right to think that a right to equality would have shifted substantive policy-making power to the courts. It was wrong,

---

128 *Quilter v Attorney General* (1998).
129 *Joslin v New Zealand* (2002).
130 Human Rights Act 1993 (NZ), s 21(1)(m).
131 Huscroft, 2003b.

however, to think that this problem could be avoided simply by omitting the word 'equality' from the Bill of Rights. Equality is the most powerful idea in modern political thought, it underlies all major political theories, and animates the very idea of a bill of rights: individuals have rights because each individual matters and matters equally. Equality-inspired claims will be made regardless of the omission of a right to equality from the Bill of Rights, and ... the right to freedom from discrimination provides a vehicle for advancing many of these claims.[132]

Gay and lesbian activists were quick to employ this new legal device to challenge the exclusion of gay and lesbian couples from the institution of marriage. In *Quilter*[133] the plaintiffs – three lesbian couples – had applied for marriage licences and had been refused on the basis that marriage for the purpose of the Marriage Act 1955 was only available to opposite-sex couples. They challenged the refusal of the Registrar of Marriages to issue marriage licences to them. They argued that to continue to confine the definition of marriage in the Marriage Act 1955 to opposite-sex couples was inconsistent with s 19 of the BORA. Consistent with the interpretive obligation in s 6 of the BORA, the definition of marriage should be interpreted as referring to a union between two persons. The Court of Appeal held that the traditional opposite-sex definition of marriage did not constitute discrimination on the basis of sexual orientation. Thomas J, in dissent on this issue, concluded that the opposite-sex common-law definition of marriage, was inconsistent with s 19 of the BORA:

> ... one cannot seriously resist the proposition that gays and lesbians are discriminated against on the ground of sexual orientation. It is the sexual preference of gays and lesbians and their resulting choice of a same-sex partner that makes them vulnerable to discrimination. Based upon this personal characteristic, gays and lesbians are denied access to a central social institution and the resulting status of married persons. ... They are denied a basic civil right in that freedom to marry is rightly regarded as a basic civil right. They lose the opportunity to choose the partner of their choice as a basic civil right of all citizens. In a real sense, gays and lesbians are effectively excluded from full membership of society.[134]

However, Thomas J concluded that it was beyond the court's power to remedy the BORA violation in the manner sought by the plaintiffs – that is, to redefine marriage in sexual orientation-neutral terms:

---

132 Huscroft, 2003b, p 367.
133 *Quilter v Attorney General* (1998).
134 Ibid, pp 536–7.

> I agree that where a breach of a fundamental right or freedom enshrined in the Bill of Rights is found to exist in any statute the Court should conscientiously strive to arrive at a meaning which will avoid that breach. ... Even adopting this approach in the present case, however, I am unable to interpret the Marriage Act in the manner sought by the appellants. The Bill of Rights is not a supreme law. The legislative history of the Bill of Rights is well known. Parliament expressly rejected a Bill of Rights which would enable the Courts to strike legislation down as invalid on the ground it is contrary to the Bill of Rights. Parliamentary or legislative supremacy was deliberately retained by the legislature. This Court has an interpretive role and while it must, in accordance with Parliament's direction prefer a meaning to any statutory provision which is consistent with the Bill of Rights, it cannot adopt a meaning which is clearly contrary to Parliament's intent. ... Declining to strain the meaning of the Act does not mean that this Court is shirking its responsibility to apply s 6. That section does not authorise the Court to legislate. Even if a meaning is theoretically possible, it must be rejected if it is clearly contrary to what Parliament intended. Consistently with what I have said above relating to the legislative history of the Bill of Rights and the Court's role, it remains for Parliament to decide whether or not legislation is required to extend marriage to gay and lesbian couples.[135]

For the other four judges of the Court of Appeal, the scope of the s 6 interpretive obligation did not need to be considered because, they concluded, the opposite-sex definition of marriage in the Marriage Act 1955 did not constitute discrimination under s 19 of the BORA. However, it is evident that the same deference to parliamentary supremacy, which underpinned Thomas J's unwillingness to endorse the remedy sought by the plaintiffs, was at the heart of the majority's conclusion that the opposite-sex definition of marriage was not discriminatory. For example, Keith J found that the fact that gay and lesbian couples could not marry under New Zealand law amounted to prima facie discrimination, but this discrimination 'is not unlawful because ... the Marriage Act prevails and thus serves to legitimise the prima facie discrimination'.[136] This is a questionable line of analysis, which seems to conflate two separate questions. It is unclear how a finding of prima facie discrimination can be neutralised by a finding that it is Parliament's intention to discriminate against gay and lesbian relationships. Parliament's intention may be relevant to the question of remedy – that is, which view of the possible definitions of marriage the courts should uphold – as Thomas J concluded, but it is not clear how it can be determinative of the

---

135 *Quilter v Attorney General* (1998), pp 541–2.
136 Ibid, p 576.

question whether the relevant legislation is consistent with s 19. This aspect of Keith J's analysis is reflective of a theme that runs throughout all judgments in *Quilter* – strong deference to Parliament. Like Thomas J, Tipping J expressed the view that 'the question whether our multicultural and secular society wishes . . . to maintain the traditional concept of marriage is essentially a question of socio-legal policy for the legislature and not for the Courts'.[137]

Placed side by side, there is a stark contrast between the manner in which the New Zealand Court of Appeal approached the sexual orientation non-discrimination demands of s 19 of the BORA in *Quilter*, and the way in which the Canadian courts have approached the equivalent question (culminating in decisions such as *Barbeau* – where the British Columbia Court of Appeal reached precisely the opposite conclusion), and the way in which the England and Wales Court of Appeal and the House of Lords approached the specific issue raised in *Mendoza*.

In fairness, it is appropriate to recognise that the Court of Appeal's decision in *Quilter* was handed down in late 1997, a year before the Supreme Court of Canada's decision in *M v H*, and more than five years before appellate courts in Canada were asked to consider the constitutionality of the traditional opposite-sex definition of marriage. The landmark decisions of the Court of Appeal and the House of Lords in *Mendoza* were several years away. In this very 'early days' context, and given that there had been no equivalent in New Zealand of the incremental claim litigation strategy, focusing on specific relationships obligations and benefits, which had proved so successful in Canada as a lead-up to the marriage challenges, it is unsurprising that the plaintiffs' action was dismissed in *Quilter*. Nonetheless, the contrast is revealing. To some extent the New Zealand/Canada difference, in both approach and outcome, can be explained relatively easily in terms of legal form – the Canadian judiciary enjoys an interpretative supremacy over the terms and demands of the Charter, including the equality guarantee in s 15, which is simply not extended to New Zealand courts under the BORA. The constraint of deference to Parliament's intention, which was clearly operative in *Quilter*, has no parallel in Canada.

As noted above, the New Zealand/UK contrast is not so readily explicable in terms of legal form. Although it is necessary to recognise that in *Mendoza* and *Quilter* the claims made by the respective plaintiffs were different in nature – the former challenged one specific incident of relationship discrimination under the Rent Act; the latter was a comprehensive challenge to the definition of marriage – in both cases the courts were called upon to exercise their authority under the interpretive obligation found in s 3 of the Human Rights Act 1998 and s 6 of the BORA, respectively. In the UK, the judges of the Court of Appeal and the House of Lords demonstrated much

---

137 *Quilter v Attorney General* (1998), p 572. For commentary on *Quilter*, see Butler, 1998; Christie, 2001; and Whiu, 2004.

less reticence than their New Zealand counterparts about 'assum[ing] the role of lawmaker'.[138]

In *Quilter*, Richardson P concluded that the definition of marriage in the Marriage Act was 'so clear that to rely on particular perspectives of human rights and social policy values to accommodate same-sex marriage would require fresh legislation, which is the function of Parliament'.[139] It could be said that the definition of 'spouse' in the Rent Act 1977 was also unequivocally heterosexual, and yet the House of Lords employed s 3 of the Human Rights Act in support of a sexual orientation-neutral interpretation of the meaning of this term. I am not suggesting that the House of Lords would necessarily have given the plaintiffs their preferred remedy if the facts and claims of *Quilter* had come before it.[140] Rather, I am drawing attention to the fact that how courts approach their legislative obligation/authority to interpret legislation in accordance with prevailing human rights standards is dictated not only by legal form, but also by elements of local legal culture – individual and corporate judicial perceptions of their role and the associated expectations of executive and legislative arms of government, and the broader society.[141]

As noted above, Butler's comparative research suggest that one of the features of New Zealand judicial culture is a disinclination on the part of judges, when compared with their counterparts in the UK, to vigorously employ their interpretive obligation under s 6 of the BORA, so as to impose their vision of the most human rights-respecting interpretation of challenged legislation.[142] This is the case, even though s 6 of the BORA extends to the judiciary an interpretive licence equivalent to that extended to the courts of the UK under s 3 of the HRA.

A subsequent communication to the United Nations Human Rights Committee by members of the *Quilter* litigant group, based on Art 26 (equality before the law), and Art 23 (the right to marry), read in light of Art 2 (the non-discrimination principle), was also unsuccessful.[143] For the Committee, the issue was settled by the terms of Art 23. Article 26 received practically no consideration. Denying same-sex couples access to the institution was not inconsistent with the ICCPR, because the right to marry in Art 23 applied only to opposite-sex couples. The Committee implicitly accepted New Zealand's argument that the claim for legal recognition of same-sex relationships in the form of 'marriage 'goes well beyond the terms of the Covenant'.[144]

138 *Quilter v Attorney General* (1998), p 526.
139 Ibid.
140 See Wintemute, 2005.
141 Hiebert, 2005.
142 Butler, 2004; see also, Hiebert, 2004.
143 *Joslin v New Zealand* (2002).
144 Ibid, para 4.2.

Two members of the Committee were at pains to leave open the possibility that Art 26 might be mobilised in the future in relation to the legal status of same-sex relationships. Rajsoomer Lallah and Martin Scheinin emphasised that the Committee's conclusion that Art 26 was not violated in the present case:

> ... should not be read as a general statement that differential treatment between married couples and same-sex couples not allowed under the law to marry would never amount to a violation of article 26. On the contrary, the Committee's jurisprudence supports the position that such differentiation may very well, depending on the circumstances of a concrete case, amount to prohibited discrimination.[145]

In *Quilter*, Thomas J, having concluded that the question of legal recognition of same-sex relationships should be left to the legislature, suggested that the New Zealand Parliament could choose from the full range of options – from doing nothing to amending the Marriage Act 1955.[146] However, after such a resounding rebuff for the argument that the BORA demanded the sexual orientation-neutral redefinition of marriage, it was unlikely that any government would pursue this option in the near future, in the absence of a legal imperative, and given the political opposition that would be encountered both inside and outside the legislature. It might be said that the *Quilter* litigation achieved precisely the opposite of its primary goal – rather than force the redefinition of marriage, it effectively struck marriage off the list of possible models for the legal recognition of same-sex relationships. In fact, those involved in the litigation were aware that the prospects of success were not good, but believed that publicity surrounding the case would nonetheless increase pressure on the New Zealand Government to commit to meaningful equality-based recognition. Nigel Christie, a lawyer and activist who was heavily involved in the domestic litigation and the Human Rights Committee communication, has observed that 'the Quilter case has played a huge role in bringing this issue to the forefront in New Zealand, and for the legal recognition of same-sex relationships becoming the subject of serious legal debate'.[147] Subsequent events support this assessment of the impact of the *Quilter* litigation.

In 1999, the recognition issue was placed firmly on the policy-making table when the Ministry of Justice produced a discussion paper on 'Same-Sex Couples and the Law'.[148] Broader developments in the area of human rights compliance were also important. When the Human Rights Act 1993 was

---

145 *Joslin v New Zealand* (2002), Appendix.
146 *Quilter v Attorney General* (1998), p 548.
147 Christie, 2002.
148 New Zealand Ministry of Justice, 1999.

enacted, the legislation specified[149] that within five years the government should ensure that all laws were consistent with New Zealand's human rights standards – including the newly added prohibition on sexual orientation discrimination. The Human Rights Commission and relevant government departments embarked on an audit project known as 'Consistency 2000' (the original 1998 target date having been extended by two years). In 1997, the National Party (conservative) Government moved to shelve the project. In 1999, the newly elected Labour Government revived the task of ensuring that New Zealand law complied with the standards set by the BORA and the Human Rights Act 1993, and in 2001 committed to a new compliance process: 'Compliance 2001'.[150] In the same year Parliament enacted the Human Rights Amendment Act 2001, which enhanced integration between the BORA and the Human Rights Act 1993, applied the non-discrimination standard set by both instruments to government activities, and provided for declarations of incompatibility (previously unavailable under the terms of New Zealand's legal regime for protecting human rights) with respect to breaches of s 19 of the BORA. In addition, Parliament enacted the Property (Relationships) Amendment Act 2001, which recognised both same-sex and opposite-sex de facto relationships for the purposes of inheritance, and spousal maintenance and property division after relationship breakdown. The Labour Party went into the 2002 national election with the enactment of civil union legislation as part of it election manifesto, and was re-elected.

Significantly then, the environment in which the Civil Union Bill Committee embarked on a concerted campaign for civil union legislation in 2001 was one in which the Labour Government and its progressive minor party allies had revitalised the human rights compliance programme, which the Government had been legislatively obliged to undertake since 1993. In particular, this project developed from a type of risk assessment exercise – spotting and rectifying areas of legislative discrimination where the government might otherwise be held liable – to a more positive affirmation and application of non-discrimination and equality principles. In this sense, while the legislative expectation created by the BORA and the Human Rights Act 1993, and reinforced by the Human Rights Amendment Act 2001, was an important motivator, it was the addition of ideological commitment from the Labour Government that made the legislative recognition of same-sex relationships a realistic goal to pursue. But there was a 'catch' of sorts. Because major party/government political will was a critical part of the favourable environment, the specific goal had to be set with reference to pragmatic political considerations – the Labour Party was not going to pursue an ideological agenda that would see it back on the Opposition benches.

---

149 Human Rights Act 1993 (NZ), s 5.
150 See also, New Zealand Ministry of Justice, 2000.

Gay and lesbian activists involved in setting the goals of the campaign decided to push for the legislative creation of a parallel relationship category for same-sex couples – civil union – rather than the legislative redefinition of marriage. (Disagreement within the gay and lesbian communities about the desirability of being able to marry was also a factor.) This approach, and the Labour Party's ultimate endorsement of it, reveals that the human right dynamic with respect to principles of non-discrimination and equality, while an important part of the New Zealand policy-making and law reform environment, was not as potent as the Canadian Charter equality dynamic.

In its submission to the Justice and Electoral Committee, the New Zealand Human Rights Commission expressed the opinion that 'full equality and non-discrimination would best be achieved by permitting access to the Marriage Act for same-sex couples'.[151] However, this was not considered to be an achievable goal. The Civil Union Bill Committee accepted, in the early stages of the campaign, that 'the New Zealand Government is sensitive to concerns about the perceived threat to the religious and "traditional" elements of marriage'.[152] In New Zealand, the general normative parameters set by the BORA and the Human Rights Act 1993 were influential, but there was still considerable space in the public discourse surrounding same-sex relationships for disagreement as to how the controversy should be resolved. The issue of same-sex relationship recognition had not been thoroughly 'legalised' in the way that it had in Canada. In this environment, it is not surprising that civil union – even though it was perceived in some quarters as incomplete equality or a 'second-class' compromise – became the preferred mechanism for addressing the controversy surrounding the legal recognition of same-sex relationships.

Following through on a non-discrimination commitment: the Civil Union Act 2004

In the public discourse surrounding the introduction of the Civil Union Bill the Government characterised the legislation as the logical next step in the long process of bringing New Zealand law into line with the non-discrimination principles embodied in s 19 of the BORA and the Human Rights Act 1993. The Government steered a careful course between justifying the bill as a legal *requirement* flowing from New Zealand's primary human rights statutes and as a manifestation of Labour's ideological commitment to gay and lesbian equality. If the proposed legislation had been perceived as a product of either of these 'extremes', it may have encountered greater resistance, both inside and outside the Parliament.

---

151 New Zealand Human Rights Commission, 2004d.
152 Civil Union Bill Committee, 2001, p 10.

In his second reading speech on the bill, the Associate Minister for Justice, Mr David Benson-Pope, observed:

> New Zealand is justifiably proud of its record on issues of human rights. It was over 11 years ago that New Zealand passed the Human Rights Act, which outlawed discrimination on the grounds of family status, marital status, and sexual orientation. This bill is one of the most important pieces of human rights legislation to be considered by the House.... The Civil Union Bill is not about being politically correct. It is about doing the correct thing—period. It is about human rights, and recognising and valuing the choices of people within our society.... The passage of this bill will help to foster a positive human rights culture in which human beings, regardless of their sexual orientation, are shown the dignity and respect to which they are entitled.[153]

The combination of factors that explained the Government's support for civil union legislation as part of the unfinished business of an equality/non-discrimination agenda – legal 'requirement', ideological commitment and political obligation – was reflected in the range of explanations offered by commentators and critics. For example, in the *New Zealand Herald*, Tunnah suggested that 'The Government is anxious to meet election pledges but is also worried that policies and legislation which recognise only married couples ... may be liable for legal challenge under human rights law'.[154] An editorial in the *Waikato Times* was sceptical about the extent to which the creation of a civil union regime was a legal necessity:

> So is the bill driven by a desire from Labour to make sure this country meets human rights laws and remove discrimination, or is it more ideological? Mr Dunne [leader of the socially conservative United Future Party] appears right in thinking it is the latter. There are plenty of ways to enshrine anti-discrimination laws, without going as far as creating a second class of marriage....[155]

Opponents of the bill attempted to exploit the ambivalence of New Zealanders about 'rights talk' and being dictated to by human rights laws. The Maxim Institute, a conservative think-tank that actively campaigned against the Civil Union Bill, argued that formal recognition of same-sex relationships was not required by New Zealand's human rights laws, because Parliament was sovereign, and s 5 of the BORA provided for 'justified limitations' on the

---

153 New Zealand House of Representatives, Hansard, 2 December 2004, pp 17386, 17388.
154 Tunnah, 2003.
155 *Waikato Times*, 2004.

application of the Act's protections – limitations that were 'not to be arrived at by a purely legal analysis, but by an assessment of the wider implications, in light of the social evidence available'.[156]

Rather than directly confront such assertions, supporters of the Civil Union Bill tended to downplay the rights angle. Certainly, the bill was portrayed as consistent with New Zealand's human rights traditions, values and laws. However, recognising the limited purchase of, and potential backlash against, abstract rights talk in New Zealand's legal culture, proponents rarely attempted to employ rights talk as a trump card.

One aspect of the public debate surrounding the Civil Union Bill which did prompt supporters to employ more explicit rights discourse was the call by some politicians for a referendum on the issue. In rejecting this course of action, the Government emphasised that it 'had a legal responsibility to remove discrimination in the law'.[157] The Campaign for Civil Union stated publicly that 'it is inappropriate for human rights issues to be decided by referendum – particularly considering that the rights in question are vehemently contested by another minority'.[158] During parliamentary debate on the bill, Green Party MP, Nandor Tanczos, opposed the referendum call in the following terms:

> I do not believe, and the Green Party does not believe, that the rights of minorities should be subject to majority veto. That is not the kind of question that should be put to a referendum. This is a basic question of: do we support human rights, or do we not? Do we support equality for all New Zealanders, or do we not? It is as simple as that.[159]

Having adopted civil union as their goal, proponents of the Civil Union Bill were sensitive to the need not to overplay the human rights card, aware that there was a significant degree of resistance in the New Zealand electorate to what might be perceived as 'political correctness'. Proponents tended to avoid relying on abstract rights invocations when advancing the case for the bill. Consideration of political pragmatism was influential, then, in shaping both the goal of the same-sex relationship recognition movement – civil union and practical non-discrimination in relation to relationship benefits and responsibilities[160] – and the strategies, arguments and rhetoric employed to this end.

The terms in which the Government made its case for why the Civil Union Bill should be enacted, and the public disagreement about its 'true' motivation underscores that, to the extent that the bill was the product of a legal

---

156 Maxim Institute, 2004.
157 New Zealand Press Association, 2004b.
158 Campaign for Civil Unions, 2004.
159 New Zealand House of Representatives, Hansard, 7 December 2004, p 17454.
160 See the Relationships (Statutory References) Act 2005 (NZ).

imperative, it was an imperative of a nature that was decidedly different to the undeniable constitutional imperative that had driven the enactment of the Civil Marriage Act 2005 in Canada. The BORA and the Human Rights Act 1993 provided the legislative infrastructure for framing a human rights-based policy with respect to the status of same-sex relationships, but because these statutes do not enjoy the same status in New Zealand legal culture as the Charter of Rights and Freedoms in Canada, the Government was careful to make the case for civil unions based on general principles of fairness, rather than a strident 'our human rights laws demand it' approach, which may have alienated potential supporters.

Like its counterpart in the UK (and unlike its counterpart in Canada) the New Zealand Government retained a significant degree of choice about how to articulate the obligations of a human rights-respecting society when it came to responding to demands for the legal recognition of same-sex relationships. In fact, the Clark Government probably enjoyed even greater latitude than the Blair Government, there being no equivalent in New Zealand of the emerging European imperative that was influential in the UK, nor any of the litigation-prompted judicial pressure that was generated in the UK by cases such as *Mendoza*.

It was also significant that in New Zealand rectification of human rights deficiencies in the state of the law – in this case: inadequate recognition of same-sex relationships – is widely regarded as a responsibility of the legislative arm of government, rather than the judicial arm. It was not just that the courts had declined the opportunity to take the lead in *Quilter*, but that the task of achieving human rights compliance is generally perceived as something to be achieved by legislation rather than court decisions. This aspect of New Zealand's policy formulation and law reform environment is a product of both legal form and legal culture.

The following plain language explanation of the Government position by David Benson-Pope, in a 'Q & A' published on the Government's 'Beehive' website is illustrative of how the pro-Civil Union Bill message was delivered to the general community – highlighting the emphasis on values of 'fairness', downplaying the 'gay and lesbian agenda' dimension of the bill, and asserting Parliament's status as the 'right place' for dealing with the issues:

> It isn't fair to deny legal rights to people unable to marry, and establishing civil union in legislation means that Parliament, rather than the judiciary, determines relationship law for New Zealand.[161]

The fact that the new relationship status to be established by the Civil Union Bill would be available to both homosexual couples and (unmarried)

---

161 Benson-Pope, 2004.

heterosexual couples may be taken as further evidence of the Government's relative autonomy on setting the policy agenda, which allowed it to make a pragmatic decision not to push the sexual orientation equality paradigm further than the electorate might be prepared to accept. Political expediency suggested that wide support for the Bill was more likely to be achieved if the measure was perceived as about unmarried couples generally, rather than about gay and lesbian equality specifically.

Ironically, one of the events that helped to consolidate the Civil Union Bill's status as a sensible product of 'New Zealand style' respect for human rights was a public protest in Wellington by opponents of the Bill. In August 2004, several thousand members of the Destiny Church, a fundamentalist Christian group, dressed in black shirts, displaying and chanting the slogan 'enough is enough', marched on Parliament. The spectacle, which was described by some observers and media commentators as reminiscent of a Nazi rally, provided civil union proponents with the opportunity to impress upon the broader community, and those parliamentarians who were still deciding how they would exercise their conscience vote on the Civil Union Bill, the extent to which opposition to the Bill was underpinned by attitudes of 'hatred and intolerance'[162] and, therefore, antithetical to New Zealand's reputation as a place where human rights are respected.

Sentiments of this sort were also reflected in the public statements of supporters of the Bill from the broader human rights community. In its submission to the Justice and Electoral Select Committee, the Human Rights Foundation emphasised New Zealand's 'tradition of fairness' and equality before the law – as demonstrated by its early support for the Universal Declaration of Human Rights, ratification of the ICCPR and domestic enactment of the both the BORA and the Human Rights Act 1993:

> Given that current legislation allows for discrimination on the basis of marital status and sexual orientation, these Bills are important components of New Zealand's efforts to address this discrimination. As such, they form important components of New Zealand's commitment to human rights for all members of our society.[163]

Benchmarking with comparable rights-respecting countries was another of the measures employed by the Government. During the course of parliamentary debate on the bill, Labour Party Minister, Chris Carter, observed:

> The previous speaker said that this legislation was out of sync with what was happening in the rest of the world, but last week the British House of

---

162 TVNZ, One News, 2004.
163 Human Rights Foundation of New Zealand, 2004, para 6.

Commons passed its civil union bill. Do we want to be a country like Britain—a modern, liberal, social democracy—or do we want to become a country like George Bush's United States of America? I know where I would rather live. I would rather live in a tolerant, liberal democracy—and that is what this bill is about.[164]

As in the UK, support for the Civil Union Bill in the gay and lesbian community was strong – which is not surprising given that the bill had its origins in the work of gay and lesbian activists who came together to form the Civil Union Bill Committee. However, some activists argued that if the Government was genuinely committed to full equality for gay men and lesbians and if its objective was to completely reform all forms of legislative discrimination on the basis of sexual orientation, it would have moved to amend the definition of marriage in the Marriage Act 1955. For example, in its submission to the Justice and Electoral Committee, PrideAlliance, the Queer Network of the Alliance Party, expressed support for the Civil Union Bill: 'Legal recognition of same sex relationships is an important step forward for tolerance and acceptance of diversity, the reduction of discrimination based on sexual orientation, and human rights in general.'[165] However, PrideAlliance emphasised that:

> [The bill] did not end discrimination against same sex couples. Retaining Marriage as an exclusively heterosexual legal institution sends a message to society that same sex relationships are still not worthy of the same level of recognition and acceptance as heterosexual relationships.[166]

Proponents of the Civil Union Bill preferred to emphasise a different message emanating from its passage. Just prior to the final vote on the Bill on 9 December 2004 – when it was passed by 65 votes to 55,[167] Chris Carter observed: 'Tomorrow, all New Zealanders will wake up in a country that has enhanced its reputation as a society that respects human rights and cares about all its peoples.'[168]

This juxtaposition of statements effectively captures the way in which the particular nature of New Zealand's human rights dynamic framed its response to the demand for recognition of same-sex relationships.[169] Both the legal form in which human rights are protected in New Zealand and the distinctive characteristics of New Zealand's human rights culture combined

---

164 New Zealand House of Representatives, Hansard, 9 December 2004, p 17660.
165 Pride Alliance, 2004, para 8.
166 Pride Alliance, 2004, para 12. See also, TVNZ, One News, 2003a.
167 New Zealand House of Representatives, Hansard, 9 December 2004, p 17662.
168 Ibid, p 17659.
169 See also Seuffert, 2006.

to create an environment in which a measured gay and lesbian activist campaign achieved its goal: the legislative creation of a parallel 'separate but equal' relationship status.

As in Canada, there is an interesting legislative postscript to New Zealand's story of the legal recognition of same-sex relationships with the enactment of the Civil Union Act 2004, which underscores the extent to which the strategic decision to aim for civil union rather than marriage was a savvy move, based on a sound understanding of the limits of the human rights dynamic in New Zealand. In May 2005, Larry Baldock from the United Future Party, a socially conservative 'family values' party that had opposed the Civil Union Bill, introduced a private member's bill with the stated purpose of confirming the traditional common-law opposite-sex definition of marriage. Having lost the fight over civil union, the United Future Party had apparently decided that at least it would do what it could to ensure that the creation of a civil union institution (which, notwithstanding the Government's public positioning, was widely understood to be primarily for the benefit of same-sex couples), was not used as a stepping stone to the sexual orientation-neutral redefinition of marriage.

The Marriage (Gender Clarification) Amendment Bill proposed that the Marriage Act 1955 should be amended so as to provide that: '... marriage may only occur between one man and one woman'; add marriage to a person of the same gender to the list of 'forbidden marriage'; and provide that foreign marriages between same-sex couples are not to be recognised as marriages under New Zealand law. Finally, the Bill proposed the addition of the following subsection to s 19 of the BORA: 'Measures taken in good faith for the purpose of assisting or advancing marriage do not constitute discrimination.' The proposed BORA amendment was, unsurprisingly, found by the Attorney General to be inconsistent with the BORA in his s 7 report to Parliament.[170] In any event the bill lapsed when Parliament was dissolved ahead of the September 2005 national election. The bill was reintroduced by the United Future Party in December 2005, but did not proceed past first reading.[171]

Australia

In August 2004, while the legislatures of the UK and New Zealand were debating civil partnership/union legislation, and while the Canadian Parliament waited on the all clear from the Supreme Court of Canada on proposed civil marriage legislation, the Australian Parliament passed the Marriage

---

170 New Zealand Attorney General, 2005.
171 New Zealand House of Representatives, Hansard, 7 December 2005, p 677.

Amendment Act 2004. Section 5 of the Australian Marriage Act 1961 now provides that 'marriage means the union of a man and a woman to the exclusion of all others, voluntarily entered into for life'. While three of Australia's traditional human rights 'peers' were moving decisively in the direction of meaningful recognition of the legitimacy of same-sex relationships, the Australian Parliament was moving precisely in the opposite direction. The legal form(lessness) of the principle of equality and non-discrimination for gay men and lesbians in Australia is certainly not the only explanation for what transpired during the course of 2004, but it is an important part of this story.

The legal environment and the lead-up to the Marriage Amendment Act 2004

In contrast to the three stories told so far in this chapter, the Australian story regarding the (non)recognition of same-sex relationships under national laws is distinguished by the *absence*, rather than the presence, of a 'suprapolitical' legal reference point with respect to equality and non-discrimination. Certainly, there has been a strong political tradition of support for principles of equality and non-discrimination, and these values have been articulated through numerous state, territorial and some federal statutes. Indeed, sexual orientation is a recognised ground of unlawful discrimination in all states and territories.[172] However, under s 51(21) of the Australian Constitution, marriage is a federal responsibility and there is no legislative prohibition against sexual orientation at the federal level. In Australia there is no equivalent of s 15 of the Canadian Charter of Rights and Freedoms, Art 14 of the ECHR, or s 19 of the New Zealand Bill of Rights Act. In 1992, the High Court considered whether a guarantee of equal treatment was implicit in the Australian Constitution. By 4:3 majority the Court said: no.[173]

Australia is a party to the ICCPR, but HRC jurisprudence on Art 26 has, at least at the present time, minimal purchase in Australian political and law reform discourse. For example, in 2003 the Human Rights Committee found that Australia was in breach of its obligations under Art 26 of the ICCPR because it denied to the surviving homosexual partner of a deceased war veteran, access to a pension to which married and de facto heterosexual partners of veterans have access.[174] The Australian Government was unmoved by the Human Rights Committee's finding.[175]

When the issue of same-sex marriage was forced onto national political and

---

172 Ronalds and Pepper, 2004, pp 27–8; O'Neill *et al*, 2004, p 503.
173 *Leeth v Commonwealth* (1992); see O'Neill *et al*, 2004, p 476.
174 *Young v Australia* (2003).
175 Australia, Human Rights and Equal Opportunity Commission, 2004; Pollard, 2006. See also, Banham, 2005.

law reform in 2004 (by a hostile government, rather than by rights-asserting gay and lesbian activists) the implications of the distinctive contours of the Australian legal environment with respect to sexual orientation equality rights became readily discernible. Not only were Australian advocates of equality for gay men and lesbians deprived of the legal ammunition that was being employed successfully by their peers in other parts of the world to advance the case for formal legal recognition of same-sex relationships at the national level, but they also found themselves without even the defensive tools necessary to repel the Government's plan to make a largely symbolic, but nonetheless powerful, statement of non-recognition and exclusion by expressly legislating for the traditional common-law definition of marriage – the very same definition that the Canadian courts and later the Canadian Parliament had determined to be incompatible with the values of equality and non-discrimination, embedded in the Charter and Canadian legal culture.

It might be said that in the broader context of the struggle for meaningful recognition of same-sex relationships, the passage of the Marriage Amendment Act 2004 was largely inconsequential. The legislation merely confirmed, without changing, the definition of marriage under Australian law, and in any event, in recent years most states and territories have extended the legislative definition of de facto relationships to include same-sex couples.[176] In Tasmania, same-sex couples have had access to a system of relationship registration since 2004,[177] and in May 2006, the Australian Capital Territory legislature enacted the Civil Unions Act 2006, which created a formal relationship category – a formal legal status for same-sex relationships.[178]

Certainly, prior to the federal government's decision to pre-empt any move towards pushing for full recognition of same-sex relationships, gay and lesbian reform activism had tended to focus on specific aspects of the disadvantage experienced by same-sex couples, such as access to a deceased partner's superannuation.[179] But one of the (unintended) effects of the events of 2004 was that they motivated many gay and lesbian activists into action in relation to an issue that they had not previously regarded as a high priority.[180] During debate on the Marriage Amendment Bill in 2004, Australian Democrats Senator, Brian Greig observed:

---

176 See Cooper, 2005; Kirby, 2005.
177 Relationships Act 2003 (Tasmania). See Darby, 2004.
178 Australian Capital Territory Department of Justice and Community Safety, 2005. The Civil Unions Act 2006 (ACT) was subsequently disallowed by the Australian Parliament, pursuant to the Australian Capital Territory (Self-Government) Act 1988 (Aust): Commonwealth Special Gazette 2006 No S93.
179 Largely achieved with the passage of the Superannuation Legislation Amendment (Choice of Superannuation Funds) Act 2004 (Aust). See now, Superannuation Industry (Supervision) Act 1993 (Aust), ss10–10A; and discussion in Australia, Human Rights and Equal Opportunity Commission, 2006b.
180 See Farouque, 2004.

> This is a clash between sex, politics and religion. It is being pushed by religious zealots and deeply conservative MPs. It is not a debate being driven by the lesbian and gay community itself. However, now that that community is under attack, it must respond. . . . It has been ironic for me to have seen this debate unfold. . . . in my 16 years of gay and lesbian rights activism and advocacy, marriage has been way down the agenda. It has never been a priority in the lesbian and gay community. Many indeed see it as a bankrupt and failing heterosexual institution based on patriarchal principles. Others feel that seeking gay marriage is heterosexual mimicry and want no part of it. But there are, of course, many long-term, same-sex couples who really do want to get married, and despite the general apathy in the gay and lesbian community around Australia, none of them have said that the option of civil marriage should be denied to same-sex couples. . . . Not wanting to get married is one thing; suddenly being told that you cannot is quite another . . .[181]

The story of Australia's distinctive response to the issue of the legal status of same-sex relationships in 2004 is not just a story of the absence of a national sexual orientation non-discrimination/equality standard, but the ascendancy, in this national legal environment, of a conservative ideology, according to which politicians have little time for gay and lesbian full equality claims, and in many cases, a degree of hostility towards them. It is not merely the formal legal gap, which has been critical in informing Australia's stance on same-sex marriage, but the (counter)values that currently occupy the 'void' in Australia's political discourse and legal culture, which is created, at least in part by the absence of a suprapolitical human rights standard for guiding and scrutinising the policy formulation process and law reform agenda. The convergence of these features created the environment in which an anti-recognition statute such as the Marriage Amendment Act could be passed – with minimal political opposition and modest popular outcry.

If the prevailing political paradigm is one that is supportive of human rights standards as a legitimate and important influence on policy development as a matter of principle or ideology (as in the Australian Capital Territory under the current Labor Government[182]), the absence of a human rights compliance imperative is likely to be less consequential. But where a commitment to human rights generally, and gay and lesbian equality specifically, is purely a matter of political preference, the opportunities for injecting human rights discourse into policy debates are contingent on the ascendancy of sympathetic political actors and values.

---

181 Australia Parliament, Hansard (Senate), 12 August 2004, pp 26507, 26508.
182 Of course, this 'pro-human rights' policy is now manifested in legal form: the Human Rights Act 2004 (ACT).

The preferences of the current Conservative Australian Government in this area had been apparent for some time. In August 2003, the Prime Minister, John Howard, made it clear that he did not support same-sex marriage: '. . . I certainly would not be initiating any moves to change the law to that effect.'[183]

By May 2004, the Government's position had hardened further still: not only would it *not* take any steps towards formal legal recognition of same-sex relationships, it would move to ensure that there was no possibility of gay and lesbian couples accessing the institution of marriage via judicial reinterpretation of the common-law definition of marriage.[184] The traditional opposite-sex common-law definition of marriage would be enshrined in the Marriage Act 1961. Although the government argued that the legislation was necessary, it is difficult to avoid the conclusion that the enactment of a statutory definition of marriage was very much a symbolic gesture – slamming a door that was already firmly shut. Even if gay and lesbian marriage advocates had considered that there might be judges who were sympathetic to their cause, they would have realised, as the government surely did, that in the Australian legal environment described above, there was simply no legal mechanism by which the court could set about the task of redefining marriage in accordance with a sexual orientation equality paradigm. The Australian judiciary, even if inclined to do so, lacked any equivalent of the constitutional or legislative bill of rights 'tools' that have been available to (though not always used by) judges in Canada, the UK and New Zealand.

The Marriage Amendment Act 2004: the impotence of human rights discourse

One of the striking features of the debate was the ease with which the Government was able to deflect criticism of the legislation on human rights grounds. The weak position of defenders of gay and lesbian equality in the Australian public debate was exacerbated by the fact that the Government's defence of traditional marriage legislation was supported by the Labour Party opposition.[185]

Certainly opponents of the Government's legislation drew on human rights discourse in their attempt to discredit the legislation. They argued that the legislation was directly inconsistent with principles of equality and non-discrimination. For example, Kendall Lovett and Mannie De Saxe from Lesbian and Gay Solidarity observed:

---

183 'Howard hits out at gay marriage', *The Age*, 5 August 2003.
184 'Gay marriage to be banned', *Sydney Morning Herald*, 27 May 2004.
185 Roxon, 2004.

Lesbian and gay men seek marriage no more and no less than their heterosexual counterparts for one reason only, and that is equal rights under the law. This is a human rights issue and one that all governments should be addressing, instead of passing regressive and retrogressive legislation.[186]

Jacqueline Tomlins (who married her female partner in Canada and had litigation pending in the Family Court seeking recognition of the marriage in Australia when the Marriage Amendment Act 2004 was passed) observed: 'Gay marriage is, very simply, an issue of equal rights; it is about some people having those rights and some people not.'[187]

The sole Green Party member in the Australian House of Representatives, Michael Organ, unequivocally characterised the bill as discriminatory in nature:

> ... the Greens oppose this bill. We object to such blatantly discriminatory legislation being brought before the parliament and we oppose the discrimination against individual Australians based upon their sexuality. ... It is an unfair and ridiculous situation that same-sex relationships all over this country – despite their longevity, despite their passion and love and despite their profound commitment – must be treated as 'different' relationships. Australia has an opportunity here to be one of the most progressive and forward thinking in the world in relation to a whole range of issues, the recognition of same-sex relationships being just one of them. However, the government and opposition bury their heads in the sand, refusing to accept and support same-sex relationships as a normal part of Australian life in 2004. For this reason I cannot support this bill and I condemn the government for bringing it before the House.[188]

In the Senate, Greens Senator Kerry Nettle also emphasised discrimination: 'The Marriage Amendment Bill 2004 legislates official discrimination against a section of our community because of their sexuality or their gender identity.'[189]

The Australian Democrats were the only other party to oppose the legislation.[190]

The decision of the Labor Party to support the legislation was read in some quarters as a pragmatic decision to deny the Government a weapon

---

186 Lesbian and Gay Solidarity, 2004.
187 Tomlins, 2004.
188 Australia Parliament, Hansard (House of Representatives), 17 June 2004, pp 30741, 30745.
189 Australia Parliament, Hansard (Senate), 12 August 2004, p 26514.
190 Senator Brian Greig, ibid, p 26507; Senator John Cherry, ibid, p 26530.

for encouraging religious and social conservative voters from deserting Labor in the lead-up to a national election. Democrats Senator, John Cherry, commented on the:

> ... shameless politicking associated with this bill. Let me make it clear – there has been no concerted lobby from the gay community for marriage rights. The legislation is not in response to some urgent legal or social issue – rather it is a pathetic attempt by John Howard to emulate the political tactics of his good friend President George W Bush and try to 'wedge' his political opponents on a 'moral' issue.[191]

Some ALP (Australian Labor Party) MPs expressly disassociated themselves from what they saw as the discriminatory sentiment underlying the legislation – while nonetheless supporting it. In the House of Representatives, Carmen Lawrence described the sentiment underlying the legislation – that same-sex relationships are not 'worthy' of the status of marriage – as 'discrimination front and centre and . . . a very cruel way of treating a minority group in our community'.[192] Senator Gavin Marshall described the legislation as perpetuating 'shameful and ridiculous discrimination' and explained his decision to support it as motivated by a determination to 'refuse John Howard the opportunity to play his nasty politics of division in the lead up to the next election . . .'.[193]

The Labor Party's position on the Marriage Amendment Act 2004 offers a further illustration of the fragility and volatility of the human rights dynamic in Australia in the absence of authoritative legal form. It is vulnerable not only to concerted ideological departures, but also strategic marginalisation for electoral purposes. Of course, the adoption of a bill of rights does not remove this possibility, but it is clearly harder to silence human rights considerations in such a context. Of course, the potency of the human rights dynamic varies not just with legal form, but also in terms of legal culture. But in the current Australian environment, human rights assertions do not draw much momentum from either source – at least in relation to gay and lesbian equality issues.

Some participants in the Australian public debate attempted to characterise human rights/equality standards as *legal* barriers to the enactment of the proposed legislation. For example, in a submission to the (short-lived[194])

---

191 Senator John Cherry, p 26530.
192 Ibid, p 30725.
193 Ibid, p 26539.
194 After being passed by the House of Representatives in June 2004, the original Marriage Legislation Amendment Bill 2004 was referred by the Senate to the Senate Legal and Constitutional Legislation Committee, which sought public submissions and was scheduled to

Senate Legal and Constitutional Committee inquiry into the proposed legislation, the Public Interest Advocacy Centre and the National Association of Community Legal Centres argued that '[t]he principle of non-discrimination is fundamental to the entire international human rights system' and that 'the proposed amendments will, without more, violate Australia's international human rights obligations, particularly Australia's commitments under the [International Covenant on Civil and Political Rights]'.[195] Specific reference was made to the provisions of the ICCPR on non-discrimination (Art 2) and equality before the law (Art 26).

The suggestion that the proposed Marriage Act amendments would place Australia in breach of its ICCPR obligations is a bit of a stretch. It is true that the Human Rights Committee has confirmed in recent years that the ICCPR does impose obligations on state parties in relation to sexual orientation equality. The case of *Young v Australia* (discussed above) is illustrative.[196] However, in *Joslin v New Zealand*[197] (also discussed earlier), the Committee had expressly rejected the argument that the maintenance of a traditional opposite-sex definition of marriage violated a state's obligation under the ICCPR.[198] This reality of the ICCPR's more modest dictates in this area was reflected in the conclusion of the PIAC/NACLC submission, which focused less on alleged violation of international human rights laws, and more on the Government's failure to respect underlying moral values:

> Amendments to any law that are completely inconsistent with Australia's obligations to protect and promote international human rights standards and *would be contrary to the fundamental values of our nation* [sic] *of fairness* must be seriously considered and justified. In this instance, PIAC and NACLC believe that the amendments are not justified.[199]

The fact that Australian human rights advocates sometimes push the limits of accepted interpretations of international human rights standards (also evident in the debate on double jeopardy reform, considered in Chapter 2)

---

report back to the Senate in October 2004. However, in August 2004 the Government effectively circumvented the committee's deliberations by introducing a revised bill – the Marriage Amendment Bill 2004 – that the Australian Labor Party Opposition was prepared to support because, unlike the original bill, it did not attempt to prevent same-sex couples from adopting children from overseas. The Senate Legal and Constitutional Legislation Committee had no choice but to abandon its inquiry.

195 Public Interest Advocacy Centre and the National Association of Community Legal Centres, 2004, p 7.
196 *Young v Australia* (2003).
197 *Joslin v New Zealand* (2002).
198 Australia, Human Rights and Equal Opportunity Commission, 2004.
199 Public Interest Advocacy Centre and the National Association of Community Legal Centres, 2004, p 8.

is an understandable reaction to the absence of domestic legal reference points for evaluating government actions. The irony is that creative invocations of international human rights standards are even easier to ignore than they are to advance – particularly in light of the dramatically reduced cache of the views of United Nations treaty monitoring bodies in Australia's contemporary legal environment.[200]

In any event, human rights objections, whether articulated in terms of moral principle or legal obligation, achieved very little purchase in the public discourse surrounding the Marriage Amendment Bill. The Government dismissed out-of-hand suggestions that the legislation discriminated against gays and lesbians. Liberal MP, Bob Baldwin, observed:

> It is important to understand that these amendments do not seek to remove any rights that homosexuals currently have with regard to marriage laws, as same-sex marriages are not currently recognised.[201]

For the Government, the exclusion of same-sex couples from the definition of marriage was not a human rights issue. Attorney General Philip Ruddock stated:

> We are not about discriminating against anybody. We are of the view that people can have their relationships. It is just that they cannot have their relationships ascribed the characteristic of marriage, as marriage is a relationship between a man and a woman. So the purpose of the bill is to give effect to that commitment, to protect the institution of marriage.[202]

One of the features of the parliamentary debate that is of particular interest in the context of the present study is the way in which the Government attempted to defend the motivation for the legislation and the timing of the bill. There is a long tradition of the UK, Australia, New Zealand and Canada looking to each other for law reform options from which to borrow. On this occasion, however, the Australian Government was not interested in following the lead of one of its traditional comparators. Rather, the Government decided that Australia needed to be 'insulated' against the possible effect of Canada's move towards full recognition of same-sex relationships in the form of an inclusive definition of marriage.

The Attorney General rejected suggestions that the Bill had been timed to

---

200 See Kinslor, 2002; Hovell, 2003; Niarchos, 2004; Charlesworth *et al*, 2006.
201 Australia Parliament, Hansard (House of Representatives), 17 June 2004, p 30718 per Mr Baldwin.
202 Ibid, p 30750.

appeal to a conservative electorate ahead of an election. Rather, Mr Ruddock explained, the Bill had been introduced quickly to head off moves by Australian same-sex couples, who had gone to Canada and been married there, to seek to have their marriages recognised by courts in Australia. According to Mr Ruddock, the timing of the Bill was 'determined by the fact that numbers of people believed that by going off-shore and entering into marriages that were permitted offshore, on return to Australia they could invite our courts to recognise those relationships'.[203] To this end, s 88EA was added to the Marriage Act 1961 (Aust): 'A union solemnised in a foreign country between: (a) a man and another man; or (b) a woman and another woman; must not be recognised as a marriage in Australia.'

Canada – the 'off-shore' destination in question – is rarely constructed as a threat to the integrity of Australia's legal standards. It is also rare for a country to be implicitly criticised for showing *too much* respect for human rights values!

It is true that two couples had initiated proceedings in the Family Court to have their Canadian marriages recognised,[204] but the prospects of this litigation succeeding were extremely slim – in the absence of any authoritative legal reference point like s 15 of the Canadian Charter, Art 14 of the ECHR or s 19 of the New Zealand Bill of Rights Act, for a judicial reformulation of the definition of marriage. Nonetheless, the Government expressed concern that 'some judges have already flagged that they believe they are custodians of the common law and that they might offer another view',[205] opposed to the Government's preference for the traditional opposite-sex definition of marriage.[206]

Democrats Senator, Brian Greig, criticised the government for pre-empting judicial consideration of the issue:

> There is no need for rush and haste. The Australian citizens who have their cases before the legal system deserve their days in court. Natural justice should have been allowed to take place. Rushing to extinguish legal avenues is despicable. Does the Prime Minister believe that no question of human rights should be left to the courts?[207]

It is hard to believe that the Government was genuinely concerned about the risk of judicial reformulation of the definition of marriage. But its expressed concerns do raise an interesting side-point here, which is relevant to my

---

203 Australia Parliament, Hansard (House of Representatives), 17 June 2004, p 30749.
204 Farouque, 2004; Goodenough, 2004; Tomlins, 2004; Wearring, 2004.
205 Australia Parliament, Hansard (House of Representatives), 17 June 2004, p 30749, per the Attorney General, Mr Ruddock.
206 Such attitudes have also influenced government bureaucratic practices: see Szego, 2006.
207 Australia Parliament, Hansard (Senate), 12 August 2004, p 26508.

examination of the relationship between human rights values and legal form. In essence, the Government was characterising the common law, under the control of judges, as a place of 'hidden dangers' and 'unknown qualities' – which executive governments and legislatures may regard as in need of control (depending on their political/values orientation).

Critics of the legislation argued that Australia should be following rather then insulating against the approach to same-sex relationships taken in traditional comparator countries. Jacqueline Tomlins, one of the 'married in Canada' Australians whose litigation was short-circuited by the Marriage Amendment Act 2004, observed: 'At a time when Canada, parts of the US, New Zealand, and big chunks of Europe are all moving to protect the rights of lesbians and gays, Australia is doing the opposite.'[208] After acknowledging the progress that had been made in relation to relationship matters within the constitutional powers of Australian states and territories, Democrats Senator, Brian Greig, also drew attention to Australia's 'odd country out' status at the national level:

> It is worth noting that as a nation we are one of very few Western countries without any national antidiscrimination laws on the grounds of sexuality or gender identity and one of very few Western countries with no partnership laws for same-sex couples.[209]

In light of the government's stated motivation for introducing the legislation when it did, it is unsurprising that it was unmoved by such arguments. In fact, National Party Senator, Bob Boswell, was emphatic that the legislation should be seen as an unequivocal rejection of not only the Canadian model of sexual orientation-neutral civil marriage, but also the New Zealand and UK models of what he termed 'counterfeit marriage' – civil union/partnership: 'A civil union is simply a marriage by another name, the only difference being that it is open to the gay and lesbian community. I will oppose that, and I will oppose any move to introduce that in to parliament.'[210]

It would be overly simplistic to explain the Australian 'counternarrative' of the (non)recognition of same-sex relationships simply in terms of the absence of a legal equality standard. The Australian Parliament did not write a heterosexual definition into the Marriage Act – a move that has been described by a former Chief Justice of the Family Court of Australia as 'one of the most shameful pieces of legislation that has ever been passed by the Australian

---

208 Tomlins, 2004.
209 Australia Parliament, Hansard (Senate), 12 August 2004, p 26511.
210 Ibid, p 26514.

Parliament'[211] – *because* of this absence, or *because* Australia does not have a bill of rights and formal procedures for injecting human rights sensitivity into the law-making process. But these gaps in Australia's legal infrastructure clearly had an influence on the process and outcomes of the public discourse surrounding the Marriage Amendment Act 2004. They contributed to the ability of the major political parties to construct the legislation, for reasons of ideology or pragmatism, as *not* a human rights issue.

In each of the other three stories about the legal status of same-sex relationships told in this chapter, governments formulated their legislative positions on the issue in a context where the expectations created by the dictates of their respective domestic legal forms with respect to human rights and gay and lesbian equality were, to a lesser or greater extent, influential. Human rights discourse was largely absent from the environment in which Australia's response was developed and implemented.

One of the ironic effects of the events of 2004 is that they have increased the profile of the issue of formal relationship recognition and marriage in the gay and lesbian activist community and among human rights lawyers and advocates more generally. Prominent activist, Rodney Croome, observed in May 2005:

> Last year's federal same-sex marriage ban changed the landscape of Australian LGBT human rights forever. It sparked a mainstream debate on marriage equality for the first time in Australian history. This debate was negative framed and cut short by the ban, but it opened the eyes of many people, including myself, to the need for marriage reform.[212]

An issue that for many had been a relatively low priority[213] is now the subject of a concerted campaign, reflected in the growth of lobby groups,[214] community and academic fora,[215] and protest rallies,[216] and the development of draft legislation. An interesting example of the latter strategy is the Same-Sex Marriage Bill, which was introduced into the Tasmanian Parliament by the Green Party in April 2005. It proposed the creation of an institution of same-sex marriage under Tasmanian state law. Proponents argued that this was constitutionally permissible because the Australian Parliament, by passing the Marriage

---

211 Nicholson, 2004. See also, Nicholson, 2005.
212 Croome, 2005.
213 Marriage was already on the agenda of some activists prior to the 2004 amendments to the Marriage Act: see Pitman, 2003.
214 The growth of the group, Australian Marriage Equality (www.australianmarriageequality.com) is illustrative.
215 For example, see Gay and Lesbian Rights Lobby, 2005; and Castan Centre for Human Rights Law, 2005.
216 Walsh and Wood, 2004; Green Left Weekly, 2005.

Amendment Act 2004, had defined its law-making authority with respect to marriage under s 51(xxi) of the Australian Constitution as limited to *heterosexual* marriage. It followed, so it was argued, that state legislatures are free to make laws on the topic of *homosexual* marriage.[217] This constitutional argument has not yet been tested – the bill did not proceed beyond first reading because it was not supported by the major parties.[218] It has also been contentious in the gay and lesbian activist community. For example, David Scamell from the Gay and Lesbian Rights Lobby observed: 'State-based marriage laws may give us the right to marry but they will not give our relationships full equality in the eyes of the law.'[219] Nonetheless, the bill, and the debate surrounding it,[220] are illustrative of one of the ways in which the issues of same-sex marriage and the full recognition of same-sex relationships has been launched onto the gay and lesbian equality agenda in Australia, ironically, fuelled by the Australian Parliament's 2004 symbolic gesture of non-recognition.[221]

Conclusions

It may not be immediately obvious, but there is a 'good news' dimension to the four stories told in this chapter for human rights advocates in Australia – particularly for those who continue to push for a national bill of rights. Comparative assessment of recent developments with respect to the legal status of same-sex relationships in Canada, the UK, New Zealand and Australia reveals that legal form *has mattered*. There is a high degree of correlation between the conventional wisdom hierarchy of legal models for the protection of human rights and the results achieved in each of the four countries. Measured against the criterion of formal legal equality, the 'best' outcome was achieved in Canada – where the civil and political rights of gay men and lesbians, including equality before the law, are constitutionally entrenched – and the 'worst' result occurred in Australia – where there is no national constitutional or legislative articulation of the principles of non-discrimination and equality in application to gay men and lesbians. In the UK and New Zealand – where the right of gay men and lesbians not to be discriminated against is protected by a statutory bill of rights – substantial (though, arguably incomplete) progress was made.

---

217 Australian Associated Press, 2005.
218 Gould, 2005a.
219 Gould, 2005b.
220 See Millbank, 2005.
221 In April 2006 the Australian Human Rights and Equal Opportunity Commission launched a National Inquiry into Discrimination against People in Same-Sex Relationships: Financial and Work-Related Entitlements and Benefits. See Australia, Human Rights and Equal Opportunity Commission, 2006a, 2006b; and Pollard, 2006.

Of course, it would be a mistake to draw too neat or direct a causal connection between the domestic legal form in which human rights are protected and the nature and outcomes of the public debate over the legal status of same-sex relationships in each of the four countries. As I have explained above, other variables apart from legal form were influential in each of the four countries. But the extent of the correlation between form and outcome does tend to support the hypothesis that a bill of rights can make a difference to how human rights controversies are resolved. This is an especially significant insight in the present context where the controversy revolved around the issue of whether established principles of equality and non-discrimination should be extended to same-sex couples.

In Australia, this question was answered (for the time being at least) in an environment where the executive and legislative arms of government were completely free to act in accordance with ideological and vote-counting strategic preferences. In this environment, and with both major parties in a two-party system adopting similar policy positions, human rights discourse was marginalised in the public discourse and largely impotent as an influence on law reform. As a result, the Australian Parliament was the only one of the four countries to offer gay and lesbian couples nothing except a legislature gesture of non-recognition or exclusion. This example tends to undermine the argument that a bill of rights is unnecessary in a society with strong traditions of respect for human rights values. Where there are few institutional mechanisms for injecting those values into the policy-making and law reform process, they are vulnerable to being trumped by competing philosophical values or pragmatic political considerations.

In each of the other three countries, human rights discourse had a significant effect on the terms in which the controversy over the formal legal status of same-sex relationships was constructed and ultimately resolved. But the human rights dynamic was not simply a generic or homogenous normative influence across Canada, the UK and New Zealand. Its shape and its potency were created locally – by reference to the distinctive attributes of the legal form for human rights protection, but also by dimensions of local legal culture.

In Canada, the human rights dynamic became a constitutional imperative – based on judicial interpretation of the equality guarantee in s 15 of the Charter of Rights and Freedoms and a firmly embedded culture of deference to judicial authority in Charter matters – which dictated that the redefinition of marriage was the only legitimate resolution of the controversy over the formal legal status of same-sex relationships. To the extent that one of the objectives of codification of human rights is to place them beyond the influence of party political preferences and pragmatic considerations, the Canadian story of the achievement of same-sex marriage might be regarded as a classic illustration of this phenomenon. As Smith has observed, in her own comparative assessment of the 'gay marriage' debate in two countries – the way in which same-sex marriage came to be characterised in Canadian public discourse as 'a question of human rights', contrasts strikingly with the US, where '[t]he discursive field of public policy and political debate defines the "gay marriage" debate as a question of moral values'.[222] At least at the federal level, the same observation applies with equal force to Australia.

The contrast between Canada and the other two countries that are the subject of the present study is less striking, but nonetheless significant. In the UK and New Zealand, a human rights dynamic centred on Art 14 of the ECHR and s 19 of the Bill of Rights Act, respectively, was influential in generating political momentum towards the legislative recognition of same-sex relationships as civil partnerships/civil unions. Consistent with the statutory bill of rights models adopted in these two countries, the role of the judiciary was less significant than it was in Canada. This was particularly so in New Zealand where the courts' main contribution was to place marriage 'off limits' as a BORA-inspired goal, thereby redirecting the relationship recognition movement to the goal of civil union, and to the strategy of legislative reform. In this setting the human rights dynamic was an important part of the environment in which the Civil Union Act 2004 came to be seen by a majority of parliamentarians as a logical extension of New Zealand's commitment to fundamental human rights values. To the extent that the BORA was seen to create a legal imperative – and there was a dimension of the public discourse that emphasised that same-sex relationship recognition was a necessary consequence of New Zealand's obligations under the BORA and the Human Rights Act 1993 – it was an imperative over which the executive and legislative arms of government exercised significant control. While the demands of legislative obligation and philosophical commitment may have combined to make the case for legislative recognition difficult to resist, there was still room in the policy-making process for other values and pragmatic considerations to be influential. In this context, a civil union regime, available to both same-sex and opposite-sex couples, which left marriage undisturbed as a heterosexual institution, marked the limits of the achievable.

In the UK, same-sex relationship status legislation was enacted at a time when neither the domestic courts nor the European Court of Human Rights had created a direct legal imperative in relation to the formal legal status of same-sex relationships. But throughout the public discourse surrounding the Civil Partnership Act 2004, there was a strong sense that ECHR/Human Rights Act 1998 jurisprudence was headed in that direction and that a broader European imperative was emerging. The significance of this influence on the policy-making and law reform process is illustrated by the considerable degree of cross-party support for the Civil Partnership Act. By contrast, although the fate of New Zealand's Civil Union Bill was decided by

---

222 Smith, 2005a, p 226.

a conscience vote, there was a strong correlation between for/against votes and party political affiliation. The comparison suggests that there is a difference in the human rights dynamic created by the bills of rights of the UK and New Zealand, which is not fully explained by their similar legal forms. The Human Rights Act's hybrid status as a domestic statute based on a European instrument (and backed by a supranational court), while undoubtedly the source of some local antagonism from those who resent 'external' interference, appears to have created a degree of separation between the demands of human rights law and political preferences, which is not as evident in New Zealand. In New Zealand, the story behind the enactment of the Civil Union Act 2004 reveals that an effective human rights imperative *can* be drawn from domestic legislative sources, but the somewhat muted status of the BORA in New Zealand's legal culture is such that the dynamic requires political will on the part of the government in order for it be effectively mobilised.

In a document released in April 2005 as part of its campaign to garner support for Bill C-38, the Canadian Department of Justice identified and rebutted a number of 'common misconceptions', including: 'Same-sex marriage is not a human right, or other countries that do not permit same-sex marriage would be human rights violators.'[223] The Department of Justice response was that, at least in Canada, the issue was a human rights one, by virtue of the equality guarantee in s 15 of the Charter. It also noted: 'Comparisons to other countries are interesting, but each country must make its own decisions, in accordance with its own values.'[224]

This chapter's examination of four countries' responses to the controversy surrounding the human rights of gay men and lesbians and the formal legal status of same-sex relationships has highlighted the way in which ostensibly universal human rights assertions are constructed and received in a local context – in different ways, by different means and to different ends. The nature and extent of the variation in the responses of Canada, the UK, New Zealand and Australia cannot be reduced simply to manifestations of legal form – in each case a range of local factors contributed to the prevailing human rights dynamic – but legal form was a critical variable in the degree of success enjoyed by proponents of equality-based legal recognition of the legitimacy of same-sex relationships.

223 Canada, Department of Justice, 2005.
224 Ibid.

Chapter 4

Balancing 'competing' human rights: Drawing the free speech/hate speech line

Introduction

When it comes to human rights controversies, few have been as enduring, and as thoroughly scrutinised, as the question of the legitimacy of legislative restriction on various forms of 'hate speech'. Provisions rendering it unlawful to engage in public conduct that incites hatred against certain identified groups are now a common component of the criminal laws or civil human rights laws of many countries. Hate speech laws, in various forms, have been enacted in all four countries that are the subject of the present study. The majority of hate speech laws are concerned with the promotion of hatred or ill-feeling (and associated action) against individuals or groups identified by ethnicity, or country of origin – motivated by the obligations to legislate assumed by all parties to the International Convention on the Elimination of All Forms of Discrimination,[1] including Canada, New Zealand, Australia and the United Kingdom (UK) – but in some jurisdictions, equivalent laws apply to hate speech directed at individuals defined by other identity characteristics, including religion and sexual orientation. At the same time, free speech is a prominent human right and democratic principle in all four countries. Indeed, a central theme in political debates, academic scholarship and litigation on hate speech laws has been whether the legal regulation of hate speech in order to support human rights in relation to cultural diversity and non-discrimination can be reconciled with the human right to exercise free speech or free expression.

Although there is significant 'common ground' across the four countries on these issues at the level of general principles, there are significant differences in terms of the manifestation of these values in legal form. The differences are relatively subtle when it comes to the non-discrimination/equality side of the equation, but are obvious in relation to the status of the right to free speech.

---

1 International Convention on the Elimination of All Forms of Discrimination, opened for signature and ratification by General Assembly Resolution 2106 (XX) of 21 December 1965 (entered into force 4 January 1969).

In Canada, the right is constitutionally protected by the Charter of Rights and Freedoms,[2] and has been the subject of detailed judicial definition and interpretation since 1982.[3] In the UK, the right to freedom of expression is expressly protected by the Human Rights Act 1998 (UK), which incorporates into domestic law Art 10 of the European Convention on Human Rights (ECHR), and which is thereby underpinned by a well-developed body of 'Strasbourg jurisprudence' regarding the legitimate scope of the right to free speech.[4] In New Zealand, s 14 of the Bill of Rights Act 1990 (BORA) expressly recognises that 'Everyone has the right to freedom of expression...'. Australia is the only one of the four countries in which the 'right' to free speech is, for the most part,[5] recognised only by the common law, leading one commentator to characterise it as a 'delicate plant'.[6]

In these circumstances it is unsurprising that neither the ubiquity of hate speech laws nor the weight of academic commentary on their merit (or lack thereof) has dampened enthusiasm for an ongoing debate about the merits of imposing legal restrictions on the expression and communication of views that have the potential to reinforce negative stereotypes and prejudices, and increase the risk of particular individuals and minority communities being exposed to tangible harms, including discrimination, abuse and violence. The New Zealand Human Rights Commission has described the operation of hate speech laws as 'notoriously difficult'.[7]

To some extent these tensions have been manifested in debates (and sometimes litigation[8]) over the *validity of* laws that restrict forms of speech and communication in the name of anti-racism, non-discrimination and multiculturalism. However, another important practical and ongoing effect of these tensions is that decision-makers in enforcement bodies (including human rights agencies and prosecution services), along with judges and tribunal members charged with adjudication responsibilities under various forms of hate speech laws, are often called on to rule on the relationship between the human right of free expression and the human right of freedom from racism/discrimination[9] – in the circumstances of a specific allegation that the line between lawful and unlawful speech has been crossed. Although it has been criticised as too narrow a conception,[10] this task is

---

2 Section 2(b) of the Canadian Charter of Rights and Freedoms, Part 1 of the Constitution Act, 1982, being Schedule B to the Canada Act 1982 (UK), 1982, c 11.
3 Moon, 2000.
4 *Thomas v News Group Newspapers Ltd* (2001), para 20 per Lord Phillips MR.
5 The implied constitutional freedom of political communication is discussed below.
6 Chesterman, 2000, p 1.
7 New Zealand Human Rights Commission, 2005a, p 3.
8 This is particularly so in Canada: see, *R v Keegstra* (1991); *Canadian Human Rights Commission v Taylor* (1990); *Saskatchewan Human Rights Commission v Bell* (1994).
9 See Sadurski, 1999, p 40.
10 See, e.g., Boyle, 1992; Foley, 1995; Braun, 2004; McGregor, 2006.

commonly characterised as a *balancing* exercise,[11] or an exercise in resolving a *conflict*.[12]

How decision-makers approach and resolve the balancing task is critical in giving meaning and shape to hate speech laws and, consequently, the degree of protection afforded to victims of racist speech. It is also important in establishing the practical parameters of abstract human rights, like the right to freedom of expression. In fact, one of the features of hate speech laws that ensures that their application (or non-application) in particular instances is frequently disputed is that they invariably require a balance to be struck between the competing human rights objectives that underpin hate speech laws. On the one hand, there are the specific obligations to legislate against 'hate propaganda' created by Art 4 of the International Convention on the Elimination of All Forms of Racial Discrimination (ICERD), as well as the general right not to be subjected to racism or other forms of discrimination, reflected in international human rights instruments including ICERD, and Art 26 of the International Covenant on Civil and Political Rights (ICCPR). On the other hand there is the right to free speech or freedom of communication, embodied in Art 19 of the ICCPR.

The human rights controversies examined in the two previous chapters surrounded the terms of resolution of a particular normative question. In the case of double jeopardy reform (Chapter 2) the central issue was whether an established human rights standard – immunity from re-prosecution after acquittal – should be *retracted*. In the case of the legal recognition of same-sex relationships (Chapter 3) the central issue was whether a developing human rights standard (sexual orientation equality) should be *extended*. In the case of the debate over hate speech laws the threshold normative question of whether legislatures should create rules for the purpose of defining the permissible bounds of public expression and communication has largely been answered: in the affirmative – as evidenced by the hate speech provisions found in the Public Order Act 1986 (UK), the Human Rights Act 1993 (NZ), the Racial Discrimination Act 1975 (Aust) and the Criminal Code 1985 (Can) (not to mention the provisions contained in the human rights/anti-discrimination legislation of almost all Canadian and Australian provincial/state/territorial legislatures[13]).

Certainly this threshold controversy is re-animated every time that a proposal for legislative extension of hate speech laws finds its way onto the policy debate and law reform agenda. Recent examples include the 2004 extension of the offence defined by s 319 of the Canadian Criminal Code to include homophobic hate speech as well as racist hate speech,[14] the 2004/2005

11 See, e.g., Coliver, 1992; and Iganski, 1999a, pp 132–3.
12 See, e.g., Sumner, 2004, p 52.
13 See McNamara, 2002, 2005.
14 2004, c 14 (Bill C-250).

inquiry by the New Zealand Parliament's Government Administration Committee into the possible introduction of expanded hate speech laws,[15] proposals for the introduction of religious vilification laws in the states of South Australia and Western Australia in 2004,[16] and the 2006 addition of provisions relating to the incitements of religious hatred to the racial hatred offences contained in the Public Order Act 1986 (UK).[17] However, even when legislative reform proposals are not on the table or the horizon, existing hate speech laws have a tendency to generate controversy and debate whenever they are the subject of public investigation or adjudication proceedings. In large part, this is because in enacting hate speech laws of a particular type, the legislative arm of government has usually only partially completed the task of 'striking a balance'[18] between competing human rights. The majority of hate speech laws are drafted in such a way as to leave significant discretion in the hands of bodies responsible for enforcement (including human rights agencies and prosecuting authorities) and adjudication (including quasi-judicial tribunals and courts) when called upon to determine whether conduct falls within the parameters of unlawful hate speech (whether defined as civil or criminal wrongs). And so, the relevant controversy surrounding the operation of hate speech laws is what I have characterised as an *enduring* one. Legislative restrictions on hate speech are constantly and routinely assessed for their free speech 'compatibility'. Authoritative free speech scrutiny does not end at the moment that the legislature enacts hate speech laws. Rather, it is an integral and enduring feature of the administration and interpretation of legislative regimes for the regulation of hate speech. The appropriate balance between the right to free speech and the human rights that underpin hate speech laws is calibrated (and recalibrated) by key decision-makers with reference to specific hate speech allegations.

Given the characteristics of the particular human rights controversy with which this chapter is concerned, the country narratives will be taking a different form than the narratives around which Chapters 2 and 3 are organised. Rather than review the public discourse surrounding particular legislative reform events, this chapter focuses on the post enactment adjudication (interpretation and application) process for hate speech laws. After a general overview of the prevailing domestic legislative framework in each country, with respect to both the right to free speech and hate speech laws, I will

---

15 New Zealand House of Representatives, 2004.
16 See Chow, 2005. Consider also the controversy surrounding the first complaint of religious vilification under Victoria's Racial and Religious Tolerance Act 2001 to be upheld by the Victorian Civil and Administrative Tribunal: *Islamic Council of Victoria v Catch the Fire Ministries Inc* (2004); *Islamic Council of Victoria v Catch the Fire Ministries Inc* (2005). At the time of writing, an appeal to the Victorian Court of Appeal was pending.
17 Racial and Religious Hatred Act 2006 (UK). See Appignanesi, 2005.
18 See Coliver, 1992.

describe what I see as the defining characteristics of the approach that has been adopted by key decision-making agencies in each of the four countries when called upon to make authoritative determinations about the parameters of legislative restrictions on hate speech. In the case of the three countries whose legislatures have codified the traditional common-law principle of free speech as an express human right (in, respectively, Canada's 1982 Charter of Rights and Freedoms, New Zealand's 1990 BORA and the UK's 1998 HRA) the discussion will focus on the operation of hate speech laws in the period after codification of the right to free speech.[19] The aim of this approach is to shed light on the question with which this study is primarily concerned: Has the adoption of a particular legal form for recognising the right to free speech had any discernable influence on the operational scope of legislative restrictions on hate speech? Discussion of the Australian experience will focus on the decade since the enactment of national racist hate speech laws, with the passage of the Racial Hatred Act 1995 (Aust), though some consideration will also be given to the operation of relevant state hate speech laws in this period.

Each of the country reviews presented in this chapter will necessarily be selective rather than comprehensive. Attention will be focused on both landmark events and recent illustrative cases. The latter will include instances in which a court (or quasi-judicial tribunal) has been called upon to rule on the scope of a specific hate speech provision, in response to an allegation (whether by the state on behalf of the community in the case of criminal proceedings or an aggrieved individual or organisation in the case of civil proceedings) that the standard of behaviour set by the legislation had been breached; as well as examples of the approach adopted by agencies responsible for key threshold decisions – such as the UK's Crown Prosecution Service (CPS) in relation to whether to proceed with criminal prosecutions, and the New Zealand Human Rights Commission in relation to whether to formally accept and proceed with individual complaints.

In addition to being well adapted to the enduring nature of the controversy surrounding hate speech laws, the other main benefit of the approach adopted in this chapter is that it will facilitate insight into the significance of differences in legal form for the judicial (and quasi-judicial) role in the protection of human rights (whereas the two previous chapters focused primarily, though not exclusively, on the legislative process).

Under these conditions, the comparative case-study method employed in this chapter is designed to illustrate the manner in which the perceived clash between competing human rights – on this occasion, the right to freedom of expression and the right not be discriminated against or subjected to the

---

19 In each case, national hate speech laws predated the adoption of a bill of rights, dating back to 1965 in the United Kingdom, 1970 in Canada and 1971 in New Zealand.

other harms associated with hate speech – has been approached and resolved in cases where human rights agencies, prosecuting authorities, tribunals and courts have been called upon to adjudicate on alleged breaches of laws prohibiting hate speech. Consistent with the underlying objectives of this book, the aim of this analysis is to reveal the extent to which the scope for legal regulation of hate speech is influenced by the legal status of competing human rights – particularly, the right to free speech, but also the right to equality/non-discrimination that underpins hate speech laws designed to offer protection to minority groups. Has the resolution of the 'clash' (both in terms of approach and outcome) varied significantly in accordance with the nature of the form of legal protection extended to the rights that need to be balanced?

International law obligations

All four countries that are the subject of the present study are parties to the ICERD, which opened for signature in December 1965, and came into force in January 1969. The Convention was ratified by the UK in March 1969, Canada in October 1970, New Zealand in November 1972 and Australia in September 1975.[20] Art 4 of ICERD states:

> States Parties condemn all propaganda and all organizations which are based on ideas or theories of superiority of one race or group of persons of one colour or ethnic origin, or which attempt to justify or promote racial hatred and discrimination in any form, and undertake to adopt immediate and positive measures designed to eradicate all incitement to, or acts of, such discrimination and, to this end, with due regard to the principles embodied in the Universal Declaration of Human Rights and the rights expressly set forth in article 5 of this Convention, inter alia:
>
> (a) Shall declare an offence punishable by law all dissemination of ideas based on racial superiority or hatred, incitement to racial discrimination, as well as all acts of violence or incitement to such acts against any race or group of persons of another colour or ethnic origin, and also the provision of any assistance to racist activities, including the financing thereof;
> (b) Shall declare illegal and prohibit organizations, and also organized and all other propaganda activities, which promote and incite racial discrimination, and shall recognize participation in such organizations or activities as an offence punishable by law;

---

20 Office of the United Nations High Commissioner for Human Rights, 2006b.

(c) Shall not permit public authorities or public institutions, national or local, to promote or incite racial discrimination.

Related obligations are also imposed by the ICCPR (Art 20: 'Any advocacy of national, racial or religious hatred that constitutes incitement to discrimination, hostility or violence shall be prohibited by law'), and the non-discrimination norm embodied in Art 26 of the ICCPR is also a relevant part of the wider international human rights law context.[21] However, since ICERD came into force, Art 4 has been widely seen as the primary international human rights reference point for motivating the enactment, and assessing the adequacy, of domestic laws dealing with racist hate speech. And yet, from its inception, this element of the obligations imposed on state parties by ICERD has been controversial, primarily because of a perceived clash with the right to free speech, which is also recognised under international human rights instruments, including Art 5 of the ICERD and Art 19 of the ICCPR. Article 19 of the ICCPR states:

1. Everyone shall have the right to hold opinions without interference.
2. Everyone shall have the right to freedom of expression; this right shall include freedom to seek, receive and impart information and ideas of all kinds, regardless of frontiers, either orally, in writing or in print, in the form of art, or through any other media of his choice.
3. The exercise of the rights provided for in paragraph 2 of this article carries with it special duties and responsibilities. It may therefore be subject to certain restrictions, but these shall only be such as are provided by law and are necessary:
    (a) For respect of the rights or reputations of others;
    (b) For the protection of national security or of public order (*ordre public*), or of public health or morals.

The level of disagreement in the international community as to whether/how racial hate speech laws can be reconciled with a commitment to the right to freedom of expression is reflected in the fact that a number of state parties, including the UK and Australia, entered, and have maintained, formal

---

21 Article 26 of the ICCPR states:

'All persons are equal before the law and are entitled without any discrimination to the equal protection of the law. In this respect, the law shall prohibit any discrimination and guarantee to all persons equal and effective protection against discrimination on any ground such as race, colour, sex, language, religion, political or other opinion, national or social origin, property, birth or other status.'

reservations with respect to Art 4.[22] Despite the existence of such reservations (or perhaps because of them), the Committee on the Elimination of Racial Discrimination (CERD) has consistently maintained that states parties should enact and enforce the laws required by Art 4.[23] In its 15th General Recommendation, issued in 1993, the Committee expressed its opinion that 'the prohibition of the dissemination of all ideas based upon racial superiority or hatred is compatible with the right to freedom of opinion and expression'.[24]

Despite such attempts by CERD to provide authoritative guidance on how the balance should be struck, the relationship between the rights

22 The United Kingdom's reservation states:

'... [T]he United Kingdom wishes to state its understanding of certain articles in the Convention. It interprets article 4 as requiring a party to the Convention to adopt further legislative measures in the fields covered by sub-paragraphs (a), (b) and (c) of that article only in so far as it may consider with due regard to the principles embodied in the Universal Declaration of Human Rights and the rights expressly set forth in article 5 of the Convention (in particular the right to freedom of opinion and expression and the right to freedom of peaceful assembly and association) that some legislative addition to or variation of existing law and practice in those fields is necessary for the attainment of the end specified in the earlier part of article 4.'

Australia's reservation states:

'The Government of Australia ... declares that Australia is not at present in a position specifically to treat as offences all the matters covered by article 4 (a) of the Convention. Acts of the kind there mentioned are punishable only to the extent provided by the existing criminal law dealing with such matters as the maintenance of public order, public mischief, assault, riot, criminal libel, conspiracy and attempts. It is the intention of the Australian Government, at the first suitable moment, to seek from Parliament legislation specifically implementing the terms of article 4 (a).'

Source: www.ohchr.org/english/countries/ratification/2.htm#reservations (accessed 15 March 2006).

New Zealand did not make a reservation in relation to Art 4 of ICERD, but did make a reservation in relation to Art 20 of the ICCPR:

'The Government of New Zealand having legislated in the areas of advocacy of national and racial hatred and the exciting of hostility and ill will against any group of persons, and having regard to the right of freedom of speech, reserves the right to not to introduce further legislation with regard to Art 20.'

The United Kingdom and Australia also entered reservations in relation to Art 20 of the ICCPR, in similar terms. The Australian reservation states:

'Australia interprets the rights provided for by articles 19, 21 and 22 as consistent with article 20; accordingly, the Commonwealth and the constituent States, having legislated with respect to the subject matter of the article in matters of practical concern in the interest of public order (*ordre public*), the right is reserved not to introduce any further legislative provision on these matters.'

Source: www.ohchr.org/english/countries/ratification/4_1.htm (accessed 15 March 2006).
23 United Nations, Committee on the Elimination of Racial Discrimination, 1985.
24 United Nations, Committee on the Elimination of Racial Discrimination, 1993, para 4.

protected by Art 4 and the free speech rights recognised by Art 5 and protected by Art 19 of the ICCPR has remained a question of considerable controversy.[25]

In this context, it is not surprising that states have adopted a variety of approaches towards meeting (or partially meeting) their obligations under Art 4 of ICERD (as well as Art 20 of the ICCPR) to legislate against hate speech. This diversity is reflected in the laws enacted by the national legislatures of: the UK (1965), Canada (1970), New Zealand (1971) and Australia (1995). Further diversity across the four countries has resulted from the adoption of various forms of hate speech laws by the majority of state/provincial/territorial legislatures in the two federations – Canada and Australia.[26]

One of the implications of the prominence of Art 4 of ICERD in the broader debate about the legitimacy of hate speech laws is that the primary focus has been on *racial* hate speech. In line with Art 20 of the ICCPR, legislatures in some countries have enacted *religious* hate speech laws (UK; the Australian states of Victoria, Queensland and Tasmania; and the Canadian provinces of Alberta, British Columbia, and Saskatchewan, as well as the Northwest Territories). Other groups at which hate speech is commonly directed, including gay men and lesbians, and transgender persons, have not had the advantage of an international human rights imperative with which to persuade law-makers into offering them the legislative protection afforded to racial minorities. Nonetheless, some jurisdictions have outlawed a broader range of types of hate speech laws, including vilification on the basis of sexual orientation (Canada, and the Australian states of New South Wales, Queensland, Tasmania, and the Australian Capital Territory).[27]

United Kingdom

History and current form of hate speech laws

The UK enacted its first hate speech statute in 1965. When the UK Parliament enacted its pioneering racial discrimination legislation – the Race Relations Act 1965 – it included a provision that prohibited the incitement of racial hatred.

---

25 Partsch, 1992; Korengold, 1993; Farrior, 1996; Boyle and Baldaccini, 2001.
26 See McNamara, 2005, 2002.
27 Provincial/territorial hate speech legislation in British Columbia, Saskatchewan, Alberta and Northwest Territories applies to all grounds on which discrimination is prohibited under the relevant statute, including sex, marital status, disability and age, as well as 'receipt of public assistance' (Saskatchewan), 'source of income' (Alberta) and 'social condition' (NWT). In Australia, NSW and ACT laws cover HIV/AIDS status and transgender identity; Tasmanian law covers disability; and Queensland law covers gender identity.

Section 6 (1) of the Race Relations Act 1965 stated:

> A person shall be guilty of an offence under this section if, with intent to stir up hatred against a section of the public in Great Britain distinguished by colour, race, or ethnic or national origin –
>
> a) he publishes or distributes written material which is threatening, abusive or insulting; or
> b) he uses in any public place or at any public meeting words which are threatening, abusive or insulting,
>
> being matters or words likely to stir up hatred against that section on grounds of colour, race, or ethnic or national origin.

The maximum penalty was two years imprisonment.

This provision, and the statute of which it was a part, came four years before the UK ratified the ICERD (in March 1969). Although international human rights law developments during the 1960s would not have been without relevance, the primary impetus for the criminalisation of racist hate speech was domestic. A proposal to include a specific racial/religious hate speech provision in the original Public Order Act 1936 failed, as did proposals in the 1940s and 1950s for the creation of a civil 'group defamation' action.[28] During the early 1960s, proposals for the enactment of legislation outlawing racist incitement gathered support within the Labour Party and formed part of its General Election Manifesto in 1964.[29]

Despite its inclusion in the Race Relations Act 1965 – that is, in what was primarily a civil anti-racial discrimination statute – s 6 created a criminal offence, which the government regarded as necessary for the maintenance of public order. Prosecutions required the consent of the Attorney General.

In *Thorne v BBC* (1967),[30] an English resident of German origin sought an injunction to stop the BBC from airing programmes that, in his view, promoted hatred against Germans. The England and Wales Court of Appeal confirmed that s 6 of the Race Relations Act 1965 did not provide any basis for aggrieved individuals to initiate civil proceedings. Lord Denning MR observed: 'It is plain to me that section 6 only creates a new criminal offence for which the proper remedy is a prosecution by or with the consent of the Attorney-General'.[31]

Although the outcome of this case was predictable, it is worthy of mention in the present context because it underscores one of the distinctive features of

---

28 Lester and Bindman, 1972, p 259.
29 Lester and Bindman, 1972, p 360.
30 *Thorne v BBC* (1967).
31 Ibid, p 1109.

the UK's experience with hate speech laws: an almost exclusive reliance on criminal law regulation. The UK is the only one of the four countries that are the subject of the present study not to have adopted some form of civil prohibition explicitly directed at hate speech.

One of the consequences of the adoption of a criminal law approach in the 1960s was that the traditional notion that subjective fault (*mens rea*) should be established before punishment could be justified was incorporated into the offence definition. Under s 6 of the Race Relations Act 1965, the prosecution had to prove not only that the conduct was 'threatening, abusive or insulting', and that it was likely to stir up racial hatred, but also that the accused *intended* to stir up hatred.

It was not long before criticism of the limitations of the UK's first hate-speech law began to be voiced. In a report on a political demonstration that turned violent in Red Lion Square in June 1974, Sir Leslie Scarman observed:

> Section 6 of the Race Relations Act is merely an embarrassment to the police. Hedged about with restrictions (proof of intent, requirement of the Attorney General's consent) it is useless to a policeman on the street. . . . The section needs radical amendment to make it an effective sanction, particularly, I think, in relation to its formulation of the intent to be proved before an offence can be established.[32]

In 1976, the offence was relocated to the Public Order Act 1936 (as s 5A) and amended in one important respect: an intention to stir up hatred was no longer an element of the offence. The Government explained the relocation of the offence on the basis that it was more appropriately placed in a criminal public order statute rather than a civil anti-discrimination statute, given that it was designed to 'prevent the stirring up of racial hatred which may beget violence and public disorder'.[33] It is worth noting that neither in its 1976 form, nor in its current form (see below), has the prohibition of inciting racial hatred contained a 'breach of the peace' component of the type traditionally found in public order legislation, such as the offence on which s 6 of the Race Relations Act 1965 and s 5A of the Public Order Act 1936 were modelled – s 5 of the Public Order Act 1936. Although it has since been re-enacted in modified form in the Public Order Act 1986 (see below), at the time, s 5 stated:

> Any person who in any public place or at any public meeting –
>
> (a) uses threatening, abusive or insulting words or behaviour, or
> (b) distributes or displays any writing, sign, or visible representation which is threatening, abusive or insulting

---

32 Scarman, 1975, cited in Bailey, Harris and Jones, 1985, p 464.
33 United Kingdom Government, 1975, cited in Bailey, Harris and Jones, 1985, p 463.

with intent to provoke a breach of the peace or where a breach of the peace is likely to be occasioned, shall be guilty of an offence.

The wording of s 5A of the Public Order Act 1986 effected a broadening of the scope of the prohibition on racist hate speech – by removing the subjective fault element. The Government defended this change on the basis that it was necessary to ensure that the legislation caught not only 'crude verbal attacks', but also conduct that 'tends to be less blatantly bigoted, to disclaim any intention to of stirring up racial hatred, and to purport to make a contribution to public education and debate'[34] – but which nonetheless was likely to stir up racial hatred. The move was by no means universally supported. During debate on the 1976 Race Relations Bill in the House of Lords, Lord Hailsham characterised as a 'constitutional outrage' the creation of an indictable offence with no subjective fault element.[35]

Ten years later the Public Order Act 1936 was replaced by the Public Order Act 1986. Section 5A was renumbered as s 18 and again amended. This time, Parliament opted for an either/or approach to whether the offence should be defined in terms of subjective intent or objectively assessed likely effect. Section 18, which is now one of a series of racial hatred provisions found in Pt 3 of the Public Order Act 1986 (UK), states:

(1) A person who uses threatening, abusive or insulting words or behaviour, or displays any written material which is threatening, abusive or insulting, is guilty of an offence if

   (a) he intends thereby to stir up racial hatred, or
   (b) having regard to all the circumstances racial hatred is likely to be stirred up thereby.

As noted above, the UK's specific racist speech offence has long been regarded as a 'companion provision' to the general disorder offence now defined by s 5 of the Public Order Act 1986. Section 5 states:

(1) A person is guilty of an offence if he –

   (a) uses threatening, abusive or insulting words or behaviour, or disorderly behaviour; or
   (b) displays any writing, sign or other visible representation which is threatening, abusive or insulting

---

34 United Kingdom Government, 1975, cited in Bailey, Harris and Jones, 1985, p 463.
35 United Kingdom Parliament, Hansard (House of Lords), 15 November 1976, 1092, cited in Australia, Human Rights Commission, 1982, p 10.

within the hearing or sight of a person likely to be caused harassment, alarm or distress thereby. . . .

(3) It is a defence for the accused to prove –

  (a) that he had no reason to believe that there was any person within hearing or sight who was likely to be caused harassment, alarm or duress, or

  (b) that he was inside a dwelling and had no reason to believe that the words or the behaviour used, or the writing, sign or other visible representation displayed, would be heard or seen by a person outside that or any other dwelling, or

  (c) that his conduct was reasonable.

Section 6(4) of the Public Order Act 1986 provides:

> A person is guilty of an offence under section 5 only if he intends . . . the writing, sign or other visible representation, to be threatening, abusive or insulting, or is aware that it may be threatening, abusive or insulting . . .

As will be discussed below, in practical terms the offence defined by s 5 is an important part of the UK's legal regime for dealing with hate speech. Although it is expressed in general terms, it has, on a number of occasions, been invoked by the police and the CPS in relation to incidents of hate speech. Recently, it has been used in conjunction with the racial/religious aggravation provisions of the Crime and Disorder Act 1998 (UK), which expose defendants to a higher penalty where their offence 'is motivated (wholly or partly) by hostility towards members of a racial or religious group'.[36]

In 2006, a new Pt 3A[37] was added to the Public Order Act 1986 by the Racial and Religious Hatred Act 2006 (UK). The offences contained in Pt 3A largely mirror those contained in Pt 3, although, due to amendments insisted upon in the House of Lords and eventually accepted in the House of Commons, the threshold for unlawful *religious* hate speech is set at a higher point than it is for unlawful *racial* hate speech. Most notably, s 29B (the 'religious' equivalent of s 18) only applies to 'threatening' words, behaviour, or displayed written material (not abusive or insulting), and the fault element for the offence is *intent* to stir up hatred (not objective likelihood). In addition, s 29B(5) states that 'This section does not apply to words

---

36 Crime and Disorder Act 1998 (UK), ss 28, 31.
37 Part 3A operates only in England and Wales: Racial and Religious Hatred Act 2006, s 3(4). In Northern Ireland incitement of both racial and religious hatred has been a criminal offence since 1970 (Prevention of Incitement to Hatred Act (Northern Ireland) 1970). See, now, Public Order (Northern Ireland) Order 1987, Pt 3.

or behaviour used, or written material displayed, solely for the purpose of being included in a programme service', and s 29J states:

> Nothing in this Part shall be read or given effect in a way which prohibits or restricts discussion, criticism or expressions of antipathy, dislike, ridicule, insult or abuse of particular religions or the beliefs or practices of their adherents, or of any other belief system or the beliefs or practices of its adherents, or proselytising or urging adherents of a different religion or belief system to cease practising their religion or belief system.

Given the very recent commencement of Pt 3A of the Public Order Act 1986, the discussion in this chapter of the operation of hate speech laws in the UK since the Human Rights Act 1998 came into force in 2000, will focus on the *racist* hate speech offences found in Pt 3 of the Public Order Act 1986, as well as the application to hate speech contexts of the offence defined by s 5 of the Public Order Act 1986. However, it is appropriate to acknowledge that the Racial and Religious Hatred Act 2006 generated enormous controversy and considerable opposition – reflected in the House of Lords' determination that the threshold for the offence of incitement to *religious* hatred provisions should be higher than the threshold for the existing offence of incitement to *racial* hatred. To a considerable extent, opposition to the Racial and Religious Hatred Bill, in the form in which it was originally introduced by the Government, was motivated by concerns that the extent of the infringement on the right to free speech would be unjustifiable. The following comment by Lord Lester, during the course of debate on the House of Lords, is illustrative:

> Freedom of speech, like equality and freedom of religion, is a fundamental civil and political right. Its protection is at the heart of our liberal democratic society. The right to freedom of speech means the right of everyone to communicate information and opinions without unnecessary state control or interference. That includes evil ideas expressed intemperately or in ways that shock, disturb or offend some sections of society. It includes insulting and offensive criticism of religious beliefs and practices— whether traditional religions or new religions or cults—provided it poses no imminent threat to public order.[38]

Finally, mention should be made of the Protection from Harassment Act 1997 (UK), s 1 of which states:

> A person must not pursue a course of conduct –
>
> (a) which amounts to harassment of another, and

---

38 United Kingdom Parliament, Hansard (House of Lords), 11 October 2005, 173.

(b) which he knows or ought to know amounts to harassment of the other.

Section 7 provides that 'references to harassing a person include alarming the person or causing the person distress', and that ' "conduct" includes speech'. Although this legislation is primarily designed to create a criminal offence (s 2), and to establish a basis for civil remedies (s 3) in relation to *stalking*, the definition of unlawful harassment is broad enough to include certain forms of hate speech.[39]

The legal form of free speech and non-discrimination/ equality rights after the Human Rights Act 1998

Article 10 of the ECHR states:

(1) Everyone has the right to freedom of expression. This right shall include freedom to hold opinions and to receive and impart information and ideas without interference by public authority and regardless of frontiers. This article shall not prevent States from requiring the licensing of broadcasting, television or cinema enterprises.
(2) The exercise of these freedoms, since it carries with it duties and responsibilities, may be subject to such formalities, conditions, restrictions or penalties as are prescribed by law and are necessary in a democratic society, in the interests of national security, territorial integrity or public safety, for the prevention of disorder or crime, for the protection of health or morals, for the protection of the reputation or rights of others, for preventing the disclosure of information received in confidence, or for maintaining the authority and impartiality of the judiciary.[40]

Of course, the coming into force of the Human Rights Act 1998 (UK) in 2000, did not represent the right to freedom of expression's first appearance in the UK's legal landscape. Since the ECHR came into force in 1953 (the UK having ratified in 1951), Art 10 and the associated jurisprudence of the European Commission on Human Rights and the European Court of Human Rights have exerted a significant influence on the decision-making practices of judges in the UK, particularly since 1966, when British residents were able to make individual petitions to Strasbourg. In addition, support for the principle of free speech has a long tradition in the common law, even

---

39 *Thomas v News Group Newspapers* (2001).
40 See also, Art 11 of the Charter of Fundamental Rights of the European Union, Official Journal C 364 of 18 December 2000.

if it was not possible to point to a positive *right* to freedom of expression.[41] In fact, a number of judges and commentators have suggested that there is no significant difference between the scope of the right to free expression under Art 10 of the ECHR and the right to free expression traditionally recognised under English common law.[42] Whether this conclusion as to complete symmetry is accepted,[43] there can be no doubt that Art 10 of the ECHR has become firmly embedded as the dominant legal touchstone for the right to freedom of expression in the UK, and this position was consolidated by the Human Rights Act 1998 (UK). One of the European Court of Human Rights' landmark decisions on Art 10 resulted from a case against the UK. In *Handyside v United Kingdom*,[44] the Court stated:

> Freedom of expression constitutes one of the essential foundations of ... a [democratic] society, one of the basic conditions for its progress and for the development of every man. Subject to paragraph 2 of Art 10, it is applicable not only to 'information' or 'ideas' that are favourably received or regarded as inoffensive or as a matter of indifference, but also to those that offend, shock or disturb the State or any sector of the population. Such are the demands of that pluralism, tolerance and broadmindedness without which there is no 'democratic society'. This means, amongst other things, that every 'formality', 'condition', 'restriction' or 'penalty' imposed in this sphere must be proportionate to the legitimate aim pursued.[45]

The only explicit counter-weights for Art 10, in the context of the legal infrastructure which frames the European balance between hate speech/free speech are Arts 14 and 17 of the ECHR:

> 14. The enjoyment of the rights and freedoms set forth in this Convention shall be secured without discrimination on any ground such as sex, race, colour, language, religion, political or other opinion, national or social origin, association with a national minority, property, birth or other status.[46]

---

41 Gardner, 1994, pp 213–14; see also Whitty *et al*, 2001, pp 380–7.
42 See *Derbyshire County Council v Times Newspapers Ltd* (1993), p 551 per Lord Keith; Gardner, 1994, p 236; Beloff, 1999, p 21; Bosma, 2000, p 301.
43 See, e.g., *R v Central Independent TV* (1994).
44 *Handyside v United Kingdom* (1979–80).
45 Ibid, para 49. See McGonagle, 2001a.
46 A 'free standing' right to non-discrimination is contained in Protocol 12 to the ECHR, which came into force in April 2005. The United Kingdom has not yet ratified Protocol 12 (see United Kingdom Parliament, Joint Committee on Human Rights, 2005). See also, Art 21 of the Charter of Fundamental Rights of the European Union, Official Journal C 364 of 18 December 2000.

17. Nothing in this Convention may be interpreted as implying for any State, group or person any right to engage in any activity or perform any act aimed at the destruction of any of the rights and freedoms set forth herein or at their limitation to a greater extent than is provided for in the Convention.

McGonagle has described s 17 as 'the rock on which most cases involving racist speech or hate speech [that is, cases in which individuals have invoked the right to freedom of expression under Art 10 in an attempt to challenge their conviction] have tended to founder'.[47]

Neither s 14 nor s 17 can be regarded as mandating the enactment of hate speech laws. There is no equivalent in the ECHR of Art 4 of the ICERD or Art 20 of the ICCPR, although in 1997 the Committee of Ministers of the Council of Europe recommended that:

> The governments of the member States should establish or maintain a sound legal framework consisting of civil, criminal and administrative law provisions on hate speech which enable administrative and judicial authorities to reconcile in each case respect for freedom of expression with respect for human dignity and the protection of the reputation or the rights of others.[48]

At the centre of this recommendation is a conviction that legal prohibitions on hate speech are an important part of domestic legal regimes, designed to protect human rights, and that such laws are compatible with commitment to the value of freedom of expression. In fact, even in the absence of a binding obligation on states parties to enact hate speech laws, a firmly established principle of European human rights law is that speech that promotes racial hatred is not entitled to the status of protected free speech. In an area dominated by fine distinctions and controversial judgment calls, one of the brightest lines drawn by the European Court of Human Rights is the line between free speech, protected by s 10(1), and unprotected hate speech, the legislative prohibition of which falls squarely within the parameters of s 10(2). In *Procurator*

---

47 McGonagle, 2003, p 46.
48 Council of Europe, Committee of Ministers, 1997. The European Commission developed a 'Proposal for a Council Framework Decision on Combating Racism and Xenophobia' (Commission of the European Communities, 2001). At the time of writing the proposal had not yet been adopted (see Council of the European Union, 2005). The Council of Europe's Cyber-Crime Convention http://conventions.coe.int/treaty/en/projects/cybercrime.htm (which came into force in July 2004) has been supplemented by an Additional Protocol Concerning the Criminalisation of Acts of a Racist and Xenophobic Nature Committed Through Computer Systems http://conventions.coe.int/Treaty/en/Treaties/Html/189.htm (which came into force in March 2006). See Akdeniz, 2006, pp 20–2.

Fiscal v Brown,[49] Lord Steyn chose the example of the unprotected status of racist hate speech under the ECHR to illustrate a more general point about the balancing of individual/community interests in the Convention:

> The inspirers of the European Convention ... the framers of the European Convention ... realised that from time to time the fundamental right of one individual may conflict with the human right of another. Thus the principles of free speech and privacy may collide. They also realised only too well that a single-minded concentration on the pursuit of fundamental rights of individuals to the exclusion of the interests of the wider public might be subversive of the ideal of tolerant European liberal democracies. The fundamental rights of individuals are of supreme importance but those rights are not unlimited: we live in communities of individuals who also have rights. ... Thus, notwithstanding the danger of intolerance towards ideas, the Convention system draws a line which does not accord the protection of free speech to those who propagate racial hatred against minorities.[50]

As will be revealed below, in the context of an examination of the operation of the UK's hate speech laws, in those relatively few cases in which the issue has come squarely before them, the courts of the UK have consistently endorsed the Strasbourg line – leaving no doubt about the legitimacy of domestic legislation that provides for criminal prohibitions on racist hate speech.

The operation of hate speech laws

When compared with criminal offences generally, racial hate speech offences have been among the most rarely prosecuted of crimes in the UK. However, when compared with the very low rate at which criminal hate speech laws have been enforced in other jurisdictions (including Canada, New Zealand and Australia, discussed below) a rather different light is shed on the UK experience. Certainly, the combined effect of a range of factors – the relatively high threshold set by offences such as the one defined by s 18 of the Public Order Act 1986; the cautious and high threshold approach of the CPS when assessing which cases to prosecute; and the vetting power of the Attorney General – is that the UK's hate speech laws have been reserved for conduct at the serious end of the spectrum. Nonetheless, the UK's hate speech laws have been an active, and not merely symbolic, component of the available legal measures for addressing particular manifestations of racism.

---

49 *Procurator Fiscal v Brown* (Scotland) (2000).
50 Ibid, citing Art 10 of the ECHR and the ECtHR's decision in *Jersild v Denmark* (1994), para 31. See also Bindman, 2003, pp 74–5.

In the 40 years that UK legislation has recognised a discrete criminal offence of inciting racial hatred, over 100 prosecutions have been initiated, with a conviction rate of almost 70%. Bailey *et al*, have reported that there were 24 prosecutions (15 convictions) under s 6 of the Race Relations Act 1965, and between 1976 and 1983, 25 prosecutions (10 convictions) under s 5A of the Public Order Act 1936.[51] In January 2005, the Attorney General, Lord Goldsmith, reported to the House of Lords that since 1987 (when the Public Order Act 1986 came into effect) there had been 65 prosecutions for offences under Pt 3 of the Act, resulting in 44 convictions.[52] During this period, the Attorney General declined to consent to a prosecution on only three occasions.[53] However, this latter figure needs to be read in the context of the very cautious approach of the CPS, including a tendency to put forward for prosecution only the strongest and more serious cases. In September 2004, the CPS reported that of the 84 case files referred to it in the preceding three-year period, only a handful of cases had been prosecuted, and only two prosecutions resulted in convictions.[54] In more recent years the CPS has adopted what it characterises as a 'robust and rigorous' approach to pursuing incitement of racial hatred cases, as exemplified by the recent prosecution of members of the British National Party (discussed below).[55]

At least some of the incidents of racist speech that are considered by the CPS to fall outside the limits of s 18 of the Public Order Act 1986 are prosecuted under the broader 'public order' offence in s 5 of the Public Order Act 1986. In fact, since it was first enacted in 1936,[56] the offence now defined by s 5 of the 1986 Act has played an active part in attempts to regulate and sanction racist hate speech in public. Because it does not attract a penalty of imprisonment,[57] the offence defined by s 5 is regarded as a less controversial infringement of the right to freedom of expression than, say, the racial incitement offence defined by s 18 of the Public Order Act 1986, which carries a maximum penalty of seven years imprisonment.[58]

The inclusion of s 5 in the 1936 Act was prompted by the activities of the British Union of Fascists (BUF), and the first person convicted under s 5 was a speaker at a London public outdoor meeting who vilified Jews.[59] More recently, members of the British National Party (BNP), including Mark

---

51 Bailey, Harris and Jones, 1985, p 464.
52 United Kingdom Parliament, Hansard (House of Lords), 31 January 2005, WA4–WA5.
53 Ibid.
54 England and Wales, Crown Prosecution Service, 2004a, p 44. For the CPS Policy on Prosecuting Cases of Racist and Religious Crime, see England and Wales, Crown Prosecution Service, 2003.
55 Seamus Taylor (Crown Prosecution Service), personal communication, 23 February 2007.
56 Public Order Act 1936, s 5.
57 The maximum penalty for an offence under s 5 is £80: The Penalties for Disorderly Behaviour (Amount of Penalty) (Amendment No.2) Order 2004 (UK).
58 Patrick Stevens (Crown Prosecution Service), personal communication, 12 November 2004.
59 Lester and Bindman, 1972, p 351.

Norwood (discussed further below), were convicted in 2002 of the offence defined by s 5 of the 1986 Act, aggravated by the motivation of hostility towards Muslims (in accordance with ss 28 and 31 of the Crime and Disorder Act 1998) after they had prepared and displayed posters that included the phrases 'Islam out of Britain' and 'Protect the British people' as well as a photo of the World Trade Centre Towers burning on 11 September 2001 and 'a Crescent and Star surrounded by a prohibition sign'.[60]

Decisions to prosecute (and decisions not to prosecute) are frequently the subject of controversy in the wider community. There is often an 'expectation gap' between the circumstances in which individuals and groups call for the invocation of hate speech laws and the circumstances in which the CPS determines that it can initiate a prosecution, given the high threshold constituted by the incitement to hatred element.[61] For example, in 2004, anti-Arab views expressed in a newspaper opinion piece by former Labour Party MP and BBC television presenter, Robert Kilroy-Silk, prompted calls for him to be charged with an offence under s 18 or s 5 of the Public Order Act 1986. The CPS declined to prosecute, and publicly defended its decision on the basis of its assessment that in relation to s 18, there was insufficient evidence that Kilroy-Silk had intended to stir up hatred or that the opinion piece was likely to stir up hatred, and in relation to s 5, it would not be able to prove that he intended his comments to be insulting or was aware that they might be.[62] The BBC cancelled Kilroy Silk's long-running television programme.

In February 2006, a Muslim cleric, Abu Hamza al-Masri, was convicted in London of numerous offences including soliciting murder and inciting racial hatred under s 18 of the Public Order Act 1986. The convictions followed a long police investigation dating back to the late 1990s. However, it was not until 2004 that the CPS decided there was sufficient evidence to prosecute Abu Hamza. Faced with criticism for not acting sooner,[63] the Metropolitan Police emphasised that it had sent three briefs to the CPS between 1999 and 2004, and that it was CPS lawyers who decided that the evidence contained in the first two submissions was insufficient to support a prosecution.[64]

Just a few days before the Abu Hamza verdicts were announced,[65] a Leeds Crown Court jury acquitted BNP leader, Nick Griffin, of two counts of inciting racial hatred, and failed to reach a verdict in relation to two other counts of inciting racial hatred. The charges were based on comments made by Griffin during speeches that were filmed by a BBC reporter who infiltrated the ranks of the BNP, and which featured in a documentary, which

---

60 *Norwood v DPP* (2003), para 6.
61 Seamus Taylor (Crown Prosecution Service), personal communication, 12 November 2004.
62 England and Wales, Crown Prosecution Service, 2004b.
63 See, e.g., Knight, 2006.
64 See England and Wales, Crown Prosecution Service and Metropolitan Police Service, 2006.
65 On the relationship between the two decisions, see Macintyre, 2006.

aired in July 2005. In the wake of the verdicts in February 2006, the CPS attracted criticism for adopting the 'high risk strategy of bringing race hate charges against the . . . BNP [which] appeared to have backfired'.[66] The CPS announced that it would proceed with a retrial.[67]

While public disagreement about the circumstances in which it is appropriate to enforce hate speech laws is common, one of the distinctive features of the UK's experience with the operation of what is now Pt 3 of the Public Order Act 1986 is that the courts have not often been called upon to adjudicate on the legitimate scope of legislative restrictions on hate speech in light of the competing goal of respecting the right of freedom of expression. Prior to the enactment of the Human Rights Act 1998 (UK), the failure of persons alleged to have engaged in hate speech – and on that basis, convicted of offences under Pt 3, or the offence defined by s 5 of the Public Order Act 1986 (whether simple or racially aggravated) – to advance free-speech based 'defences' or grounds of appeal might have been explained with reference to the relatively passive recognition extended to the 'right' to freedom of expression at common law. Implicit in the approach of Lord Reid in the 1973 decision of the House of Lords in *Brutus v Cozens*[68] was the view that there was no warrant for narrowly construing, let alone doubting, the legitimacy of, the prohibition contained in s 5 of the Public Order Act 1936 (the forerunner of s 5 of the Public Order Act 1986), given that Parliament had already built into the statutory offence definition what it considered to be appropriate limits:

> Parliament had to solve the difficult question of how far freedom of speech or behaviour must be limited in the general public interest. It would have been going much too far to prohibit all speech or conduct likely to occasion a breach of the peace because determined opponents might not shrink from organising or at least threatening a breach of the peace in order to silence a speaker whose views they detest. Therefore vigorous and it may be distasteful or unmannerly speech or behaviour is permitted so long as it does not go beyond any one of three limits. It must not be threatening. It must not be abusive. It must not be insulting. I see no reason why any of these should be construed as having a specially wide or a specially narrow meaning. They are all limits easily recognisable by the ordinary man. Free speech is not impaired by ruling them out.[69]

Given that the coming into force of the Human Rights Act 1998 has inspired ECHR-based litigation in a wide range of areas,[70] it might have been anticipated that hate speech prosecutions in the UK after 2000 would be more

66 Herbert, 2006.
67 Wainwright, 2006.
68 *Brutus v Cozens* (1973).
69 Ibid, p 862.
70 Schmidt and Halliday, 2004.

likely to be met with objections that provisions like ss 5 and 18 of the Public Order Act 1986 were incompatible with the right to free speech protected by Art 10 of the ECHR, or that their enforcement in the particular circumstances of the case was an infringement of the defendant's rights under Art 10. In fact, challenges of this sort have been rare. Where advanced they have usually been disposed of by the courts with relative ease.

The case of Mark Norwood is illustrative. As noted above, Norwood was charged with an aggravated offence under s 5 of the Public Order Act 1986 after displaying a BNP poster that carried anti-Muslim words and images. In 2002, he was convicted in the Magistrates' Court and fined £300. He appealed to the High Court where he argued that his conviction contravened Art 10 of the ECHR.[71] Counsel for Norwood foreshadowed, but did not ultimately advance, an argument that the aggravated version of the s 5 offence was incompatible with Art 10. Rather, it was argued that:

> . . . in construing section 5 in its aggravated form and in its application to the facts, courts should give proper weight to the individual's right to freedom of expression in Art 10.1 when deciding where to draw the line between, on the one hand, racial or religious threats, abuse or insults intended as such or with an awareness that they might be such, and, on the other, the right to speak openly and frankly, and to express opinions or convey ideas on matters, including those that may be of public interest or concern.[72]

Auld LJ agreed that Art 10.1 should be taken into account in the context of assessing whether the accused had acted 'reasonably' for the purpose of s 5(3) of the Public Order Act 1986 (see above), and emphasised that 'the restrictions in Article 10.2 should be narrowly construed and convincingly established'.[73] However, the High Court concluded that there was no basis for overturning the trial judge's finding that the elements of the offence with which Norwood had been charged were made out, and the appeal was dismissed.

Norwood made an application to the European Court of Human Rights, where he again argued that his conviction violated his right to freedom of expression under Art 10 of the ECHR (as well as his right not to be discriminated against under Art 14).[74] The Court's response was blunt: it would not countenance an attempt to invoke the right to freedom of expression in purported justification of conduct that was directly inconsistent with Art 17 of the ECHR (see above):

---

71 *Norwood v DPP* (2003), para 11.
72 Ibid, para 36 per Auld LJ.
73 Ibid, para 37.
74 *Norwood v United Kingdom* (2004).

> The general purpose of Art 17 is to prevent individuals or groups with totalitarian aims from exploiting in their own interests the principles enunciated by the Convention. The Court, and previously, the European Commission of Human Rights, has found in particular that the freedom of expression guaranteed under Art 10 of the Convention may not be invoked in a sense contrary to Art 17. . . .
>
> The Court notes and agrees with the assessment made by the domestic courts, namely that the words and images on the poster amounted to a public expression of attack on all Muslims in the United Kingdom. Such a general, vehement attack against a religious group, linking the group as a whole with a grave act of terrorism, is incompatible with the values proclaimed and guaranteed by the Convention, notably tolerance, social peace and non-discrimination. The applicant's display of the poster in his window constituted an act within the meaning of Art 17, which did not, therefore, enjoy the protection of Articles 10 or 14.[75]

In reaching this conclusion, the Court emphasised that the characterisation of racial or religious hate speech as falling outside the parameters of Convention-protected freedom of expression, was firmly established within Strasbourg jurisprudence. It cited a series of prior decisions to this effect, from the 1979 decision of the former European Commission for Human Rights in *Glimmerveen and Hagenbeek v The Netherlands*,[76] to the Court's 2003 decision in *Garaudy v France*.[77]

Article 10 has, on a small number of occasions, been successfully deployed to challenge hate speech-related criminal convictions. For example, in *Jersild v Denmark*[78] the Strasbourg Court ruled that a journalist who recorded and broadcast the racist hate speech of others was entitled to the protection of Art 10.[79] In *Percy v DPP*[80] a woman was convicted of an offence under s 5 of the Public Order Act 1986, after she had written the words 'Stop Star Wars' on a flag of the United States of America, before placing it on the ground and standing on it. Percy was participating in a protest against US military policy, and the Star Wars National Missile Defence System in particular, at a US air base in England. Military personnel from the US witnessed Percy's conduct. The trial judge conclude that Percy's 'behaviour with the flag was insulting to American citizens at whom it was directed'.[81] On

---

75 *Norwood v United Kingdom* (2004), p 4.
76 *Glimmerveen and Hagenbeek v The Netherlands* (1979).
77 *Garaudy v France* (2003).
78 *Jersild v Denmark* (1994).
79 For a summary, see Mowbray, 2001, p 473. See also the European Court of Human Rights decision in *Lehideux and Isorni v France* (1998).
80 *Percy v DPP* (2001).
81 Ibid, para 2.

appeal, the High Court quashed Percy's conviction. Hallett J noted that Percy was protesting in relation to 'a matter of legitimate public debate',[82] and emphasised that s 5 of the Public Order Act 1986 was not designed to criminalise 'peaceful protest'.[83] In deciding whether a person had crossed the line between 'legitimate protest'[84] and criminal behaviour under s 5, it was necessary for the Court to:

> ... presume that the appellant's conduct in relation to the American flag was protected by Art 10 unless and until it was established that a restriction on her freedom of expression was strictly necessary.[85]

Hallett J concluded (Kennedy LJ concurring) that, in the particular circumstances of the case, a s 5 conviction was 'incompatible with the appellant's rights under the European Convention on Human Rights'.[86]

The defendants in *Jersild* and *Percy* were able to gain the protection of Art 10 of the ECHR because the conduct in which they had engaged was not ultimately regarded as constituting hate speech. Generally, however, in both the decisions of the Strasbourg Court and the courts of the UK, conduct considered to fall within the category of hate speech has, as McGonagle observes, been 'consistently held to be beyond the *ne plus ultra* of protected expression'.[87] It is not that the courts have regarded Art 10 as irrelevant to the interpretation and application of hate speech laws. On the contrary, in *Hammond v DPP*,[88] May LJ emphasised that when faced with the task of interpreting s 5 of the Public Order Act 1986, s 3 of the Human Rights Act 1998 required the courts to take Art 10 into account both when assessing 'reasonableness' and when defining 'insulting'.[89] On the facts of the case, the High Court declined to interfere with the trial court's finding that Hammond – an evangelical Christian preacher who publicly displayed a sign which carried the phrases, 'Stop Immorality', 'Stop Homosexuality', and 'Stop Lesbianism'[90] – had engaged in conduct prohibited by s 5.[91]

The relative 'brightness' of the European line between protected free speech and unlawful hate speech was also evident in the approach adopted by

---

82 *Percy v DPP* (2001), para 29.
83 Ibid, para 25.
84 Ibid.
85 Ibid, para 27.
86 Ibid, para 33.
87 McGonagle, 2001a, p 24. See also, McGoldrick and O'Donnell, 1998, pp 464–9; Lester and Pannick, 2004, pp 349–50.
88 *Hammond v DPP* (2004).
89 Ibid, para 21.
90 Ibid, para 5.
91 Ibid, paras 32–3.

the Court of Appeal in the case of an attempt to obtain civil remedies for racist hate speech via an action under the Protection from Harassment Act 1997 (UK) (see above). In *Thomas v News Group Newspapers*[92] a woman initiated a civil action under s 3(2), alleging that a series of newspaper articles in which she featured, constituted racist harassment that was unlawful under s 1 of the Act.

On 6 July 2000, *The Sun* newspaper published an article titled 'Beyond a Joke – Fury As Police Sarges Are Busted After Refugee Jest'. The article reported that three police officers from Bishopsgate had been disciplined for making racially discriminatory comments about a Somali refugee who had sought assistance from the police in finding her way to an asylum centre in Croydon. The article conveyed indignation that the officers had been demoted over what *The Sun* implied was a minor incident. The article was implicitly critical of Esther Thomas, an administrative employee (referred to in *The Sun* as 'a black clerk') at the police station who had overheard the conversation between the police officers and whose complaint was a factor in the decision to institute disciplinary proceedings. A week later, a follow-up article expressing similar sentiments appeared in *The Sun*. The article quoted from a number of readers' letters, including the following: 'The treatment of these officers is diabolical. Had it been two black officers and a white asylum seeker it would have been dismissed as the trivial incident it was.'[93] A third article, published a week later, included the following: 'All three were hauled in front of a disciplinary tribunal after a black civilian clerk complained about a series of exchanges at Bishopsgate last July.'[94]

Esther Thomas commenced proceedings under the Protection from Harassment Act 1997 in the Lambeth County Court. She alleged that the publication of the newspaper articles (after which she received hate mail), which had left her 'terrified and scared to go to work',[95] constituted an unreasonable course of conduct that amounted to unlawful harassment. Specifically, Thomas claimed that the articles had incited racial hatred: she asserted that it had been unnecessary and unreasonable for the articles to describe her as a 'black clerk' and for her name and place of work to be published.

In the County Court, Judge Cox refused an application from News Group to strike out the claim, rejecting the argument that a series of newspaper articles did not fall within the definition of harassment for the purpose of the Protection from Harassment Act 1997. News Group appealed this decision and the matter was removed to the Court of Appeal.

Before the Court of Appeal, News Group argued that a series of newspaper articles could only be regarded as constituting a course of conduct

92 *Thomas v News Group Newspapers* (2001).
93 Ibid, para 8.
94 Ibid, para 9.
95 Ibid, para 11.

amounting to harassment in the most extreme circumstances: '... such conduct would have to be extreme and be devoid of any true desire either to exercise freedom of speech or to fulfil the newspaper's responsibility to inform the public.'[96] In support of this submission News Group argued that s 12(4) of the Human Rights Act 1998 required the court to interpret and apply the relevant provisions of the Protection from Harassment Act 1997 in conformity with the right to freedom of expression recognised by Art 10 of the ECHR.

The Court of Appeal unequivocally accepted the submission from News Group that the European Court of Human Rights attached great significance to freedom of expression, with Lord Phillips MR quoting and endorsing the following statement of principle from the European Court of Human Rights' judgment in *Nilsen and Johnsen v Norway*.[97]

> According to the Court's well-established case law, freedom of expression constitutes one of the essential foundations of a democratic society and one of the basic conditions for its progress and for each individual's self-fulfilment. Subject to Art 10(2), it is applicable not only to 'information' or 'ideas' that are favourably received or regarded as inoffensive or as a matter of indifference, but also to those that offend, shock or disturb. Such are the demands of that pluralism, tolerance and broadmindedness without which there is no 'democratic society'. As set forth in Art 10, this freedom is subject to exceptions, which must, however, be construed strictly, and the need for any restrictions must be established convincingly.
>
> The test of 'necessity in a democratic society' requires the Court to determine whether the 'interference' corresponded to a 'pressing social need', whether it was proportionate to the legitimate aim pursued and whether the reasons given by the national authorities to justify it are relevant and sufficient.[98]

Lord Phillips MR emphasised that even prior to the enactment of the Human Right Act 1998, the English common law had embodied these principles.[99] Lord Phillips MR was dismissive of News Group's attempts to rely on US Supreme Court First Amendment jurisprudence in support of a narrow interpretation of the scope of unlawful harassment under the Protection from Harassment Act 1997, concluding that 'I have not found that the American jurisprudence affords any assistance that is not available on this side of the

---

96 *Thomas v News Group Newspapers* (2001), para 14.
97 *Nilsen and Johnsen v Norway* (1999).
98 Ibid, para 43.
99 *Thomas v News Group Newspapers* (2001), para 23.

Atlantic.[100] However, it was not in dispute that the duty to give effect to the right of freedom of expression was an 'an important consideration to any court when considering whether an offence or civil tort has been committed contrary to . . .' the Protection from Harassment Act 1997.

The Court also noted that it was:

> . . . common ground between the parties . . . and properly so, that before press publications are capable of constituting harassment, they must be attended by some exceptional circumstances which justifies sanctions and the restriction on the freedom of expression that they involve.[101]

Significantly, the parties agreed that one such exceptional circumstance was the publication of newspaper articles that were 'calculated to incite racial hatred of an individual'.[102] This concession was endorsed by the Court of Appeal on the basis that 'the Convention right of freedom of expression does not extend to protect remarks directly against the Convention's underlying values' – such as racist speech. The Strasbourg Court's decisions in *Jersild*[103] and *Lehideux*[104] were cited in support of this assessment.

Consequently, the outcome of the case before the Court of Appeal turned on what Lord Phillips MR described as a 'relatively narrow . . . central issue':[105] had Esther Thomas pleaded an arguable case that in publishing the series of articles *The Sun* had 'intended to provoke hostility on the part of its readers against her on the grounds of her race'?[106] Lord Phillips MR concluded that she had:

> When the three publications are considered together . . . I am satisfied that the respondent has pleaded an arguable case that the appellants harassed her by publishing racist criticism of her which was foreseeably likely to stimulate a racist reaction on the part of their readers and cause her distress.[107]

Consequently, the appeal against the decision of Judge Cox to refuse News Group's strike-out application was dismissed.[108]

---

100 *Thomas v News Group Newspapers* (2001), para 25.
101 Ibid, para 35.
102 Ibid, para 37.
103 *Jersild v Denmark* (1994).
104 *Lehideux and Isorni v France* (1998).
105 *Thomas v News Group Newspapers* (2001), para 38.
106 Ibid, para 38.
107 Ibid, para 49.
108 The case did not proceed to a final determination.

Key features of the United Kingdom balance

The specific question of the implications of Art 10 of the ECHR for the prohibitions on racist hate speech in Pt 3 of the Public Order Act 1986 has not, since the Human Rights Act 1998 came into operation in 2000, been raised squarely before an appellate court in the UK.[109] At first glance, this is surprising, particularly when compared with the willingness of individuals in many jurisdictions (including Canada, and, to a lesser extent, Australia) to advance free speech-based objections to findings that they had engaged in unlawful hate speech. However, when consideration is given to a number of features of the operation of hate speech laws in the UK, the absence of ECHR-inspired challenges is unsurprising.

Relevant factors include:

- the nature of hate speech laws in the UK (criminal offences with relatively high fault threshold and onerous evidentiary requirements);
- CPS prosecution policy under which only a small minority of the most serious alleged violations of Pt 3 of the Public Order Act 1986 are pursued as prosecutions; and
- the jurisprudence of the Strasbourg Court and the courts of the UK on the unavailability of Art 10 as a 'defence' for expression which promotes racial hatred or other forms of hate speech.

To the extent that it is possible to discern a 'European' conception of the scope of the right to free speech, one of its strong elements is antipathy towards hate speech, and racist hate speech in particular. Gearty has described 'the struggle against racism' as 'a constituent element of the European identity'.[110] In a similar vein, McGonagle has noted that 'the long and sinister shadow of the hatred unleashed by Nazism in the last century continues to inform public and judicial policy-making in Europe'.[111]

Such observations underscore the importance of appreciating that the terms in which the balance between unlawful hate speech and protected free speech is struck in the UK – leaving considerable scope for the statutory prohibition of various forms of hate speech – are not a simple product of the legal form in which the competing interests are recognised, under the ECHR and the Human Rights Act 1998. More significant is an underlying

---

109 In *Wilson v Procurator Fiscal* (2005), the defendant attempted, belatedly, to advance an Art 10 argument in the Scottish High Court in support of an appeal against his conviction for distributing written material that incited racial hatred under s 19 of the Public Order Act 1986. However, the Court declined to address the question on procedural grounds.
110 Gearty, 1999, p 327. See also, McGonagle, 2001a.
111 McGonagle, 2001a, p 25.

thread within contemporary European and British legal culture,[112] heavily informed by Europe's Second World War and Holocaust experiences – a conviction that the promotion of racial hatred (and by extension, the promotion of hatred on other identity grounds) should not be tolerated, and a conviction that the right to freedom of expression must necessarily yield when it comes into conflict with principles of equality, non-discrimination and anti-racism. The prominence of these values within the legal environment of the UK pre-dated the Human Rights Act 1998, although they have been reinforced by the closer incorporation of relevant Strasbourg jurisprudence into domestic judicial decision-making processes.

Canada

History and current form of hate speech laws

Most analyses of the origins of hate speech laws in Canada begin with the 1965 'Report of the Special Committee on Hate Propaganda in Canada',[113] which resulted in the addition of a series of new offences to the Canadian Criminal Code in June 1970. In fact, the first racial hate speech was enacted by the province of Manitoba in 1934 in the form of a statutory tort.[114] Even at the federal level, establishment of the special committee and the eventual enactment of criminal legislation were preceded by a long period of lobbying by community groups, committee reviews and consideration of draft legislation dating back to the early 1950s.

In 1965, the Canadian Minister of Justice, Guy Favreau, established a special committee 'to study and report upon the problems related to the dissemination of varieties of "hate propaganda" in Canada'.[115] The Cohen committee (named for its chair, Maxwell Cohen, then Dean at the Law School, McGill University) was established as a response to concern about a rise in hate propaganda activity by neo-Nazi organisations in Canada at the time[116] and concern about the inadequacy of existing legal measures. This perceived inadequacy was reinforced by the terms of the international obligations that Canada was soon going to assume as a signatory to the ICERD.[117]

---

112 See Leben, 1999, p 95.
113 Cohen, 1966.
114 An Act to amend 'The Libel Act', SM 1934, c 23. See now Defamation Act 1987 (Manitoba), s 19.
115 Ross, 1994, p 152.
116 Kayfetz, 1970; Kaplan, 1993.
117 The ICERD was adopted by the United Nations General Assembly on 21 December 1965, then signed and ratified by Canada on 24 August 1966 and 14 October 1970, respectively (Office of the United Nations High Commissioner for Human Rights, 2006b).

The Cohen Committee recommended the addition of a range of new offences to the Canadian Criminal Code, including offences of promoting genocide and inciting racial hatred. The *criminalisation* of racist hate speech was the only regulatory approach considered (and ultimately recommended) by the Cohen Committee. In the 1960s in Canada, civil anti-discrimination and human rights laws were in a fledgling state and were simply not conceived of as a feasible alternative to traditional criminal law-based prohibition and enforcement. In addition, the Cohen Committee was a special committee established by the Federal Minister of Justice, under a constitutional structure in which authority to enact criminal laws was a matter for the federal legislature.[118] The Cohen Committee explained its approach as follows:

> The Committee considered its terms of reference to include all legal aspects that might be relevant to a Canadian system of correction or control should the facts seem to warrant such recommendations. Such a view, of course, made it necessary to have some limited interest in those non-criminal legal aspects essentially under provincial jurisdiction. Since at least one Canadian Province – Manitoba – had enacted legislation as early as 1934 attempting to deal with 'group libel', essentially through restraining orders, this was an experience which the Committee could not ignore. Nevertheless, for obvious reasons the Committee's primary focus tended to be directed to areas within federal jurisdiction wherever legal controls were involved and essentially this meant a concentration on the criminal law.[119]

More generally, as in the UK and New Zealand during the same era, the types of locally prevalent racist hate speech which were considered to require a legislative response (along with the virulent anti-Semitism and other forms of racism associated with Nazism that were the primary motivation for the inclusion of Art 4 in the ICERD) were such that criminal law-based regulation was regarded as the only possible legislative response.

Bill C-53, modelled on the recommendations of the Cohen Committee, was introduced into the Canadian Parliament in October 1969. It was passed and came into force on 11 June 1970.

The Canadian 'Criminal Code' now contains three offences dealing with hate speech directed at members of an 'identifiable group'. When first enacted in 1970 the Criminal Code provisions were only concerned with *racist* hate speech, and so 'identifiable group' was defined as 'any section of the public distinguished by colour, race, religion or ethnic origin.' In 2004, the Canadian

---

118 The Constitution Act, 1867 (UK), 30 and 31 Victoria, c 3, s 91(27).
119 Cohen, 1966, p 4.

Parliament enacted Bill C-250 to expand the definition of 'identifiable group' to include sexual orientation.[120]

Section 318 of the Code creates an offence of advocating genocide:

> (1) Every one who advocates or promotes genocide is guilty of an indictable offence and liable to imprisonment for a term not exceeding five years.

Genocide is defined in s 318(2) as the act of killing members of an identifiable group or of deliberately inflicting conditions on an 'identifiable group' calculated to bring about the destruction of that group, in whole or in part. According to s 318(4) an ' "identifiable group" means any section of the public distinguished by colour, race, religion or ethnic origin'. No prosecution can commence without the consent of the Attorney General.

Under s 319(1) it is an offence to incite hatred against an identifiable group 'where such incitement is likely to lead to a breach of the peace'. This offence carries a maximum penalty of two years imprisonment.

Section 319(2) of the Criminal Code creates an offence of wilfully inciting hatred:

> Every one who, by communicating statements, other than in private conversation, wilfully promotes hatred against any identifiable group is guilty of
>
> (a) an indictable offence and is liable to imprisonment for two years; or
> (b) an offence punishable on summary conviction.

Section 319(3) provides for a range of defences in an effort to limit the effect of s 319(2) on freedom of expression:

> (3) No person shall be convicted of an offence under subsection (2)
>
> (a) if he establishes that the statements communicated were true;
> (b) if, in good faith, the person expressed or attempted to establish by an argument an opinion on a religious subject or an opinion based on a belief in a religious text;
> (c) if the statements were relevant to any subject of public interest, the discussion of which was for the public benefit, and if on reasonable grounds he believed them to be true; or
> (d) if, in good faith, he intended to point out, for the purpose of removal, matters producing or tending to produce feelings of hatred toward an identifiable group in Canada.

---

120 Criminal Code, RS, 1985, c C-46, s 318(4); 2004, c 14, s 1.

The consent of the relevant provincial Attorney General is required for prosecution under this section.[121]

In 1977, the hate speech provisions of the Criminal Code were supplemented by a prohibition contained in the Canadian Human Rights Act – a broad anti-discrimination statute applicable in areas of federal jurisdiction. Section 13 of the Human Rights Act is directed at the 'telephonic' communication of hate speech. In its current form, it states:

> 13. (1) It is a discriminatory practice for a person or a group of persons acting in concert to communicate telephonically or to cause to be so communicated, repeatedly, in whole or in part by means of the facilities of a telecommunication undertaking within the legislative authority of Parliament, any matter that is likely to expose a person or persons to hatred or contempt by reason of the fact that that person or those persons are identifiable on the basis of a prohibited ground of discrimination.
>
> (2) For greater certainty, subsection (1) applies in respect of a matter that is communicated by means of a computer or a group of interconnected or related computers, including the Internet, or any similar means of communication . . .[122]

The very specific nature of the prohibition contained in s 13 of the Canadian Human Rights Act 1977 – limited as it is to a particular mode of communication – is explained by the fact that in the mid-1970s, when federal human rights legislation was being drafted, telephone hate lines became a popular technique employed by right-wing racist organisations, particularly in the province of Ontario. In October 1976, following further media coverage and controversy regarding the use of a telephone hate line by the Western Guard in Toronto, the Minister of Justice explained that the new federal human rights legislation would 'contain certain provisions prohibiting the sending of hate messages over the telephone . . .'.[123] According to the Minister the new legislative measures were 'designed to provide an effective supplement to the provisions in the Criminal Code for combatting this particularly revolting . . . practice of tape-recorded, racially biased messages going out over the telephone'.[124] In his second reading speech on the Canadian Human Rights Bill, the Justice Minister observed:

---

121 Criminal Code, s 319(6).
122 Subsection 2 was added to s 13 in 2001: Anti-terrorism Act 2001, c. 41, s. 88. It confirmed what the Canadian Human Rights Tribunal had recently decided: that s 13 applied to internet-based communication (*Citron and Toronto Mayor's Committee v Zundel* (2002)). See, generally, Bailey, 2004.
123 Canada Parliament, Hansard (House of Commons), 25 October 1976, p 418.
124 Ibid.

I think those of us who were here in parliament at the time, felt that we had dealt with this issue in the amendments to the Criminal Code which were passed relating to hate, but new practices have emerged. Under this bill the sending of repeated hate messages over federally regulated telephones would be prohibited. The measure is more rigorous than section 281.1 [now s 319] of the Criminal Code, but it avoids—or I have endeavoured to draft it in such a way as to avoid interference with legitimate expression of opinion.[125]

In 1984, a House of Commons Special Committee on Visible Minorities[126] recommended a broadening of s 13 to allow the Canadian Human Rights Commission to deal with complaints of hate speech no matter how the 'message' was communicated. That is, the Committee recommended that the scope of s 13 be expanded beyond telephonic communication to the public dissemination of hate propaganda by any means. Section 13 was not amended in this way, and no such laws have subsequently been enacted at the national level. However, a number of provinces/territories have created a civil wrong of 'hate speech' in the context of anti-discrimination legislation.

In Alberta, British Columbia, Saskatchewan and the Northwest Territories it is unlawful to engage in public conduct that promotes hatred or contempt of any of the identified groups against whom discrimination is unlawful.[127] Section 3 of Alberta's Human Rights, Citizenship and Multiculturalism Act is illustrative:

(1) No person shall publish, issue or display or cause to be published, issued or displayed before the public any statement, publication, notice, sign, symbol, emblem or other representation that

    (a) indicates discrimination or an intention to discriminate against a person or class of persons, or

    (b) is likely to expose a person or a class of persons to hatred or contempt because of the race, religious beliefs, colour, gender, physical disability, mental disability, age, ancestry, place of origin,

---

125 Canada Parliament, Hansard (House of Commons), 11 February 1977, p 2976. Interestingly, one commentator has argued for the 'transfer' of the prohibition on telephonic hate messages from the Canadian Human Rights Act to the Criminal Code: Taylor, 1995.
126 Canada, House of Commons, 1984.
127 Alberta: s 2 of the Human Rights, Citizenship and Multiculturalism Act, RSA 2000, c H-14; British Columbia: s 7 of the Human Rights Code, RSBC 1996, c 210; Saskatchewan: s 14 of the Saskatchewan Human Rights Code, RSS 1979, c S-24.1; Northwest Territories: s 13 of the Consolidation Of Human Rights Act, RSNT 2002, c 18. A prohibition of this sort was added to Manitoba's human rights legislation in 1976, but repealed in 1987: McNamara, 2005, p 5.

marital status, source of income or family status of that person or class of persons.

(2) Nothing in this section shall be deemed to interfere with the free expression of opinion on any subject.

Anti-discrimination legislation in other Canadian jurisdictions contains only a narrow prohibition on the display of discriminatory 'signs and symbols'.[128]

The legal form of free speech and non-discrimination/ equality rights after the Canadian Charter of Rights and Freedoms 1982

Canada is unique among the four countries that are the subjects of the present study in that human rights on both sides of the hate speech/speech balance are constitutionally recognised in the Canadian Charter of Rights and Freedoms:

2. Everyone has the following fundamental freedoms:
...
(b) freedom of thought, belief, opinion and expression, including freedom of the press and other media of communication.

15. (1) Every individual is equal before and under the law and has the right to the equal protection and equal benefit of the law without discrimination and, in particular, without discrimination based on race, national or ethnic origin, colour, religion, sex, age or mental or physical disability.

27. This Charter shall be interpreted in a manner consistent with the preservation and enhancement of the multicultural heritage of Canadians.

In addition to these specific provisions, other aspects of the legal and institutional design for the protection of human rights in Canada (outlined in Chapter 1) are significant. First, s 1 of the Charter provides that the rights and freedoms protected by the Charter are not absolute: they can be subjected 'to such reasonable limits prescribed by law as can be demonstrably justified in a free and democratic society'. Second, subject to s 33 of the

---

128 See McNamara, 2005, pp 7–34. Two provinces have created statutory torts of 'racial defamation' – see s 19 of Manitoba's Defamation Act, RSM 1987, c D20; and British Columbia's Civil Rights Protection Act, RSBC 1996, c 49 – but these statutes are rarely invoked. See McNamara, 2005, pp 35–42.

Charter,[129] the Supreme Court of Canada is the authoritative arbiter of the meaning of the Charter's provisions and their implications for common law rules and legislation.

Moon has observed that:

> In its elaboration of freedom of expression under section 2(b) of the Charter, the Supreme Court of Canada has made some grand state ments about the freedom's value. The court has said that freedom of expression is 'an essential feature of Canadian parliamentary democracy'; that a 'democracy cannot exist without' it; that it is 'one of the fundamental concepts that has formed the basis for the historical development of the political, social and educational institutions of western society'; that it is 'the means by which the individual expresses his or her personal identity and sense of individuality'; that it is an important way of 'seeking and attaining truth'; and, more generally, that its 'vital importance ... cannot be over-emphasized'. While these statements are general and underdeveloped, they are understood by the court to add up to a substantial justification for the constitutional protection of freedom of expression.[130]

But as Moon points out, it does not follow that the category of speech protected as a constitutional right is as wide as the broad conception of 'freedom of expression as political ideal',[131] that is commonly asserted in the liberal tradition, including by opponents of hate speech laws. In Canada, this distinction must inevitably be drawn in the context of constitutional adjudication, given that the Charter embodies principles – including the rights and values recognised in ss 15 and 27 – with which the right to freedom of expression will sometimes collide.

The contribution that s 15 of the Charter has made to the achievement of genuine equality in Canada is keenly debated, and criticism of the Supreme Court of Canada's equality jurisprudence is prevalent in the academic literature.[132] Few would argue that s 15 has effected a dramatic transformation, especially outside of the context of direct discrimination.[133] But in the specific context of debate over the merits and limits of hate - speech laws, the Charter's general equality guarantee in s 15, along with its specific articulation of Canada's commitment to multiculturalism in s 27, have been important components of the judicial and broader public discourse.

---

129 See Chapter 1.
130 Moon, 2000, p 33 (case citations omitted).
131 Moon, 2000, p 219.
132 See Schneiderman and Sutherland, 1997; McAllister and Dodek, 2002; Magnet *et al*, 2003.
133 See, e.g., Porter, 2005.

The operation of hate speech laws

When the offence of wilful incitement of racial hatred was added to the Canadian Criminal Code in 1970, it appeared that the Canadian Parliament had taken a decisive step towards the effective regulation of racist hate speech. In response to concern about the deleterious impact of racist hate propaganda, and consistent with Canada's international obligations under Art 4 of ICERD, the Canadian Parliament had decided to bring to bear the 'toughest' of the regulatory mechanisms available – the criminal law.

But from its inception, the offence now defined by s 319(2) of the Code was infrequently prosecuted. The first reported case involving a charge of wilfully inciting hatred served to further emphasise the high threshold that would need to be met in order to secure criminal convictions. In *R v Buzzanga*,[134] the Ontario Court of Appeal overturned the conviction of two men who had been found guilty of inciting racial hatred after they handed out flyers vilifying the local French-Canadian community. (They were in fact members of that community and were aiming to garner support for the community in relation to a controversial new French language school.) Martin JA held that the inclusion of 'wilfully' in the statutory definition meant that the prosecution had to prove that the accused subjectively sought to promote hatred or foresaw that this was very likely. This could not be said of the defendants, given that they had a contrary intention. Martin JA noted that:

> ... the use of the word 'wilfully' ... reflects Parliament's policy to strike a balance in protecting the competing social interests of freedom of expression on the one hand, and public order and group reputation on the other hand.[135]

Three years later, the formal legal context in which decisions about Canadian hate speech were to be made, changed significantly, with the enactment of the Canadian Charter and Rights and Freedoms in 1982. During the 1980s, attempts to enforce Canada's two primary national hate speech laws – s 319(2) of the Criminal Code, and s 13 of the Canadian Human Rights Act – attracted widespread media coverage, generated considerable controversy, and eventually led, in 1990, to Supreme Court of Canada rulings on the constitutional validity of both statutory provisions.[136]

In 1984, Jim Keegstra was charged with wilfully promoting hatred contrary to the Criminal Code. Keegstra was a high-school teacher in Eckville, Alberta, from the early 1970s until 1982, when he was dismissed. Keegstra

---

134 *R v Buzzanga* (1979).
135 Ibid, p 382.
136 *R v Keegstra* (1991).

was accused of communicating anti-Semitic statements to his students.[137] Keegstra was convicted in 1985 in the Alberta Court of Queen's Bench, sentenced to five months imprisonment and fined $5,000. He appealed successfully to the Alberta Court of Appeal on the basis that s 319(2) offended rights guaranteed by the Canadian Charter of Rights and Freedoms, including the right to freedom of expression in s 2(b). The Crown appealed to the Supreme Court of Canada.[138]

In 1985, Donald Andrews and Robert Smith – members of the Nationalist Party of Canada – were charged with wilfully promoting hatred, after publishing and circulating anti-Semitic and racist material. They were convicted in the District Court of Ontario and sentenced to prison for 12 months and 7 months, respectively. Appeals to the Ontario Court of Appeal were dismissed (although the sentences were reduced to three months and one month). Andrews and Smith appealed to the Supreme Court of Canada.[139]

In 1979, the Canadian Human Rights Commission received complaints about an anti-Semitic recorded telephone message produced and advertised in Toronto by the Western Guard Party, headed by John Ross Taylor. A tribunal established by the Commission found that the message breached s 13 of the Canadian Human Rights Act and ordered Taylor and the Western Guard Party to refrain from communicating the message. They did not, and were convicted of contempt in the Federal Court of Canada. Taylor was jailed for one year and the Western Guard Party was fined $5,000. Taylor submitted a communication to the United Nations Human Rights Committee alleging that, by its enforcement of s 13 of the Canadian Human Rights Act against him, Canada was in breach of its obligations under the ICCPR, including with respect to the right to freedom of expression in Art 19. The Committee ruled that the communication was inadmissible, because the conduct in relation to which Taylor sought the protection of the ICCPR – the advocacy of racial or religious hatred – was conduct that, by virtue of Art 20 of the ICCPR, Canada had an obligation to prohibit.[140]

In 1983, the Commission sought further orders in the Federal Court on the basis that the Western Guard was still communicating anti-Semitic telephone messages. Taylor argued unsuccessfully in the Federal Court and the Federal Court of Appeal that s 13 of the Canadian Human Rights Act was invalid by virtue of inconsistency with s 2(b) of the Charter. Taylor appealed to the Supreme Court of Canada.[141]

The Supreme Court of Canada handed down its decisions in *Keegstra, Andrews* and *Taylor* concurrently on 13 December 1990. By a 4:3 majority,

---

137 See Bercuson and Wertheimer, 1985.
138 *R v Keegstra* (1991).
139 *R v Andrews* (1990).
140 *Taylor v Canada* (1983), para 8.
141 *Canadian Human Rights Commission v Taylor* (1990).

led by Dickson CJ, the Supreme Court of Canada ruled that: s 319(2) of the Criminal Code[142] and s 13 of the Canadian Human Rights Act[143] did infringe the right to freedom of expression protected by s 2(b) of the Charter, but that the limitation was a reasonable one for the purpose of s 1 of the Charter. Both statutory hate speech provisions were, therefore, constitutionally valid. The minority, led by McLachlin J, concluded that neither s 319(2) nor s 13 was a reasonable limit on the right to freedom of expression.[144]

In *Keegstra*, Dickson CJ emphasised 'the principles of equality and the inherent dignity of all persons that infuse both international human rights and the Charter'.[145] He noted:

> CERD and ICCPR demonstrate that the prohibition of hate promoting expression is considered to be not only compatible with a signatory nation's guarantee of human rights, but is as well an obligatory aspect of this guarantee.[146]

Hate speech was characterised as having only a 'tenuous connection ... with s 2(b) values'.[147]

The Chief Justice acknowledged the limitations of criminal legislation as a mechanism for 'advancing the goals of equality and multicultural tolerance in Canada...',[148] observing that '[i]t is important in my opinion, not to hold any illusions about the ability of this one provision [s 319(2)] to rid our society of hate propaganda and its associated harms'.[149] Nonetheless, such was 'the enormous importance of the objective fueling s 319(2)' that 'even the severe response of criminal prohibition' was justified.[150]

In *Taylor*, a similar conclusion was reached about s 13 of the Canadian Human Rights Act: the prohibition on messages promoting hatred or contempt did infringe s 2(b) of the Charter, but was a reasonable limit saved from invalidity by s 1:

> In seeking to prevent the harms caused by hate propaganda, the objective behind s 13(1) is obviously one of pressing and substantial importance sufficient to warrant some limitation upon the freedom of expression. It

---

142 *R v Keegstra* (1991); *R v Andrews* (1990).
143 *Canadian Human Rights Commission v Taylor* (1990).
144 See, generally, Moon, 2000, ch 5; McGoldrick and O'Donnell, 1998; Elman, 1994; Weinrib, 1991.
145 *R v Keegstra* (1991), p 48.
146 Ibid.
147 Ibid, p 79.
148 Ibid, 71.
149 Ibid.
150 Ibid, p 73.

is worth stressing, however, the heightened importance attached to this objective by reason of international human rights instruments to which Canada is a party and ss 15 and 27 of the Charter.[151]

The values reflected in ss 15 and 27 were described by Dickson CJ as 'linchpin Charter principles'.[152]

The majority rejected the argument that the phrase 'hatred or contempt' in s 13 of the Canadian Human Rights Act set too low or too vague a harm threshold. It endorsed the Canadian Human Rights Tribunal's interpretation[153] of the threshold reflected in the words of s 13 as referring 'to unusually strong and deep-felt emotions of detestation, calumny and vilification'.[154]

Significantly, in terms of the broader questions of the relative merits of *criminal* hate speech laws and *civil* hate speech laws (debate over which has been especially prominent in Australia, see below), Dickson CJ continued:

> To the extent that the section [s 13] may impose a slightly broader limit upon freedom of expression than does s 319(2) of the Criminal Code, however, I am of the view that the conciliatory bent of a human rights statute renders such a limit more acceptable than would be the case with a criminal provision.[155]

In contrast to what has been characterised as the majority's 'harm-based approach',[156] the minority adopted a strong 'pro-speech' position. In *Keegstra*, McLachlin J conceded that '[h]ate literature presents a great challenge to our conceptions about the value of free expression'.[157] Of two possible normative reference points for determining the scope and nature of the Canadian Charter's protection of free speech, McLachlin J noted that the 'conception of freedom of expression' reflected in international and European human rights laws was quite different from the way in which free speech was conceived in the United States' First Amendment jurisprudence:

> Both the American and international approach recognize that freedom of expression is not absolute, and must yield in some circumstances to other values. The divergence lies in the way the limits are determined. On the international approach, the objective of suppressing hatred appears

---

151 *Canadian Human Rights Commission v Taylor* (1990), p 919 per Dickson CJ.
152 Ibid, p 920.
153 *Nealy v Johnston* (1989).
154 *Canadian Human Rights Commission v Taylor* (1990), p 928 per Dickson CJ.
155 Ibid, pp 928–9.
156 See New Zealand Human Rights Commission, 2004a, paras 2–7.
157 *R v Keegstra* (1991), p 92.

to be sufficient to override freedom of expression. In the United States, it is necessary to go much further and show clear and present danger before free speech can be overridden.[158]

In addressing the implications of s 2(b) of the Charter for s 319(2) of the Criminal Code and s 13 of the Canadian Human Rights Act, the minority adopted an approach that drew heavily on the American-style enlarged conception of protected speech. McLachlin J did not accept that the scope of s 2(b) should be read down by virtue of the inclusion in the Charter of s 15 (equality) and s 27 (multiculturalism). To the extent that there was a perceived conflict between s 2(b) and s 15, it was 'a conflict, ... not between *rights*, but rather between philosophies'.[159] Section 27 was characterised as a mere 'principle of construction'.[160]

In *Keegstra*, McLachlin J concluded that s 319(2) was not a reasonable limit on the right to freedom of expression and so was not saved by s 1 of the Charter:

> Accepting that the objectives of the legislation are valid and important and potentially capable of overriding the guarantee of freedom of expression, I cannot conclude that the means chosen to achieve them – the criminalization of the potential or foreseeable promotion of hatred – are proportionate to those ends.[161]

In *Taylor*, McLachlin J concluded that s 13 also failed to satisfy the requirements of s 1 of the Charter. 'The section is too broad and too invasive; it overreaches its objectives and ultimately cannot be justified by them.'[162]

Canada is the only one of the four countries that are the subject of the present study to have had the 'benefit' of judicial assessment of the protected free speech/unlawful hate speech by the supreme appellate/constitutional court in the country. Of course it is not all that surprising that the issue came before Canada's highest court relatively quickly. In the UK, New Zealand and Australia, there is no equivalent of the Supreme Court of Canada's express power to strike down federal or provincial legislation on the basis of Charter incompatibility.

In this context, the Supreme Court's decisions in *Keegstra, Andrews* and *Taylor* might have been expected to substantially resolve doubts about the legitimacy of Canada's speech laws. This was especially important in the

---

158 *R v Keegstra* (1991), p 100.
159 Ibid, p 108.
160 Ibid, p 110.
161 Ibid, p 133.
162 *Canadian Human Rights Commission v Taylor* (1990), p 970.

case of s 319(2) of the Criminal Code, given that there was evidence prior to 1990 of reluctance on the part of some Attorneys General to consent to prosecutions.[163] However, partly because there was such fundamental disagreement among the judges of the Supreme Court of Canada about the constitutional validity of Canada's national hate speech legislation, the trio of 1990 cases did not conclusively settle the question of where the line should be drawn between free speech protected by the Charter and hate speech justifiably subjected to statutory prohibition. The decisions in *Keegstra Andrews* and *Taylor* did at least resolve the formal question of the constitutional validity of s 319(2) of the Criminal Code and s 13 of the Canadian Human Rights Act. Despite the narrow margin by which these two provisions were upheld, since 1990, the Supreme Court has shown no inclination to revisit the question of validity.[164] Constitutional challenges to the validity of provincial hate speech laws have also failed, with appellate courts applying the principles and approach endorsed by the majority in *Keegstra* and *Taylor*.[165]

Since 1990, provincial authorities have launched a small number of criminal prosecutions under s 319(2) of the Criminal Code. For example, in 1994 the Appeal Division of the Prince Edward Island Supreme Court upheld the conviction of Michel Safadi for wilfully promoting hatred against Jews.[166] Over a number of years Safadi had circulated letters that vilified Christianity. Safadi had made the letters 'appear to originate from a Jewish source with the intention that their contents would promote in the letters' recipients hatred against the Jews'.[167]

In 2001, the Court of Appeal for Ontario dismissed an appeal against Mark Harding's conviction for wilfully promoting hatred against Muslims.[168] During 1997, Harding, 'a self-described Christian pastor',[169] had distributed pamphlets and made available recorded telephone messages that included seriously derogatory assertions about Muslims in general – including that they were 'violent and hateful', and 'underneath their false sheep's clothing, are raging wolves, seeking whom they may devour, and Toronto is definitely on their hit list'.[170]

In 2005, David Ahenakew, a prominent Saskatchewan First Nations politician was convicted of wilfully promoting hatred against Jews.[171] In 2002, at a

---

163 Elman, 1994; Ross, 1994.
164 See, e.g., *R v Krymowski* (2005).
165 See, e.g., the Saskatchewan Court of Appeal's decision concerning s 14 of the Saskatchewan Human Rights Code: *Saskatchewan Human Rights Commission v Bell* (1994).
166 *R v Safadi* (1994).
167 *R v Safadi* (1993), p 80.
168 *R v Harding* (2001).
169 Ibid, para 1.
170 Ibid, para 7.
171 *R v Ahenakew* (2005).

conference organised by the Federation of Saskatchewan Indian Nations, Ahenakew made a speech and later gave a media interview that included a number of anti-Semitic comments, including the assertion that the 'Second World War was created by the Jews'[172] and a reference to Jews as 'a disease' that had been determined to take over Germany.[173]

These examples of post-*Keegstra* prosecutions under s 319(2) of the Criminal Code suggest that while they continue to be used sparingly, decisions about the enforcement of Canada's criminal hate speech laws are no longer complicated by the high levels of uncertainty and disagreement about the propriety of applying criminal sanctions to harmful speech that prevailed prior to 1990. Of course, s 319(2) prosecutions still generate controversy, and a degree of resistance is sometimes discernible in the approach of trial judges. For example, in *R v Elms* (2005), the Ontario Superior Court of Justice upheld a Crown appeal against the acquittal of Mark Elms on charges of wilfully promoting hatred against a number of identified groups by distributing CDs at a 'skinhead' concert at a Toronto bar. The CDs contained song titles and lyrics that promoted hatred of Jews, Blacks, Hispanics, East Asians and Muslims. Hawkins J ruled that the trial judge had erred in requiring the Crown to prove that Elms was *selling* the CDs, given that s 319(2) was not limited to this particular form of distribution. A new trial was ordered. In *R v Krymowski* (2005), the Supreme Court of Canada upheld a Crown appeal against the acquittal of six persons charged with promoting hatred against Roma at a demonstration against a number of Roma refugees who were seeking permission to remain in Canada. The trial judge dismissed the case on the basis that whereas the Crown alleged that the defendants had wilfully promoted hatred against *Roma*, the conduct in question – including the display of the following slogans: 'Honk if you hate Gypsies; You're a cancer on Canada' – was directed at '*Gypsies*'. The Supreme Court ruled unanimously that the trial judge had erred in failing to take judicial notice of the fact that the terms 'Roma' and 'Gypsy' were commonly used interchangeably.[174]

Notably, in both of these cases, the appeal process was employed successfully by the Crown to invoke the authoritative voice of appellate courts. In both cases, additional evidentiary hurdles introduced at the trial stage, which effectively made it harder for the Crown to secure convictions, were removed as incompatible with the terms of s 319(2) and the legitimate scope of the statutory prohibition thereby imposed on hate speech.

In the case of the hate speech provisions contained in the Human Rights Act, since *Taylor*, the Canadian Human Rights Commission has continued

---

172 *R v Ahenakew* (2005), para 8.
173 Ibid, para 11. At the time of writing Ahenakew had commenced an appeal in the Saskatchewan Court of Queen's Bench (Bernhardt 2006).
174 *R v Krymowski* (2005), para 24.

to enforce the limited prohibition contained in s 13 against the activities of organised right-wing groups and the racist and homophobic hate speech in which they engage via telephone and the internet.[175] The Canadian Human Rights Tribunal has continued to reject arguments that s 13 should be construed narrowly or that its constitutional validity should be re-assessed.[176] In March 2006, the Tribunal found that the communication of racist hate speech via the World Wide Web involved a breach of s 13 of the Canadian Human Rights Act, not only by the individuals responsible for the specific websites in question, but also by the internet service provider that hosted the websites.[177]

Provincial hate speech laws[178]

The significance of the Supreme Court of Canada's 1990 constitutional jurisprudence on the relationship between hate speech laws and s 2(b) of the Canadian Charter of Rights and Freedoms has not been limited to national legislation. Adjudicators addressing alleged violations of provincial hate-speech prohibitions in Saskatchewan, British Columbia and Alberta have located their deliberations firmly in the shadow of *Keegstra* and *Taylor*.[179] This is not surprising. What *is* surprising is that this context has not generated the relative confidence and clarity that has generally been observable in the post-1990 operation of s 319(2) of the Criminal Code and s 13 of the Canadian Human Rights Act (albeit, sometimes only as a result of appellate review). Tribunals and courts have generally had little time for 'head-on' challenges to the constitutional validity of provincial hate speech laws. Arguments along these lines have been consistently rejected. However, one of the most striking features to emerge from an examination of post-1990 adjudications under provincial hate speech laws is that the 'Canadian-style' free speech scrutiny adopted by the majority of the Supreme Court of Canada in *Keegstra* and *Taylor* has had a significant, though somewhat uneven, impact on the resolution of complaints, even where the specific issue of Charter/constitutional validity has not been squarely before the tribunal or court.

One of the important threads that runs consistently, even if not universally, through the recent history of adjudication under provincial hate speech laws is a lingering unease about the legitimacy of legislative restrictions on the

---

175 Section 13 proceedings have been taken against groups such as the Heritage Front, the Manitoba Knights of the Ku Klux Klan, the Church of Christ in Israel and Canadian Liberty Net, as well as Ernst Zundel.
176 *Schnell v Machiavelli and Associates Emprize Inc and Micka* (2002).
177 *Warman v Kulbashian* (2006).
178 This section draws on material previously published in McNamara, 2005.
179 See, generally, McNamara, 2005, pp 48–81.

communication of ideas – even ideas of racism, homophobia or other forms of prejudice directed at a particular group. This unease has been manifested in the preference of a number of judicial and quasi-judicial decision-makers for a narrow construction of the scope of provincial hate speech prohibitions, particularly in those jurisdictions where the legislature has expanded the prohibition beyond the traditional, and reasonably innocuous, prohibition on discriminatory signs and symbols.[180] Even in cases where this approach has been taken, some complainants have been able to satisfy the elevated threshold for establishing that the conduct in question was unlawful. However, in a number of cases, the direct effect of the raising of the legal threshold has been that the complainant, and the wider community which the complainant represented, have been denied legal redress. In terms of the more general and long-term impact, the tendency towards a narrow construction of provincial hate speech prohibitions in public adjudications sends a powerful symbolic message to the broader community about the practical breadth of the category of protected speech upon which hate speech laws should not be permitted to impinge.

This tendency towards a restrictive interpretation of hate speech prohibitions is not universal. Beneath this dominant thread is a counter-tendency, observable in a smaller number of cases, towards giving legislation a fuller or even expansive definition, without apparent concern for the consequences for freedom of expression. In fact, surprisingly, in a context where the jurisprudential landscape for the right to freedom of expression has been well developed in the last 15 years, there is still a notable amount of inconsistency and divergence among adjudicators with respect to central questions about how similar legislative restrictions on hate speech should be interpreted in light of 'Charter' and free speech sensitivities. This finding demonstrates that it by no means follows that formal resolution of the *legal* (or constitutional) status of competing sets of values – in this case, 'free speech' and 'equality' – will necessarily put an end to wider moral and political debates about the relative importance of those values.[181] To the extent that Canadian legal culture continues to be characterised by a degree of ambivalence about the legitimate scope of legislative restrictions on hate speech – particularly at the generally less serious end of the spectrum occupied by provincial statutes – the associated tensions are reflected in the interpretive strategies employed by adjudicators, including the adoption of an approach to statutory interpretation, which borrows heavily, though not always helpfully, from the Supreme Court of Canada's constitutional validity jurisprudence. The following example is illustrative.

180 For examples, see McNamara, 2005, pp 48–81.
181 See Moon, 2000, p 219.

Kane v Alberta Report

On 31 October 1997, an article appeared in the *Alberta Report* magazine entitled 'A Canmore Mall Project Ends in a Bitter Feud'. The article addressed events that had occurred during the negotiations between a Canadian builder, Fred Schickedanz, and an American promoter, Benson Flanzbaum, associated with a failed commercial property development. The article included references to the amount of gold jewellery worn by Mr Flanzbaum as well as to his 'open shirts' and 'hirsute chest'. The article also contained the following passage:

> One professional planner comments on the failed project: 'North American commercial real estate is dominated by firms that often happen to be Jewish owned [eg Oshawa and Canmore Development]. The retail sector is much the same. Like cliques everywhere, some of these people tend to deal with each other, and Mr. Schickedanz is an outsider.'[182]

A complaint was lodged with the Alberta Human Rights and Citizenship Commission by the Jewish Defence League of Canada and Harvey Kane in May 1998, alleging that the publication of the article contravened what was then s 2 of the Alberta Human Rights, Citizenship and Multiculturalism Act 1996 (now s 3 – see above). After attempts to resolve the complaint by conciliation failed, the complaint was dismissed. This decision was appealed and the matter was referred to the Alberta Human Rights and Citizenship Commission Panel for determination. Before determining the merits of the complaint the Panel submitted a number of questions of law to the Alberta Court of Queen's Bench for an opinion.

The questions of law considered by the Court of Queen's Bench that are relevant for present purposes were:

3. Can a breach of s 2(1) of the *Act* be found in the face of a defence based on s 2(2)? That is, does s 2(2) bar the Panel from finding a breach of 2(1) when the alleged wrongdoer can establish that he/she is freely expressing his/her opinion?
4. If s 2(2) is not a bar to finding a breach of s 2(1), can s 2(2) be used after a finding of breach of s 2(1) in order to justify that breach?
5. What standards must the Panel apply to determine whether a representation 'is likely to expose a person or a class of persons to hatred or contempt'? Are different considerations applied to questions of 'contempt' as opposed to questions of 'hatred'?

---

182 *Kane v Alberta Report* (2001), para 2.

In relation to the significance of s 2(2) of the Act (that is, questions 3 and 4) Rooke J opined that s 2(2) provides neither a defence nor a justification for a breach of s 2(1). He observed that several cases have established that protection from hate/contempt-based expression 'is a pressing and substantial objective, and is justified in a free and democratic society'.[183] If the protection afforded by legislative restrictions on hate speech could simply be overridden by allowing a respondent to place his/her conduct outside the scope of the prohibition by showing that s/he was just expressing an opinion, the rights would be meaningless and defeat the purpose of the legislation. Rooke J noted that 'excluding opinions from the reach of s 2(1) would go a long way in defeating the purpose of the legislation'.[184]

According to Rooke J, although s 2(2) does not create a defence, it does require that in the interpretation and application of s 2(1) freedom of expression must be balanced against the objective of eliminating discrimination.[185] This involves a two-step process. First, the terms 'hatred' and 'contempt' must be interpreted with an awareness of the need to achieve this balance – ensuring that only serious harms are caught by the prohibition. Second, 'once a *prima [facie] breach* is found, the Panel must go on to specifically balance freedom of expression against the particular breach'.[186] Apart from stating that an '*Oakes* analysis'[187] was not necessary unless the constitutional validity of the legislation was challenged, it is not clear from the reasons of Rooke J what is involved in the 'second step' inquiry mandated by s 2(b), other than 'an examination of the nature of the statement in a full, contextual manner which recognizes the objectives and goals of the legislation and is *Charter* sensitive'.[188]

On the meaning of the phrase 'likely to expose ... to hatred or contempt' (question 5) Rooke J first endorsed the *Taylor*[189] interpretation of the harm threshold established by the reference to 'hatred or contempt'. In determining the meaning of 'likely to expose', Rooke J considered and rejected the approach adopted by the British Columbia Human Rights Tribunal in *Canadian Jewish Congress v North Shore Free Press Ltd and Collins* (*CJC*)[190] – which focused on whether the conduct was likely to *increase the risk* of exposure to hatred or contempt – on the basis that this would set too low a threshold:

---

183 *Kane v Alberta Report* (2001), para 67.
184 Ibid, para 70.
185 Ibid, para 73, following Dickson CJ in *Canadian Human Rights Commission v Taylor* (1990).
186 Ibid, para 77.
187 A test of constitutional validity developed by the Supreme Court of Canada in *R v Oakes* (1986) based on s 1 of the Charter, and employed by the Court in *R v Keegstra* (1990) and *Canadian Human Rights Commission v Taylor* (1990).
188 *Kane v Alberta Report* (2001), para 85.
189 *Canadian Human Rights Commission v Taylor* (1990).
190 *Canadian Jewish Congress v North Shore Free Press Ltd and Collins* (1997).

The test proposed in *CJC* would admit of a breach where there is a 1% chance of being exposed to hatred or contempt which is increased by .01%. This would effectively allow a finding of a contravention of the Act, despite that the target group is still not 'likely' to be exposed to hatred or contempt. I do not believe this is what is intended by the Act.[191]

There is a certain irony in this observation. In *CJC* the British Columbia Human Rights Tribunal was at great pains to interpret s 7 of the BC Human Rights Code in a manner that was highly sensitive to the need to minimally infringe on free speech, and yet the substance of Rooke J's criticism is that the Tribunal adopted an interpretation of equivalent legislation, which infringed too heavily on the right to freedom of expression. This difference of opinion demonstrates that there is considerable scope for divergence when it comes to the articulation and application of free speech sensitivity while setting the parameters of legislative restrictions on hate speech.

Rooke J preferred to articulate an 'analytical framework rather than a template to be mechanically applied in every case',[192] but expressed approval of the following test:

> Does the communication itself express hatred or contempt of a person or group on a basis of one or more of the listed grounds? Would a reasonable person, informed about the context, understand the message as expressing hatred or contempt?
>
> Assessed in its context, is the likely effect of the communication to make it more acceptable to others to manifest hatred or contempt against the person or group concerned? Would a reasonable person consider it more likely than not to expose members of the target group to hatred and contempt?[193]

It is interesting that even as he expressed doubts about the necessity of a single 'test', Rooke J nonetheless felt compelled to spell out what he considered to be an acceptable approach in just such terms. This tendency to rely heavily on legal 'tests', which substantially augment the wording of the legislation – a distinctive feature of Canadian hate speech cases – appears to be a direct consequence of the high degree of '*Charter* consciousness' and free speech sensitivity that is associated with such determinations in Canada. It is not clear that this heavily 'legalistic' approach is an effective device for

---

191 *Kane v Alberta Report* (2001), para 122.
192 Ibid, para 124.
193 Ibid, para 125.

achieving the balancing of interests and values which are at the heart of the interpretation and application exercise.

The Alberta Human Rights and Citizenship Panel accepted that the Opinion provided by Rooke J was binding. Turning to the facts of the case, the Panel found that the article contained 'a very powerful image or caricature that amounts to a negative stereotype of Jewish people, more specifically of Jewish businessmen'.[194] The message of the article went far beyond that of a failed business deal; the focus was on the religion of Mr Flanzbaum. The image conveyed was considered in the context of the Jewish experience, which included, as LaForest J had noted in the Supreme Court of Canada's decision in *Ross v New Brunswick School District No. 15*,[195] the fact that Jews are 'an historically disadvantaged group that has endured persecution on the largest scale'. It was further noted 'that many of the leading *Charter* cases on freedom of expression and discrimination involve anti-Semitic communications'.[196] According to the Panel, the article in question subtly reinforced a notion of Jews being rich, powerful and conspiring to control business to the exclusion of others.

The Panel observed that the fact that a publication contains anti-Semitic messages does not necessarily mean that it conveys hatred or contempt as per s 2(1)(b) of the Act. It held that although the article in the *Alberta Report* perpetuated a damaging stereotype of Jewish people, it did 'not express the extreme level of communication required to amount to hatred or contempt'.[197] However, it did 'indicate discrimination' and was therefore unlawful by virtue of the alternative harm/risk threshold in s 2(1)(a) of the Act. The Panel held that 'the stereotype of Jews contained in the Art indicates discrimination because it discloses a discriminatory belief or attitude that will reinforce prejudice against them'.[198]

The Panel noted that in reaching its overall decision it had 'carefully balanced the interests of freedom from discrimination and that of the freedom of expression . . .'.[199] It found that s 2(1) was 'directed towards achieving such pressing and sufficiently important objectives that it warrants limiting freedom of expression in this case'.[200] In the present case, the respondent's freedom of expression was minimally impaired – the respondents could have avoided the reach of the restriction imposed by s 2(1) simply by excluding the final quotation (attributed to the unnamed 'professional planner') from the article. The Panel made no order as to remedies, being satisfied that the

---

194 *Kane and Jewish Defence League of Canada v Alberta Report et al* (2002), p 11.
195 *Ross v New Brunswick School District No 15* (1996).
196 *Kane v Alberta Report* (2002), p 12.
197 Ibid, p 13.
198 Ibid, p 16.
199 Ibid, p 17.
200 Ibid.

respondents' offer of space in the magazine in which the complaints could raise their concerns was sufficient.[201]

Key features of the Canadian balance

During the 1980s the Charter of Rights and Freedoms cast a significant shadow over the operation of Canadian hate speech laws, manifesting in the form of uncertainty and disagreement about whether legislative restrictions on hate speech could be reconciled with a constitutionally entrenched right to freedom of expression. Since the decisions in *Keegstra, Andrews* and *Taylor* in 1990, the Charter's direct influence has been replaced by the 'shadow effect' of the Supreme Court of Canada's hate speech/free speech jurisprudence. Decisions regarding the scope and application of hate speech laws are made within the terms of the balance struck by the Supreme Court. Free speech sensitivity remains a significant normative influence on decision-making processes in relation to specific allegations of hate speech, but that influence is filtered through the lens of the Court's hate speech/free speech jurisprudence. The most obvious and predictable feature of the post-1990 environment is that the *validity* of hate speech laws is, for the most part, a non-issue. In some cases, validity arguments are still advanced in the context of litigation – most often in the case of provincial hate speech laws on which the Supreme Court of Canada has not specifically ruled – but they tend to be routinely rejected by adjudicators.

Another feature of the post-1990 environment is less predictable, but perhaps of even greater significance in light of this book's underlying inquiry into the impact of legal form on the construction and resolution of human rights controversies. Significantly, and reflecting the characteristic features of the legal form in which human rights are protected in Canada, the authoritative terms of the hate speech/free speech balance were resolved judicially, and articulated in the distinctive legal discourse of the Supreme Court of Canada's Charter jurisprudence. Even though the question of constitutional validity has been settled, it is often possible to continue to observe the tensions and disagreements that prompted validity challenges in the first place, not far beneath the surface of the adjudication process. Specifically, adjudicators

---

201 The Panel's decision was later overturned by the Alberta Court of Queen's Bench (*Alberta Report v Alberta Human Rights and Citizenship Commission* (2002)), on the basis that the Panel had erred in taking into account expert evidence presented in two British Columbia decisions dealing with equivalent legislative provisions – *Canadian Jewish Congress v North Shore Free Press Ltd and Collins* (1997); *Abrams v North Shore Free Press Ltd and Collins* (1999) – without bringing this to the attention of the parties and giving them an opportunity to make submissions in relation to the admissibility of, or weight to be attached to, the evidence. Clark J ordered that the matter be remitted back to the Alberta Human Rights Panel for rehearing. However, the matter was settled.

in hate speech cases commonly draw on the principles, rules, tests and techniques used by Supreme Court of Canada to resolve the question of constitutional validity, when called upon to interpret the scope of statutory hate speech prohibitions and their application in particular instances. The result, as illustrated by the decision in *Kane v Alberta Report*,[202] is a cautious, rule-based and relatively *legalistic* approach to interpretation and adjudication. This is not an approach that necessarily results in the adoption of a restrictive scope for hate speech prohibitions, but it does tend to exaggerate the extent to which what are unavoidably political judgments can be reduced to technical quasi-constitutional decisions.

One of the expectations that is commonly associated with the constitutionally entrenched model of human rights protection is the opportunity for the judiciary to provide authoritative resolution of controversies over how competing rights and interests should be balanced. But one of the by-products of this approach is that subsequent decision-making in relation to the subject of controversy is influenced, not only by the outcome, but also by the nature of the discursive style of its resolution. This may militate against broader resolution of the underlying tension – which invariably lingers beyond the moment of 'official' resolution, as it has in the case of continued political disagreement in Canada about the legitimacy of legislative restrictions on hate speech.[203]

New Zealand

History and current form of hate speech laws

Legislative restriction on racist hate speech was first introduced as part of the Race Relations Act 1971, and was enacted in response to New Zealand's international obligations under the ICERD, which New Zealand signed in 1965 and ratified in 1972. Section 25 of the Act provided that:

> Any person who publishes or distributes written material or who broadcasts or speaks publicly in a threatening, abusive or insulting manner

---

202 See also the approach to the construction of the hate speech prohibition in the Saskatchewan Human Rights Code (s 14) endorsed by the Saskatchewan Court of Appeal in *Saskatchewan Human Rights Commission v Bell* (1994): discussed in McNamara, 2005, pp 54–8.

203 See, e.g., the controversy surrounding the decision of a Saskatchewan Board of Inquiry that a newspaper advertisement that 'consisted of four passages from the Bible in red ink, followed by an equal sign and two stick men holding hands inside a red circle with a line through the stick men' breached s 14 of the Saskatchewan Human Rights Code in that it was likely to expose homosexuals to hatred or ridicule: *Hellquist v Owens and Sterling Newspapers* Co (2001). This decisions was affirmed by the Saskatchewan Court of Queen's Bench in *Hellquist v* Owens (2002), but subsequently overturned by the Saskatchewan Court of Appeal: *Owens v Saskatchewan Human Rights Commission* (2006).

with intent to excite hostility or ill will against, or bring into contempt or ridicule, any group of persons in New Zealand on the grounds of their colour, race or national origins is committing an offence.

Although the Race Relations Office received a significant number of complaints alleging breaches of s 25 during the 1970s, it had no jurisdiction to use its investigation and conciliation functions in relation to what was a criminal offence (unlike the racial discrimination provisions elsewhere in the Race Relations Act 1971, which provided for victim-initiated complaints and civil remedies).[204] Very few criminal prosecutions for the offence defined by s 25 were undertaken by the police and prosecutorial authorities.[205]

In response to dissatisfaction with the operational limitations of s 25, the New Zealand Parliament amended the Race Relations Act 1971 in 1977, with the addition of a new s 9A:

(1) It shall be unlawful for any person –

    (a) to publish or distribute written matter which is threatening, abusive, or insulting, or to broadcast by means of radio or television words which are threatening, abusive, or insulting; or

    (b) to use in any public place . . . or within the hearing of persons in any such place or at any meeting to which the public are invited or have access, words which are threatening, abusive, or insulting

– being matter or words likely to excite hostility or ill will against, or bring into contempt or ridicule, any group of persons in New Zealand on the ground of colour, race, or ethnic or national origins of that group of persons.

Section 9A quickly became the most frequently invoked provision of the Race Relations Act 1971. In the decade between 1979 and 1989, the Office of Race Relations (RRO) received 1,065 s 9A complaints, representing more than 60 per cent of the total number of complaints under all provisions of the Act.[206] As Walter Hirsh (Race Relations Conciliator, 1985–1989) has explained, dissatisfaction soon resurfaced – that the Act's hate speech provisions were now *over*-inclusive:

> Problems with the section began very soon after its introduction in 1977. The public, the media and many politicians soon began to express discontent with the section. The RRO was flooded with complaints under the section and several cases under 9A gained comprehensive national

---

204 Hirsh, 1990.
205 See, e.g., *King-Ansell v Police* (1979).
206 Hirsh, 1990, p 19.

media coverage, which in some cases did little more than bring the Office into disrepute. Discontent grew steadily in the 1980s . . .[207]

In December 1989, the New Zealand Parliament repealed s 9A of the Race Relations Act.

Hirsh has suggested that free speech sensitivity made an indirect, though significant, contribution to the demise of s 9A, because it had been influential in the decision to limit the enforcement powers of the RRO to a conciliation paradigm:

> So, what went wrong with Section 9A? On the face of it, the section seemed to be very suitable. However, the Section reflected a reluctance by Parliament to interfere with the freedom of speech as indicated . . . [by New Zealand's ICCPR Art 20 reservation]. This position has been strongly maintained in New Zealand. The provisions of Section 9A granted some remedy to groups of people, but not to individuals. The section gave jurisdiction to the Race Relations Conciliator and ascribed the very difficult task of seeking a settlement between parties in cases where a complaint was found to have substance. My experience, and that of my predecessor, showed that achieving a settlement in Section 9A cases was extremely difficult. Time and time again we had been unsuccessful in convincing people, and the media management in particular, that they had acted in a racist manner and that they should do or say something by way of amends. So unsuccessful had we been in conciliation in Section 9A cases that we began to wonder if it was possible.[208]

Matters could be referred to a tribunal for adjudication (at the time, the Equal Opportunities Tribunal), either by the Race Relations Conciliator or the complainant, but this step was rarely taken. In *Neal v Sunday News*,[209] the Tribunal ruled that a newspaper article that contained jokes which 'imputed stupidity or general inferiority to Australians',[210] did not breach s 9A because it was not likely to 'excite hostility or ill will' against Australians or expose them to 'contempt or ridicule'.[211]

In 1993 the Race Relations Act 1971 and the Human Rights Commission Act 1977 were replaced by the Human Rights Act 1993. Section 25 of the original 1971 Act (creating a criminal offence of inciting racial disharmony)

---

207 Hirsh, 1990, p 21. See also, Huscroft, 1995, p 194.
208 Hirsh, 1990, pp 21–2.
209 *Neal v Sunday News Auckland Newspaper Publications Ltd* (1985).
210 Ibid, p 234.
211 Ibid, p 240.

was reproduced in the 1993 Act with only minor modifications.[212] Section 9A was reintroduced, with significant amendments, as s 61:

(1) It shall be unlawful for any person –

    (a) to publish or distribute written matter which is threatening, abusive, or insulting, or to broadcast by means of radio or television words which are threatening, abusive, or insulting; or

    (b) to use in any public place . . . or within the hearing of persons in any such public place, or at any meeting to which the public are invited or have access, words which are threatening, abusive, or insulting; or

    (c) to use in any place words which are threatening, abusive, or insulting if the person using the words knew or ought to have known that the words were reasonably likely to be published in a newspaper, magazine, or periodical or broadcast by means of radio or television,

– being matter or words likely to excite hostility against or bring into contempt any group of persons in or who may be coming to New Zealand on the ground of the colour, race, or ethnic or national origins of that group of persons.

(2) It shall not be a breach of subsection (1) to publish in a newspaper, magazine, or periodical or broadcast by means of radio or television a report relating to the publication or distribution of matter by any person or the broadcast or use of words by any person, if the report

---

212 Section 131 of the Human Rights Act 1993 states:

'(1) Every person commits an offence and is liable on summary conviction to imprisonment for a term not exceeding 3 months or to a fine not exceeding $7,000 who, with intent to excite hostility or ill-will against, or bring into contempt or ridicule, any group of persons in New Zealand on the ground of the colour, race, or ethnic or national origins of that group of persons:

(a) publishes or distributes written matter which is threatening, abusive, or insulting, or broadcasts by means of radio or television words which are threatening, abusive, or insulting; or

(b) uses in any public place (as defined in section 2(1) of the Summary Offences Act 1981), or within the hearing of persons in any such public place, or at any meeting to which the public are invited or have access, words which are threatening, abusive, or insulting:

being matter or words likely to excite hostility or ill-will against, or bring into contempt or ridicule, any such group of persons in New Zealand on the ground of the colour, race, or ethnic or national origins of that group of persons.

(2) For the purposes of this section, "publishes or distributes" and "written matter" have the meaning given to them in section 61.'

of the matter or words accurately conveys the intention of the person who published or distributed the matter or broadcast or used the words.

The key difference between s 61 of the Human Rights Act 1993 and its predecessor in the Race Relations Act 1971 is that the degree of potential harm is limited to 'hostility' (rather than 'hostility or ill-will') and 'ridicule' (rather than 'contempt or ridicule') – effectively raising the threshold of the legislative proscription.

In August 2004, the New Zealand Parliament's Government Administration Select Committee began an inquiry into 'whether or not further legislation to prohibit or restrain hate speech legislation is warranted'.[213] The inquiry was prompted by the controversy surrounding a failed attempt to ban the distribution in New Zealand of two videos that contained materials that was alleged to constitute hate speech directed at gay men and lesbians. New Zealand's Film and Literature Board of Review had originally classified the videos as 'objectionable' under the Films, Videos and Publications Classification Act 1993. In *Living Word Distributors Ltd v Human Rights Action Group*,[214] the New Zealand Court of Appeal overturned this decision on the basis that the videos did not fall into the category of content that could be considered 'objectionable' under s 3 of the Act because it did not deal with 'sex, horror, crime, cruelty, or violence'. It followed that there was no basis for the Board to go on to consider whether the availability of the videos was 'likely to be injurious to the public good'.[215] The reference to 'sex' in s 3 was interpreted as a reference to sexual 'activity rather than to the expression of opinion or attitude'[216] – for example, about the morality of homosexuality. In reaching its conclusion the Court emphasised that the legislation had to be interpreted in light of the guarantee, in s 14 of the BORA, that 'everyone has the right to freedom of expression'.[217]

The decision in the *Living Word* case drew attention to an apparent gap in the regulatory regimes established by New Zealand legislation. Specifically, neither the censorship regime established by the Films, Videos and Publications Classification Act 1993, nor the Human Rights Act 1993 dealt with homophobic hate speech. In its response to the Government Administration Committee's 2003 report on the operation of the Films, Videos and Publications Classification Act 1993,[218] the Government indicated that it would consider whether laws dealing with hate speech 'may need to be strengthened

---

213 New Zealand House of Representatives, 2004.
214 *Living Word Distributors Ltd v Human Rights Action Group* (2000).
215 Films, Videos and Publications Classification Act 1993, s 3(1).
216 *Living Word Distributors Ltd v Human Rights Action Group* (2000), para 39.
217 Ibid, paras 35–45. See also, *Moonen v Film and Literature Board of Review* (2000).
218 New Zealand House of Representatives, Government Administration Committee, 2003.

and whether this is an appropriate matter for censorship or human rights law reform'.[219] In August 2004, the Government Administration Committee announced its Inquiry into Hate Speech. While the inquiry's terms of reference were broad, it was widely regarded as primarily concerned with the question of whether the protection of hate speech laws should be extended to gay men and lesbians.[220]

Although the Committee received written submissions in late 2004 and held some public hearings in the first half of 2005, at the time of writing the inquiry was in hiatus, and is not expected to pursue the option of legislative reform.[221] Following the September 2005 general election, one of the policy concessions made by the Labour Government, in return for a commitment from the United Future Party that it would 'provide confidence and supply for the term of this Parliament', was that it would 'not support any legislative initiatives to place limits on freedom of expression through so called "hate speech" laws'.[222]

The legal form of free speech and non-discrimination/equality rights after the BORA 1990

The principles of free speech and non-discrimination are both expressed in the BORA.

> 14. Everyone has the right to freedom of expression, including the freedom to seek, receive, and impart information and opinions of any kind in any form.
>
> 19. (1) Everyone has the right to freedom from discrimination on the grounds of discrimination in the Human Rights Act 1993.

The New Zealand Court of Appeal has characterised the right to freedom of expression recognised by s 14 as 'as wide as human thought and imagination'.[223] But the true extent of the BORA's support for free speech can only be assessed in light of the operation of s 5 of the BORA – which, as explained in Chapter 1, allows for the legal imposition of 'such

---

219 New Zealand Government, 2003, p 3.
220 Dye, 2005.
221 New Zealand Human Rights Commission, 2006, para 2.5. Nonetheless, as recently as November 2006, the Inquiry into Hate Speech was still formally on the agenda of the Government Administration Committee: www.parliament.nz/en-NZ/SC/summary/
222 United Future, 2005. See also New Zealand Human Rights Commission, 2006, para 2.5.
223 *Moonen v Film and Literature Board of Review* (2000), para 15. See Huscroft, 2003c, p 311.

reasonable limits . . . as can be demonstrably justified in a free and democratic society'.[224] Huscroft has observed that 'the acid test of any commitment to freedom of expression is not the generosity with which the right is defined, but the strictness of the standard against which limitations on the right are assessed'.[225] Huscroft's assessment is that, to date, the New Zealand approach (represented in the adjudication activities of the courts, and the law-making activities of the legislature) to articulating the practical scope of the right to freedom of expression protected by the BORA has left considerable room for legislative limitations on speech:

> Experience to date suggests that content-based limitations on the right are likely to be considered reasonable and demonstrably justified in a wide variety of contexts. Indeed, extensive limitations have been established by Parliament and the courts since passage of the Bill of Rights.[226]

Huscroft points to the fact that the (re)inclusion of a civil racial disharmony provision as part of New Zealand law in 1993, in the form of s 61 of the Human Rights Act 1993, generated relatively little public controversy; an illustration of New Zealand's relatively 'laid back' attitude towards speech limitations.[227]

For present purposes, what is particularly relevant about Huscroft's analysis of the status of the right to freedom of expression in New Zealand is that, contrary to common assumptions about the enhanced protection associated with the legal form of a bill of rights, it suggests that the adoption of the BORA in 1990 may not have been a particularly transformative event. The *legal form* of the traditional value of freedom of expression may have changed – from a 'cherished' value in 'the Anglo–New Zealand [common law] legal tradition'[228] to a BORA right – but the potency of free speech sensitivity as a feature of New Zealand legal culture has changed little. Whether this is regarded as a 'good' or 'bad' news story will depend, of course, on one's personal preferences with respect to the breadth of the immunity against restriction that an express right to freedom of expression should support. Huscroft, who employs the broad freedom underpinned by the First Amendment in the US as a normative reference point, laments the fact that s 14 of the BORA has not inspired New Zealanders – whether politicians,

---

224 BORA 1990, s 5.
225 Huscroft, 2003c, p 315.
226 Ibid.
227 Huscroft, 1995. See also *Jeffrey v Police* (1994), an unsuccessful appeal against an obscene language conviction that Huscroft identifies as a further illustration of the New Zealand judiciary's tendency to narrowly construe the immunity against speech restrictions underpinned by s 14 of the BORA (Huscroft, 2003c, pp 330–1).
228 Huscroft, 2003c, p 308.

judges, or the broader community – to 'get serious about freedom of expression'.[229]

Certainly Huscroft is right that neither the legislature nor the judiciary has seized on s 14 as a justification for dramatically transforming the traditional common law support for a (malleable) free speech principle into a robust constitutional impediment to attempts at legislative curtailment. As he acknowledges, it would be naive to expect the BORA, given its form, to be a catalyst for dramatic change of this type.[230] But a closer look at the operation of hate-speech laws in New Zealand in recent years (see below) suggests that, at least in this particular context, s 14 of the BORA has developed some real 'teeth'.

Within the BORA, the other side of the free speech/hate speech balance is provided by s 19. As noted in Chapter 3, despite the New Zealand Parliament's conscious adoption of the language of 'non-discrimination' rather than the language of 'equality', the inclusion of s 19 in the BORA necessarily ensured that equality – 'the most powerful idea in modern political thought'[231] – would occupy a prominent place in New Zealand's policy development, lawmaking and adjudication processes. Although chiefly understood in terms of its explicit legal effect – prohibiting various forms of discrimination in New Zealand (including racial discrimination)[232] – s 19 has also formed part of the broader backdrop for debates and adjudications over the racial disharmony provisions of the Human Rights Act 1993, as well as other New Zealand laws mobilised against hate speech.

In the *Living Word* case (discussed above), the Court of Appeal addressed the question of the relationship between ss 14 and 19 of the BORA, in the context of an attempt to mobilise New Zealand's censorship regime against material that was regarded as homophobic hate speech. The Court of Appeal criticised the High Court for having characterised the BORA framework for approaching the task of interpreting and applying the Films, Videos and Publications Classification Act 1993 as one involving a 'direct clash of rights'.[233] Moreover, according to the Court of Appeal, it was an error to treat s 19 as 'trumping' s 14.[234] Richardson P offered no further guidance on how adjudicators should approach the task of interpreting legislative speech restrictions in the light of the inclusion of both ss 14 and 19 in New Zealand's primary human rights statute.

---

229 Huscroft, 1995, p 212; also, pp 172–3.
230 Ibid, p 172.
231 Huscroft 2003b, p 367.
232 See Chapter 3 for a discussion of the Court of Appeal's approach to s 19 in *Quilter v Attorney General* (1998).
233 *Living Word Distributors Ltd v Human Rights Action Group* (2000), para 41.
234 Ibid, para 42; see also, paras 78–9 per Thomas J.

The operation of hate speech laws

Since the enactment of the BORA in 1990 and the HRA in 1993, the operation of New Zealand's hate speech laws has been characterised by very infrequent formal enforcement. In the case of the criminal offence created by s 131, this was a continuation of a pattern observable since the enactment of the Race Relations Act 1971. In 35 years, there has only been one prosecution under s 131 of the HRA or its predecessor, s 25 of the Race Relations Act.[235]

More surprising is the very small number of cases in which the s 61 (civil) racial disharmony prohibition has been found to have been breached. It is not simply that there have been only a very small number of formal tribunal adjudications involving alleged violations of s 61. This is fairly typical of the experience of other jurisdictions where legislation has made hate speech a civil wrong enforceable in a complaint-based anti-discrimination system.[236] Nor is it the case that the number of complaints lodged with the Human Rights Commission has dropped dramatically. Over the last decade the New Zealand Human Rights Commission has received several hundred complaints alleging a breach of s 61 of the HRA (see below). What is most striking about the operation of s 61 in recent years is that in the overwhelming majority of cases, the Human Rights Commission has declined to proceed on the basis that the conduct does not fall within the legislative definition of unlawful racist hate speech. It would have been reasonable to expect an increase in the rate of complaint rejection, when compared with the operation of s 9A of the Race Relations Act 1971 in the 1980s – given that in the drafting of s 61 of the HRA 1993, there was a deliberate narrowing of the scope of the definition of unlawful hate speech (by establishing higher harm thresholds). But the rate of rejection in recent years has been of a magnitude that cannot be fully explained by the statutory adjustments. In 2002–2003 the New Zealand Human Rights Commission received 280 complaints alleging a breach of s 61. None of these complaints were pursued by the Commission as formal complaints.[237] During the 12 month period from July 2004 to June 2005 the Commission received almost 250 enquiries or complaints regarding racial disharmony.[238] None of the complaints was considered to fall within the parameters of s 61.[239]

In its 2005 submission to the Government and Administration Committee's Inquiry into Hate Speech, the Human Rights Commission defended its

---

235 *King-Ansell v Police* (1979). See Hodge, 1981; Moses, 1996, p 187; Huscroft, 2003c, p 324.
236 See McNamara, 2002; McNamara, 2005.
237 New Zealand Human Rights Commission, 2005a, pp 8–9.
238 The Commission reports that it received a total of 7,344 enquiries and complaints during this period, 3.4% of which were categorised as relating to the racial disharmony provisions of the Human Rights Act 1993: New Zealand Human Rights Commission, 2005c, p 10.
239 Robert Hallowell, Senior Legal Adviser, New Zealand Human Rights Commission, personal communication, 18 August 2005.

current approach to handling s 61 complaints as a necessary product of the combined effect of the rewording of the racial disharmony provision in 1993 and the need to take into account the right to freedom of expression protected by the BORA:

> The introduction of the NZBoRA in 1990, added the right to freedom of expression to the mix. In order to balance the right to express opinions that may be unpopular or controversial against material that is likely to expose people to hatred or contempt, the Commission has adopted the practice of requiring some evidence that the material or comment will increase the risk of manifestation of hostility or contemptuous behaviour.... As a result of the Commission's approach few complaints reach the necessary threshold.... While the current threshold at which the Commission accepts complaints as within jurisdiction is set at a high level, the Commission believes that this is necessary in order to respect the right to freedom of expression and so as not to trivialize genuine grievances.[240]

Before the Government and Administration Committee's Inquiry into Hate Speech, the Human Rights Commission characterised the working balance that has been struck by the Commission in recent years when handling s 61 complaints – under which no conduct has been considered to be sufficiently serious to fall within the scope of the legislative prohibition – as 'about right'.[241] What this assessment suggests is that while racist hate speech laws are 'on the books' in New Zealand, in practice they are currently being interpreted as involving such a high threshold that they are effectively beyond the reach of the vast majority of situations in response to which individuals and organisations may seek to facilitate their enforcement.

A pattern of narrow interpretation of hate speech laws is not unique to New Zealand. As discussed above, a similar (albeit somewhat uneven) pattern can be observed in Canada. But what is distinctive about the New Zealand experience is that it has been neither the legislature nor the courts or tribunals that have initiated or encouraged a narrow construction of s 61, based on fee speech sensitivity. The Human Rights Commission and the Race Relations Commissioner (currently Joris de Bres) have been the primary architects of this approach.

When the New Zealand Parliament reintroduced a civil racial disharmony provision in 1993 (in the form of s 61 of the HRA) after a four-year hiatus, it undoubtedly recalibrated the harm threshold that would need to be reached before the legislative standard could be considered to have been breached. At

---

240 New Zealand Human Rights Commission, 2005a, pp 8–9, 17–18.
241 New Zealand Human Rights Commission, 2005b. See also New Zealand Human Rights Commission, 2004c.

the same time, the very act of reintroducing a statutory prohibition necessarily involved articulation of the position that certain types of racist hate speech should not be 'protected' by the right to freedom of expression. That is, Parliament struck the balance in such a way as to leave room for the legitimate restriction of certain types of racist expression. Implicit in the inclusion of s 61 in the HRA is parliamentary acceptance of the proposition that the legislative regulation of hate speech is not incompatible with a commitment to the BORA-protected right to free speech.

Nor can the courts be considered to have driven the Human Rights Commission to adopt a narrow conception of the scope of the legislative prohibition on racist hate speech. On the few occasions when New Zealand quasi-judicial or judicial adjudicators have been called upon to adjudicate on the reach of s 61, they have not been particularly receptive to arguments that s 61 should be narrowly construed so as to avoid infringing the right to free speech.

In *Archer*,[242] the Human Rights Tribunal considered a complaint that Derek Archer had breached s 61 of the Human Rights Act 1993, when, during the course of radio broadcasts in 1994, he made derogatory comments about Chinese people and Japanese people. On the central issue of how the harm/risk threshold set by s 61 should be interpreted and applied, the Tribunal ruled that whether the conduct was 'threatening, abusive or insulting' should be assessed objectively – from the point of view of the 'ordinary sensible citizen'[243] – and whether the conduct was likely to 'excite hostility or bring into contempt' should be assessed with reference to the 'significant number of New Zealanders who are less perceptive or sensitive on racial issues than others and who might be susceptible to the meaning we have found the offending words to have'.[244] The Tribunal concluded that Archer had breached s 61 and ordered him to refrain from engaging in the same or similar conduct.

Huscroft has described the standard employed by the Tribunal with respect to hostility/contempt as 'the lowest common denominator that can be imagined'.[245] However, it is clear that Huscroft's objections do not centre simply on the approach adopted by the Tribunal in *Archer*, but on the very terms of s 61 (and s 131):

> The problem, in essence, is this: both provisions facilitate the suppression of expression based on conjecture that it may cause others to adopt racist attitudes. The requirement that it be 'likely' that expression have this consequence does not guarantee adequate protection for the right to

---

242 *New Zealand Human Rights Commission, Proceedings Commissioner v Archer* (1996).
243 Ibid, p 128.
244 Ibid, p 129.
245 Huscroft, 2003a, p 324.

freedom of expression, because the consequences of expression simply cannot be reduced to anything approaching likelihood.[246]

Huscroft's analysis reflects his position about the implications of the inclusion of s 14 in the BORA: whatever its status and significance may have been in its pre-1990 common law form, the right to free speech is now expressly recognised in New Zealand's primary domestic human rights instrument and should be protected to the fullest extent possible when it comes up against competing interests. Huscroft has clearly and powerfully articulated his own preference as to the scope of s 14's free speech guarantee – and the concomitant arguments that ss 61 and 131 of the Human Rights Act 1993 'cannot be justified as reasonable limitations on freedom of expression because they are overbroad in their application'.[247] With specific reference to s 61, he has observed: 'It is a mystery to me how a law this bad came to be re-enacted in the face of the Bill of Rights.'[248]

Whether Huscroft is right that s 14 *should* operate as a broad and robust constraint on the law-making functions of the New Zealand Parliament and the interpretation and adjudication activities of courts and tribunals with respect to 'hate speech' is a moot point, but it has not often been regarded as such by those organs of governments. Huscroft himself notes (albeit with surprise and disappointment) that when the bill that resulted in the Human Rights Act 1993 came before the New Zealand Parliament, the Attorney General did not issue a report under s 7 of the BORA indicating that ss 61 and 131 constituted unjustifiable infringements of the right to freedom of expression protected by the BORA.[249] In *Archer* the Human Rights Tribunal appeared to be quite at ease with the notion that s 61 of the HRA can sit comfortably alongside s 14 of the BORA:

> We accept that where there are rights enshrined in ... [the BORA] which in a particular context can be regarded as competing the balance may be determined by reference to other legislation. In this case the Human Rights Act 1993 reinforces the right of freedom from discrimination by particularising which rights should be protected and by prescribing specific remedies to assist in that protection. The Human Rights Act 1993 is a justified limitation in terms of s 5 Bill of Rights Act 1990 as are the laws of defamation. The existence of these rights by definition limits the right to freedom of expression. The right to

---

246 Huscroft, 2003a, p 234.
247 Huscroft, 1995, p 204.
248 Ibid, p 209.
249 On s 7 reports, see Chapter 1.

freedom of expression carries with it the responsibility not to infringe the rights of others.[250]

It is noteworthy that the Tribunal expressly drew the non-discrimination principle in s 19 of the BORA into the debate over the legitimate scope of New Zealand's hate speech laws. Notwithstanding its obvious relevance, at least in terms of the general philosophical and legal underpinnings of provisions such as s 61 of the Human Rights Act 1993, it has not featured prominently in New Zealand's public discourse over the hate speech/free speech controversy.[251]

In an analogous situation – a case involving Wellington City Council's use of an abatement notice under the Resource Management Act 1991 to deal with two swastikas, which a man painted on the outside of his house[252] – Grieg J, in the High Court, was unmoved by the argument that s 14 of the BORA represented a barrier to the use of the abatement notice to prohibit the display of racist symbols: 'I think there can be little doubt that the objective of the Resource Management Act is such as to warrant the overriding of the freedom of expression.'[253]

The tenor of the Court of Appeal's subsequent decisions in *Living Word*[254] and *Moonen*[255] indicate that, if given the opportunity, it may scrutinise more closely the question of how easily the right protected by s 14 of the BORA can be 'trumped' by other values and rights, such as those embodied in laws that regulate/sanction hate speech. For the time being, however, there is little to suggest that the New Zealand Human Rights Commission's current approach to the scope of s 61 of the HRA has been driven by the dictates of authoritative judicial or quasi-judicial decision-makers. In fact, a recent s 61 case before the Human Rights Tribunal suggests that there may be some divergence between the preferred approaches of the Commission and the Human Rights Tribunal.

A pamphlet circulated by Winston Peters MP and the New Zealand First Party in 2003 prompted Bruce Bissett to attempt to invoke the prohibition in s 61 of the HRA.[256] The pamphlet purported to highlight the 'dangers' posed by 'third-world immigrants', including 'soaring crime levels' and exposure to 'third-world diseases'. Although the text of the pamphlet did not refer to a particular 'race', ethnicity or country of origin, the pamphlet also featured a

---

250 *New Zealand Human Rights Commission, Proceedings Commissioner v Archer* (1996), pp 129–30.
251 *Cf* New Zealand Human Rights Commission, 2005a, p 5.
252 *Zdrahal v Wellington City Council* (1995).
253 Ibid, p 711. See discussion in West-Newman, 2001, pp 251–3.
254 *Living Word Distributors Ltd v Human Rights Action Group* (2000).
255 *Moonen v Film and Literature Board of Review* (2000).
256 TVNZ, One News, 2003b.

Balancing 'competing' human rights 221

graph that indicated that the majority of New Zealand's immigrants were 'Asian'.[257] In May 2004, the Human Rights Commission reached the conclusion that the pamphlet did not breach s 61. Bissett nonetheless decided to pursue the matter in the Human Rights Tribunal himself – an option that is available under the Human Rights Act 1993, but rarely taken up by complainants.[258]

In the Tribunal the defendant applied to have the matter struck out on the basis that it was 'frivolous and vexatious'. The Tribunal declined to do so, and instead invited the parties to make submission on a range of relevant issues. Significantly, the Tribunal also invited the Human Rights Commission, which was not a party to the proceedings, to make a submission. The Tribunal appears to have been motivated to take this course of action because it had 'some reservations about the approach adopted by the Commission'[259] in deciding that the distribution of the pamphlet did not fall within the category of unlawful racist hate speech set by s 61. In particular, the Tribunal noted that the Commission had explained its decision to Bissett by observing that 'In order for the words [in the pamphlet] to be considered unlawful they would have had to *invite a hostile action* against a particular group, in this case, Asians'.[260] The Tribunal's specific reservations about the approach to s 61 adopted by the Commission were that it:

(a) seems to import into the section a need to establish that the words invite 'hostile action' against the subject group, which is not quite the same as what section 61 says, and
(b) does not mention a second issue under section 61, namely whether or not the words in issue might bring the subject into contempt.[261]

In essence, the Tribunal's concern was that the Commission appeared to have raised the already high threshold set by the words of s 61 even further by refashioning the 'excite hostility' arm of the two-limbed harm threshold into a requirement that the conduct must 'actively invite hostility against a group of people',[262] and by apparently disregarding the 'bring into contempt' limb of the harm threshold.

In its submission to the Tribunal, the Commission distinguished between a 'civil libertarian approach' to the interpretation of the legitimate breadth of hate speech laws in light of the need to simultaneously respect the right to

---

257 *Bissett v Peters* (2004), paras 26, 32.
258 Human Rights Act 1993 (NZ), s 92B.
259 *Bissett v Peters* (2004), para 10.
260 Cited in *Bissett v Peters* (2004), para 8 (emphasis added).
261 *Bissett v Peters* (2004), para 10.
262 Cited in *Bissett v Peters* (2004), para 9.

free speech, and a 'harms-based approach' to this same task.²⁶³ Its self-described 'position in deciding whether a complaint has contravened s 61 is more akin to the civil libertarian approach' – which 'reflects the need to balance the requirements of the section against s 14 of the NZBoRA and freedom of expression'.²⁶⁴

Interestingly, the Commission illustrated the difference between the 'harm-based' and 'civil libertarian' approaches with reference to the majority and minority positions adopted by the judges of the Supreme Court of Canada in *R v Keegstra* and *Canadian Human Rights Commission v Taylor*.²⁶⁵ The Commission consciously lined up its position on how the right to free speech/hate speech law balance should be struck with the position of the *minority* judges in *Keegstra* – who held that s 319 of the Canadian Criminal Code and s 13 of the Canadian Human Rights Act were constitutionally invalid as unjustifiable infringements on the right to freedom of expression protected by s 2(b) of the Canadian Charter of Rights and Freedoms. It is unsurprising then, that the Human Rights Commission has adopted a narrow definition of the scope of the racist hate speech provisions of the Human Rights Act 1993, and that it has justified this position as a necessary consequence of the inclusion of s 14 in the BORA. On the other hand, it is unusual for a human rights agency in New Zealand to justify its preferred interpretation of New Zealand legislation with reference to a minority opinion on the scope of equivalent legislation in another country – particularly in the context of the New Zealand BORA where the courts, let alone the Human Rights Commission, are not empowered to strike down legislation on the basis of incompatibility with human rights (in this case, the right to freedom of expression).

In response to the Tribunal's specific query as to the justification for the view that only conduct that incited 'hostile action' contravened s 61, the Commission emphasised its 'civil libertarian' orientation, and indicated that its approach also reflected its mindfulness 'of the potential for trivial complaints to dominate the disputes process'.²⁶⁶ The Commission quoted with approval Huscroft's recommended approach to the interpretation of s 61:

> It is incumbent upon the Human Rights Commission and the . . . Tribunal to adopt interpretation of relevant terms that protect the right to the [greatest] extent possible. The . . . Commission and the . . . Tribunal should be slow to conclude that expression is likely to cause contempt or hostility regardless of how obnoxious they may consider the expression to be.²⁶⁷

---

263 New Zealand Human Rights Commission, 2004a, paras 2–7.
264 Ibid, para 9.
265 *R v Keegstra* (1990); *Canadian Human Rights Commission v Taylor* (1990).
266 New Zealand Human Rights Commission, 2004a, para 15.
267 Huscroft, 2003a, quoted in New Zealand Human Rights Commission, 2004a, para 17.

The Commission defended its adoption of a narrow interpretation of the phrase, 'bring into contempt',with reference to the approach of Canadian court and tribunals to comparable provisions in hate speech laws.[268] Again, it attached particular significance to the minority view of the Supreme Court of Canada in *Taylor* that the word 'contempt' was too vague, broad and susceptible to subjective interpretation to be included in a statutory prohibition on hate speech. its inclusion necessarily and unjustifiably infringed the right to freedom of expression.[269]

Key features of the New Zealand balance

Divergent views about where the balance should be struck between sanctioning hate speech and protecting freedom of expression are, of course, par for the course – in each of the four countries that are the subject of the present study, and in many other parts of the world. That they should prompt debate in New Zealand over the appropriate interpretation and application of ss 61 and 131 of the Human Rights Act 1993 is to be expected. But aspects of the New Zealand experience are particularly interesting for the light they shed on the significance of legal form for the operational 'shape' of human rights.

Currently, a 'pro-speech position'[270] dominates the interpretation and application of racial disharmony laws in New Zealand, with the effect that it is extremely rare for any conduct to be authoritatively characterised as unlawful. This state of affairs exists in a broader context where, notwithstanding its express recognition in s 14 of the BORA, the right to freedom of expression has not generally been regarded by the New Zealand Parliament or the New Zealand judiciary as a potent barrier to restrictions on speech in the pursuit of other policy goals (including anti-racism and respect for equality and non-discrimination). The Court of Appeal has made it clear that the inclusion of s 14 in the BORA was not without consequence in terms of the significance and resilience to be thereafter attributed to the right to freedom of expression in New Zealand,[271] but there is nothing in the approach of the courts or specialist tribunals like the Human Rights Review Tribunal to suggest that s 14 had introduced a 'shield' of First Amendment-like proportions into the New Zealand legal environment. And yet, that is how the Human Rights Commission has employed s 14 in recent years, at least in the specific context of interpretation and application of hate speech laws.

---

268 New Zealand Human Rights Commission, 2004a, paras 26–31.
269 The proceedings were subsequently discontinued by Bissett, and so a final decision on the merits was never handed down by the New Zealand Human Rights Tribunal.
270 This is the label applied by West-Newman (2001) to the position advanced by Grant Huscroft in Huscroft, 1995 (and also in Huscroft, 2003c). West-Newman (2001) offers an alternative 'from the bottom' perspective.
271 *Moonen v Film and Literature Board of Review* (2000).

My chief concern here is not that issue should be taken with the Human Rights Commission's approach. My personal position on the legitimacy of hate speech laws would place me more comfortably in the 'harms-based' camp, rather than the 'civil libertarian' camp – if one were forced to identify in terms of the dichotomy identified by the Commission[272] – but for present purposes, that is beside the point. Rather, I want to highlight what the recent New Zealand experience reveals about the significance of legal form in terms of the potency of human rights-based arguments in the context of a controversy over how competing interests/rights should be balanced. As noted in Chapter 1, the particular legal regime for human rights protection adopted by New Zealand in 1990 involved a conscious decision to avoid setting up a 'trump card' bill of rights. It was anticipated that the BORA would be an important influence, but by no means the only influence, on processes of policy development, law-making and adjudication. But in the (perhaps unique) context of the jurisdiction in which New Zealand's racist hate speech laws operate, it is not the legislature, nor the courts, nor even the Human Rights Review Tribunal, whose preferred interpretations have had the greatest impact on the practical scope of the hate speech provisions of the Human Rights Act 1993. It is the Human Rights Commission, as the initial, and in many cases, only arbiter of where the line should be drawn between unlawful hate speech and protected free speech, whose approach to interpretation and application is pivotal. The New Zealand Parliament has provided guidance, in the form of ss 61 and 131 of the Human Rights Act 1993, but the terms of the legislation are such that there is considerable scope for divergent interpretations. (The Commission has conceded that, over the years, 'the interpretation of the applicability of s 61 has fluctuated according to who has administered it . . . '.[273])

Section 14 is not irrelevant to these events either. The public statements of the Human Rights Commission in recent years provide a solid basis for suggesting that it has been emboldened, in presenting a relatively broad conception of the scope of the right to freedom of expression (and a commensurately narrow conception of the allowable limits of hate speech prohibitions), by the presence of s 14 of the BORA as part of New Zealand's legal environment. Section 14 may not (yet) be widely regarded as *mandating* a broad conception of protected speech in New Zealand – in the same way that the First Amendment, and to a lesser extent, s 2(b) of the Charter are regarded in the US and Canada, respectively – but the example of s 61's operation in recent years suggests that s 14 can be an effective mechanism for anchoring and amplifying a robust right to freedom of expression. It is unlikely that the Human Rights Commission's current approach to the scope of the racial disharmony provisions of the Human Rights Act 1993 would have been

---

272 New Zealand Human Rights Commission, 2004a, paras 2–7.
273 New Zealand Human Rights Commission, 2005a, p 21.

sustainable in the absence of s 14 of the BORA, even if the same 'civil libertarian' values were in the ascendancy within the Commission. One of the features of New Zealand's post-1990 legal environment is the *potential* to elevate particular norms or policy directions that are contentious or controversial, by articulating them as legal or even 'quasi-constitutional' rights as opposed to 'mere' political, ideological or philosophical preferences. A theme I will take up in Chapter 5, based on reflections across the three case studies, is that this technique – a type of low level 'trumping' – tends to be employed in a fairly pragmatic and sometimes cynical way in New Zealand: depending on the assumed synergy between the ostensibly relevant BORA standard and the preferred policy outcome. But it is apparent in the present context that the Human Rights Commission has taken the considered position that its current approach to the construction of s 61 strikes an appropriate balance between free speech and non-discrimination. For the time being at least, the Human Rights Commission appears to have taken up Huscroft's challenge to 'take freedom of expression seriously'.[274]

Australia[275]

History and current form of hate speech laws

In 1974, the Australian Government moved to introduce legislation so as to meet Australia's obligations as a party to the ICERD. Despite Australia's reservation in relation to Art 4, the Racial Discrimination Bill 1974 included a prohibition on racist hate speech (cl 28):

> A person shall not, with intent to promote hostility or ill-will against, or to bring into contempt or ridicule, persons included in a group of persons in Australia by reason of the race, colour or national or ethnic origin of the persons included in that group –
>
> (a) publish or distribute written matters;
> (b) broadcast words by means of radio or television; or
> (c) utter words in any public place, or within the hearing of persons in any public place, or at any meeting to which the public are invited or have access,
>
> being written matter that promotes, or words that promote, ideas based on –
>
> (d) the alleged superiority of persons of a particular race, colour or

---

274 Huscroft, 1995, p 173. See also, McGregor, 2006.
275 This section draws on material previously published in McNamara, 2002.

national or ethnic origin over persons of a different race, colour or national or ethnic origin; or

(e) hatred of persons of a particular race, colour or national or ethnic origin.

Penalty: $5,000.[276]

The Liberal Party-Country Party Coalition, in Opposition, did not support the inclusion of this clause in Australia's first national anti-discrimination statute. During debate in the House of Representatives, the Liberal Party Member for Bennelong, John Howard (since 1996, Australia's Prime Minister), expressed the Opposition's concerns about the proposed criminalisation of racial vilification:

> ... [T]o attempt to proscribe dissemination of ideas, however base many people in this chamber might find those ideas, is to get into an area which in the view of the Opposition is so dangerous and could infringe on such a basic right that the Opposition very strongly opposes the inclusion in the Bill of this clause.[277]

The Attorney General, Mr Enderby, defended the inclusion of cl 28 on the basis that it reflected Australia's obligation under the ICERD, and because 'the criminal law does not only provide a penalty; it expresses a sense of community outrage at certain types of behaviour'.[278]

Faced with a hostile Senate (where the Liberal/Country Coalition held the balance of power), the Labour Party proposed a compromise amendment that would limit the prohibition of racial vilification to conduct that was done with 'intent to provoke a breach of the peace'.[279] However, the Coalition did not accept the amendments and maintained its complete opposition to the clause in its entirety. Clause 28 was deleted[280] from the Racial Discrimination Act 1975 (Aust) (RDA).

The prospect of national racial vilification legislation was again raised during the 1980s, when proposals to add incitement to racial hatred and racial defamation provisions to the RDA 1975 were considered. The Human Rights Commission proposed the addition of two new provisions to the RDA 1975 that would:

> ... make it unlawful for a person to publicly utter or publish words

---

276 Parliament of Australia, Hansard (House of Representatives), 9 April 1975, p 1408.
277 Ibid, pp 1408–9.
278 Ibid, p 1409.
279 Parliament of Australia, Hansard (Senate), 29 May 1975, p 2036 per Senator McClelland.
280 Ibid.

which, having regard to all the circumstances, are likely to result in hatred, intolerance or violence against a person or persons, or a group of persons, distinguished by race, colour, descent or national or ethnic origin [and] ... make it unlawful to publicly insult or abuse an individual or group, or hold that individual or group up to contempt or slander, by reason of their race, colour, descent or national or ethnic origin.[281]

The Commission recommended that publication be defined broadly 'to cover the print and electronic media, sign boards, abusive telephone calls etc and that both the individual making the statements and the owners and controllers of the issuing medium would be covered ...'.[282] Significantly, the Human Rights Commission explained that 'Setting the provisions within the ambit of the Racial Discrimination Act makes it possible to retain the very considerable advantages of adopting conciliation procedures in such cases', and argued that 'Avoiding a criminal law approach maintains the parallel with the defamation of individuals and increases the educative role of the law'.[283] The Commission's proposals were not enacted into legislation.[284]

In the early 1990s, the Labour Government again moved to introduce legislative restrictions on racist hate speech, motivated by the recommendations of the Human Rights and Equal Opportunity Commission (HREOC)'s National Inquiry into Racist Violence (1991),[285] the Royal Commission into Aboriginal Deaths in Custody (1991),[286] and the Australian Law Reform Commission's reference on Multiculturalism and the Law (1992).[287] Each of these reports identified racial vilification as a sufficiently serious problem in Australia to warrant the making of such conduct unlawful, although there were divergent views as to the most appropriate form of legal regulation. The primary point of divergence was over whether criminal law was an appropriate form of regulation, or whether conciliation-based human rights law was more appropriate.

In November 1994, the Racial Hatred Bill was introduced into the House of Representatives. It was based on a two-pronged approach to the proscription of racial vilification, proposing changes to both the Crimes Act 1914 (Aust) and the RDA 1975. The 1994 bill proposed that three new criminal offences be created. The first would have prohibited specific threats to persons where motivated by the race, colour or national or ethnic origin

---

281 Australia, Human Rights Commission 1983, p 2.
282 Ibid at 3.
283 Ibid.
284 See also Australia, Human Rights Commission, 1984; and Pettman, 1982.
285 Australia, Human Rights and Equal Opportunity Commission, 1991.
286 Australia, Royal Commission into Aboriginal Deaths in Custody, 1991.
287 Australian Law Reform Commission, 1992.

of the person or persons threatened, while the second would have prohibited racially motivated threats to property. The third amendment to the Crimes Act 1914 (Aust) proposed by the 1994 bill was the creation of an offence of intentionally inciting racial hatred punishable by imprisonment for one year:

> A person must not, with the intention of inciting racial hatred against another person or a group of people, do an act, otherwise than in private, if the act:
>
> (a) is reasonably likely, in all the circumstances, to incite racial hatred against the other person or group of people; and
> (b) is done because of the race, colour or national or ethnic origin of the other person or of some or all of the people on the group.

The 1994 bill also proposed that the RDA 1975 be amended so as to make it unlawful to do a public act that was likely to 'offend, insult, humiliate or intimidate' members of a group defined by race, colour, or national or ethnic origin. No evidence of intention, knowledge or recklessness with respect to the adverse effect of the conduct would be required, but the proposed section contained a long list of exemptions or 'defences'.[288]

The Racial Hatred Bill 1994 was passed in the House of Representatives on 16 November 1994, notwithstanding the opposition of the Coalition. In the Senate both the Labour Party and the Australian Democrats supported the bill. The Coalition Opposition, again, opposed it in its entirety primarily on free speech grounds. The Western Australian Greens (who held two Senate seats) supported the regulation of racial vilification via civil human rights law and processes as reflected in the proposed amendment to the RDA 1975. However, the WA Greens refused to support the inclusion of criminal sanctions within the regulatory framework for racial vilification. As a result of amendments introduced in the Senate by the WA Greens, the provisions which would have added three new offences to the Crimes Act 1914 (Aust) were deleted from the legislation before it was passed on 24 August 1995.[289]

In its present form, s 18C(1) of RDA 1975 states:

> It is unlawful for a person to do an act, otherwise than in private, if:
>
> (a) the act is reasonably likely, in all the circumstances, to offend, insult, humiliate or intimidate another person or a group of people; and

---

288 For commentary, see Eastman, 1994; Akmeemana and Jones, 1995; Johns, 1995.
289 For further analysis of the parliamentary debate on the Racial Hatred Bill 1994, see McNamara and Solomon, 1996, pp 272–7; and McNamara, 2002, pp 40–9.

(b) the act is done because of the race, colour or national or ethnic origin of the other person or of some or all of the people in the group.[290]

Section 18C(1) applies only to conduct that is likely to have the effect of causing offence, insult, humiliation or intimidation, if the conduct occurs 'otherwise than in private'. Section 18C(2)–(3) states that:

(2) For the purpose of subsection (1), an act is taken not to be done in private if it:
   (a) causes words, sounds, images or writing to be communicated to the public; or
   (b) is done in a public place; or
   (c) is done in the sight or hearing of people who are in a public place.
(3) In this section:
   'public place' includes any place to which the public have access as of right or by invitation, whether express or implied and whether or not a charge is made for admission to the place.

Section 18D of the Act limits the scope of the proscription of racist hate speech by creating a number of exemptions/defences:

Section 18C does not render unlawful anything said or done reasonably and in good faith:

(a) in the performance, exhibition or distribution of an artistic work; or
(b) in the course of any statement, publication, discussion or debate made or held for any genuine academic artistic or scientific purpose or any other genuine purpose in the public interest; or
(c) in making or publishing:
   (i) a fair and accurate report of any event or matter of public interest; or
   (ii) a fair comment on any event or matter of public interest if the comment is an expression of a genuine belief held by the person making the comment.

---

290 Section 18B states:

If:

(a) an act is done for 2 or more reasons;

(b) one of the reasons is the race, colour or national or ethnic origin of a person (whether or not it is the dominant reason or a substantial reason for doing the act);

then, for the purpose of this Part, the act is taken to be done because of the person's race, colour, national or ethnic origin.

In addition to ongoing pressure exerted on Australia by international human rights agencies such as the United Nations Committee on the Elimination of Racial Discrimination – to lift its reservation in relation to Art 4 and enact legislation of the type expected of state parties to ICERD[291] – another factor that prompted the then Labour Government to introduce racist hate speech legislation in the mid-1990s was that in the 20 years since such laws had been first contemplated by the Australian Parliament, the legislative landscape in relation to racism and discrimination had changed significantly. During the 1970s and 1980s, anti-discrimination was enacted by state and territory legislatures.[292] In 1989, New South Wales became the first Australian jurisdiction to enact legislation that made public racist hate speech unlawful.[293] Other states/territories followed suit shortly thereafter: Western Australia[294] in 1990, the Australian Capital Territory[295] and Queensland[296] in 1991. Since the Australian Parliament's enactment of the Racial Hatred Act 1995, hate-speech legislation has been enacted in the remainder of Australian jurisdictions with the exception of the Northern Territory: South Australia in 1996,[297] Tasmania in 1998,[298] and Victoria in 2001.[299]

Western Australia is the only jurisdiction to have *criminalised* the incitement of hatred, along the lines of the offences which operate in the UK[300] and Canada,[301] and which is on the statute books, in a modified form, in New Zealand.[302] A number of offences relating to racist hate speech were added to the Criminal Code 1913 (WA) 1990 and revamped in 2004.[303] The current offences include: the intentional promotion of animosity towards, or harassment of, members of a racial group (14 years imprisonment);[304] and engaging in conduct which is likely to promote animosity towards, or harassment of, members of a racial group (five years imprisonment).[305] In other state/territorial jurisdictions that have enacted hate speech laws, hate speech

---

291 See United Nations, Committee on the Elimination of Racial Discrimination, 1994, para 549.
292 See generally, O'Neill *et al*, 2004; Ronalds and Pepper, 2004.
293 See now Anti-Discrimination Act 1977 (NSW), ss 20B–20C, 38R–38T, 49ZS–49ZTA, 49ZXA–ZXC.
294 See now Criminal Code 1913 (WA), Pt II, Div XI.
295 Discrimination Act 1991 (ACT), Pt 6.
296 See now Anti-Discrimination Act 1991 (Qld), s 124A.
297 Racial Vilification Act 1996 (SA).
298 See Anti-Discrimination Act 1998 (Tas), s 19.
299 Racial and Religious Tolerance Act 2001 (Vic).
300 Public Order Act 1986 (UK), s 18.
301 Criminal Code, RS, 1985, c C-46, s 319(2).
302 Human Rights Act 1993 (NZ), s 131.
303 Criminal Code Amendment (Racial Vilification) Act 2004 (WA).
304 Criminal Code 1913 (WA), s 77.
305 Criminal Code 1913 (WA), s 78.

per se is not a crime, but it is a criminal offence to engage in what might be termed 'aggravated' hate speech – that is, combining hate speech with actual or threatened personal violence or property damage. Section 4 of the South Australian Racial Vilification Act 1996 is illustrative:[306]

> A person must not, by a public act, incite hatred towards, serious contempt for, or severe ridicule of, a person or group of persons on the ground of their race by –
>
> (a) threatening physical harm to the person, or members of the group, or to property of the person or members of the group; or
> (b) inciting others to threaten physical harm to the person, or members of the group, or to property of the person or members of the group.[307]

The legal form of free speech and non-discrimination/equality rights in Australia

Australia is distinctive among the four countries that are the subject of the present study in that there is no express articulation of a right to freedom of expression in a national statute.[308] In a recent decision, Kirby J put it as follows:

> Unlike the basic laws of most nations, the Australian Constitution does not contain an express guarantee of freedom of expression, such as that included in the *Constitution of the United States* and now in the *Canadian Charter of Rights and Freedoms*. Nor has legislation providing such a guarantee been enacted at a federal or State level in Australia, as it has in New Zealand and more recently in the United Kingdom. In this respect, Australia's constitutional arrangements are peculiar and now virtually unique.[309]

Traditionally, the legal foundation for assertions based on the importance of free expression is the common-law principle that 'everybody is free to do

---

306 See also, Anti-Discrimination Act 1977 (NSW), ss 20D, 38T, 49ZTA, 49ZXC; Discrimination Act 1991 (ACT), s 67; Anti-Discrimination Act 1991 (Qld), 131A; Racial and Religious Tolerance Act 2001 (Vic), ss 24–5.
307 Maximum penalty: 3 years imprisonment or $5,000 fine ($25,000 if the offender is a corporation).
308 Only in the Australian Capital Territory and Victoria has the right been 'codified' in a bill of rights: see Human Rights Act 2004 (ACT), s 16(2); Charter of Human Rights and Responsibilities Act 2006 (Vic), s 15.
309 *Coleman v Power* (2004), para 208.

anything, subject only to the provisions of the law'.[310] However, since the 1990s the High Court has moved to articulate a more tangible constitutional and legal framework for the principle of respect for freedom of expression.

In 1992, the High Court ruled, for the first time, that a 'freedom of political communication' was implicit in the Australian Constitution, as a necessary concomitant of Australia's system of responsible government.[311] The implicit constitutional guarantee of freedom of communication is relatively limited in terms. In *Lange v ABC*, a unanimous High Court stated:

> The freedom of communication which the Constitution protects is not absolute. It is limited to what is necessary for the effective operation of that system of representative and responsible government provided for by the Constitution. . . . The freedom will not invalidate a law enacted to satisfy some other legitimate end if the law satisfies two conditions. The first condition is that the object of the law is compatible with the maintenance of the constitutionally prescribed system of representative and responsible government. . . which the Constitution prescribes. The second is that the law is reasonably and appropriately adapted to that end.[312]

In *Coleman v Power*,[313] a majority of the High Court endorsed a modified version of the second limb of the test – previously articulated by Kirby J in *Levy v Victoria*:

> [D]oes the law which is impugned have the effect of preventing or controlling communication upon political and governmental matters *in a manner which is inconsistent* with the system of representative government for which the Constitution provides?[314]

Coleman v Power is worthy of note in the present context, because in it a number of judges described the status of the right to free speech in Australia as more than the 'residue' that remains after statutory limitations are accounted for, and not a 'mere' common-law right. McHugh J described the right to free speech as a 'fundamental right',[315] while Gummow and Hayne JJ placed it in the category of 'fundamental common law rights'.[316] The significance of the *fundamental* designation has been said to lie in the degree of precision

---

310 *Lange v Australian Broadcasting Corporation* (1997), p 560.
311 *Australian Capital Television v Commonwealth of Australia* (1992); *Nationwide News Pty Ltd v Wills* (1992).
312 *Lange v ABC* (1997), p 561.
313 *Coleman v Power* (2004).
314 *Levy v Victoria* (1997), p 646, cited in *Coleman v Power* (2004), para 95 per McHugh J.
315 *Coleman v Power* (2004), para 65.
316 Ibid, para 185.

and expression required of any legislative provision that purported to limit the right in question. McHugh J stated: 'Except by necessary implication, courts should not extend the natural and ordinary meaning of words that create an offence, especially when the statute is regulating such a fundamental right as that of free speech.'[317] According to Gummow and Hayne JJ, 'Fundamental common law rights are not to be eroded or curtailed save by clear words'.[318]

Notwithstanding the High Court's recent attempts to bolster the legal and constitutional foundation for free speech values in Australia, it would appear, on the face of it, that to the extent that it is possible to identify a 'right' to freedom of expression in Australia's legal environment, it is a right that is relatively fragile and circumscribed. This assessment is reflected in Chesterman's characterisation:

> [F]reedom of speech is ... a 'delicate plant' within Australian law. It is alive as an important value to be protected, and it is growing. But the plant needs to be nurtured. It is not so robust or so strongly established that it could never wither away on account of destructive or unsympathetic treatment.[319]

Given its relative fragility and legal form(lessness), it might be assumed that the right to free speech would be a relatively benign influence on the enactment and operation of hate speech laws. As will be explained below, this has not proven to be the case.

At least in terms of legal *form*, the principle of non-discrimination has a more explicit status in the Australian legal environment than free speech – albeit in a selective, 'group specific' manner. There is no Australian equivalent of the 'generic' equality/non-discrimination provision found in the UK, via Art 14 of the ECHR, in Canada, via s 15 of the Charter of Rights and Freedoms, and New Zealand, via s 19 of the BORA. In addition, the High Court has declined to find a guarantee of 'equal treatment' to be implicit in the Australian Constitution.[320] However, national, state and territorial legislation gives expression to the principle of non-discrimination in relation to a variety of groups who have traditionally been subjected to, or are otherwise susceptible to, discrimination.[321] Most notably, in the present context (given that the majority of hate speech laws only proscribe *racist* hate speech), the right not to be discriminated against on the basis of 'race, colour, descent or

---

317 *Coleman v Power* (2004), para 65. See also, *Gifford v Strang Patrick Stevedoring Pty Ltd* (2003), para 33.
318 Ibid, para 185.
319 Chesterman, 2000, p 1. See also, Gelber, 2002a, pp 98–100; O'Neill *et al*, 2004, pp 369–71; Rice, 2005.
320 *Leeth v Commonwealth* (1992); see O'Neill *et al*, 2004, p 476.
321 For an overview, see O'Neill *et al*, 2004, ch 18; Ronalds and Pepper, 2004.

national or ethnic origin' is embodied in the Racial Discrimination Act 1975 (Aust)[322] – the statute to which a prohibition on racist hate speech was belatedly added in 1995.

The operation of hate speech laws

One of the distinctive features of Australia's experience with hate speech laws is that, although they have been in operation for the shortest period of any of the four countries that are the subjects of the present study, they have been formally invoked more frequently than comparable laws in the UK, Canada and New Zealand. To some extent this is a predictable consequence of fact that Australia has largely eschewed criminal law regulation in preference to the complaint-based civil regulation model, with lower harm thresholds (albeit alongside relatively broad exceptions and defences). Where prosecuting authorities in all countries routinely vet alleged breaches of criminal hate-speech statutes in terms of the prospects of securing a conviction (including satisfaction of the criminal 'beyond reasonable doubt' standard of proof), individuals or representative organisations in Australia that consider that they have been the victims of unlawful vilification can invoke civil hate speech laws with relative ease – in the case of many jurisdictions, by lodging a complaint with the relevant jurisdiction's human rights/anti-discrimination agency. In addition, and in contrast to the approach adopted by the New Zealand Human Rights Commission in recent years, Australian agencies have generally not applied an especially high threshold when making a prima facie assessment of whether the conduct complained of falls within the parameters of the legislative prohibition.

Between October 1995 – when the racist hate speech provisions of RDA 1975 came into force – the Human Rights and Equal Opportunity Commission received over 800 complaints alleging that 18C had been breached.[323] Complaints under state laws have also been relatively 'high volume'. For example, in NSW, the state where hate speech laws have been in operation for the longest period (since 1989), the Anti-Discrimination Board of Board has received approximately 1,000 complaints alleging a breach of the Anti-Discrimination Act 1977 (NSW)'s prohibitions on hate speech directed at a range of target groups.[324] There have been only two prosecutions under Western Australia's racist hate speech laws (resulting in one conviction and one acquittal[325]), and none under the various criminal hate speech offences that

---

322 Racial Discrimination Act 1975 (Aust), s 9.
323 Source: HREOC annual reports, available at www.hreoc.gov.au/publications/index.htmlñrep and McNamara, 2002, pp 62–3.
324 Source: ADB of NSW annuals reports, available at www.lawlink.nsw.gov.au/lawlink/adb/ ll_adb.nsf/pages/adb_annual_report_index and McNamara 2002, pp 144–5.
325 See ABC News Online, 2005; Taylor, 2006.

are on the books in New South Wales, the Australian Capital Territory, Queensland, South Australia and Victoria.

The majority of the complaints alleging breaches of civil anti-discrimination laws, whether national or state/territorial, have not proceeded far beyond complaint lodgement. Only a small proportion has resulted in a mediated or 'settled' outcome, and an even smaller proportion has been resolved by way of authoritative tribunal or court adjudication.[326] While the outcomes achieved by mediation are confidential – one of the characteristics of the anti-discrimination regimes onto which hate speech laws have tended to be 'grafted' in Australia (as in New Zealand and Canada) – the public record of tribunal and court decisions offer a valuable window into the manner in which adjudicators in Australia have approached the task of balancing the competing values that are at issue in the interpretation and application of legislative prohibitions on hate speech.

Mirroring the Canadian experience, albeit to a more modest extent, the most explicit manifestation of free speech sensitivity in the context of public adjudication on alleged breaches of Australian hate speech has been that on a number of occasions persons against whom civil proceedings have been initiated under various Australian hate speech laws have argued that the relevant legislation is invalid by virtue of inconsistency with the implied freedom of political communication (outlined above). Such arguments have consistently failed. In *Jones v Scully*,[327] the Federal Court of Australia applied the *Lange* test and confirmed that the racist hate speech provisions in Pt IIA of RDA 1975 were a justifiable infringement of freedom of expression. Ely J endorsed the approach and conclusion of Commissioner Cavanough in earlier proceedings regarding the same matter:

> It is conceivable that the restrictions imposed by s 18C(1) of the RDA might in certain circumstances effectively burden freedom of communication about government and political matters. However, it seems to me that, bearing in mind the exceptions or exemptions available under s 18D, Part IIA as a whole is 'reasonably appropriate and adapted to serve a legitimate end the fulfilment of which is compatible with the maintenance of the system of government prescribed by the Constitution'.[328]

In *Kazak v John Fairfax Publications Ltd*,[329] the NSW Administrative

---

326 McNamara, 2002, pp 109, 205.
327 *Jones v Scully* (2002).
328 *Hobart Hebrew Congregation and Jones v Scully* (2000), p 11, discussed in McNamara, 2002, p 75.
329 *Kazak v John Fairfax Publications Ltd* (2000).

Decisions Tribunal reached the same conclusion about the racial vilification provisions of the Anti-Discrimination Act 1977 (NSW).[330]

Despite the relative ease with which tribunal members and judges have reached the conclusion that Australia's hate speech laws pass constitutional muster, it remains the case that no appellate court has yet been called upon to squarely address the issue. Consequently, a degree of uncertainty remains and some respondents continue to challenge the constitutional validity of legislative restrictions on hate speech.[331] Those who oppose hate speech laws on free speech grounds might have been encouraged by the High Court's 2004 decision in *Coleman v Power*.[332] A majority of the court held that a criminal offence of using 'threatening, abusive and insulting words' in public,[333] was invalid as an unjustified limitation on the constitutional freedom of political communication. Douglas has suggested:

> Opponents of vilification legislation may also take heart from *Coleman v Power*, but given the defences which typically exist under such legislation, and division in the High Court as to the extent of the implied freedom, it is likely that vilification legislation would withstand constitutional attack.[334]

Interpreting the scope of hate speech laws

Challenges to the *validity* of legislation are only the most obvious manifestation of free speech sensitivity when it comes to the operation of hate speech laws. In the context of the underlying concerns of this book, of equal importance is the question of what effect Australia's version of the 'right' to freedom of expression has had on judicial and quasi-judicial interpretations of the scope of hate speech prohibitions (and associated defences and exceptions).

In an earlier study of adjudications under NSW and national racist hate-speech laws during the 1990s,[335] I found that there had been considerable case-to-case variation as adjudicators endeavoured to apply the language and underlying values of legislative prohibitions on hate speech. The importance of upholding the value of 'free speech' has been routinely affirmed in the

---

330 *Kazak v John Fairfax Publications Ltd* (2000), para 96. See McNamara, 2002, pp 170–2. The Tribunal's substantive decision on whether s 20C had been breached in this case was overturned on appeal (*John Fairfax Publications Ltd v Kazak* (2002)), but the Appeal Panel did not express a view on the constitutional validity question.
331 See, e.g., *Radio 2UE Sydney Pty Ltd v Burns* (2005). At the time of writing, an appeal to the Appeal Panel of the NSW Administrative Decisions Tribunal which addresses the constitutional validity of the hate speech provisions of the Anti-Discrimination Act 1977 (NSW) was pending.
332 *Coleman v Power* (2004).
333 Vagrants, Gaming and Other Offences Act 1931 (Qld) (since repealed).
334 Douglas, 2005, p 27. See also, Akmeemana and Jones, 1995; Flahvin, 1995; McNamara and Solomon, 1996; Clarke, 2005, pp 410–20; Meagher, 2005.
335 McNamara, 2002.

context of the evolution of Australia's various regulatory regimes for dealing with hate speech. However, a wide range of views were advanced by different adjudicators on the breadth of the category of speech which should, in a democratic society such as Australia, remain 'free' – that is, unregulated by legislation – and a diversity of conclusions have been reached on the appropriate shape of hate speech legislation, which is intended to respect this value.

Contrary to the assumption that the relatively limited foundation for the 'right' to free speech in Australia might serve to minimise the impact of free speech sensitivity on the shape of hate speech laws, the absence of an authoritative barometer for identifying the limits of protected free speech – in the form of express constitutional, legislative or substantive common-law guidelines – appears to have created space for the exercise of considerable discretion in the interpretation of a category of protected speech upon which hate speech laws should not be permitted to impinge.

In recent years,[336] tribunals and courts have begun to develop greater clarity and consistency – partly as a result of a number of cases working their way through to appellate levels, but also as adjudicators have come to terms with the full significance of the High Court's articulation of a narrow, but constitutionally guaranteed, category of protected political speech.

In its 2002 decision in *Veloskey v Karagiannakis*, the Appeal Panel of the NSW Administrative Decisions Tribunal conceded that the interpretation of the definition of unlawful racist hate speech in s 20C(1) of the Anti-Discrimination Act 1977 (NSW)[337] had 'not always been consistent'.[338] The Panel endeavoured to provide authoritative guidance on those elements of the definition of unlawful conduct on which there had been disagreement and inconsistency in earlier decisions.[339] In *John Fairfax Publications Pty Ltd v Kazak*, also decided in 2002, the Appeal Panel addressed the other side of the statutory ledger: the scope of the exceptions contained in s 20C(2) of the Act.[340] In a case that arose out of the publication in the *Australian Financial Review* of an opinion piece that was highly critical of, and vitriolic towards, Palestine's leadership at the time, the Panel ruled that, at first instance, the Tribunal had erred by setting too high a threshold in order to be satisfied that it had acted reasonably and in good faith for a purpose in the public interest (s 20C(2)c)). The Panel ruled that:

> The proviso [under s 20C(2)] requires an objective assessment of the motives of the Appellant in deciding to publish the subject article,

---

336 See also, Chapman, 2004; Meagher, 2004; Chapman and Kelly, 2005; Gelber, 2005.
337 Anti-Discrimination Act 1977 (NSW), s 20C.
338 *Veloskey v Karagiannakis* (2002), para 20.
339 Ibid, paras 21–35.
340 *John Fairfax Publications Pty Ltd v Kazak* (2002).

provided the act of publication is carried out for a purpose in the public interest. Discussion or debate about any matter is within the public interest. It is not the author's motives in choosing the terminology, or in casting the article in certain language, which is relevant to this issue; it is the rationale behind the decision to publish.[341]

Although the Appeal Panel did not expressly defend its preferred interpretation of the scope of s 20C(2) with reference to free speech principles, it is reasonable to assume that the goal of minimal impairment of freedom of expression was influential – even if only indirectly, in the sense of recognising that this was the rationale for the inclusion of statutory exceptions or provisos when hate speech provisions were first added to the Anti-Discrimination Act 1977 (NSW) in 1989.[342]

Since the enactment of the Racial Hatred Act 1995 (Aust), adjudication of complaints under Pt IIA of RDA 1975 has followed a similar pattern. Early decisions were characterised by the articulation and application of a wide range of views about the scope of the legislative prohibition on racist hate speech in s 18C and the exemptions contained in s 18D – particularly prior to 2000, when the Human Rights and Equal Opportunity Commission retained an adjudicative function, and HRECOC Commissioners were the primary adjudicators of complaints under racist hate speech complaints under RDA 1975.[343] The discernible influence of free speech sensitivity on the approach adopted by different commissioners sometimes varied widely.[344]

As in NSW, a greater consistency of approach has been achieved in recent years. A series of decisions involving a cartoon published in a Western Australian newspaper provide a useful illustration of how adjudicators have tended to tackle the task of balancing the competing values and interests which come into play in relation to complaints under Pt IIA of RDA 1975.

The 'Alas Poor Yagan' case

On 6 September 1997, a cartoon by Dean Alston was published in *The West Australian*. Titled 'Alas Poor Yagan', the cartoon appeared in the context of publicity regarding attempts by members of the Nyungar community to have

---

341 *John Fairfax Publications Pty Ltd v Kazak* (2002), para 35.
342 Anti-Discrimination (Racial Vilification) Amendment Act 1989 (NSW).
343 See McNamara, 2002, pp 66–107.
344 Compare, for example, *Jacobs v Fardig* (1999) and *McGlade v Lightfoot* (1999), discussed in McNamara, 2002, pp 102–6. The latter decision was subsequently overturned on appeal: *McGlade v Human Rights and Equal Opportunity Commission* (2000), and the original complaint was later upheld: *McGlade v Lightfoot* (2002).

Balancing 'competing' human rights 239

the head of Yagan (an ancestor of the complainants) returned from a museum in London to Western Australia. The cartoon portrayed Yagan in a demeaning manner (preferring to stay in London and drink beer than return to the Nyungar community), ridiculed the mixed ancestry of members of the Nyungar community (including a number of the complainants) and contained disrespectful references to the Waugyl, a significant cultural and spiritual figure for Nyungar communities.

On 24 September 1997, a complaint was lodged by Hannah McGlade on behalf of the Nyungar Circle of Elders, alleging that the publication of the cartoon by West Australian Newspapers Ltd was unlawful by virtue of s 18C of RDA 1975. In March 1998, the Race Discrimination Commissioner decided that the conduct complained of was not unlawful by virtue of the exemptions contained in s 18D. The complainants then exercised their statutory entitlement to have the matter referred to a Human Rights and Equal Opportunity Commission (HREOC) public inquiry. In April 2001, the Commission ruled that the publication of the cartoon did fall within the definition of unlawful racist hate speech in s 18C, but dismissed the complaint on the basis that the respondent could rely on the exemptions in ss 18D(a) and 18D(b).

The Commission's findings began with an extended discussion of the 'right' to free speech in Australia and the debate over whether racist hate speech legislation was 'an unfair intrusion on freedom of speech'.[345] Commissioner Innes noted that in 'crafting' its legislative response to calls for legislative proscription of hate speech 'the Commonwealth Parliament appears to have intended to strike a balance between two rights: the right to freely express or communicate certain matters and ideas and the right to live free from vilification'.[346] The Commissioner saw this balance as embedded in the structure of Pt IIA of RDA 1975:

> The structure of the legislation provides the framework within which this balancing exercise must take place. The general protection for individuals or groups from harassment or fear because of their race, colour, national or ethnic origin is set out in s 18C. Section 18D then sets out what can be viewed as a protection of freedom of particular forms of expression, by outlining certain exemptions to which the general prohibition of s 18C will not apply. The exemptions . . . aim at preventing the stifling of activities which, although likely to offend etc are done reasonably and in good faith.[347]

---

345 *Corunna v West Australian Newspapers Ltd* (2001), p 75462.
346 Ibid, p 75465.
347 Ibid.

There is no evidence of any tendency to narrowly define the scope of unlawful conduct under s 18C in *Corunna*. On the contrary, Commissioner Innes adopted a relatively broad interpretation of the s 18C definition. For example, in considering whether the publication of the cartoon was '*reasonably likely* . . . to offend, insult, humiliate or intimidate', the Commissioner adopted the 'reasonable victim test', which meant that, in the circumstances of the case, the likely effect of the respondent's publication of the allegedly vilifying cartoon was assessed from the point of view of the 'reasonable Nyungar or Aboriginal person test'. The Commissioner explained his preference for this interpretation of the reasonable likelihood requirement in s 18C:

> It seems to me that, in the context of remedial legislation such as the RDA, and noting the comments in Australian cases and articles, and US and Canadian cases, the reasonable victim test is the appropriate test to adopt. This addresses the difficulty inherent in the reasonable person test of continuing the dominance of the dominant class or group, yet recognises that the views of a hypersensitive 'victim' or member of the relevant class will not prevail.[348]

Consistent with Commissioner Innes' analysis of the relationship between the structure of Pt IIA and the 'balancing' of competing rights, the impact of free speech sensitivity on the decision in *Corunna* is to be found in his (ultimately determinative) handling of the respondent's submission that even if the definition of s 18C was found to be satisfied, the publication of the cartoon was not unlawful because it fell within at least one of the exemption categories in s 18D.

The Commissioner commenced his analysis of this submission by observing that 'the exemptions [in s 18D] should be read broadly rather than narrowly'.[349] In support of this approach, Commissioner Innes quoted from the decision of Commissioner Johnston in a previous s 18C HREOC public inquiry (*Bryl v Melbourne Theatre Company*[350]):

> This is consistent with the presumption that a fundamental tenet of the common law is freedom of expression . . . Incursions by statute into freedom of expression should not be lightly assumed. A statutory provision that purports to have that effect should be strictly construed.[351]

Commissioner Innes continued:

---

348 *Corunna v West Australian Newspapers Ltd* (2001), p 75468.
349 Ibid, p 75469.
350 *Bryl v Melbourne Theatre Company* (1999).
351 Quoted in *Corunna v West Australian Newspapers Ltd* (2001), p 75469.

Freedom of expression is not, of course, absolute. It is, when viewed in relation to a provision like section 18D, a consideration to be taken into account when determining whether conduct is exempt, even if it otherwise would contravene section 18C. Section 18D is a corrective provision to prevent government from stifling non-conformity or ideas that may displease, or which some find offensive.[352]

There would appear to be something of a 'double-counting' of free speech sensitivity in this analysis, with important consequences for the overall scope of RDA 1975's legislative regime for the regulation of racist hate speech. The implicit argument is that free speech sensitivity demands not only the *inclusion* of s 18D in the legislative formulation but, in addition, the *broad definition* of those exemptions once included. In the result, to the extent that the Commonwealth Parliament consciously reserved a certain 'space' for free speech in setting the parameters (albeit with limited precision) for the legislative prohibition of racist hate speech, that 'space' may be considered to have been further expanded by a broad definition of the s 18D exemptions in *Corunna*.

Commissioner Innes ruled that the respondent had acted reasonably in publishing the cartoon. It was not, according to the Commissioner, 'sufficiently exaggerated or prejudiced . . . to breach the standard of reasonableness'. The respondent had not acted outside what Commissioner Johnston had described in *Bryl v Melbourne Theatre Company* as the ' ". . . margin of tolerance" [which] should be exercised in deciding what is reasonable'.[353] With respect to the good faith requirement:

> There was no evidence before me which suggested that the conduct of the respondent smacked of 'dishonesty or fraud' to follow Commissioner Johnston's formulation for the good faith requirement. Nor was there evidence of 'malice' on the part of the respondent.[354]

Commissioner Innes concluded that the respondent's conduct was exempted from the operation of s 18C on the basis of s 18D(a) – because 'a cartoon is an artistic work in the sense intended by the legislators'[355] – and s 18D(b) – because 'the cartoon was published in the course of encouraging public discussion or debate about the return of Yagan's head to Australia'.[356]

On appeal to the Federal Court of Australia, Nicholson J rejected the

---

352 *Corunna v West Australian Newspapers Ltd* (2001).
353 Ibid, p 75470.
354 Ibid.
355 Ibid, p 75471.
356 Ibid, p 75473.

argument that the Commissioner had erred in endorsing and applying a broad interpretation of the exemptions in s 18D.[357]

A further appeal to the Full Federal Court was also dismissed.[358] French J characterised the appeal as one which:

> ... raises the question of the appropriate balance, in *the Racial Discrimination Act*, between the prohibition of racial vilification and the protection of freedom of expression and, in particular, the statutory requirement of reasonableness and good faith in the exercise of that freedom.[359]

Before turning to the specific matters under appeal, French J reviewed in some detail the relevant international legal standards, including Art 19 of the ICCPR and Art 4 of the ICERD. He drew attention to the considerable controversy that surrounded the drafting of the latter, and which has continued since.[360] In this context, and given the 'fundamental' nature of the 'general principle that people should enjoy freedom of speech and expression',[361] French J confirmed that it was appropriate 'that s 18D be construed broadly rather than narrowly'.[362] However, it did not follow that the 'good faith' elements of the exemptions be read simply as 'subjective honesty' or the absence of subjective malice:

> A person acting in the exercise of a protected freedom of speech or expression under s 18D will act in good faith if he or she is subjectively honest, and objectively viewed, has taken a conscientious approach to advancing the exercising of that freedom in a way that is designed to minimize the offence of insult, humiliation or intimidation suffered by people affected by it.[363]

On this issue, French J found no fault with the approach of Commissioner Innes at first instance and dismissed the appeal. Carr J also dismissed the appeal. Lee J (in dissent) disagreed: the Commissioner had approached the issue of good faith as an inquiry about whether West Australian Newspapers

---

357 *Bropho v Human Rights and Equal Opportunity Commission and West Australian Newspapers Ltd* (2002), para 31.
358 *Bropho v Human Rights and Equal Opportunity Commission and West Australian Newspapers Ltd* (2004).
359 Ibid, para 3.
360 Ibid, para 60, citing Boyle and Baldaccini, 2001. See also, *Toben v Jones* (2003) paras 88–113 per Allsop J.
361 Ibid, para 72.
362 Ibid, para 73.
363 Ibid, para 102.

had acted with ' "dishonesty or fraud" or "malice" – an approach that was too broad an interpretation of the scope of the exemptions in s 18D'.[364]

The decision of the Full Court might be regarded as having effected a modest recalibration of the precise terms of the 'good faith' inquiry for the purpose of s 18D of RDA 1975. However, its real significance in the present context is that it confirms just how important the goal of minimal impairment of the right free speech is considered, when addressing the balance which the legislation strikes between protected free speech and unlawful hate speech. Even where the implied freedom of political communication and the question of constitutional validity are not on the table, free speech sensitivity remains a very real part of the interpretive mix. To a large extent, this is a direct flow-on effect on the prominence of free speech sensitivity in the public discourse and political negotiations over the Racial Hatred Act 1995 (Aust). The tensions and compromises that characterised the parliamentary debates during 1994–1995 have been embedded in the legislative definition of unlawful racist hate speech, constructed out of the combined effect of ss 18C and 18D of RDA 1975.

Turning to the United Nations

A final event in the short history of the operation of hate speech laws in Australia is the story of Aboriginal activist Stephen Hagan's attempts to invoke hate speech laws to force the Toowoomba Sports Ground Trust to remove the word 'nigger' from a grandstand. The stand was named the 'ES "Nigger" Brown Stand' in honour of a well-known (non-Indigenous) rugby league player and later local politician, who died in 1972, and whose nickname was 'Nigger'.[365] The Federal Court dismissed Hagan's complaint that the continued display of the word was unlawful under s 18C of the Racial Discrimination Act 1975 (Aust).[366] Drummond J held that in the context in which it was displayed, the word 'nigger' was not likely to offend, insult, humiliate or intimidate persons of colour.[367] Hagan's appeal to the Full Federal Court was dismissed,[368] and an application for special leave to appeal to the High Court was denied.[369]

---

364 *Toben v Jones* (2003), para 144.
365 Hagan, 2005; Willheim, 2003.
366 *Hagan v Trustees of Toowoomba Sports Ground Trust* (2000).
367 Ibid, para 8.
368 *Hagan v Trustees of Toowoomba Sports Ground Trust* (2001).
369 *Hagan v Trustees of the Toowoomba Sports Ground Trust* B17/2001 (19 March 2002) www.austlii.edu.au/au/other/hca/transcripts/. See Hagan, 2005, pp 244–7; Willheim, 2003.

As of March 2006, Australia was one of only 47 of the 170 state parties to the ICERD,[370] and the only one of the four countries that are the subjects of the present study, to have consented to the individual complaint procedure under Art 14 of the ICERD. Article 14 provides:

> A State Party may at any time declare that it recognizes the competence of the Committee to receive and consider communications from individuals or groups of individuals within its jurisdiction claiming to be victims of a violation by that State Party of any of the rights set forth in this Convention. No communication shall be received by the Committee if it concerns a State Party which has not made such a declaration.

In 2002, Hagan lodged a communication with the CERD Committee, alleging that the continued display of the word 'nigger' at the Toowoomba Sports Ground placed Australia in breach of its obligations under the ICERD. The Committee agreed:

> ... [T]he Committee considers that that use and maintenance of the offending term can at the present time be considered offensive and insulting, even if for an extended period it may not have necessarily been so regarded. The Committee considers, in fact, that the Convention, as a living instrument, must be interpreted and applied taking into the circumstances of contemporary society. In this context, the Committee considers it to be its duty to recall the increased sensitivities in respect of words such as the offending term appertaining today. . . . The Committee recommends that the State party take the necessary measures to secure the removal of the offending term from the sign in question, and to inform the Committee of such action it takes in this respect.[371]

The Australian Government, the Queensland Government and the Toowoomba Sports Ground Trust were all unmoved by the Committee's findings and recommendation, and declined to take steps to remove or alter the sign.[372]

---

370 Office of the United Nations High Commissioner for Human Rights, 2006c; Office of the United Nations High Commissioner for Human Rights, 2006b.
371 *Hagan v Australia* (2003), paras 7–3. 8. See also, Hagan, 2005, pp 248–56.
372 Roberts, 2003; Hagan, 2005, pp 264–7. At the time of writing, a complaint by Hagan under s 124A of the Anti-Discrimination Act 1991 (Qld) (as amended in 2001) was pending. Section 24A(1) provides: 'A person must not, by a public act, incite hatred towards, serious contempt for, or severe ridicule of, a person or group of persons on the ground of the race, religion, sexuality or gender identity of the person or members of the group.' See, further, Graham, 2006.

Key features of the Australian balance

Notwithstanding the relative fragility of the legal form in which the right to freedom of expression is recognised in Australia, concern about the implications for free speech has been a recurring theme in the story of the enactment, operation and interpretation of hate speech legislation in Australia over the course of the last two decades. The consistent effect of free speech sensitivity in the drafting legislative approval, and adjudication processes has been to operate as a 'brake' on hate speech legislation – with respect to both the form in which it has been enacted, and the manner in which it has been interpreted and applied by tribunals and courts.

Free speech sensitivity has been a central factor behind the distinctive pattern in Australian hate speech legislation of minimal reliance on *criminalisation* as a regulatory response. Australia is the only one of the four countries that are the subject of the present study, not to have enacted a nationally applicable criminal offence of inciting racial hatred. The decision of the Australian Parliament to exclude such an offence from the Racial Hatred Act 1995, prior to enactment, is a vivid illustration of the Australian tendency to regard the criminalisation of hate speech as incompatible with a continued commitment to the value of free speech. As a result, with the exception of Western Australia, all Australian jurisdictions have characterised hate speech as a civil wrong rather than a criminal offence. In most cases the category of 'unlawful hate speech' has been grafted onto complaint-based civil human rights regimes originally established to deal with breaches of anti-discrimination laws. Ironically, the very same concerns regarding the objective of minimal impairment of free speech that have prompted the UK to rely exclusively on criminal law regulation,[373] have prompted Australian makers to eschew criminal sanctions in favour of civil remedies.

Free speech sensitivity has also been an importance influence on the post-enactment operation of Australian hate speech laws. First, and somewhat surprisingly – given the absence of an express constitutional or statutory right to free speech and the very limited authority of Australian courts to invalidate laws on grounds of human rights incompatibility – there have been a number of challenges to the constitutional validity of state and national hate-speech laws. These have tended to take the form of attempts by opponents of hate speech laws to mobilise the implied freedom of political communication developed by the High Court of Australia during the 1990s. Given the relatively modest parameters of the guarantee, and the room that the High Court has left for the imposition of limits on communication in the pursuit of legitimate policy goals, hate speech laws have to date, been considered to pass muster. Second, Australia's version of the right of free speech – sourced in

---

373 Gelber, 2002a, p 106.

common-law tradition, embraced in parliamentary discourse and fortified by the implied constitutional guarantee as well as the High Court's recent emphasis on its character as a 'fundamental right' – has been an important part of the interpretive context in which tribunals and courts have approached the task of applying the different forms of hate speech laws that operate across Australia. On the whole, this had not led tribunal members and judges to adopt a narrow construction of the scope of legislative prohibitions *per se*. However, it *has* led adjudicators to broadly interpret the scope of legislative 'defences' (or 'exemptions') – most notably in cases under Pt IIA of RDA 1975. Exemption provisions like s 18D of RDA 1975 are not incidental to legislative definitions of hate speech. Rather, they are an integral part of the legislative framework for delimiting unlawful hate speech from protected free speech. Their inclusion in Australian hate speech legislation, and their broad interpretation by adjudicators, vividly illustrate the significance of free speech sensitivity as a normative influence in Australia's legal culture – even in the absence of an express constitutional or legislative right to freedom of expression.

Conclusions

One of the reservations sometimes expressed by supporters of hate speech laws about the prospects of a bill of rights in Australia, is that such a move would inevitably involve the express recognition of the right to freedom of expression, and that this would, in turn, threaten the validity, or encourage a narrow interpretation, of hate speech laws. The stories of the operation of hate speech laws in the UK, Canada, New Zealand and Australia told in this chapter suggest that such concerns may be ill-founded. First, free speech sensitivity has long been a significant constraint on the shape of hate speech laws in Australia, notwithstanding its relatively 'delicate' legal form. Second, the evidence from Canada, New Zealand and the UK does not suggest that codification of the right to free speech (via the Charter, BORA or HRA, respectively) necessarily increases the breadth of the category of protected speech, or necessarily effects a corresponding diminution in the operational scope of hate speech laws. In fact, of the three case studies examined in this book, the enduring controversy over the balance to be struck between protected free speech and unlawful hate speech has been the case in which the evidence for the significance of legal form is the weakest.

A number of concluding observations can be drawn from the four stories in this chapter about the significance of legal form for the manner in which the balance is struck between the right to freedom of expression and the right to non-discrimination.

First, there is no correlation between the intensity of the controversy over the legitimate scope of hate speech and the form in which 'competing' human rights are recognised. The public discourse in all four countries has been characterised, at various points, by heated debate over whether the right to freedom of expression can legitimately be infringed in pursuit of non-discrimination and anti-prejudice goals, irrespective of the legal form in which domestic systems recognise free speech and equality rights.

Second, the degree of jurisdictional variation – in terms of both the scope of the statutory definition of unlawful hate speech and the preferred enforcement mechanism (from conciliation-based complaint handling to criminal prosecution) – suggest that, even at the stage of law creation, there is no 'natural' outcome of the task of balancing respect for freedom of expression and non-discrimination/equality. Notwithstanding their common obligations under Art 4 of the ICERD, national legislators in the four countries (as well as state/provincial/territorial legislators in Canada and Australia) have adopted a variety of models for the legal regulation of racist hate speech, and some jurisdictions have extended protection to other groups who are subjected to hate speech. These variations cannot be explained in terms of the legal form of the competing rights in question. For example, it is in Australia, despite the 'delicate' legal shape of the right to free speech in that country, that free speech sensitivity has been most strongly manifested in the form of a reluctance to *criminalise* hate speech, and a preference for civil mechanisms and sanctions. In Canada, the constitutional form of the right to freedom of expression in s 2(b) of the Charter (as well as the right to equality in s 15 and the commitment to multiculturalism in s 27) has influenced the *approach* of the courts to the interpretation of hate speech laws, but it has not resulted in an unduly restrictive approach to setting the parameters of hate speech restrictions. Canada has proved to be a more receptive legal and political environment for the employment of *criminal law* in the regulation of vilification than Australia. Given that the imposition of criminal penalties by the state is generally regarded as the most serious of the range of available regulatory options,[374] it might be assumed that a right to free speech, which enjoyed express constitutional protection – as in Canada – would be more likely to be regarded as constituting an insurmountable barrier to the criminalisation of hate speech than a 'right' to free speech that received no equivalent constitutional (or statutory) protection – as in Australia. Instead, it is in *Australia* that a relatively enlarged free speech sensitivity has been pivotal in the confinement of criminal law regulation to a marginal and practically inoperative role vis-à-vis other Australian hate speech statutes, whereas in Canada, prosecutions for criminal hate speech remain an important (albeit, infrequently invoked) component of the network of Canadian hate speech statutes.

Third, legal form has exerted a somewhat uneven, and relatively weak, influence, on the manner in which decision-makers have approached the task

---

374 See Australian Law Reform Commission, 2002.

of balancing competing rights in the context of specific invocations of hate speech laws. That is, it has not generally been the case that those countries in which the right to freedom of expression receives an ostensibly 'stronger' form of protection (that is, constitutional entrenchment, or bill of rights codification) have tended to construe hate speech laws narrowly. Rather, it is factors attributable to local legal culture (of which, of course, formal institutional arrangements are a part) that have operated as strong influences on the balancing exercise and its outcomes. In the UK, a firmly established European conviction about the unacceptability of racist hate speech and the necessity of legal regulation, has produced an environment in which the line between legitimate and protected free speech, and illegitimate and punishable (racist) hate speech, is a relatively bright and constant one. Against the backdrop of the European Court of Human Rights' jurisprudence – which has consistently and unequivocally placed the protection of Art 10 of the ECHR beyond the reach of those who engage in hate speech – courts in the UK have rarely been called upon to adjudicate on free speech-inspired arguments for the invalidation or narrow interpretation of hate speech laws.

To those familiar with the jurisprudence of the European Court of Human Rights, this aspect of the story of the operation of hate speech laws in the UK may come as little surprise. However, to those more familiar with the judicial and quasi-judicial interpretations of hate speech laws in Australia and Canada, the degree of jurisprudential consensus and certainty in the UK about where the line should be drawn between legitimate media expression and unlawful hate speech is striking. To a significant extent, the tensions and uncertainties that continue to impact on Australian and Canadian microdecisions (see below) appear to have been largely settled in the UK. Whether or not this sort of institutionalised certainty is desirable is open to debate. For example, Iganski has observed that European policy formulation in relation to racist hate speech has often been 'formulated with a degree of generality that demonstrates little sensitivity to the conflicts over "rights" which impede policy intervention'.[375] In a similar vein, McGonagle has expressed reservations about what he sees as the tendency of European judicial and quasi-judicial bodies to 'spurn . . . the limited opportunities that have arisen for lengthy analysis' of the compatibility of 'freedom of expression and anti-racism'.[376] Nonetheless, the confidence with which prohibited hate speech is demarcated from the speech which warrants protection from legal restriction is, in the context of the present comparative exercise, a distinctive feature of the UK story.

In contrast to the established European position on the legitimacy and necessity of hate speech laws, in New Zealand, a different set of ideological

---

375 Iganski, 1999b. See, e.g., European Commission against Racism and Intolerance, 2001.
376 McGonagle, 2001b.

values has, in recent times, informed a different balancing approach. The less entrenched, but currently ascendant, libertarian philosophical preferences of the New Zealand Human Rights Commission have seen the hate speech provisions of the Human Rights Act 1993 (NZ) interpreted narrowly, in deference to the goal of minimal impairment of the right to freedom of expression. If legal form *per se* was an influential variable, greater similarity between these two countries would have been expected.

Fourth, even though legal form has not had a strong impact on the terms of the balance ultimately struck when it comes to the operation of hate-speech laws, the particular legal form of competing human rights in each country has exerted an influence on the discursive styles, strategies and interpretive techniques of the free speech/hate speech debate in each of the countries. For example, the distinctive characteristics of the Canadian model of human rights protection – constitutional entrenchment and (effective) judicial supremacy – has encouraged litigants to advance head-on challenges to the validity of hate speech laws, and has prompted adjudicators to employ interpretative techniques drawn from the Supreme Court of Canada's Charter validity jurisprudence. However, as noted above, this has not resulted in a more 'free speech-weighted' Canadian balance than the balance that has been struck elsewhere. In New Zealand, although there is little evidence that s 14 has *caused* the current approach to the interpretation of s 61 of the Human Rights Act 1993, the status of the right to freedom of expression as a 'BORA right' has been highlighted by the New Zealand Human Rights Commission on those occasions where it has sought to explain and defend the terms in which it strikes the free speech/hate speech balance.

Finally, codification of competing human rights – in the present context, the right to free speech and the right to equality/non-discrimination – has not necessarily injected greater stability, consistency, or predictability into the balancing exercise. In Canada and Australia – countries that occupy opposite ends of the legal form spectrum – interpretations of the scope of hate speech prohibitions in the context of specific allegations that a civil legislative standard has been breached, are still characterised by a considerable degree of adjudicator-to-adjudicator variation. To some extent this is a product of the nature of the quasi-judicial anti-discrimination jurisdiction onto which hate speech laws have usually been grafted in these jurisdictions, where the influence of precedent is weak and the availability of appellate court guidance, often modest. But it also serves as a reminder about the tensions that are embedded in legislative attempts to articulate a line between protected free speech and prohibited hate speech, and the limitations of codification as a mechanism for firmly setting the parameters for one of liberal democracy's most enduring human rights controversies.

Chapter 5

Conclusion: Does legal form matter?

In writing this book, I have not set out to offer a normative assessment of whether it was the 'right thing' for Canada to enact the Charter of Rights and Freedoms 1982, for New Zealand to enact the Bill of Rights Act 1990, or for the United Kingdom to enact the Human Rights Act 1998. As an outsider, and without a more comprehensive examination of the evaluative research and scholarship which has been produced in Canada over more than two decades,[1] and which is emerging in the UK[2] and to a lesser extent, New Zealand,[3] to have embarked on any such exercise would have been, to say the least, presumptuous. Nor has it been my aim to produce a general theory of the relationship between legal form and respect for human rights. Even if this were considered possible or desirable, a four-country examination of three human rights controversies would clearly provide an inadequate foundation for such a task.

My goals have been more modest. Motivated by the meandering (though recently reinvigorated) debate in Australia over the desirability of adopting a bill of rights, I set out to investigate some of the common assumptions about the utility of this approach to the goal of injecting human rights considerations into domestic processes of policy development, law reform and legal decision-making. Rather than undertake it in the abstract, this investigation has been grounded in the stories of three human rights controversies – as they have played out in Australia, Canada, New Zealand and the UK in recent years – each of which illustrates different expectations commonly associated with domestic legal arrangements for the recognition and protection of human rights.

Chapter 2 examined legislative moves to limit the scope of the immunity

---

1 See, e.g., Mandel, 1994; Bakan, 1997; Knopff, 2000; Manfredi, 2001; Hiebert, 2002; James *et al*, 2002; McAllister and Dodek, 2002; Magnet *et al*, 2003; Beaudoin, 2005; Kelly, 2005; Sharpe and Roach, 2005; MacIvor, 2006.
2 See, e.g., Jowell and Cooper, 2003; Halliday and Schmidt, 2004; Clements and Thomas, 2005; Harvey, 2005; Lester and Pannick, 2004.
3 See Rishworth *et al*, 2003; Butler and Butler, 2005.

against re-prosecution after acquittal underpinned by the traditional rule against double jeopardy. This controversy was generated by what was essentially a head-on assault on the scope of an established human right, bringing into play the expectation that human rights discourse has a *defensive* function – to provide individuals with a degree of insulation from the potentially negative effects of governmental actions, by constituting a constraint on the range of permissible policy options.

Chapter 3 examined the manner in which national governments and legislatures in each of the four countries have responded to demands for legal recognition of same-sex relationships. In this case, human rights law has been deployed to support the full *extension* of principles of equality and non-discrimination to gay men and lesbians, reflecting the expectation that human rights discourse should facilitate just policy-making in response to 'new' human rights assertions advanced by equality-seeking groups and individuals.

Chapter 4 considered recent developments in the enduring controversy over the creation and operation of hate speech laws – a controversy dominated by debate over the implications of the perceived clash between competing human rights: the equality and non-discrimination rights not to be subjected to the harms associated with hate speech and the right to freedom of expression. In this context, human rights law has been mobilised on both sides of the dispute, creating an expectation that human rights discourse should provide a framework for weighing up and *balancing* competing interests and rights.

In this final chapter I aim to consolidate the central insights to have emerged from the three case studies about each of the four different domestic legal regimes for the recognition and protection of human rights. Consistent with the primary objective of this book, the focus will be on the role that legal form has (or has not) played in shaping public discourse and influencing the terms of resolution of the controversy. Concluding observations about the significance of legal form for the protection of human rights within local legal cultures – that is, for the creation of a 'rights-supportive culture' will follow a country-by-country overview.[4]

Canada

In 2000, Michael Ignatieff made the following observation about the 'rights revolution' in Canada:

> ... [R]ights talk ... has widened the democratic conversation of societies like ours [Canada]. I grew up in a Canada where the conversation of the country was firmly in the hands of a political and economic elite. Since

---

4   Hirschl, 2004, p 154.

the 1960s, the rights revolution has brought to the table new groups that were never heard before, and the debate about what kind of society this should be has become noisier, less controllable, and democratic than it was before. For this, we have to thank the rights revolution.[5]

Since 1982, the Charter of Rights and Freedoms has been at the centre of the rights revolution. More specifically, the defining features of the Canadian model of domestic human rights regime – constitutionally entrenched rights (albeit, primarily of the civil and political variety) and effective judicial supremacy over their interpretation and application – have had 'a transformative impact on political discourse'.[6]

One of the features of the Canadian human rights landscape that emerges strongly from the Canadian stories told in this book, is that, to a greater extent than in any of the other three countries, Canada's legal arrangements for the protection of human rights have the capacity to transform certain policy options into constitutional imperatives. That is, the Charter has not simply ensured that human rights considerations feature prominently in the public discourse on controversial political questions, but that Charter rights play a major role in shaping the contours of that discourse.

The power of the Charter to place certain 'anti-human rights' measures off limits to legislative actors is illustrated by the (non) story of double jeopardy reform in Canada. Whereas governments in the UK, New Zealand and Australia have been tempted to diminish the scope of the established immunity against re-prosecution after acquittal in pursuit of 'law and order' style criminal justice agendas, s 11(h) of the Charter is generally regarded as creating a discursive environment in which such a move would be regarded as beyond contemplation.

The power of the Charter to mandate the pursuit of a particular policy path is vividly illustrated by Canada's unique resolution of the controversy over the legal status of same-sex relationships. Despite continuing political disagreement, s 15 of the Charter was successfully mobilised by advocates of same-sex marriages and employed by Canadian judges (and ultimately, legislators) to render the re-definition of marriage in inclusive, sexual orientation-neutral terms as the only constitutionally viable alternative. As a matter of pure legal form, legislative insistence on a different solution (such as a parallel civil union regime, along the lines of the UK or New Zealand legislative models), was possible, via invocation of the s 33 legislative override. But the

---

5   Ignatieff, 2000, p 26.
6   Hirschl, 2004, p 221. Hiebert, 2002, p 201, has observed, with specific reference to gay and lesbian equality claims, that the Charter has played 'a dynamic role ... in changing the assumptions and expectations of the polity': Hiebert, 2002, p 201. See also, Smith, 2005c, p 25.

Charter's potency is not merely a product of legal form; it is strengthened by the extent to which a commitment to *de facto* judicial supremacy over the dictates of the Charter has become embedded in Canada's legal culture.

Both of these case studies serve to add force to the claim – at the heart of the legal form hierarchy commonly endorsed by human rights advocates – that a domestic human rights model based on constitutionalisation and effective judicial supremacy is the best way of placing human rights considerations outside of the overtly political realms of executive and legislative decision-making. Whether this feature should be regarded as a *strength* or *weakness* of the Canadian model – that is, whether a country's legal and institutional arrangements *should* take controversial human rights questions out of the hands of elected politicians – is contested, even by some advocates of a highly visible and influential place for human rights considerations in processes of policy development and law reform.[7] The relative attractiveness of New Zealand or UK-style bills of rights (and associated vetting and supremacy arrangements) is considered further below.

The third and final Canadian story told in this book – of the resolution of the tension between the right to freedom of expression and the right to equality/non-discrimination in the context of the creation and application of hate speech laws – tells a more equivocal tale about the Charter's capacity to deliver on the expectation that a domestic legal framework for the protection of human rights should facilitate the striking of an appropriate balance between rights that are said to be in competition. To a considerable extent the Charter has provided such a framework. Canadian courts have consistently (though not always unanimously) rejected arguments that hate speech laws cannot be reconciled with the express recognition of the right to freedom of expression in s 2(b) of the Charter. The mere fact of constitutional entrenchment has not transformed free speech values into a force that is fatal to the survival of hate speech laws. At the same time, in the context of specific hate-speech allegations, particularly under provincial human rights legislation, adjudicators continue to grapple with the demands of demarcating speech that is constitutionally protected from speech that is legitimately caught by hate speech prohibitions. The Charter may have provided the constitutional and interpretive framework within which such decisions are made. In some respects it has complicated and 'over-legalised' the line-drawing exercise in which tribunals and courts are required to participate, which in turn, tends to refuel, rather than dampen, the fires of disagreement about the legitimate scope of hate speech restrictions.

A strong overall theme to emerge from the Canadian component of the present study is that the Charter of Rights and Freedoms, and the associated institutional arrangements for scrutiny and review, have made a significant

---

7 See Campbell, 1999; Ignatieff, 2000; Hiebert, 2004.

contribution to ensuring that human rights (at least those rights reflected in the Charter) feature prominently in the discourses surrounding legal decision-making. Charter considerations are not only prominent, but consistently potent: with the power to foreclose, as well as to mandate, policy directions. A feature of the Canadian model as it has taken shape, that may have been unanticipated in 1982, is the tendency for the Charter to be regarded as a tool of the judiciary, and for litigation to be seen as the default strategy of Charter engagement. As a result, governments have not always been pro-active in fulfilling their own obligations to advance human rights goals. The manner in which the courts led, and the legislatures, for the most part, reluctantly followed, the application of the s 15 equality guarantee to same-sex relationships is illustrative.

United Kingdom

The stated objective of the Blair Government, in introducing the Human Rights Act 1998, was to 'bring rights home'.[8] Ironically, perhaps, one of the strongest themes to emerge from the UK component of this study is that since the HRA came into force in 2000, the supranational standards embodied in the European Convention on Human Rights (ECHR) have emerged as the paramount legal reference point for the injection of human rights considerations into UK policy development, law reform and scrutiny procedures. While this was neither accidental nor a hasty move – the UK had assumed an obligation to comply with the ECHR more than 40 years previously – the irony is that the three case studies tell a story, not so much of the domestication of a previously 'foreign' set of human rights standards, but of the creation of a powerful external yardstick for prompting, defending and critiquing government policy agendas. However, in contrast to the powerful and relatively independent nature of the Charter imperative that has developed in Canada since 1982, the European imperative generated by the 1998 incorporation of the ECHR into UK law – with implications for executive policy development, legislative scrutiny and judicial decision-making – has, at least in the case of the three controversies examined in this book, operated within parameters largely controlled by the executive and legislative arms of government.

The relatively smooth path to double jeopardy reform in the UK serves as an interesting illustration of the enthusiasm with which a government can embrace the concept of an undeniable human rights imperative, where such an embrace is consistent with the pursuit of a preferred policy option and law reform outcome. The new evidence exception to the immunity against re-prosecution after acquittal was introduced via Pt 10 of the Criminal Justice Act 2003, not because the UK Government was required to do so by

---

8 United Kingdom Government, 1997.

virtue of its European human rights law obligations. The ECHR is silent on this aspect of the rights of a criminal accused, and at the time the UK was not party to Protocol 7 – Art 4 of which expresses the European *ne bis in idem* principle. Rather, the UK's renewed commitment to European human rights standards via its enactment of the HRA, provided a convenient and highly effective discursive strategy for justifying the erosion of one of the common law's oldest human rights as a necessary incident of the pursuit of the Government's criminal justice policy agenda.

The UK Government's public articulation of the case for the Civil Partnership Act 2004 as a measure that was consistent with the principle of equality/non-discrimination embodied in Art 14 of the ECHR, was also partly strategic. However, in the case of the controversy surrounding the legal recognition of same-sex relationships, the influence of an emerging, but apparently inevitable, European imperative was discernible. Nonetheless, where, by 2003, it was considered to be reasonably clear that Canadian law-makers had little choice but to endorse full equality in the form of gay and lesbian access to the legal institution of marriage, in the UK, the Government and Parliament retained the freedom to stake their claim to the parallel institution of civil partnership as the appropriate form of legal recognition. There were at least two relevant reasons for this. First, the nascent European human rights paradigm of equality for same-sex couples had not (and has still not) reached the point where nothing other than the re-definition of marriage would be satisfactory. Second, although the courts were beginning to show a preparedness to vigorously employ their interpretive responsibility under s 3 of the HRA in support of the removal of sexual orientation discrimination from the UK's laws, the limits on judicial power under the HRA, and the principle of parliamentary supremacy that those limits reflect, ensured that the final decision as to the terms on which relationship recognition would be offered to gay men and lesbians would be left to Parliament.

The enactment of the HRA was of only modest significance for the manner in which decision-makers in the UK approached the free speech/hate speech balance. Well before the HRA came into force – in fact, from the time of the enactment of the first racist incitement laws in the 1960s – UK law exhibited the hallmarks of the European approach to the regulation of racist hate speech: a legislative preference for the criminalisation of serious forms of racist hate speech, and an interpretive approach that drew a relatively firm distinction between expression that should be immune from legislative imposition, and expression that should be condemned and punished for its propensity to foster discrimination and disorder. Since 2000, on those few occasions when courts have been called upon to adjudicate on the free speech/hate speech balance, judges in the UK have strongly endorsed the established Strasbourg approach to the construction of the right to freedom of expression in Art 10 of the ECHR.

In adopting the 'Commonwealth model' as the basis for the framework established by the HRA, the UK Parliament made a conscious decision to institute a domestic environment for policy development, law reform and decision-making processes, which would simultaneously guarantee that (European-based) human rights standards would feature prominently in deliberation and public debate, but would not necessarily mandate the pursuit of particular outcomes. That is, the executive Government and the Parliament would have the last word on the resolution of human rights controversies, but their decisions would be made in a context where the standards embodied in the ECHR were neither mere rhetorical tropes nor absolute dictates. In the case of hate speech laws, the parameters had already been largely set, in accordance with a common feature of the legal cultures of many European states: the conviction that racist hate speech laws were both legitimate and necessary. The more direct invocation of Art 10 of the ECHR after 2000 merely served to reinforce the relatively stable balance between the right to freedom of expression and the right not to be subjected to discrimination that had been struck by prosecutors and judges in the UK since the late 1960s. The enactment of Pt 10 of the Criminal Justice Act 2003 and the Civil Partnership Act 2004 were legislative events with more overt foundations in the particular model of domestic human rights infrastructure adopted by the UK in 1998, and to that extent more readily illustrate the significance of legal form.

New Zealand

With its enactment of the Bill of Rights Act 1990 (BORA), the New Zealand Parliament's stated objective was 'to affirm, protect, and promote human rights and fundamental freedoms in New Zealand'.[9] Whereas the Canadian approach to an equivalent goal involved an institutional design and distribution of interpretative authority that relied heavily on the judicial arm of government, the New Zealand model opted for weighting the compliance responsibility in favour of the executive and legislative arms of government. Consequently, the BORA provides a relatively weak foundation for judicial scrutiny, with no power to invalidate BORA-inconsistent laws, and only modest powers with respect to the issuance of declarations of incompatibility. If one of the objectives of New Zealand's formal bill of rights arrangements was to ensure that final judgments about the appropriate influence of human rights considerations on policy development processes and law reform outcomes should lay with elected politicians – in Cabinet and in the Parliament – the three case studies examined in this study indicate a considerable degree of success. On the other hand, for those who expected the BORA to provide a domestic human rights touchstone of the 'trump' variety – a role that is played by the Charter in Canada, and, to a lesser extent, the HRA in the UK – then the New Zealand stories told in this book may disappoint.

9 Bill of Rights Act 1990 (NZ), Preamble.

The failure of the BORA to transform human rights discourse into an imperative, outside or above the mix of ideological ebb and flow, pragmatic compromise, opportunism and populism that is characteristic of political discourse in liberal democracies (particularly in the multi-party legislature, minority government and shifting coalitions of post-1996 New Zealand under MMP[10]) is powerfully illustrated by the erosion of the rule against double jeopardy to be effected by the Criminal Procedure Bill. Despite its long tradition of common law protection, and its express articulation in s 26(2) of the BORA, the immunity against re-prosecution after acquittal underpinned by the rule against double jeopardy appears to be a relatively easy target for legislative overhaul. The broader significance of New Zealand's story of double jeopardy reform does not lay in the mere fact that statutory exceptions are set to be introduced, but that the BORA has been relatively marginal to the public discourse surrounding the Criminal Procedure Bill, both inside and outside the Parliament, and has provided little resistance to the Government's legislative agenda.

If the BORA has been at the periphery of the double jeopardy debate, it occupied a more prominent position in the public discourse surrounding the Civil Union Act 2004 (NZ). A key difference was that on this occasion the non-discrimination principle embodied in s 19 was not a potential barrier to the Government's legislative agenda, but an important ally. Alert to the perceived antagonism of the New Zealand electorate towards American (or Canadian) style 'human rights talk', neither the Government nor civil union campaigners advanced an aggressive case for equality-based formal recognition of same-sex relationships as a strong legal imperative. Rather, the case for the creation of a civil union regime (primarily for same-sex couples, but, strategically perhaps, made available for unmarried opposite-sex couples too) was firmly advanced as a logical extension of New Zealand's stated commitment to the principle of non-discrimination, as reflected in both the BORA and the Human Rights Act 1993. Not only was this approach strategic in its discursive preference for the language of non-discrimination values over hard-edged BORA rights, the legal model of relationship recognition was a compromise, at least for those in the gay and lesbian community who sought the same outcome as their peers in Canada – access to a sexual orientation-neutral definition of marriage. As in the UK – perhaps to an even greater extent, in the absence of judicial engagement or any normative influence equivalent to the emerging European imperative on same-sex equality – the New Zealand Government retained a significant degree of choice over the mechanism of recognition that it was prepared to endorse.

---

10 MMP is an abbreviation for the Mixed Member Proportional system of electoral voting, which has operated in New Zealand since 1996, one of the effects of which has been to increase the number of political parties with seats in the New Zealand House of Representatives.

The New Zealand theme of the strategic (im)mobilisation of the BORA in the context of the public discourse surrounding human rights controversies is reflected yet again in the recent operation of the hate speech provisions of the Human Rights Act 1993, albeit in different circumstances. From the early 1970s, legislators and administrative decision-makers have struggled to find an acceptable balance between the objectives of respecting the classic liberal democratic right to freedom of expression and providing legal redress to targets or victims of racist hate speech, consistent with the values of a bicultural and increasingly diverse society. Almost from its initial creation in 1971, the criminal offence of inciting racial disharmony has been regarded as a primarily symbolic gesture, so its dormancy was predictable. That the modified civil racial disharmony prohibition, which was reintroduced in 1993, has been equally dormant is more surprising, particularly given that s 61 of the Human Rights Act 1993 can be presumed to have been drafted and endorsed by Parliament with cognizance of the terms of s 14 of the BORA, enacted just three years earlier. The explanation lies, to a considerable extent, in what might be characterised as the libertarian position taken by the current administration of the New Zealand Human Rights Commission with respect to the free speech/hate speech balance. The point is, that while the formal legal status of the right to freedom of expression since 1990 does not *mandate* a narrow or high threshold construction of the scope of hate speech legislation, it does provide a powerful discursive mechanism with which to defend a philosophical preference for a free speech-weighted balance.

In the case of the three case studies examined here, human rights sensitivity has exerted a rather uneven influence on New Zealand's public discourse surrounding controversial law and policy questions. Since 1990, BORA compliance scrutiny has become a routine feature of New Zealand's legal environment, but this does not guarantee that human rights considerations are pre-eminent among the mix of competing values and political considerations. To a greater extent than in Canada or the UK, the executive and legislative arms of government exert a strong influence over the parameters and potency of control BORA-based human rights discourse in the context of specific controversies. This pattern is consistent with the institutional design and authority distribution characteristics of the regime put in place by the BORA, but it also speaks to more established features of New Zealand's legal culture, including a relatively pronounced tendency to regard the inherently political judgments involved in the resolution of human rights controversies as the legitimate domain of Parliament rather than the courts.

Australia

The first and most obvious general observation about Australia to be drawn from the three case studies is that despite the absence of a national bill of rights, human rights sensitivity is still a prominent feature of Australian public discourse. In the case of each of the controversies examined in this study, human rights considerations have formed part of the mix of arguments and counter-arguments. The prominence of human rights discourse in Australia's legal culture in undeniable. However, a significant point of distinction between Australia, and Canada and the UK, and, to a lesser extent, New Zealand, is that whether *prominence* translated into *purchase* and *potency* in the case of particular human rights controversies was highly variable. To the extent that a primary domestic reference point for human rights scrutiny renders the discursive parameters – though not necessarily the outcomes – of human rights controversies more predictable, the absence of a bill of rights in Australia has contributed to the fluctuating fortunes of human rights-based claims. The point is, that human rights sensitivity is not a consistently weak influence in Australia. On the contrary, even in the absence of a national bill of rights (and associated scrutiny mechanisms), it can be surprisingly influential. The controversies surrounding double jeopardy reform and hate speech laws are illustrative.

Although one state legislature (NSW) eventually took the step, in October 2006, to introduce statutory 'fresh and compelling' evidence and tainted acquittal exceptions,[11] nationally, Australia's version of the right not to be prosecuted after acquittal, underpinned by the common law rule against double jeopardy, has proven to be more resilient in the face of proposed legislative curtailment, than the equivalent right in the UK and New Zealand – despite the fact that Australian governments have faced similar populist and media-fuelled campaigns.

In the case of hate speech laws, free speech sensitivity has operated as a brake on the nature and scope of legislative restrictions on hate speech to an extent, and with a consistency that belies the ostensibly 'delicate' legal form of the right to freedom of expression in Australia. Australia's version of the right to freedom of expression has exerted at least as great a constraining influence as the constitutionally entrenched right to freedom of expression in Canada. In at least one respect, free speech considerations have exerted a more powerful influence on the shape of hate speech laws than in Canada: with the exception of the state of Western Australia, legislatures, including the Australian Parliament, have generally eschewed the regulatory strategy of criminalising hate speech. In addition, a characteristic of Australian legislative definitions of civil hate speech prohibitions is the standard inclusion of broad free speech-inspired exemptions or defences. Although there has been a degree of case-to-case variation (as in Canada), for the most part, quasi-judicial and judicial decision-makers have given these provisions the expansive operation that has been deemed to be the parliamentary intention

---

11 See now Crimes (Appeal and Review) Act 2001 (NSW), as amended by the Crimes (Appeal and Review) Amendment (Double Jeopardy) Act 2006 (NSW).

behind their inclusion – with the net effect that the parameters of hate speech restrictions have been narrowed.

Although it is firmly embedded in Australia legal culture – even if only faintly articulated in its formal legal infrastructure – the right to free speech has not operated so powerfully as to invalidate or seriously marginalise hate speech laws enacted in pursuit of non-discrimination/equality objectives. Hate speech laws are an established, and not merely symbolic, part of Australia's human rights regulatory framework.

It is in the case of the controversy over the legal recognition of same-sex relationships that the implications of Australia's unique 'bill of rights-less' status are most vividly revealed. To a greater extent than in any of the other three countries, the capacity to transform a human rights-inspired political assertion into a legal imperative has been shown to be heavily contingent on the degree to which the claimed right is considered to align with the ascendant philosophies and policy preferences of executive/legislative government. While the immunity against re-prosecution after acquittal and both the right to free speech and the right not to be harmed by hate speech are all, more or less, embedded in Australia's legal culture, the principle of full sexual orientation equality is demonstrably not. In this environment, the fact that Australian law does not articulate a national standard of non-discrimination for gay men and lesbians, has left those members of the Australian gay and lesbian community who seek formal legal recognition of their same-sex relationships exposed to the aggressive resistance of the current Australian Government. In the absence of an authoritative domestic legal reference point for demanding equality-based relationships – such as was available to same-sex marriage/civil partnership/civil union campaigners in Canada, the UK and New Zealand – gay and lesbian activists have not only struggled to achieve purchase when attempting to articulate their goals as human rights imperatives, they have been legally powerless to resist the diametrically opposed (non-recognition) policy direction pursued by the Howard Government, and endorsed by the Australian Parliament in the form of the Marriage Amendment Act 2004.

Drawing on research undertaken in the mid-1990s, Stychin observed in 1998 that the failure to adopt a bill of rights 'does not mean that a discourse of individual rights is without currency in Australia. In the 1990s, rights have played a substantial role within public discourse'.[12] I concur with Stychin's central point, but almost a decade on, during which time a Liberal-National (conservative) Coalition Government has been elected and remained in power at the national level, the implications of Australia's bill of rights-less status need to be revisited.

The recent story of the non-recognition of same-sex relationships in

---

12 Stychin, 1998, p 155.

Australia suggests an underlying fragility in Australia's human rights culture, when it comes to efforts to expand the parameters of existing rights concepts – like equality. Although the difficulty of advancing a compelling human rights argument for equality-based recognition of same-sex relationships in Australia's current political climate cannot be neatly explained as a direct result of the absence of a bill of rights-embedded equality/non-discrimination guarantee, the comparative analysis presented in this book supports the conclusion that legal form – or the lack thereof – has made a difference in Australia. To varying degrees, the equality/non-discrimination provisions of the Charter, HRA and BORA, respectively, played an important role in the discursive strategies employed successfully by proponents of recognition. In Australia, the combined effect of ascendant conservative moral values and a domestic legal framework which provided nowhere to ground an alternative human rights-based normative argument goes a long way to explaining why the recent story of the (non)recognition of same-sex relationships in Australia differs so dramatically from the stories that have unfolded in Canada, the UK and New Zealand in the same period.

How legal form matters

I introduced this book by admitting my sympathetic scepticism towards the claims commonly advanced by advocates of an Australian bill of rights. Twelve stories and 250 pages later, it seems only fair to conclude by confessing my surprise at what this comparative study has revealed. Detailed examination of the public discourse surrounding controversies over double jeopardy reform, the legal recognition of same-sex relationships, and the operation of hate speech laws had revealed that legal form *does* matter. The relevant point of distinction is not simply between having a bill of rights and not having one – although the Australian experience does suggest that the latter carries real risks that human rights considerations can be subverted by alternative normative visions. The present study suggests that the differences in legal form between the domestic bills of rights that currently operate in Canada, the UK and New Zealand translate into discernible differences in the shape and potency of human rights discourse in terms of its capacity to *defend* and *extend* human rights values.

The Charter's characteristics of constitutional entrenchment and effective judicial supremacy have served to insulate due process rights such as the immunity against double jeopardy, and energise the non-discrimination principle in support of full legal equality for same-sex couples to a greater extent than has occurred under either of the bill of rights models that operate in the UK and New Zealand. Identifiable differences in terms of the relative capacity of the different legal models to provide a framework for the effective *balance* of competing human rights were less obvious. Elements of legal culture were more influential in the case of the controversy surrounding hate speech laws.

The relationship between the utility of the human rights dynamic and legal form is not a simple one. The specific norms and institutional arrangements introduced by a bill of rights sit within, rather than apart from, the broader legal culture out of which they have emerged – in the case of a largely organic 'home grown' instrument like the Canadian Charter of Rights and Freedoms – or into which they have been placed – in the case of an 'external' instrument like the European Convention on Human Rights. In turn, legal form exerts an influence on legal culture – creating (or foreclosing) strategic options, shaping public discourse, affecting the way in which lines of agreement and disagreement are drawn, providing access points for individual or collective agency, allocating responsibility for scrutiny and the assessment of compliance, and redistributing the balance of authority between the executive, legislative and judicial arms of government.

The domestic legal form ultimately favoured in any given jurisdiction is likely to be determined, to a considerable extent, by philosophical preferences as to the status that human rights sensitivity should occupy, relative to the range of values and considerations involved in political decision-making.

Those who prefer a supreme 'beyond majoritarian politics' conception of human rights, located outside the realm of legitimate political disagreement, can be expected to argue for the Canadian constitutional model – although they will need to confront the defenders of parliamentary supremacy and the opponents of judicial law-making. For those who embrace, or are resigned to, the predominance of the concept of human rights, but who oppose judicial hegemony over the resolution of human rights controversies,[13] and would prefer them to be ultimately resolved in the political arena, where reasonable minds may reasonably disagree, and the influence of pragmatism and opportunism is a tolerable part of the bargain, the 'Commonwealth' model – versions of which operate in New Zealand and the UK – will be regarded as an acceptable compromise. For those who would prefer human rights discourse to operate as an essentially conservative and easily harnessed normative influence – protecting the rights of the status quo, and mobilised in new contexts only in pursuit of goals that resonate with ascendant party political preferences – the current Australian model will remain attractive.

---

13 See, e.g., Hiebert, 2004; also, Ignatieff, 2000.

Bibliography

Akdeniz, Y, 2006, *Stocktaking on Efforts to Combat Racism on the Internet*. Background Paper. Intergovernmental Working Group on the Effective Implementation of the Durban Declaration and Programme of Action, Commission on Human Rights, E/CN.4/2006/WG.21/BP.1.

Akmeemana, S and Jones, M, 1995, 'Fighting Racial Hatred' in Human Rights and Equal Opportunity Commission, Race Discrimination Commissioner, *The Racial Discrimination Act: A Review*, Canberra: Australian Government Publishing Service.

Allan, J, 2001, 'Take Heed Australia – A Statutory Bill of Rights and its Inflationary Effect', 6 *Deakin Law Review* 322–33.

ALSO Foundation, 2004, *Relationship Recognition*, Federal Issues Paper, 10 September www.also.org.au/discover/projectsandservices/Lobbypapers.htm (accessed 20 October 2005).

Alston, P (ed), 1994, *Towards an Australian Bill of Rights*, Canberra/Sydney: Centre for International and Public Law, Australian National University/Human Rights and Equal Opportunity Commission.

Alston, P (ed), 1999, *Protecting Human Rights Through Bills of Rights: Comparative Perspectives*, Oxford: Oxford University Press.

Alston, P and Crawford, J, 2000, *The Future of UN Human Rights Treaty Monitoring*, Cambridge: Cambridge University Press.

Angenot, M, 2004, 'Social Discourse Analysis: Outlines of a Research Project', 17 *The Yale Journal of Criticism* 199–215.

Appignanesi, L (ed), 2005, *Free Expression is No Offence*, London: English PEN.

Arcioni, E, 2003, 'Politics, Police and Proportionality – An Opportunity to Explore the *Lange* Test: *Coleman v Power*', 25 *Sydney Law Review* 379–90.

Arden, M, 2000, *The Common Law in the Age of Human Rights*, Holdsworth Club, University of Birmingham.

Arthurs, H and Arnold, B, 2005, 'Does the Charter Matter? 11 *Review of Constitutional Studies* 35–117.

Ashworth, A, 2004, 'Criminal Justice Act 2003 (2) Criminal Justice Reform: Principles, Human Rights and Public Protection', *Crim LR* 516–32.

Auchmuty, R, 2004, 'Same-Sex Marriage Revived: Feminist Critique and Legal Strategy', 14 *Feminism & Psychology* 101–26.

Auld, R, 2001, *Review of the Criminal Courts of England and Wales*, September www.criminal-courts-review.org.uk/auldconts.htm (accessed 28 April 2006).

Australia, Human Rights Commission, 1982, *Incitement to Racial Hatred: The International Experience*, Canberra: AGPS.

Australia, Human Rights Commission, 1983, *Proposed Amendments to the Racial Discrimination Act Concerning Racial Defamation*, Discussion Paper No 3, Canberra: Human Rights Commission.

Australia, Human Rights Commission, 1984, *Proposal for Amendment to the Racial Discrimination Act to Cover Incitement to Racial Hatred and Racial Defamation*, Report No 7, Canberra: AGPS.

Australia, Human Rights and Equal Opportunity Commission, 1991, *Racist Violence: Report of National Inquiry into Racist Violence in Australia* Canberra: AGPS.

Australia, Human Rights and Equal Opportunity Commission, 2004, Submission to the Senate Legal and Constitutional Legislation Committee on the Provisions of the Marriage Legislation Amendment Bill 2004, 30 July, Sydney: HREOC www.hreoc.gov.au/legal/submissions/marriage_leg.html (accessed 28 April 2006).

Australia, Human Rights and Equal Opportunity Commission, 2005, *Annual Report 2004–2005*, Sydney: HREOC.

Australia, Human Rights and Equal Opportunity Commission, 2006a, 'Same-Sex: Same Entitlements National Inquiry – Discrimination against People in Same-Sex Relationships: Financial and Work-Related Entitlements and Benefits', Media Release, 3 April 2006, www.hreoc.gov.au/media_releases/2006/18_06.htm (accessed 18 May 2006).

Australia, Human Rights and Equal Opportunity Commission, 2006b, *Same Sex: Same Entitlements*, Discussion Paper, Sydney: HREOC.

Australia, Ministry of Justice and Customs, 2004, 'Double jeopardy reform still on the agenda', Media Release, 22 March, www.ag.gov.au/agd/WWW/justiceminister Home.nsf/Page/Media_Releases (accessed 26 May 2006).

Australia, Model Criminal Code Officers Committee of the Standing Committee of Attorneys-General (MCCOC), 2003, *Issue Estoppel, Double Jeopardy and Prosecution Appeals Against Acquittals*, Discussion Paper, November.

Australia, Model Criminal Code Officers Committee of the Standing Committee of Attorneys-General (MCCOC), 2004, *Double Jeopardy*, MCCOC Report, March.

Australia, Royal Commission into Aboriginal Deaths in Custody, 1991, *National Report*, Canberra: AGPS.

Australian Associated Press, 2005, 'Loophole could allow gay marriage', *The Age*, 11 April.

Australian Broadcasting Corporation, ABC TV, 2003, 'Australian Story: Double Bind', 7 April, www.abc.net.au/austory/content/2003/s932472.htm (accessed 25 May 2006).

Australian Broadcasting Corporation, ABC News Online, 2005, 'Former white supremacist jailed for synagogue attack', 20 December, www.abc.net.au/news/newsitems/200512/s1535272.htm (accessed 22 December 2006).

Australian Broadcasting Corporation, Radio National, 2005, 'The Law Report: Double Jeopardy', 27 September, www.abc.net.au/rn/talks/8.30/lawrpt/stories/s1468272.htm (accessed 28 April 2006).

Australian Broadcasting Corporation, ABC Radio, 2006, 'PM: Law Council urges against double jeopardy changes', 27 January, www.abc.net.au/pm/content/2006/s1556915.htm (accessed 26 May 2006).

Australian Capital Territory Bill of Rights Consultative Committee, 2003, *Towards an ACT Human Rights Act*, Canberra: ACT Bill of Rights Consultative Committee.

Australian Capital Territory Department of Justice and Community Safety, 2005, *The Recognition of Same Sex Relationships in the ACT: Discussion Paper*, Canberra: ACT Department of Justice and Community Safety.

Australian Law Reform Commission, 1992, *Multiculturalism and the Law*, Report No 57, Canberra: Australian Government Publishing Service (AGPS).

Australian Law Reform Commission, 1994, *Equality Before the Law*, Report No 69, Canberra: AGPS.

Australian Law Reform Commission, 2002, *Principled Regulation: Civil and Administrative Penalties in Australian Federal Regulation*, Report No 95, Canberra: AGPS.

Australian Parliament, 2006, Standing orders and other orders of the Senate, www.aph.gov.au/Senate/pubs/standing_orders/index.htm (accessed 25 May 2006).

Bagaric, M and Neal, L, 2005, 'Double Jeopardy in Australia: The Illusion of an Absolute Protection and the Prosecution Process as Punishment', 8 *Canberra Law Review* 87–110.

Bailey, J, 2004, 'Private Regulation and Public Policy: Toward Effective Restriction of Internet Hate Propaganda', 49 *McGill LJ* 59–103.

Bailey, P, 1999, 'Implementing Human Rights – The Way Forward', 5 *Australian Journal of Human Rights* 167–77.

Bailey, S, Harris, D and Jones, B, 1985, *Civil Liberties: Cases and Materials*, 2nd edn, London: Butterworths.

Bakan, J, 1997, *Just Words: Constitutional Rights and Social Wrongs*, Toronto: University of Toronto Press.

Banakar, R, 2004, 'When Do Rights Matter? A Case Study of the Right to Equal Treatment in Sweden', in S Halliday and P Schmidt (eds), *Human Rights Brought Home: Socio-Legal Studies of Human Rights in the National Context*, Oxford: Hart.

Banham, C, 2005, 'Same-sex pension revoked', *Sydney Morning Herald*, 4 November, p 7.

Bayefsky, A, 2001, *The UN Human Rights Treaty System: Universality at the Crossroads*, Ardsley: Transnational Publishers.

Beaudoin, G, 2005, *The Canadian Charter of Rights and Freedoms*, 4th edn, Toronto: LexisNexis Butterworths.

Behrendt, L, 2003, 'It's Broke So Fix It: Arguments For a Bill of Rights', 9 *Australian Journal of Human Rights* 257–62.

Bell, L, Nathan, A and Peleg, I, 2000, *Negotiating Culture and Human Rights*, New York: Columbia University Press.

Beloff, M, 1999, ' "What Does it All Mean?" Interpreting the Human Rights Act 1998', in L Betten (ed), *The Human Rights Act 1998: What it Means. The Incorporation of the European Convention on Human Rights into the Legal Order of the United Kingdom*, The Hague/London/Boston: Martin Nijhoff Publishers.

Benson-Pope, D, 2004, 'Questions and Answers on Civil Union and Relationships (Statutory References) Bills', 21 June, www.beehive.govt.nz/ViewDocument.aspx?DocumentID=20064 (accessed 28 April 2006).

Bercuson, D and Wertheimer, D, 1985, *A Trust Betrayed: The Keegstra Affair*, Toronto: Doubleday Canada.
Bernhardt, D, 2006, 'Ahenakew appeals hate conviction', *The StarPhoenix*, 4 April, www.canada.com/saskatoonstarphoenix/index.html (accessed 11 April 2006).
Bierbrauer, G, 1994, 'Toward an Understanding of Legal Culture: Variations in Individualism and Collectivism Between Kurds, Lebanese, and Germans', 28 *Law and Society Review* 243–64.
Billingsley, B, 2002, 'Section 33: The *Charter's* Sleeping Giant', 21 *Windsor Yearbook of Access to Justice* 331–46.
Bindman, G, 2003, 'Racism and Freedom of Expression', in B Clarke (ed), *Challenging Racism: Using the Human Rights Act*, London: Lawrence & Wishart.
Blackburn, R, 2001, 'The United Kingdom', in R Blackburn and J Polakiewicz (eds), *Fundamental Rights in Europe: The European Convention on Human Rights and its Member States, 1950–2000*, Oxford: Oxford University Press.
Blackshield, T and Williams, G, 2006, *Australian Constitutional Law and Theory: Commentary and Materials*, 4th edn, Sydney: Federation Press.
Blankenberg, E, 1998, 'Patterns of Legal Culture: The Netherlands Compared to Neighbouring Germany', 46 *American Journal of Comparative Law* 1–41.
Boniface, D, 2003, 'If at first you don't succeed... chipping away at the Human Rights and Equal Opportunity Commission', 12 *Human Rights Defender* 8–9.
Bosma, H, 2000, *Freedom of Expression in England and Under the ECHR: in Search of Common Ground. A Foundation for the Application of the Human Rights Act 1998 in English Law*, Antwerpen/Groningen/Oxford: Intersentia/Hart.
Bourassa, K and Varnell, J, 2002, *Just Married: Gay Marriage and the Expansion of Human Rights*, Toronto: DoubleDay Canada.
Boyd, S, 1996, 'Best Friends or Spouses? Privatization and the Recognition of Lesbian Relationships in M v. H', 13 *Canadian Journal of Family Law* 321–41.
Boyd, S, 1999, 'Family, Law and Sexuality: Feminist Engagements', 8 *Social and Legal Studies* 369–89.
Boyd, S and Young, C, 2003, ' "From Same-Sex to No Sex"?: Trends Towards Recognition of (Same-Sex) Relationships in Canada', 1 *Seattle Journal for Social Justice* 757–93.
Boyle, K, 1992, 'Overview of a Dilemma: Censorship Versus Racism', in S Coliver (ed), *Striking A Balance: Hate Speech, Freedom of Expression and Non-Discrimination*, London and Colchester: Article 19, International Centre Against Censorship and Human Rights Centre, University of Essex.
Boyle, K and Baldaccini, A, 2001, 'A Critical Evaluation of International Human Rights Approaches to Racism', in S Fredman (ed), *Discrimination and Human Rights: The Case of Racism*, Oxford: Oxford University Press.
Braun, S, 2004, *Democracy Off Balance: Freedom of Expression and Hate Propaganda Law in Canada*, Toronto: University of Toronto Press.
British Broadcasting Corporation, BBC News, 2005, 'Double jeopardy law ushered out', 3 April, http://news.bbc.co.uk/1/hi/uk/4406129.stm (accessed 29 May 2006).
Broadbridge, S, 2002, *The Criminal Justice Bill: Double Jeopardy and Prosecution Appeals*. House of Commons Library Research Paper 02/74.
Bronitt, S and Jobling, P, 2005, 'Democratic and Human Rights under the Commonwealth Constitution', 17 *Legaldate* 1–3.

Brown, W and Halley, J, 2002, *Left Legalism/Left Critique*, Durham: Duke University Press.

Brysk, A (ed), 2002, *Globalization and Human Rights*, Berkeley: University of California Press.

Burke, A and Gelber, K, 2005–2006, 'Can Human Rights Save Us?' 80 *Arena Magazine* 43–45.

Burton, F and Carlen, P, 1979, *Official Discourse; On Discourse Analysis, Government Publications, Ideology and the State*, London: Routledge.

Burton, K, 2004, 'Reform of the double jeopardy rule on the basis of fresh and compelling DNA evidence in New South Wales and Queensland', 11 *James Cook University LR* 84–107.

Butler, A, 1997, 'The Bill of Rights Debate: Why the New Zealand Bill of Rights Act 1990 is a Bad Model for Britain', 17 *Oxford Journal of Legal Studies* 323–45.

Butler, A, 1998, 'Same-sex Marriage and Freedom from Discrimination in New Zealand', *Public Law* 396–406.

Butler, A, 2000, 'Strengthening the Bill of Rights', 31 *Victoria University of Wellington Law Review* 129–47.

Butler, A and Butler, P, 2005, *The New Zealand Bill of Rights Act: A Commentary*, Wellington: LexisNexis NZ.

Butler, P, 2004, 'Human Rights and Parliamentary Sovereignty in New Zealand', 35 *Victoria University of Wellington Law Review* 341–66.

Calhoun, C, 2000, *Feminism, the Family and the Politics of the Closet: Lesbian and Gay Displacement*, Oxford: Oxford University Press.

Campaign for Civil Unions, 2004, 'Referendum an inappropriate and dangerous precedent', Media Release, 7 December, www.civilunions.org.nz/formedia (accessed 25 October 2005).

Campbell, T, 1999, 'Human Rights: A Culture of Controversy', 26 *Journal of Law and Society* 6–26.

Campbell, T, Goldsworthy, J and Stone, A (eds), 2006, *Human Rights Without a Bill of Rights: Institutional Performance and Reform in Australia*, Aldershot: Ashgate.

Canada, Department of Justice, 2002, *Marriage and Legal Recognition of Same-Sex Unions: A Discussion Paper*, Ottawa: Department of Justice.

Canada, Department of Justice, 2005, 'Bill C–38 – *the Civil Marriage Act:* Common Misconceptions', http://canada.justice.gc.ca/en/news/fs/2005/doc_31440.html (accessed 28 April 2006)

Canada, Department of Public Safety and Emergency Preparedness, 2005, 'Deputy Prime Minister and Minister of Public Safety and Emergency Preparedness announces appointment of the Honourable Bob Rae to lead the Air India Flight 182 review and inquiry', News Release, 25 November, www.psepc.gc.ca/media/nr/20051125-en.asp (accessed 9 January 2006).

Canada, House of Commons, 1984, *Equality Now! Report of the Special Committee on Visible Minorities*, Ottawa: Supply and Services.

Canada, Office of the Prime Minister, 2006, 'Prime Minister Harper announces inquiry into Air India bombing', Media Release, 1 May, http://pm.gc.ca/eng/media.asp?category=1&id=1145 (accessed 23 May 2006).

Canadian Broadcasting Corporation, CBC News, 2005a, '2 acquitted in Air India bombings', 17 March, www.cbc.ca/story/canada/national/2005/03/16/air-india-advance050316.html (accessed 9 January 2006).

Canadian Broadcasting Corporation, CBC News, 2005b, 'Reactions to the Air India verdicts: Victims' families and friends', 16 March, www.cbc.ca/news/background/airindia/reaction_victimsfamilies.html (accessed 9 January 2006).

Canadians for Equal Marriage, 2006, Majority of MPs Oppose Re-opening Marriage: Opponents of Equal Marriage call for Vote Delay', Media Release, 16 May, www.equal-marriage.ca/resource.php?id=501 (accessed 23 May 2006).

Cape, E, 2004, *Reconcilable rights?: Analysing the Tension Between Victims and Defendants*, London : Legal Action Group.

Carr, B, 2001, 'The Rights Trap: How a Bill of Rights Could Undermine Freedom', 17 *Policy* 19–21.

Cartwright, S, 2001, 'The Harkness Henry Lecture: Some Human Rights Issues', 9 *Waikato Law Review* 13–23.

Casanovas, P, 1999, *Pragmatics and Legal Culture: A General Framework*, Working Party No 159, Barcelona: Institut de Ciencies Politiques i Socials, Universitat Autonoma de Barcelona.

Castan Centre for Human Rights Law, 2005, 'Same Sex Marriage Forum, 26 May 2005', www.law.monash.edu.au/castancentre/public-edu/ssmforum.html (accessed 28 April 2006).

Chapman, A, 2004, 'Australian Racial Hatred Law: Some Comments on Reasonableness and Adjudicative Method in Complaints Brought by Indigenous People', 30 *Monash University Law Review* 27–48.

Chapman, A and Kelly, K, 2005, 'Australian Anti-vilification Law: a Discussion of the Public/Private Divide and the Work Relations Context', 27 *Sydney LR* 203–36.

Charlesworth, H, 2002a, *Writing in Rights: Australia and the Protection of Human Rights*, Sydney: UNSW Press.

Charlesworth, H, 2002b, 'Concepts of Equality in International Law' in G Huscroft and P Rishworth (eds), *Litigating Rights: Perspectives from Domestic and International Law*, Oxford: Hart.

Charlesworth, H, Chiam, M, Hovell, D and Williams, G, 2006, *No Country is an Island: Australia and International Law*, Sydney: UNSW Press.

Chesterman, M, 2000, *Freedom of Speech in Australian Law: A Delicate Plant*, Aldershot: Ashgate.

Chow, R, 2005, 'Inciting Hatred or Merely Engaging in Religious Debate? The Need for Religious Vilification Laws', 30 *Alternative Law Journal* 120–2, 145.

Christie, N, 2001, 'The New Zealand Same-Sex Marriage Case: From Aotearoa to the United Nations', in R Wintemute and M Andenaes (eds), *Legal Recognition of Same-Sex Partnerships: A Study of National, European and International Law*, Oxford: Hart.

Christie, N, 2002, *LeGaLE: Lesbian and Gay Legal Equality*, http://homepages.paradise.net.nz/nigelchr/About_Nigel.htm (accessed 29 May 2006).

Civil Union Bill Committee, 2001, *Legal Recognition of Same-Sex Couples in New Zealand: An Analysis* (unpublished).

Clarke, T, 2005, *Racism, Pluralism and Democracy in Australia: Re-conceptualising Racial Vilification Legislation*, PhD Thesis, Faculty of Law, University of New South Wales.

Clements, L and Thomas, P (eds), 2005, *The Human Rights Act: A Success Story?*, Oxford: Blackwell.

Clements, R, 2000, 'Bringing It All Back Home: "Rights" in English Law Before the Human Rights Act 1998', 21 *Human Rights Law Journal* 134–42.

Clennell, A and Norrie, J, 2006, 'Embattled Iemma boosts police numbers', *Sydney Morning Herald*, 20 March, www.smh.com.au/news/national/embattled-iemma-boosts-police/2006/03/19/1142703217980.html (accessed 26 May 2006).

Cohen, M, 1966, *Report of the Special Committee on Hate Propaganda in Canada*, Ottawa: Queen's Printer.

Cole, M, 2005, 'Double jeopardy reform shelved', *[Brisbane] Courier-Mail*, 23 May.

Coliver, S (ed), 1992, *Striking A Balance: Hate Speech, Freedom of Expression and Non-Discrimination*, London and Colchester: Article 19, International Centre Against Censorship and Human Rights Centre, University of Essex.

Commission of the European Communities, 2001, Proposal for a Council Framework Decision on Combating Racism and Xenophobia, COM 664 final, 2001/0270 (CNS), Brussels, 28 November.

Commonwealth of Australia, 2005, *Australia's National Framework For Human Rights: National Action Plan*.

Conservative Party of Canada, 2006, *Standing Up For Canada: Conservative Party of Canada Federal Election Platform*, www.conservative.ca/media/20060113-Platform.pdf (accessed 23 May 2006).

Cooper, D, 2005, 'For richer or poorer, in sickness and in health: Should Australia embrace same-sex marriage?', 19 *Australian Journal of Family Law* 153–74.

Corns, C, 2003, 'Retrial of Acquitted Persons: Time for Reform of the Double Jeopardy Rule?', 27 *Criminal Law Journal* 80–101.

Cossman, B, 2002, 'Lesbians, Gay Men and the Canadian Charter of Rights and Freedoms', 40 *Osgoode Hall Law Journal* 223–49.

Cotler, I, 2005, 'Bill C-38 – the Civil Marriage Act. Open Letter from the Minister of Justice Concerning Alternative Approaches', http://canada.justice.gc.ca/en/fs/ssm/open_letter.html (accessed 28 April 2006).

Cotterrell, R, 1997, 'The Concept of Legal Culture', in D Nelken (ed), *Comparing Legal Cultures*, Aldershot: Dartmouth.

Cotterrell, R, 2002, 'Seeking Similarity, Appreciating Difference: Comparative Law and Communities', in A Harding and E Orucu (eds), *Comparative Law in the 21st Century*, The Hague: Kluwer Law International, 2002.

Cotterrell, R, 2004, 'Law in Culture', 17 *Ratio Juris* 1–14.

Council of Europe, Committee of Ministers, 1997, *Recommendation No R (97) 20 of the Committee of Ministers to Member States on 'Hate Speech'*, www.coe.int/T/CM/adoptedTexts_en.asp (accessed 1 May 2006).

Council of the European Union, 2005, Note from Presidency to Council re 'Proposal for a Council Framework Decision on Combating Racism and Xenophobia', 8994/05, Droipen 24, 19 May, Brussels, http://register.consilium.eu.int/pdf/en/05/st08/st08994.en05.pdf (accessed 2 May 2006).

Cowan, J, Dembour, M-B and Wilson, R (eds), 2001, *Culture and Rights: Anthropological Perspectives*, Cambridge: Cambridge University Press.

Cowan, R, 2005, 'First double jeopardy trial given go-ahead', 11 November, www.guardian.co.uk.

Cram, I, 2002, *A Virtue Less Cloistered: Courts, Speech and Constitutions*, Oxford: Hart.

Croome, R, 2005, 'Standing before history's judge', Address at Newtown Hotel,

1 May, www.rodneycroome.id.au/other_more?id=1692_0_2_10_M13 (accessed 28 April 2006).

Curry, B and Galloway, G, 2005, 'Same-sex bill finally passes: After bitter two year political battle, divisive legislation moves to Senate', *The Globe and Mail*, 29 June, A1.

Dalberg-Larsen, J, 2001, 'Human Rights and National Legal Cultures: The Case of Labour Law', in K Hastrup (ed), *Legal Cultures and Human Rights: The Challenge of Diversity*, The Hague: Kluwer Law International.

Darby, A, 2004, 'Tasmania accepts same-sex partners', *The Age*, 3 January.

Darrow M and Alston, P, 1999, 'Bills of Rights in Comparative Perspective', in P Alston (ed), *Protecting Human Rights Through Bills of Rights: Comparative Perspectives*, Oxford: Oxford University Press.

Davies, A, 2004, 'Labor caucus fights shy of disturbing ancient double jeopardy rule', *Sydney Morning Herald*, 17 November.

Davis, D, 2003, 'Constitutional Borrowing; The Influence of Legal Culture and Local History in the Reconstitution of Comparative Influence: The South African Experience', 1 *International Journal of Constitutional Law* 181–95.

Debeljak, J, 2003a, 'The Human Rights Act 1998 (UK): The Preservation of Parliamentary Supremacy in the Context of Rights Protection', 9 *Australian Journal for Human Rights* 183–235.

Debeljak, J, 2003b, 'Rights and Democracy: A Reconciliation of the Institutional Debate' in T Campbell, J Goldsworthy and A Stone (eds), *Human Rights Protection: Boundaries and Challenges*, Oxford: Oxford University Press.

Dennis, I, 2000, 'Rethinking double jeopardy: Justice and finality in the criminal process', *Criminal Law Review* 933–51.

Dingwall, G, 2000, 'Prosecutorial Policy, Double Jeopardy and the Public Interest', 63 *Modern Law Review* 268–80.

Donnelly, J, 2002, *Universal Human Rights in Theory and Practice*, New York: Cornell University Press.

Dorf, M, 2004, 'Interpretive Holism and the Structural Method, or How Charles Black Might Have Thought about Campaign Finance Reform and Congressional Timidity', 92 *Georgetown Law Journal* 833–57.

Douglas, R, 2005, 'The Constitutional Freedom to Insult: The Insignificance of Coleman v Power', 16 *Public Law Review* 23–38.

Douzinas, C, 1996, 'Justice and Human Rights in Postmodernity', in C Gearty and A Tomkins (eds), *Understanding Human Rights*, London: Pinter.

Douzinas, C, 2000, *The End of Human Rights*, Oxford: Hart.

Doyle, J and Wells, B, 1999, 'How Far Can the Common Law Go Towards Protecting Human Rights?', in P Alston (ed), *Protecting Human Rights Through Bills of Rights: Comparative Perspectives*, Oxford: Oxford University Press.

Dye, S, 2005, 'Backlash on hate speech proposal', *The New Zealand Herald*, 18 March, www.nzherald.co.nz (1 May 2006).

Eastman, K, 1994, 'Drafting Vilification Laws: Legal and Policy Issues', 1 *Australian Journal of Human Rights* 285–98.

Eberts, M, 1999, 'The Canadian Charter of Rights and Freedoms: A Feminist Perspective', in P Alston (ed), *Protecting Human Rights Through Bills of Rights: Comparative Perspectives*, Oxford: Oxford University Press.

Egale Canada, 2006, '104 Law Profs ask Harper for Supreme Court reference: Passage of unconstitutional law would lead to legal swamp', Media Release, 17 January, www.egale.ca/index.asp?lang=E&menu=20&item=1277 (accessed 23 May 2006).

Egale Canada/Canadians for Equal Marriage, 2005, *Equal Marriage: a Constitutional Imperative*, Submission to the Bill C–38 Legislative Committee, www.equalmarriage.ca/resource.php?id=431 (accessed 28 April 2006).

Elman, B, 1994, 'Combating Racist Speech: The Canadian Experience', 32 *Alberta Law Review* 623–66.

Emmerson, B and Ashworth, A, 2001, *Human Rights and Criminal Justice*, London: Sweet and Maxwell.

England and Wales, Crown Prosecution Service, 2003, *Racist and Religious Crime – CPS Prosecution Policy*, London: CPS Equality and Diversity Unit and Policy Directorate.

England and Wales, Crown Prosecution Service, 2004a, *Addressing Equality and Diversity in the Crown Prosecution Service: A Stocktake Report*, London: CPS Equality and Diversity Unit.

England and Wales, Crown Prosecution Service, 2004b, 'CPS decision on article by Robert Kilroy-Silk', Media Release, 1 July, www.cps.gov.uk/news/pressreleases/archive/2004/131_04.html (accessed 2 May 2006).

England and Wales, Crown Prosecution Service, 2006, 'William Dunlop sentenced in first double jeopardy case', Media Release, 6 October, www.cps.gov.uk/news/press-releases/155_06.html (accessed 8 October 2006).

England and Wales, Crown Prosecution Service and Metropolitan Police Service, 2006, 'Joint CPS and Metropolitan Statement – Abu Hamza', Media Release, 8 February, www.cps.gov.uk/news/pressreleases/106_06.html (accessed 2 May 2006).

England and Wales Law Commission, 1999, *Double Jeopardy: A Consultation Paper*, Consultation Paper No 156, London: The Stationery Office.

England and Wales Law Commission, 2001, *Double Jeopardy and Prosecution Appeals*, Report No 267, London: The Stationery Office.

Epp, C, 1996, 'Do Bills of Rights Matter? The Canadian Charter of Rights and Freedoms', 90 *The American Political Science Review* 765–79.

Eskridge, W, 2002, *Equality Practice: Civil Unions and the Future of Gay Rights*, New York: Routledge.

Ettelbrick, P, 2004, 'Since When is Marriage a Path to Liberation?' in R Baird and S Rosenbaum (eds), *Same Sex Marriage: The Moral and Legal Debate*, 2nd edn, Amherst: Prometheus Books.

European Commission against Racism and Intolerance, 2001, *Legal Measures to Combat Racism and Intolerance in the Member States of the Council of Europe*, CRI(98)80 Rev 2, Strasbourg: Council of Europe.

European Parliament, 2000, *Resolution on Respect for Human Rights in the European Union (1998–1999)*, 16 March, A5–0050/2000.

European Parliament, 2006, *Resolution on Homophobia in Europe*, 18 January, P6_TA-PROV(2006) 0018.

Evans, C, 2004, 'Responsibility for Rights: The ACT *Human Rights Act*' 32 *Federal Law Review* 291–309.

Evans, T, 2005, 'International Human Rights Law as Power/Knowledge', 27 *Human Rights Quarterly* 1046–68.

Falk, R, 2000, *Human Rights Horizons: The Pursuit of Justice in a Globalizing World*, New York: Routledge.

Farouque, F, 2004, 'Gay "husbands" to test their marriage in court', *The Age*, 4 February.
Farrar, D, 2003, 'Double-jeopardy caution required', *The Canberra Times*, 24 April, p 17.
Farrior, S, 1996, 'Moulding the Matrix: The Historical and Theoretical Foundations of International Law Concerning Hate Speech', 14 *Berkeley Journal of International Law* 1–98.
Feldman, D, 2002, 'Parliamentary Scrutiny of Legislation and Human Rights', *Public Law* 323–48.
Fenson, M, 1964–65, 'Group Defamation: Is the Cure Too Costly?', 1 *Manitoba Law School Journal* 255–81.
Fitzpatrick, B, 2002, 'Tinkering or Transformation? Proposals and principles in the White Paper, "Justice for All"' 5 *Web Journal of Current Legal Issues*, http://webjcli.ncl.ac.uk/2002/issue5/fitzpatrick5.html (accessed 28 April 2006).
Fitzpatrick, B, 2003, 'Double Jeopardy: One idea and two myths from the Criminal Justice Bill 2002', *The Journal of Criminal Law* 149.
Flahvin, A, 1995, 'Can Legislation Prohibiting Hate Speech be Justified in Light of Free Speech Principles?', 18 *UNSW Law Journal* 327–40.
Fletcher, M, 2003, 'Some Developments to the *ne bis in idem* Principle in the European Union: Criminal Proceedings Against Huseyn Gozutok and Klaus Brugge', 66 *Modern Law Review* 769–80.
Foley, C, 1995, *Human Rights, Human Rights: The Alternative Report to the United Nations Human Rights Committee*, London: Rivers Oram Press.
Freeman, C, 1988, 'Double Jeopardy Protection in Canada: A Consideration of Development, Doctrine and a Current Controversy', 12 *Crim LJ* 3–27.
Friedland, M, 1969, *Double Jeopardy*, Oxford: Clarendon Press.
Friedland, M, 2004, 'Criminal Justice in Canada Revisited', 48 *Criminal Law Quarterly* 419–73.
Friedland, M and Roach, K, 1994, *Criminal Law and Procedure: Cases and Materials*, 7th edn, Toronto: Emond Montgomery Publications.
Friedman, L, 1975, *The Legal System: A Social Science Perspective*, New York: Russell Sage Foundation.
Friedman, L, 1994, 'Is There a Modern Legal Culture', 7 *Ration Juris* 117–31.
Friedman, L, 1997, 'The Concept of Legal Culture: A Reply', in D Nelken (ed), *Comparing Legal Cultures*, Aldershot: Dartmouth.
Friedman, L and Perez-Perdomo, R (eds), 2003, *Legal Culture in the Age of Globalization: Latin America and Latin Europe*, Palo Alto: Stanford University Press.
Galligan, D and Sandler, D, 2004, 'Implementing Human Rights', in S Halliday and P Schmidt (eds), *Human Rights Brought Home: Socio-Legal Studies of Human Rights in the National Context*, Oxford: Hart.
Gardbaum, S, 2001, 'The New Commonwealth Model of Constitutionalism', 49 *American Journal of Comparative Law* 707–60.
Gardner, J, 1994, 'Freedom of Expression', in C McCrudden and G Chambers (eds), *Individual Rights and the Law in Britain*, Oxford: Clarendon Press.
Garland, D, 2001, *The Culture of Control: Crime and Social Order in Contemporary Society*, Oxford: Oxford University Press.
Gay and Lesbian Humanist Association, 2004, 'Why are gays being fobbed off with

second-best? Asks gay group', Press Release, 30 March, www.galha.org/press/2004/03_30.html (accessed 28 April 2006).
Gay and Lesbian Rights Lobby, 2004, *Key Issues in Federal Gay and Lesbian Law Reform,* www.glrl.org.au/issues/federal_relationship_recognition.htm (accessed 28 April 2006).
Gay and Lesbian Rights Lobby, 2005, *Federal Relationship Recognition Forum—18 June 2005; Briefing Paper*, www.glrl.org.au/issues/RelationRecogForum2005/Recognition%20models.pdf. (accessed 28 April 2006).
Gearty, C, 1993, 'The European Court of Human Rights and the Protection of Civil Liberties: An Overview', 52 *Cambridge Law Journal* 89–127.
Gearty, C, 1999, 'The Internal and External "Other" in the Union Legal Order: Racism, Religious Intolerance and Xenophobia in Europe', in P Alston (ed), *The EU and Human Rights*, New York: Oxford University Press.
Gelber, K, 2002a, *Speaking Back: The Free Speech versus Hate Speech Debate*, Philadelphia: John Benjamins Publishing Company.
Gelber, K, 2002b, 'Free Speech, Hate Speech and an Australian Bill of Rights', 2 *The Drawing Board: An Australian Review of Public Affairs* 107–18.
Gelber, K, 2005, 'Hate Speech in Australia: Emerging Questions', 28 *UNSW Law Journal* 861–7.
Gerlach, N, 2004, *The Genetic Imaginary: DNA in the Canadian Criminal Justice System*, Toronto: University of Toronto Press.
Gessner, V, Hoeland, A and Varga, C (eds), 1996, *European Legal Cultures*, Aldershot: Dartmouth.
Gibbs, K, 2004, 'Double jeopardy in the remaking', *Lawyers Weekly*, 13 April, www.lawyersweekly.com.au (accessed 26 May 2006).
Glendon, M, 1991, *Rights Talk: The Impoverishment of Political Discourse*, New York: Free Press.
Glenn, P, 2003, 'The Internationalisation of Law and Legal Culture', in P Cane and M Tushnet (eds), *The Oxford Handbook of Legal Studies*, Oxford: Oxford University Press.
Goldfarb, M, 2005, 'A Canada defined by the Charter', *The Globe and Mail*, 14 July, p A17.
Goodenough, P, 2003, 'Videos on Homosexuality: Free Speech or Hate Speech?', CNSNews.com, 12 March, www.cnsnews.com (accessed 24 March 2006).
Goodenough, P, 2004, 'Australian Homosexuals "Marry" in Canada, Challenge Laws at Home', CNSNews.com, 5 February, www.cnsnews.com/ForeignBureaus/Archive/200402/FOR20040205c.html (accessed 28 April 2006).
Goodman, R, 2004, 'The Difference Law Makes: Research Design, Institutional Design, and Human Rights', 98 *American Society of International Law Proceedings* 198–202.
Goodman, R and Jinks, D, 2003, 'Measuring the Effects of Human Rights Treaties', 14 *European J Int'l Law* 171–83.
Goodman, R and Jinks, D, 2004, 'How to Influence States: Socialization and International Human Rights Law', 54 *Duke LJ* 621–703.
Gould, I, 2005a, 'Tas rejects gay marriage', *Sydney Star Observer*, 21 April, www.ssonet.com.au/archives/display.asp?articleID=4948 (accessed 28 April 2006).
Gould, I, 2005b, 'Community Divided on Marriage', *Sydney Star Observer*, 5 May, www.ssonet.com.au/archives/display.asp?articleID=4987 (accessed 28 April 2006).

Graham, C, 2006, 'Our no brainer', *National Indigenous Times*, 4 May, p 4.
Green, L, 2004, 'What's Left of Critique?', 16 *Yale Journal of Law & the Humanities* 399–404.
Green Left Weekly, 2005, 'National protests for same-sex marriage rights', *Green Left Weekly*, 17 August, www.greenleft.org.au/back/2005/638/638p2b.htm (accessed 28 April 2006).
Green, M (2001) 'What We Talk About When We Talk About Indicators: Current Approaches to Human Rights Measurement', 23 *Human Rights Quarterly* 1062–1097.
Gregory, A, 2001, 'Double jeopardy goes on trial', *The New Zealand Herald*, 28 March.
Griffith, G, 2000, *The Protection of Human Rights: A Review of Selected Jurisdictions*, Briefing Paper No 3/2000, Sydney: NSW Parliamentary Library Research Service.
Griffith, G, 2006, *A NSW Charter of Rights? The Continuing Debate*, Briefing Paper No 5/2006, Sydney: NSW Parliamentary Library Research Service.
Grover, S, 2005, 'Democracy and the Canadian Charter Notwithstanding Clause: Are They Compatible?', 9 *International Journal of Human Rights* 479–90.
Gunther, K, 1999, 'The Legacies of Injustice and Fear: A European Approach to Human Rights and their Effects on Political Culture', in P Alston (ed), *The EU and Human Rights*, Oxford: Oxford University Press.
Gyllenspertz, H, 2002, 'Justice at last for Julie', 17 July, www.thisisthenortheast.co.uk/the_north_east/news/campaigns/criminalinjustice/pages/170702_1.html (accessed 8 January 2006).
Haesler, A, 2003, 'The Rule against Double Jeopardy. Its Tragic Demise in New South Wales. A Tale of Woe. Another Victim of the Law "n" Order Regime', Lawyers Reform Association Seminar Series, 18 June.
Hagan, S, 2005, *The N Word: One Man's Stand*, Broome: Magabala Books.
Halliday, S & Schmidt, P (eds), 2004, *Human Rights Brought Home: Socio-Legal Studies of Human Rights in the National Context*, Oxford: Hart.
Harland, C, 2000, 'The Status of the International Covenant on Civil and Political Rights (ICCPR) in the Domestic Law of State Parties: An Initial Global Survey Through UN Human Rights Committee Documents', 22 *Human Rights Quarterly* 187–260.
Harris, J, 2005, 'Matrix barrister takes stand on same-sex marriage recognition', *The Lawyer*, 7 March 2005, www.thelawyer.com/cgi-bin/item.cgi?id=114292&d=11&h=24&f=23 (accessed 28 April 2006).
Harvey, C (ed), 2005, *Human Rights in the Community: Rights as Agents for Change*, Oxford: Hart.
Hastrup, K (ed), 2001a, *Legal Cultures and Human Rights: The Challenge of Diversity*, The Hague: Kluwer Law International.
Hastrup, K, 2001b, 'Accommodating Diversity in a Global Culture of Rights: An Introduction', in K Hastrup (ed), *Legal Cultures and Human Rights: The Challenge of Diversity*, The Hague: Kluwer Law International.
Hathaway, O, 2002, 'Do Human Rights Treaties Make a Difference?', 112 *Yale LJ* 1935–2042.
Havers, P and English, R, 2000, *An Introduction to Human Rights and the Common Law*, Oxford: Hart.
Healey, J (ed), 2003, *The Cloning Debate*, Thirroul, NSW: Spinney Press.

Hele, M, 2003, 'Teary mum pleads for law change', *The [Brisbane] Courier Mail*, 12 November, p 12.
Henzel, J, 2004, 'Goff's Plan Election Stunt, Say Critics', *New Zealand Herald*, 18 May.
Herbet, I, 2006, 'BNP leader walks free as race-hate prosecution fails', *The Independent* (Online Edition), 3 February, http://news.independent.co.uk/uk/legal/article342857.ece (accessed 15 February 2006).
Herman, D, 1994, *Rights of Passage: Struggles for Lesbian and Gay Legal Equality*, Toronto: University of Toronto Press.
Herman, D, 1997, 'The Good, the Bad, and the Smugly: Sexual Orientation and the Perspectives on the Charter', in D Schneiderman and K Sutherland (eds), *Charting the Consequences: The Impact of Charter Rights on Canadian Law and Politics*, Toronto: University of Toronto Press.
Heyns, C and Viljoen, F, 2001, 'The Impact of the United Nations Human Rights Treaties on the Domestic Level', 23 *Human Rights Quarterly* 483–535.
Heyns, C and Viljoen, F, 2002, *The Impact of the United Nations Human Rights Treaties on the Domestic Level*, The Hague: Kluwer Law International.
Hiebert, J, 2002, *Charter Conflicts: What is Parliament's Role?*, Montreal & Kingston: McGill-Queen's University Press.
Hiebert, J, 2003, 'Parliament and Rights', in T Campbell, J Goldsworthy and A Stone (eds), *Protecting Human Rights: Instruments and Institutions*, Oxford: Oxford University Press.
Hiebert, J, 2004, 'New Constitutional Ideas: Can New Parliamentary Models Resist Judicial Dominance When Interpreting Rights?', 82 *Texas Law Review* 1963–87.
Hiebert, J, 2005a, 'Interpreting a Bill of Rights: The Importance of Legislative Rights Review', 35 *British Journal of Political Science* 235–55.
Hiebert, J, 2005b, 'Rights-Vetting in New Zealand and Canada: Similar Idea, Different Outcomes', 1 *New Zealand Journal of Public and Int'l Law* 63–103.
Hiebert, J, 2006a, 'Parliament and the Human Rights Act: Can the JCHR help facilitate a culture of rights?', 4 *Int'l J Con Law* 1–38.
Hiebert, J, 2006b, 'Parliamentary Bills of Rights: An Alternative Model?', 69 *Modern LR* 7–28.
Hinch, D, 2003, 'Sometimes the law passes use-by date', *The [Melbourne] Sunday Herald Sun*, 16 February, p 75.
Hirschl, R, 2000, ' "Negative" Rights vs "Positive" Entitlements: A Comparative Study of Judicial Interpretations of Rights in an Emerging Neo-Liberal Economic Order', 22 *Human Rights Quarterly* 1060–98.
Hirschl, R, 2004, *Towards Juristocracy: The Origins and Consequences of the New Constitutionalism*, Cambridge: Harvard University Press.
Hirsh, W, 1990, 'The New Zealand Experience: Exciting Racial Disharmony and the Law', 1 *Without Prejudice* 18–26.
Hodge W, 1981, 'Incitement to Racial Hatred in New Zealand', 30 *ICLQ* 918–26.
Hogg, R and Brown, D, 1998, *Rethinking Law & Order*, Sydney: Pluto Press.
Hovell, D, 2003, 'The Sovereignty Stratagem: Australia's Response to UN Human Rights Treaty Bodies', 28 *Alternative Law Journal* 297–301.
Howard, J, 2004, 'Transcript of the Prime Minister the Hon John Howard MP

Interview with John Laws, Radio 2UE', 8 March, www.pm.gov.au/news/interviews/Interview738.html (accessed 28 April 2006).
Human Rights Foundation of New Zealand, 2004, *Submission to the Justice and Electoral Committee on the Civil Union Bill and the Relationships (Statutory References) Bill*, www.humanrights.co.nz/index.html (accessed 29 May 2006).
Hunt, M, 1999, 'The Human Rights Act and Legal Culture: The Judiciary and the Legal Profession', 26 *Journal of Law and Society* 86–102.
Hunter, J, 1985, 'The development of the rule against double jeopardy', 5 *The Journal of Legal History* 3–19.
Hurlburt, W, 1986, *Law Reform Commissions in the United Kingdom, Australia and Canada*, Edmonton: Juriliber.
Hurley, M, 2005, *Sexual Orientation and Legal Rights*, Current Issues Review 92–1E, Ottawa: Parliamentary Information and Research Service, Library of Parliament.
Huscroft, G, 1995, 'Defamation, Racial Disharmony, and Freedom of Expression', in G Huscroft and P Rishworth (eds), *Rights and Freedoms: The New Zealand Bill of Rights Act 1990 and the Human Rights Act 1993*, Wellington: Brooker's.
Huscroft, G, 2002, 'Rights, Bill of Rights, and the Role of Courts and Legislatures', in G Huscroft and P Rishworth (eds), *Litigating Rights: Perspectives from Domestic and International Law*, Oxford: Hart.
Huscroft, G, 2003a, 'The Attorney General's Reporting Duty', in P Rishworth, G Huscroft, S Optican and R Mahoney, *The New Zealand Bill of Rights*, Melbourne: Oxford University Press.
Huscroft, G, 2003b, 'Freedom From Discrimination', in P Rishworth, G Huscroft, S Optican and R Mahoney, *The New Zealand Bill of Rights*, Melbourne: Oxford University Press.
Huscroft, G, 2003c, 'Freedom of Expression', in P Rishworth, G Huscroft, S Optican and R Mahoney, *The New Zealand Bill of Rights*, Melbourne: Oxford University Press.
Huscroft, G and Rishworth, P (eds), 2002, *Litigating Rights: Perspectives from Domestic and International Law*, Oxford: Hart.
Iganski, P, 1999a, 'Legislating against hate: outlawing racism and antisemitism in Britain', 19 *Critical Social Policy* 129–41.
Iganski, P, 1999b, 'Legislating morality, and competing "rights": legal instruments against racism and antisemitism in the European Union', 25 *Journal of Ethnic and Migration Studies* 509–16.
Ignatieff, M, 2000, *The Rights Revolution*, Toronto: Anansi Press.
Ignatieff, M, 2001, *Human Rights as Politics and Idolatry*, Princeton: Princeton UP.
International Lesbian and Gay Association, 2003, 'Brazilian Resolution: The resolution on human rights and sexual orientation, 2 December, www.ilga.org (accessed 29 May 2006).
International Lesbian and Gay Association, 2004, 'Canada and New Zealand statement at the UNCHR in support of the Brazilian resolution', 26 April, www.ilga.org (accessed 29 May 2006).
International Lesbian and Gay Association, 2005, 'UN: 32 Countries Support New Zealand', 20 April, www.ilga.org (accessed 29 May 2006).
International Lesbian and Gay Association – Europe, 2005, 'Same-Sex Marriage and Partnership: Country-by-Country', www.ilga-europe.org/europe/issues/marriage_and_partnership/same_sex_marriage_and_partnership_country_by_country (accessed 29 May 2006).

James, A, Taylor, N and Walker, C, 2000, 'The Reform of Double Jeopardy', 5 *Web Journal of Current Legal Issues* http://webjcli.ncl.ac.uk/2000/issue5/james5.html (accessed 28 April 2006).

James P, Abelson, D and Lusztig, M (eds), 2002, *The Myth of the Sacred: The Charter, the Courts, and the Politics of the Constitution in Canada*, Montreal/Kingston: McGill-Queen's University Press.

Jayawickrama, N, 2002, *The Judicial Application of Human Rights Law: National, Regional and International Jurisprudence*, Cambridge: Cambridge University Press.

Johns, L, 1995, 'Racial Vilification and ICERD in Australia', 2 *E Law* www.murdoch.edu.au/elaw/issues/v2n1/johns.txt (accessed 28 April 2006).

Johns, R, 2003, *Double Jeopardy*, NSW Parliamentary Library Research Service Briefing Paper No 16/03.

Joseph, P, 1999, 'The New Zealand Bill of Rights Experience', in P Alston (ed), *Protecting Human Rights Through Bills of Rights: Comparative Perspectives*, Oxford: Oxford University Press.

Joseph, S, Schultz, J and Castan, M, 2004, *The International Covenant on Civil and Political Rights: Cases, Materials, and Commentary*, 2nd edn, Oxford: Oxford University Press.

Jowell, J and Cooper, J, 2003, *Delivering Rights: How the Human Rights Act is Working*, Oxford: Hart.

Justice, 2001, *A Human Rights Commission for the United Kingdom? Submission of Justice to the Joint Committee on Human Rights*, July.

Justice, 2002, *Justice For All: Justice response to the White Paper*, October.

Justice, 2003, *Criminal Justice Bill, Parts 1–11. Briefing for the Second Reading and Committee Stages in the House of Lords*, June.

Kahana, T, 2001, 'The Notwithstanding Mechanism and Public Discussion: Lessons From the Ignored Practice of Section 33 of the Charter', 44 *Canadian Public Administration* 255.

Kaplan, W, 1993, 'Maxwell Cohen and the Report of the Special Committee on Hate Propaganda', in W Kaplan and D McRae (eds), *Law, Policy, and International Justice: Essays in Honour of Maxwell Cohen*, Montreal and Kingston: McGill-Queen's University Press.

Kavanagh, A, 2004, 'The Elusive Divide between Interpretation and Legislation Under the Human Rights Act', 24 *Oxford Journal of Legal Studies* 259–85.

Kayfetz, B, 1970, 'The Story Behind Canada's New Anti-Hate Law', 4 *Patterns of Prejudice* 5.

Keith, K, 1997, 'A Bill of Rights: Does it Matter? A Comment', 32 *Texas International Law Journal* 393–9.

Kelly, J, 2005, *Governing with the Charter: Legislative and Judicial Activism and Framers' Intent*, Vancouver: UBC Press.

Kennedy, S, 2004, 'Editorial Opinion – Jeopardy change erodes our basic human rights', *The Ashburton Guardian*, 29 May, www.ashburtonguardian.co.nz/index.asp?articleid=3125 (accessed 28 April 2006).

Kinley, D (ed), 1998, *Human Rights in Australian Law: Principles, Practice and Potential*, Sydney: Federation Press.

Kinley, D, 1999, 'Parliamentary Scrutiny of Human Rights: A Duty Neglected?', in P Alston (ed), *Protecting Human Rights Through Bills of Rights: Comparative Perspectives*, Oxford: Oxford University Press.

Kinslor, J, 2002, ' "Killing Off" International Human Rights Law: An Exploration of the Australian Government's Relationship with United Nations Human Rights Committees', 8 *Aust J of Human Rights* 79–99.

Kirby, M, 1999, 'Domestic Implementation of International Human Rights Norms', 5 *Aust J of Human Rights* 109–25.

Kirby, M, 2003, 'Judgements to lift the burden of fear', *The [Sydney] Sun-Herald*, 5 October, p 71.

Kirby, M, 2003b, 'Carroll, double jeopardy and international human rights law', 27 *Crim LJ* 231–45.

Kirby, M, 2005, 'Sexuality and Australian Law', in H Graupner and P Tahmindjis, *Sexuality and Human Rights: A Global Overview*, Binghamton: Harrington Park Press.

Klare, K, 1998, 'Legal Culture and Transformative Constitutionalism', 14 *South African J of Human Rights* 146–88.

Klotzko, A, 2004, *A Clone of Your Own? The Science and Ethics of Cloning*, Oxford: Oxford University Press.

Klug, F, 2004, 'The United Kingdom Experience', in C Debono and T Colwell (eds), *Comparative Perspectives on Bills of Rights*, Canberra: National Institute of Social Sciences and Law.

Knight, L, 2002, 'Pricey defence costs taxpayers', *North Shore News*, 10 July, www.nsnews.com/issues02/w070802/072202/opinion/072202op2.html (accessed 6 January 2006).

Knight, S, 2006, 'Police defend Hamza inquiry as blame game begins', *TimesOnline* 8 February, www.timesonline.co.uk (accessed 2 May 2006).

Knopff, R, 2000, *The Charter Revolution and the Court Party*, Peterborough: Broadview Press.

Koch, C, 2003, 'Envisioning a Global Legal Culture', 25(1) *Michigan Journal of International Law* 1–76.

Korengold, M, 1993, 'Lessons in Confronting Racist Speech: Good Intentions, Bad Results and Article 4(a) of the Convention on the Elimination of All Forms of Racial Discrimination', 77 *Minnesota Law Review* 719–37.

Kritzer, H and Zemans, F, 1993, 'Local Legal Culture and the Control of Litigation', 27 *Law & Society Review* 535–57.

Lahey, K and Alderson, K, 2004, *Same-Sex Marriage: The Personal and the Political*, Toronto: Insomniac Press.

Landman, T, 2002, 'Comparative Politics and Human Rights', 24 *Human Rights Quarterly* 890–923.

LaViolette, N, 2002, 'Waiting in a New Line at City Hall: Registered Partnerships As an Option For Relationship Recognition Reform in Canada', 19 *Can J of Fam L* 115–72.

LaViolette, N and Whitworth, S, 1994, 'No Safe Haven: Sexuality as a Universal Human Right and Gay and Lesbian Activism in International Politics', 23 *Millenium: Journal of International Studies* 563–88.

Law Commission of Canada, 2001, *Beyond Conjugality: Recognizing and Supporting Close Personal Relationships*, Ottawa: Law Commission of Canada.

Law Institute of Victoria, 2004, *Submission to the Model Criminal Code Officers' Committee of the Standing Committee of Attorneys-General on its Discussion Paper*

'Issue Estoppel, Double Jeopardy and Prosecution Appeals Against Acquittals' (November 2003), 17 March.
Law Society of England and Wales, 2002, 'The Law Society response to the Criminal Justice White Paper *Justice for All*', October, London: Law Society of England and Wales.
Leane, G, 2004, 'Enacting Bills of Rights: Canada and the Curious Case of New Zealand's "Thin" Democracy', 26 *Human Rights Quarterly* 152–88.
Leben, C, 1999, 'Is There a European Approach to Human Rights?' in P Alston (ed), *The EU and Human Rights*, Oxford: Oxford University Press.
Leckie, S, 1998, 'Another Step Towards Indivisibility: Identifying the Key Features of Violations of Economic, Social and Cultural Rights', 20(1) *Human Rights Quarterly* 81–124.
Legal Aid Queensland, 2004, *Response to 'Discussion Paper: Issue Estoppel, Double Jeopardy & Prosecution Appeals Against Acquittals'*.
Legrand, P, 1999, *Fragments on Law as Culture*, Deventer: Tjeenk Willink.
Lesbian and Gay Solidarity, 2004, 'Same-Sex Marriage. Homophobia and Religion in Australia in 2004 – The Same-Sex Marriage Debate', www.zipworld.com.au/~josken/samesex.htm (accessed 28 April 2006).
Lester, A, 2002, *Parliamentary Scrutiny of Legislation Under the Human Rights Act 1998*, Occasional Paper No 8, New Zealand Centre for Public Law, Faculty of Law, Victoria University of Wellington.
Lester, A and Bindman, G, 1972, *Race and Law*, Harmondsworth: Penguin.
Lester, A and Pannick, D (eds), 2004, *Human Rights Law and Practice*, London: LexisNexis UK.
Liberty, 2002a, *Liberty's briefing on the 'Criminal Justice Bill' – 2nd Commons reading*, November.
Liberty, 2002b, 'Criminal Justice Bill: Liberty Response', Press Release, 21 November, www.liberty-human-rights.org.uk/news-and-events/1-press-releases/2002/ (accessed 28 April 2006).
Liberty, 2003, *Liberty's briefing on the 'Criminal Justice Bill' for the House of Lords*, June.
Liberty, 2005, 'Couple challenge UK stance on Gay Marriage', Press Release, 21 September, www.liberty-human-rights.org.uk/news-and-events/1-press-releases/2005/ (accessed 28 April 2006).
Liberty, Legal Action Group, Bar Council, Criminal Bar Association, 2002, 'Government's criminal justice plans for the Queen's Speech: joint statement from Liberty, Legal Action Group, Bar Council, Criminal Bar Association', Press Release, 10 November, http://liberty-human-rights.org.uk/press/press-releases-2002/ (accessed 8 January 2006).
Loughlin, M, 2001, 'Rights, Democracy, and Law', in T Campbell, K Ewing and A Tomkins (eds), *Sceptical Essays on Human Rights*, Oxford: Oxford University Press.
Macintyre, B, 2006, 'Sworn enemies find a common cause', *TimesOnline*, 8 February, www.timesonline.co.uk/article/0,,2–2030041,00.html (accessed 2 May 2006).
MacIvor, H, 2006, *Canadian Politics and Government in the Charter Era*, Toronto: Thomson/Nelson.
Macpherson, W, 1999, *The Stephen Lawrence Inquiry – Report of an Inquiry by Sir William Macpherson of Cluny*, Cm 4262, London: Stationery Office.

Magnet, J, Beaudoin, G, Gall, G and Manfredi, C (eds), 2003, *The Canadian Charter of Rights and Freedoms: Reflections on the Charter after twenty years*, Toronto: LexisNexis Butterworths.

Mahoney, R, 1990, 'Previous Acquittal and Previous Conviction in New Zealand: Another Kick at the Cheshire Cat', 7 *Otago LR* 222–65.

Maiman, R, 2004, '"We've had to Raise our Game": Liberty's Litigation Strategy under the Human Rights Act 1998', in S Halliday and P Schmidt (eds), *Human Rights Brought Home: Socio-Legal Studies of Human Rights in the National Context*, Oxford: Hart.

Mandel, M, 1994, *The Charter of Rights and the Legalization of Politics in Canada*, Toronto: Thompson Education Publishing.

Manfredi, C, 2001, *Judicial Power and the Charter: Canada and the Paradox of Liberal Constitutionalism*, Toronto: Oxford University Press.

Manfredi, C, 2003, 'Same-Sex Marriage and the Notwithstanding Clause', *Policy Options*, October, p 21.

Manfredi, C, 2004, *Feminist Activism in the Supreme Court: Legal Mobilization and the Women's Legal Education and Action Fund*, Vancouver: UBC Press.

Marshall, D, 2005, *Justice in Jeopardy: The Unsolved Murder of Baby Deidre Kennedy*, Sydney: Random House.

Marshall, G, 2002, 'The United Kingdom Human Rights Act, 1998', in V Jackson and M Tushnet (eds), *Defining the Field of Comparative Constitutional Law*, Westport/London: Praeger.

Mathew, P, 1995, 'International Law and the Protection of Human Rights in Australia: Recent Trends', 17 *Sydney Law Review* 177–203.

Mathews, J, 2003, *Advice to the Attorney General: Safeguards in Relation to Proposed Double Jeopardy Legislation*, 27 November, www.lawlink.nsw.gov.au/lawlink/clrd/ll_clrd.nsf/pages/CLRD_reports (accessed 26 May 2006).

Maxim Institute, 2004, 'Oral Submission to the Justice and Electoral Select Committee on the Civil Union Bill and the Relationships (Statutory References) Bill', 27 September, www.maxim.org.nz/civilunions/index.php (accessed 25 October 2005).

McAllister, D and Dodek, A (eds), 2002, *The Charter at Twenty: Law and Practice 2002*, Toronto: Ontario Bar Association.

McCrudden, C, 2000, 'A Common Law of Human Rights? Transnational Judicial Conversations on Constitutional Rights', in K O'Donovan and G Rubin (eds), *Human Rights and Legal History*, Oxford: Oxford University Press.

McGee, G and Caplan, A, 2004, *The Human Cloning Debate*, Berkeley: Berkeley Hills Books.

McGoldrick, D and O'Donnell, T, 1998, 'Hate-Speech Laws: Consistency With National and International Human Rights Law', 18 *Legal Studies* 453–85.

McGonagle, T, 2001a, 'Wresting (Racial) Equality From Tolerance of Hate Speech', 23 *Dublin University Law Journal* 21–54.

McGonagle, T, 2001b, 'Freedom of Expression and Limits on Racist Speech: A Difficult Symbiosis', 13 *Interights Bulletin – A Review of the International Centre for the Legal Protection of Human Rights* 135–6.

McGonagle, T, 2003, 'Protection of Human Dignity, Distribution of Racist Content (Hate Speech)', in S Nikoltchev (ed), *IRIS Special: Co-Regulation of the Media in Europe*, Strasbourg: The European Audiovisual Observatory.

McGregor, J, 2006, 'Balancing responsibilities with rights: freedom of expression and hate speech in New Zealand', EEO Commissioner, New Zealand Human Rights Commission, Address to the Ministry of Justice Symposium on the Bill of Rights Act, 8 February, www.hrc.co.nz/home/hrc/newsandissues/balancing responsibilitieswithrights.php (accessed 31 March 2006).

McLachlin, B, 1996, 'The Canadian Charter and the Democratic Process', in C Gearty and A Tomkins (eds), *Understanding Human Rights*, London: Pinter.

McLean, J, 2001, 'Legislative Invalidation, Human Rights Protection and s 4 of the New Zealand Bill of Rights Act', *New Zealand Law Review* 421–48.

McNamara, L, 2002, *Regulating Racism: Racial Vilification Laws in Australia*, Sydney: Institute of Criminology, University of Sydney.

McNamara, L, 2005, 'Negotiating the Contours of Unlawful Hate Speech: Regulation Under Provincial Human Rights Laws in Canada', 38 *University of British Columbia Law Review* 1–82.

McNamara, L and Solomon, T, 1996, 'The Commonwealth Racial Hatred Act 1995: Achievement or Disappointment?', 18 *Adelaide Law Review* 259–88.

Meagher, D, 2004, 'So Far So Good?: A Critical Evaluation of Racial Vilification Laws in Australia', 32 *Federal Law Review* 225–53.

Meagher, D, 2005, 'The Protection of Political Communication under the Australian Constitution', 28 *UNSW Law Journal* 30–68.

Meckled-Garcia, S and Cali, B (eds), 2006, *The Legalization of Human Rights: Multi-disciplinary Perspectives on Human Rights and Human Rights Law*, London: Routledge.

Millbank, J, 2005, 'Advice to GLRL on Same-Sex Marriage Bill', 19 May, www.glrl.org.au/issues/advicefinal.pdf (accessed 28 April 2006).

Milner, A, 2005, 'Criminal Procedure Bill ignores real issues', 30 *NZ Lawyer*, 25 November, pp 1, 4.

Moon, R, 2000, *The Constitutional Protection of Freedom of Expression*, Toronto: University of Toronto Press.

Moses, J, 1996, 'Hate Speech: Competing Rights to Freedom of Expression', 8 *Auckland ULR* 185–203.

Mowbray, A, 2001, *Cases and Materials on the European Convention on Human Rights*, London: Butterworths.

Murphy, J, 2004, 'Some Wrongs and (Human) Rights in the English Same-Sex Marriage Debate', 18 *BYU Journal of Public Law* 543–67.

Nason, D and Emerson, S (2002) 'Mason joins push for review', *The Australian*, 13 December, p 1.

Nelken, D, 1995, 'Disclosing/Invoking Legal Culture: An Introduction', 4 *Social & Legal Studies* 435–52.

Nelken, D (ed), 1997, *Comparing Legal Cultures*, Aldershot: Dartmouth.

Nelken, D and Feest, J (eds), 2001, *Adapting Legal Cultures*, Oxford: Hart.

New South Wales Council for Civil Liberties, 2005, 'CCL supports a Human Rights Act for all Australians', www.nswccl.org.au/issues/bill_of_rights/index.php (accessed 28 April 2006).

New South Wales Council for Civil Liberties and the UNSW Council for Civil Liberties, 2004, *Submission to the Model Criminal Code Officers' Committee's Issue Estoppel, Double Jeopardy and Prosecution Appeals Against Acquittals*, 17 February, www.nswccl.org.au/publications/submissions.php (accessed 26 May 2006).

New South Wales Government, 2003, *Explanatory Note on the Consultation Draft Bill – Criminal Appeal Amendment (Double Jeopardy) Bill 2003*, Sydney: NSW Parliamentary Counsel's Office.
New South Wales Law Reform Commission, 1995, *Directed Verdicts of Acquittal*, Discussion Paper 37, Sydney: NSW Law Reform Commission.
New South Wales, Office of the Premier, 2003, 'Carr Government to Overhaul "Double Jeopardy" Rule', Media Release, 9 February.
New South Wales Parliament, Legislation Review Committee, 2005, *Annual Review, July 2004–June 2005*, Sydney: Parliament of NSW.
New Zealand Attorney General, 2004, *Report of the Attorney General under the New Zealand Bill of Rights Act 1990 on the Criminal Procedure Bill*, Presented to the House of Representatives pursuant to Section 7 of the New Zealand Bill of Rights Act 1990 and Standing Order 264 of the Standing Orders of the House of Representatives.
New Zealand Attorney General, 2005, *Report of the Attorney General under the New Zealand Bill of Rights Act 1990 on the Marriage (Gender Clarification) Amendment Bill 2005*, Presented to the House of Representatives pursuant to Section 7 of the New Zealand Bill of Rights Act 1990 and Standing Order 264 of the Standing Orders of the House of Representatives.
New Zealand Government, 2003, *Government Response to Government Administration Committee Report on its Inquiry into the Operation of the Films, Videos, and Publications Classification Act 1993 and Related Issues*, www.justice.govt.nz/pubs/reports/2003/gac/Govt_Response_to_GAC_Report.pdf (accessed 30 May 2006).
New Zealand Herald, 2004, 'Editorial: Valid foundation for double jeopardy change', *New Zealand Herald*, 18 May.
New Zealand House of Representatives, Government Administration Committee, 2003, *Inquiry into the operation of the Films, Videos, and Publications Classification Act 1993 and related issues*, www.clerk.parliament.govt.nz/Content/SelectCommitteeReports/i5a.pdf (accessed 30 May 2006).
New Zealand House of Representatives, 2004, 'Government Administration Committee Inquiry into Hate Speech, Media Release, 5 August.
New Zealand House of Representatives, 2005, *Standing Orders*, www.clerk.parliament.govt.nz/Publications/Other/ (accessed 24 May 2006).
New Zealand House of Representatives, Law and Order Committee, 2005, *Criminal Procedure Bill*, Wellington: House of Representatives.
New Zealand Human Rights Commission, 2004a, *Submission on the Criminal Procedure Bill to the Law and Order Committee*, 4 August.
New Zealand Human Rights Commission, 2004b, 'Submissions by the Human Rights Commission re the Matter Between Bruce William Bissett and the Right Hon Winston Peters, MP Before the Human Rights Review Tribunal', HRRT 50/03 30 September.
New Zealand Human Rights Commission, 2004c, *Human Rights in New Zealand Today: Nga Tika Tangata O Te Motu*, Wellington: Human Rights Commission.
New Zealand Human Rights Commission, 2004d, *Submission on the Civil Union and Relationships (Statutory References) Bills to the Justice and Electoral Select Committee*, 6 August.
New Zealand Human Rights Commission, 2005a, 'Submission to the Government Administration Committee into the Inquiry into Hate Speech, 5 May, www.

hrc.co.nz/home/hrc/newsandissues/submissiontotheinquiryintohatespeech.php (accessed 15 March 2006).
New Zealand Human Rights Commission, 2005b, 'Balance "about right", hate speech inquiry told', Media Release, 5 May, www.hrc.co.nz/home/hrc/newsandissues/hatespeechbalanceaboutright.php (accessed 15 March 2006).
New Zealand Human Rights Commission, 2005c, *Annual Report*, Wellington: Human Rights Commission.
New Zealand Human Rights Commission, 2006, *Race Relations in 2005*, Wellington: Human Rights Commission.
New Zealand Law Commission, 2000, *Acquittal Following Perversion of the Course of Justice: A Response to R v Moore*, NZLC PP42, Wellington: Law Commission.
New Zealand Law Commission, 2001, *Acquittal Following Perversion of the Course of Justice*, NZLC R70, Wellington: Law Commission.
New Zealand Law Society, 2004a, 'Second double jeopardy exception more controversial', 31 May, www.nz-lawsoc.org.nz/lawtalk/625double%20jeopardy.htm (accessed 28 April 2006).
New Zealand Law Society, 2004b, *Submissions on the Criminal Procedure Bill*, 27 August.
New Zealand Law Society, 2005, 'Double jeopardy changes likely, despite strong opposition', www.nz-lawsoc.org.nz/lawtalk/652criminal%20procedure.htm (accessed 28 April 2006).
New Zealand Ministry of Justice, 1999, *Same-Sex Couples and the Law*, Discussion Paper, Wellington: Ministry of Justice.
New Zealand Ministry of Justice, 2000, *Re-evaluation of Human Rights Protections in New Zealand*, Discussion Paper, Wellington: Ministry of Justice.
New Zealand Minister of Justice, 2004a, 'Exceptions to double jeopardy to be introduced', Media Release, 16 May, www.beehive.govt.nz/ViewDocument.aspx?DocumentID=19705 (accessed 28 April 2006).
New Zealand Minister of Justice, 2004b, 'Bill to improve fairness, efficiency of proceedings', Media Release, 1 July, www.beehive.govt.nz/ViewDocument.aspx?DocumentID=20196 (accessed 28 April 2006).
New Zealand Parliamentary Library, 2006, *Criminal Procedure Bill 2004 (Supplementary Order Papers 2006 Nos 50 and 51 (Opposition))*, Bill Digest No 1408, 2 and 3 August, Wellington: Parliamentary Library.
New Zealand Press Association, 2004a, 'Legal changes "eating into human rights"', *New Zealand Herald*, 20 October.
New Zealand Press Association, 2004b, 'Civil Union backers reject referendum calls', *New Zealand Herald*, 1 December, www.nzherald.co.nz/search/story.cfm?storyid=DD8A2912-39E2-11DA-8E1B-A5B353C55561 (accessed 28 April 2006).
Niarchos, N, 2004, 'Human Rights in Australia: a Retreat from Treaties', 26 *Law Society Bulletin* [South Australia] 23–30.
Nicholson, A, 2004, 'The "reform" that shames Australia', *The Age*, 20 September.
Nicholson, A, 2005, 'The Legal Regulation of Marriage', 29 *Melbourne University Law Review* 556–68.
Niemi, H, 2003, *National Implementation of Findings by United Nations Human Rights Treaty Bodies: A Comparative Study*, Turcu: Institute for Human Rights, Abo Akademi University.

Odysseus Trust, 2005, 'Civil Partnership Act 2004', www.odysseustrust.org/text/civilpartnerships.html (accessed 28 April 2006).
Office of the United Nations High Commissioner for Human Rights, 2006a, *Ratifications and Reservations: International Covenant on Civil and Political Rights*, 8 May, www.ohchr.org/english/countries/ratification/4.htm (accessed 24 May 2006).
Office of the United Nations High Commissioner for Human Rights, 2006b, *Ratifications and Reservations: International Convention on the Elimination of All Forms of Racial Discrimination*, 8 May, www.ohchr.org/english/countries/ratification/2.htm (accessed 24 May 2006).
Office of the United Nations High Commissioner for Human Rights, 2006c, *Statistical survey of individual complaints considered under the procedure governed by article 14 of the International Convention on the Elimination of All Forms of Racial Discrimination*, 15 March, www.ohchr.org/english/bodies/cerd/stat4.htm (accessed 5 April 2006).
Offord, B, 2003, *Homosexual Rights as Human Rights: Activism in Indonesia, Singapore and Australia*, Bern: Peter Lang.
O'Gorman, T, 2002, 'Review risks presumption of innocence', *The Australian*, 20 December, p 9.
Ogus, A, 2002, 'The Economic Basis of Legal Culture: Networks and Monopolization', 22 *Oxford Journal of Legal Studies* 419–34.
O'Neill, N, Rice, S and Douglas, R, 2004, *Retreat from Injustice: Human Rights Law in Australia*, 2nd edn, Sydney: Federation Press.
Opeskin, B and Weisbrot, D (eds), 2005, *The Promise of Law Reform*, Sydney: Federation Press.
Optican, S, 2003, 'Retroactive Penalties and Double Jeopardy', in P Rishworth, G Huscroft, S Optican and R Mahoney, *The New Zealand Bill of Rights*, Melbourne: Oxford University Press.
Orlin, T and Scheinin, M, 2000, 'Introduction' in T Orlin, A Rosas and M Scheinin (eds), *The Jurisprudence of Human Rights Law: A Comparative Interpretive Approach*, Turcu: Institute for Human Rights, Abo Akademi University.
Orlin, T, Rosas, A and Scheinin, M (eds), 2000, *The Jurisprudence of Human Rights Law: A Comparative Interpretive Approach*, Turcu: Institute for Human Rights, Abo Akademi University.
Otto, D and Wiseman, D, 2001, 'In Search of "Effective Remedies": Applying the International Covenant on Economic, Social and Cultural Rights to Australia', 7 *Australian Journal of Human Rights* 5–46.
Outrage!, 2003, 'Outrage! Rejects Government's Civil Partnership Proposal', Press Release, 30 September.
Outrage!, 2005, 'Royal Wedding – Gays demand marriage rights too', Press Release, 9 April, www.petertatchell.net/ (accessed 30 November 2006).
Panetta, A, 2005, 'Senate can't stop same-sex marriage, Cotler says', *Globe and Mail*, 12 July.
Pannick, D, 2000, 'Let's leave politics out of double jeopardy debate', *The Times*, 23 May, www.lawteacher.net/Articles/0411.htm (accessed 8 January 2006).
Parkinson, C, 2003, 'Double jeopardy reform: The new evidence exception for acquittals', 26 *UNSWLJ* 603–21.
Parliamentary Assembly of the Council of Europe, 2005, *Legal Recognition of Same-Sex Partnerships in Europe*, Doc 10640, 5 July.

Partsch, K, 1992, 'Racial Speech and Human Rights: Article 4 of the Convention on the Elimination of All Forms of Racial Discrimination', in S Coliver (ed), *Striking A Balance: Hate Speech, Freedom of Expression and Non-Discrimination*, London and Colchester: Article 19, International Centre Against Censorship and Human Rights Centre, University of Essex.

Patman, R (ed), 2000, *Universal Human Rights*, Basingstoke: Macmillan.

Pentony, P and Rice, S, 2004, 'When the story ends, close the book: discussing the double jeopardy rule', *On Line Opinion*, 21 May, www.onlineopinion.com.au (accessed 8 October 2006).

Pettman, R, 1982, *Incitement to Racial Hatred: Issues and Analysis*, Human Rights Commission Occasional Paper No 1, Canberra: AGPS.

Pitman, T, 2003, 'Same Sex Marriage: The Next Big Thing', *DNA Magazine*, April, www.freedomint.org/marriageforall/index.htm (accessed 28 April 2006).

Pollard, R, 2006, 'Give us a break: same-sex couples step up fight for entitlements', *Sydney Morning Herald*, 4 April, p 6.

Porter, B, 2005, 'Twenty Years of Equality Rights: Reclaiming Expectations', 23 *Windsor Yearbook of Access to Justice* 145–92.

Potter, P, 2000, 'Globalisation and Local Legal Culture: Dilemmas of China's Use of Liberal Ideals of Private Property Rights', 2 *Australian Journal of Asian Law* 1–33.

Prakash, N, 2002–2003, 'R v Carroll: Double Jeopardy Under Fire', 22 *U Queensland LJ* 267–71.

Pride Alliance, 2004, 'Submission to the Justice and Electoral Committee on the Civil Union Bill and the Relationships (Statutory References) Bill, 5 August.

Public Interest Advocacy Centre and the National Association of Community Legal Centres, 2004, *Joint Submission on the Marriage Amendment Bill* www.piac.asn.au/publications/pubs/submab_20040804.html (accessed 29 May 2006).

Rae, B, 2005, *Lessons to be Learned. The report of the Honourable Bob Rae, Independent Advisor to the Minister of Public Safety and Emergency Preparedness, on outstanding questions with respect to the bombing of Air India Flight 182*, Ottawa: Air India Review Secretariat.

Rajan, S, 2005, 'Racial Vilification Legislation: The Western Australian Model', 9 *Australian Mosaic* 38.

Rice, S, 2005, 'Do Australians have equal protection against hate speech?', Democratic Audit of Australia, 1 August, http://arts.anu.edu.au/democraticaudit/papers/200508_rice_hate_speech.pdf (accessed 6 April 2006).

Richardson, I, 2004, 'The New Zealand Bill of Rights: Experience and Potential, Including the Implications for Commerce', 10 *Canterbury Law Review* 259–72.

Rishworth, P, 2003a, 'The New Zealand Bill of Rights', in P Rishworth, G Huscroft, S Optican and R Mahoney, *The New Zealand Bill of Rights*, Melbourne: Oxford University Press.

Rishworth, P, 2003b, 'Interpreting Enactments: Sections 4, 5, and 6', in P Rishworth, G Huscroft, S Optican and R Mahoney, *The New Zealand Bill of Rights*, Melbourne: Oxford University Press.

Rishworth, P, 2003c, 'Interpreting and Applying the Bill of Rights', in P Rishworth, G Huscroft, S Optican and R Mahoney, *The New Zealand Bill of Rights*, Melbourne: Oxford University Press.

Rishworth, P, Huscroft, G, Optican, S and Mahoney, R, 2003, *The New Zealand Bill of Rights*, Melbourne: Oxford University Press.

Risse, T, Ropp, S and Sikkink, K (eds), 1999, *The Power of Human Rights: International Norms and Domestic Change*, Cambridge: Cambridge University Press.

Roach, K, 1999, *Due Process and Victim's Rights: The New Law and Politics of Criminal Justice*, Toronto: University of Toronto Press.

Roberts, G, 2003, ' "Offensive" Stand to Stay', *The Australian*, 24 April, www.theage.com.au/articles/2003/04/23/1050777305889.html (accessed 6 April 2006).

Roberts, G, 2005, 'State to move on double jeopardy', *The Australian*, 31 August, p 7.

Roberts, P, 2002a, 'Justice For All? Two Bad Arguments (and Several Good Suggestions) For Resisting Double Jeopardy Reform', 6 *International Journal of Evidence and Proof* 197–217.

Roberts, P, 2002b, 'Double Jeopardy Law Reform: A Criminal Justice Commentary', 65 *Modern Law Review* 393–424.

Robinson, M, 2004, 'Advancing Economic, Social and Cultural Rights: The Way Forward', 26 *Human Rights Quarterly* 866–72.

Robinson, S, 2005, 'Pride topples prejudice', *Globe and Mail*, 4 July, p A13.

Rock, P, 2004, *Constructing Victims' Rights: The Home Office, New Labour, and Victims*, Oxford: Oxford University Press.

Ronalds, C and Pepper, R, 2004, *Discrimination Law and Practice*, 2nd edn, Sydney: Federation Press.

Ross, J, 1994, 'Hate Crime in Canada: Growing Pains With New Legislation', in M Hamm (ed), *Hate Crime: International Perspectives on Causes and Control*, Cincinnati: ACJS/Anderson.

Roth, K, 2004, 'Defending Economic, Social and Cultural Rights: Practical Issues Faced by an International Human Rights Organization', 26 *Human Rights Quarterly* 63–73.

Roxon, N, 2004, 'Marriage will remain a union between a man and a woman, but same sex couples are entitled to recognition as de factos', Australian Labor Party News Statement, 1 June, www.alp.org.au/media (accessed 3 June 2004).

Rozenberg, J, 2005, 'Murder reviews with end of "double jeopardy"', 4 April, www.telegraph.co.uk (accessed 8 January 2006).

Rubenstein, L, 2004, 'How International Human Rights Organizations Can Advance Economic, Social and Cultural Rights: a Response to Kenneth Roth', 26 *Human Rights Quarterly* 845–65.

Sadurski, W, 1999, *Freedom of Speech and Its Limits*, Dordrecht/Boston/London: Kluwer Academic Publishers.

Sanders, D, 1996, 'Getting Lesbian and Gay Issues on the International Human Rights Agenda', 18 *Human Rights Quarterly* 67–106.

Saunders, D, 2005, ' "What more do you want me to tell you?" PM says as Air-India families gather', *Globe and Mail*, 24 June, p 1.

Sayers, M, 2005, 'Co-operation across Frontiers', in B Opeskin and D Weisbrot (eds), 2005, *The Promise of Law Reform*, Sydney: Federation Press.

Scarman, L, 1975, *Red Lion Square disorders of 15 June 1974: Report of inquiry by the Rt Hon Lord Justice Scarman, OBE*, Cmnd 5919, London: HMSO.

Schmidt, P and Halliday, S, 2004, 'Introduction: Socio-Legal Perspectives on Human Rights in the National Context', in S Halliday and P Schmidt (eds), *Human Rights Brought Home: Socio-Legal Studies of Human Rights in the National Context*, Oxford: Hart.

Schneiderman, D and Sutherland, K (eds), 1997, *Charting the Consequences: The Impact of Charter Rights on Canadian Law and Politics*, Toronto: University of Toronto Press.

Scott, C, 1999, 'Reaching Beyond (Without Abandoning) the Category of "Economic, Social and Cultural Rights"', 21 *Human Rights Quarterly* 633–60.

Sedley, S, 2005, 'The Rocks or the Open Sea: Where is the Human Rights Act Heading?', 32 *Journal of Law and Society* 3–17.

Seuffert, N, 2006, 'Sexual Citizenship and the Civil Union Act 2004', 37 *Victoria University of Wellington LR* 281–306.

Sharpe, R and Roach, K, 2005, *The Charter of Rights and Freedoms*, 3rd edn, Toronto: Irwin Law.

Sigler, J, 1969, *Double Jeopardy: The Developments of a Legal and Social Policy*, New York: Cornell University Press.

Skeers, J, 2003, 'Australia: State election descends into law-and-order bidding war', www.wsws.org/articles/2003/mar2003/nsw-m14.shtml (28 April 2006).

Smith, M, 1999, *Lesbian and Gay Rights in Canada: Social Movements and Equality-Seeking, 1971–1995*, Toronto: University of Toronto Press.

Smith, M. 2005a, 'The Politics of Same-Sex Marriage in Canada and the United States', *PS: Political Science & Politics* (April) 225–8.

Smith, M, 2005b, 'Social Movements and Judicial Empowerment: Courts, Public Policy and Lesbian and Gay Organizing in Canada', 33 *Politics & Society* 327–53.

Smith, M, 2005c, 'Explaining Human Rights Protections: Institutionalist Analysis in the Lesbian and Gay Rights Case', paper presented at the Annual Meeting of the Canadian Political Science Association, University of Western Ontario, London, 2–4 June, www.cpsa-acsp.ca (accessed 23 May 2006).

Starrenburg, N, 2004, 'Interpretive Theories in New Zealand Bill of Rights Jurisprudence', 10 *Auckland University Law Review* 115–42.

Steiner, H and Alston, P, 2001, *International Human Rights in Context: Law, Politics, Morals*, 2nd edn, Oxford: Oxford University Press.

Stonewall, 2005, 'Housing: The Mendoza Case', www.stonewall.org.uk/information_bank/partnership/housing/default.asp (accessed 28 April 2006).

Stonewall, 2006, 'Civil Partnership Act: Frequently Asked Questions', www.stonewall.org.uk/information_bank/partnership/civil_partnership_act/152.asp (accessed 30 May 2006).

Stott Despoja, N, 2000, 'The Evidence Points to the Need For an Australian Bill of Rights', 15 November, www.onlineopinion.com.au/view.asp?article=1282 (accessed 28 April 2006).

Strang, H, 2004, *Repair or Revenge?: Victims and Restorative Justice*, Oxford: Oxford University Press.

Stychin, C, 1998, *A Nation By Rights*, Philadelphia: Temple University Press.

Stychin, C, 2004, 'Same-Sex Sexualities and the Globalization of Human Rights Discourse', 49 *McGill Law Journal* 951–68.

Sullivan, T, Warren, E and Westbrook, J, 1994, 'The Persistence of Local Legal Culture: Twenty Years of Experience From the Federal Bankruptcy Courts', 17 *Harvard Journal of Law and Public Policy* 801–65.

Sumner, L, 2004 *The Hateful and the Obscene: Studies in the Limits of Freedom of Expression*, Toronto: University of Toronto Press.

Symonides, J, 2003, *Human Rights: International Protection, Monitoring Enforcement*, Burlington, VT: Ashgate.

Szego, J, 2006, 'Embassies unhelpful with gay marriages', *Sydney Morning Herald*, 14–15 January, p 3.

Tahmindjis, P, 2005, 'Sexuality and International Human Rights Law', in H Graupner and P Tahmindjis, *Sexuality and Human Rights: A Global Overview*, Binghamton: Harrington Park Press.

Talbott, W, 2005, *Which Rights Should Be Universal?*, New York: Oxford University Press.

Taylor, E, 1995, 'Hanging up on Hate: Contempt of Court as a Tool to Shut Down Hatelines', 5 *National Journal of Constitutional Law* 163–82.

Taylor, J, 2004, 'Human Rights Protection in Australia: Interpretation Provisions and Parliamentary Supremacy', 32 *Federal Law Review* 57–77.

Taylor, P, 2006, ' "Street language" ruled not vilification', *The Australian*, 15 September, www.theaustralian.news.com.au/story/0,20867,20415043-29677,00.html (accessed 17 September 2006).

Thampapillai, V, 2005, *A Bill of Rights for New South Wales and Australia*, Discussion Paper, Sydney: The Law Society of NSW.

Thomas, E, 2004, 'A Bill of Rights: the New Zealand Experience', in C Debono and T Colwell (eds), *Comparative Perspectives on Bills of Rights*, Canberra: National Institute of Social Sciences and Law.

Tomlins, J, 2004, 'When I do becomes you can't', *The Age*, 3 September, A3.

Tomlinson, H, 2001, *Interpreting Convention Rights: Essential Human Rights Cases of the Commonwealth*, London: Butterworths.

Tribe, L, 1988, *American Constitutional Law*, 2nd edn, Mineola, NY: The Foundation Press.

Tunnah, H, 2003, 'Government moves to allow gay couples to legally "tie the knot" ', *New Zealand Herald*, 16 July.

Tushnet, M, 1996, 'Living With A Bill of Rights', in C Gearty and A Tomkins (eds), *Understanding Human Rights*, London: Pinter.

TVNZ, One News, 2003a, 'Mixed reaction to Civil Union Bill', 17 July, http://tvnz.co.nz/view/page/423466/206121 (accessed 28 April 2006).

TVNZ, One News, 2003b, 'Uproar over "racist" pamphlet', 2 December, http://tvnz.co.nz/view/page/425825/240200 (accessed 28 April 2006).

TVNZ, One News, 2004, 'Civil Union Bill raises tensions', 23 August, http://tvnz.co.nz/view/news_national_story_skin/443454%3Fformat=html (accessed 28 April 2006).

Twomey, A, 1994, 'Laws Against Incitement to Racial Hatred in the United Kingdom', 1 *Aust J Human Rights* 235–48.

United Future, 2005, *United Future Policy Statement – Confidence and Supply Agreement*, http://unitedfuture.org.nz/successes/cs.php (accessed 24 March 2006).

United Kingdom Government, 1975, *Racial Discrimination*, Cmnd 6234, London: HSMO.

United Kingdom Government, 1997, *Rights Brought Home: The Human Rights Bill*, Cm 3782, London: TSO.

United Kingdom Government, 2002, *Justice For All*, Cm 5563, London: TSO.

United Kingdom Government, Department for Constitutional Affairs, 2003, Declarations of Incompatibility made under s4 of Human Rights Act 1998, www.humanrights.gov.uk/decihm.htm (accessed 11 May 2006).

United Kingdom Government, Women and Equality Unit, 2003a, *Civil Partnership: A Framework for the Legal Recognition of Same-Sex Couples*, London: Department of Trade and Industry.

United Kingdom Government, Women and Equality Unit, 2003b, *Responses to Civil Partnership: A Framework for the Legal Recognition of Same-Sex Couples*, London: Department of Trade and Industry.

United Kingdom Parliament, House of Commons Select Committee on Home Affairs, 2000, *The Double Jeopardy Rule*, Third Report of Session 1999–2000, HC 190, 8 June.

United Kingdom Parliament, House of Commons Select Committee on Home Affairs Committee, 2003, *Criminal Justice Bill*, Second Report of Session 2002–03, HC 83, 4 December.

United Kingdom Parliament, Joint Committee on Human Rights, 2003a, *Criminal Justice Bill*, Second Report of Session 2002–03, HC374/HL40, 31 January.

United Kingdom Parliament, Joint Committee on Human Rights, 2003b, *Criminal Justice Bill: Further Report*, Eleventh Report of Session 2002–03, HC666/HL96, 13 June.

United Kingdom Parliament, Joint Committee on Human Rights, 2004, *Civil Partnership Bill*, Fifteenth Report of Session 2003–04, HL136/HC 885, 7 July.

United Kingdom Parliament, Joint Committee on Human Rights, 2005, *Review of International Human Rights Instruments*, Seventeenth Report of Session 2004–05, HC264/HL99, 31 March.

United Kingdom, Royal Commission on Criminal Justice, 1993, *Report* Cm 2263, London: HMSO.

United Nations, Committee on the Elimination of Racial Discrimination, 1985, *General Recommendation No. 07: Legislation to eradicate racial discrimination (Art. 4)*, 23 August.

United Nations, Committee on the Elimination of Racial Discrimination, 1993, *General Recommendation No. 15: Organized violence based on ethnic origin (Art. 4)*, 23 March.

United Nations, Committee on the Elimination of Racial Discrimination, 1994, *Concluding observations of the Committee on the Elimination of All Forms of Racial Discrimination: Australia* (19 September) A/49/18.

United Nations, Human Rights Committee, 1984, *CCPR General Comment No. 13: Equality before the courts and the right to a fair and public hearing by an independent court established by law (Art. 14)*: 13 April.

University of NSW Council for Civil Liberties, 2003, *Submission to the NSW Attorney-General's Community Consultation of the Draft Criminal Appeal Amendment (Double Jeopardy) Bill*, October, www.nswccl.org.au/publications/submissions.php (accessed 26 May 2006).

Varga, C, 1992, *Comparative Legal Cultures*, Aldershot: Dartmouth.

Vasta, A, 2006, 'Double Jeopardy: To Amend or Not to Amend? 72 *Precedent* 18–21.

Victoria, Human Rights Consultation Committee, 2005, *Rights, Responsibilities and Respect: The Report of the Human Rights Consultation Committee*, Melbourne: Department of Justice.

Vincent, F, 2003, 'Human Rights and the Criminal Law', 14th Sir Leo Cussen Memorial Lecture, 16 October, www.leocussen.vic.edu.au (accessed 31 January 2006).

Waaldijk, K, 2001, 'Small Change: How the Road to Same-Sex Marriage Got Paved in the Netherlands', in R Wintemute and M Andenaes (eds), *Legal Recognition of Same-Sex Partnerships: A Study of National, European and International Law*, Oxford: Hart.

Waikato Times, 2004, 'Editorial: Slowing the push for "gay marriage"', *Waikato Times*, 13 May.

Wainright, M, 2006, 'Retrial ordered after Griffin walks free', *Guardian Unlimited*, 3 February, www.guardian.co.uk/farright/story/0,,1701242,00.html (accessd 2 May 2006).

Walker, J, 2003, 'Body of Evidence', *The Weekend Australian*, 15–16 February.

Walsh, K and Wood, M, 2004, 'Same-sex marriage ban "not decent and not fair"', *The Sun-Herald*, 15 August.

Watson, A, 1982, 'Legal Change: Sources of Law and Legal Culture', 131 *University of Pennsylvania Law Review* 1121–57.

Wearring, M, 2004, 'Aussie face of gay marriage', *Sydney Star Observer*, Issue 716, 3 June, www.ssonet.com.au/archives/display.asp?articleID=4000 (accessed 28 April 2006).

Weatherburn, D, 2004, *Law and Order in Australia: Rhetoric and Reality*, Sydney: Federation Press.

Webber, J, 2006, 'A Modest (but Robust) Defence of Statutory Bills of Rights', in T Campbell, J Goldsworthy and A Stone (eds), *Human Rights Without a Bill of Rights: Institutional Performance and Reform in Australia*, Aldershot: Ashgate.

Weinberg, R, 2004, 'Try, Try Again; If at first they don't succeed, criminal prosecutions in England now get a second chance', *Legal Times*, 16 February.

Weinrib, L, 1991, 'Hate Promotion in a Free and Democratic Society: *R v Keegstra*', 36 *McGill LJ* 1416–49.

West-Newman, C, 2001, 'Reading Hate Speech From the Bottom in Aotearoa: Subjectivity, Empathy, Cultural Difference', 9 *Waikato Law Review* 231–64.

Whitty, N, Murphy, T and Livingstone, S, 2001 *Civil Liberties Law: The Human Rights Act Era*, Oxford: Oxford University Press.

Whiu, L, 2004, 'Same-sex Marriage: Equality or Compulsory Heterosexuality', in L Alice and L Star (eds), *Queer in Aotearoa New Zealand*, Palmerston North: Dunmore Press.

Wilets, J, 2003, 'The Inexorable Momentum Toward National and International Recognition of Same-Sex Relationships: An International, Comparative, Historical and Cross-Cultural Perspective', in L Wardle *et al* (eds), *Marriage and Same-Sex Unions: A Debate*, Westport; Praeger.

Willheim, E, 2003, 'Australia's Racial Vilification Laws Found Wanting? The "Nigger Brown" Saga: HREOC, the Federal Court, the High Court and the Committee on the Elimination of Racial Discrimination', 4 *Asia Pacific Journal on Human Rights and the Law* 86–129.

Williams, D, 2003, 'Against Constitutional Cringe: The Protection of Human Rights in Australia', 9 *Australian Journal of Human Rights* 1–9.

Williams, G, 2000, A Bill of Rights for Australia, Sydney: UNSW Press.

Williams, G, 2004, *The Case For an Australian Bill of Rights: Freedom in the War on Terror*, Sydney: UNSW Press.

Williams, G, 2005, 'Advice re proposed Same-Sex Marriage Act', 22 March, http://tglrg.org/more/82_0_1_0_M3/ (accessed 28 April 2006).

Wintemute, R, 2004a, 'Sexual Orientation and the Charter: The Achievement of Formal Legal Equality (1985–2005) and Its Limits', 49 *McGill LJ* 1143–80.

Wintemute, R, 2004b, 'International Trends in Legal Recognition of Same-Sex Couples', paper presented at the *European Convention on Human Rights Act 2003 Review and Human Rights in Committed Relationships Conference*, Irish Human Rights Commission and Law Society of Ireland, Dublin, 16 October.

Wintemute, R, 2005, 'Sexual Orientation and Gender Identity', in C Harvey (ed), *Human Rights in the Community: Rights as Agents for Change*, Oxford: Hart.

Woodiwiss, A, 2003, *Making Human Rights Work Globally*, London: Glasshouse Press.

Young, A, 2002, 'Judicial Sovereignty and the Human Rights Act 1998', 61 *Cambridge Law Journal* 53–65.

Index

Abu Hamza al-Masri 178
acquittal, immunity from re-prosecution after *see* double jeopardy
Ahenakew, David 199–200
Alston, Dean 238
Andrews, Donald 195
appeals
  exhaustion of 41
  rights to 76
Archer, Derek 218
Auld Report (UK) 49
Australia 7–8, 10, 11, 12, 15, 19, 259–62
  bill of rights campaigns 3, 13, 33–4
  common traditions and contemporary differences 32–5
  double jeopardy 37, 38, 39, 41–2, 78–80, 93, 96–7, 260
    from *Carroll* to the status quo 80–2
    merits of double jeopardy under scrutiny 43, 44, 45, 46–7
    profile and impact of human rights discourse 82–92
  freedom of expression/hate speech restriction 160, 167, 247, 249, 260–1
    'Alas Poor Yagan' case 238–43
    history and current form of hate speech laws 225–31
    interpreting scope of hate speech laws 236–8
    key features of Australian balance 245–6
    legal form of free speech and non-discrimination/equality rights 231–4
    operation of hate speech laws 234–6
    United Nations and 243–4

  same-sex relationships 99–100, 104, 110, 142–3, 155, 261–2
    impotence of human rights discourse 146–54
    legal environment and lead-up to Marriage Amendment Act 2004 143–6
autrefois convict/autrefois acquit pleas 39, 48, 60

Baldock, Larry 142
Baldwin, Bob 150
Bar Council (UK) 56
Barker, Rick 63, 72
Belgium, same-sex relationships 103
Benson-Pope, David 102–3, 137, 139
bills of rights 2–3, 7, 13, 15
  bill of rights campaigns in Australia 3, 13, 33–4
Bissett, Bruce 220, 221
Boswell, Bob 152
Bradley, Trevor 46
Brazil, same-sex relationships 103
British Irish Rights Watch 57
British National Party (BNP) 177–8, 178–9, 180
British Union of Fascists (BUF) 177
Brittan of Spennithorne, Lord 38–9
Bush, George W. 148

Campaign for Civil Union (NZ) 138
Canada 9, 10, 11, 13, 19, 252–5
  common traditions and contemporary differences 21–4
  double jeopardy 38, 39, 41, 42, 48, 63, 74–8, 93, 253
    merits of double jeopardy under scrutiny 47

freedom of expression/hate speech
  restriction 160, 167, 247, 249, 253
history and current form of hate
  speech laws 187–92
Kane v Alberta Report case 203–7
key features of Canadian balance
  207–8
legal form of free speech and non-
  discrimination/equality rights
  after Charter of Rights and
  Freedoms 192–3
operation of hate speech laws
  194–201
provincial hate speech laws 201–7
same-sex relationships 17, 99, 103, 104,
  105, 150, 151, 154, 155–6, 157,
  253
Bill C-38 and the Charter imperative
  108–19
legal environment and lead-up to
  Civil Marriage Act 2005 105–8
Carmody, Tim 78, 79
Carr, Bob 44, 91
Carroll, Raymond 46–7
Carter, Chris 140–1
Cherry, John 148
Chrétien, Jean 107
Christie, Nigel 134
Clark, Helen 72
cloning 44
Cohen, Maxwell 187
Cohen Committee (Canada) 187–8
common law protection of human rights
  3, 7, 10–11, 16, 17, 19–21, 33, 35,
  38, 39, 40, 42, 43, 47–8, 50, 51, 52
common traditions and contemporary
  differences 19–21
  Australia 32–5
  Canada 21–4
  New Zealand 24–8
  United Kingdom 28–32
comparative analysis 8–10
constitutional protection of human
  rights 2–3, 7–13, 15, 17, 19–20,
  21–4
Cotler, Irwin 112–13
Council for Civil Liberties (Australia) 91
Council for Civil Liberties (NSW) 12, 88
  double jeopardy and 85, 87
Criminal Bar Association (UK) 56, 57
Croome, Rodney 153
Crown Prosecution Service (UK),
  freedom of expression/hate
  speech restriction and 163, 177,
  178, 179, 186

de Bres, Joris 217
De Saxe, Mannie 146–7
Debus, Bob 82
Destiny Church (NZ) 140
DNA technology 44, 74
Donaldson, Lord 20
double jeopardy 5, 7, 37–43, 92–7, 161,
  252
  age of rule on 38–9, 43, 50
  Australia 37, 38, 39, 41–2, 43, 44, 45,
    46–7, 78–80, 93, 96–7, 260
    from *Carroll* to the status quo 80–2
    profile and impact of human rights
      discourse 82–92
  Canada 38, 39, 41, 42, 47, 48, 63, 74–8,
    93, 253
  as human right 37–8, 41–2
  human rights discourse and
    Australia 82–92
    Canada 75–6, 77–8
    New Zealand 62, 63, 65–72, 73
    United Kingdom 49, 50–60
  'law and order' campaigns and 45–7,
    60–1, 78–9, 80, 90
  merits of double jeopardy protection
    under scrutiny 43–7
  new evidence and 38, 44, 49, 52, 58, 60,
    61, 62–3, 72, 78, 81, 90–1
  New Zealand 38, 39, 41, 42, 43, 45–6,
    48, 60–73, 86, 95–6, 258
  perjury and 41, 46–7, 48, 76, 77, 79
  tainted acquittal and 38, 60, 61, 63–4,
    68, 74, 77, 81, 90
  United Kingdom 38–9, 41, 42, 43, 44,
    45, 46, 47–8, 64, 67–8, 70–1, 86,
    93, 94–5, 255–6
  shape and impact of human rights
    discourse 50–60
  from the Stephen Lawrence Inquiry
    to the Criminal Justice Act 2003
    48–50
Dunlop, Billy 46, 93
Dutton, Peter 78, 80, 90, 91

East Timor 19
Egale (Canada) 116
Elms, Mark 200
equality before the law 7, 101, 102

European Union, same-sex relationships and 120, 125, 127
evidence, double jeopardy and new evidence 38, 44, 49, 52, 58, 60, 61, 62–3, 72, 78, 81, 90–1
expectations 6

Favreau, Guy 187
freedom of expression/hate speech restriction 5, 7, 159–64, 246–9, 252
  Australia 160, 167, 247, 249, 260–1
    'Alas Poor Yagan' case 238–43
    history and current form of hate speech laws 225–31
    interpreting scope of hate speech laws 236–8
    key features of Australian balance 245–6
    legal form of free speech and non-discrimination/equality rights 231–4
    operation of hate speech laws 234–6
    United Nations and 243–4
  Canada 160, 167, 247, 249, 253
    history and current form of hate speech laws 187–92
    Kane v Alberta Report case 203–7
    key features of Canadian balance 207–8
    legal form of free speech and non-discrimination/equality rights after Charter of Rights and Freedoms 192–3
    operation of hate speech laws 194–201
    provincial hate speech laws 201–7
  international law obligations 164–7
  New Zealand 160, 167, 248–9, 259
    history and current form of hate speech laws 208–13
    key features of New Zealand balance 223–5
    legal form of free speech and non-discrimination/equality rights after BORA 1990 213–15
    operation of hate speech laws 216–23
  United Kingdom 160, 167, 248, 256–7
    history and current form of hate speech laws 167–73
    key features of UK balance 186–7
    legal form of free speech and non-discrimination/equality rights after HRA 1998 173–6
    operation of hate speech laws 176–85
Friedland, Martin 37, 74

gender discrimination 101
Gill, Peter 74, 77
globalisation 16
Goff, Phil 62
Goldsmith, Lord 39, 47, 177
Government Administration Committee (NZ), freedom of expression/hate speech restriction and 162, 212, 213, 216–17
Greig, Brian 144–5, 151, 152
Griffin, Nick 178
Guess, Gillian 74

Hailsham, Lord 170
Hampton, Nigel 72
Harding, Mark 199
Harper, Stephen 75, 112, 118, 119
hate speech restriction *see* freedom of expression/hate speech restriction
Herman, D. 9, 117
Heyns, C. 4, 14
Hiebert, J. 1, 22, 23, 25–6, 31, 32, 65, 116
Hirsh, Walter 209–10
Hogg, Julie 46, 93
Home Affairs Committee (UK), double jeopardy and 49, 53, 57
homosexual relationships *see* same-sex relationships
Howard, John 89, 146, 148, 226
Human Rights Commission (Australia), freedom of expression/hate speech restriction and 226–7, 234
Human Rights Commission (Canada), freedom of expression/hate speech restriction and 195, 200–1
Human Rights Commission (NZ)
  double jeopardy and 67, 69–70, 71, 72
  freedom of expression/hate speech restriction and 160, 163, 216–18, 220–3, 224–5
  same-sex relationships and 136
Human Rights Foundation (NZ), same-sex relationships and 140
human rights issues 1–5

approaching correlation between form and quality 11–13
double jeopardy and human rights discourse
  Australia 82–92
  Canada 75–6, 77–8
  New Zealand 62, 63, 65–72, 73
  United Kingdom 49, 50–60
human rights discourse 1–2, 5–7, 9–10, 14, 36, 49–50, 63, 73, 82
present study 5
rationale for case study selection 6–8
rationale for comparative analysis 8–10
rationale for country selection 10–11
same-sex relationships and human rights discourse 104–5
  Australia 146–54
  Canada 108–19
  New Zealand 136–42
  United Kingdom 121–3, 125, 127–8
Huscroft, G. 22, 25, 26, 28, 66, 214, 215, 218–19

Ignatieff, Michael 252–3
international human rights law 4, 11, 14, 19, 32, 35, 39, 164–7
International Lesbian and Gay Law Association 103
interpretation issues 4

Joint Committee on Human Rights (UK)
  double jeopardy and 53, 54–6, 64, 67–8
  same-sex relationships and 125–6
Justice (UK) 57

Keating, Paul 89
Keegstra, Jim 194–5
Kennedy, Baroness 59
Kennedy, Deirdre 46, 47
Kennedy, Faye 78, 80, 90
Kilroy-Silk, Robert 178
Kirby, Michael 12, 88, 89
Kitzinger, Celia 127–8

'law and order' campaigns, double jeopardy and 45–7, 60–1, 78–9, 80, 90
Law and Order Committee (NZ), double jeopardy and 66–8, 72

Law Commission (NZ), double jeopardy and 60–1, 68, 71
Law Commission (UK), double jeopardy and 49, 53, 61, 84
Law Reform Commission (Canada), double jeopardy and 74
law reforms, human rights and 2
Law Society (NZ), double jeopardy and 67, 70, 72
Law Society (UK), Criminal Law Committee 57
Lawrence, Carmen 148
Lawrence, Stephen 46, 48, 69
Lawyers for Human Rights (Australia) 85
Layton, Jack 99, 100
Legal Action Group (UK) 56
legal culture 1, 2, 3, 4, 7, 15–18, 22, 23, 28, 42
legal forms for human rights protection 4, 5, 7, 13–15, 17–18, 262–3
  correlation between form and quality 11–13
  measuring effect of legal form 18–19
  proactivity and 36
Legislation Review Committee (NSW), double jeopardy and 88–9
Leigh, Edward 126
Lesbian and Gay Solidarity (Australia) 146–7
Lester, Lord 32, 122, 172
Liberty (UK) 128
  double jeopardy and 56, 57, 58
localisation 16
Lovett, Kendall 146–7

Macpherson Report (UK) 46, 48–9, 69
Marshall, Gavin 148
Martin, Paul 107, 109, 111, 113–14
Mathews, Jane 81, 82–3
Maxim Institute (NZ) 137–8
Ming, Ann 46
Mitchell, Chris 80
Model Criminal Code Officers Committee (MCCOC; Australia), double jeopardy and 64, 81, 83, 84, 87, 88, 90
Monaghan, Karon 128
Moore, Kevin 46, 60–1

National Association of Community Legal Centres (Australia), same-sex relationships and 149

ne bis in idem principle 39, 41, 48, 94, 256
Neill of Bladen, Lord 39, 47
Netherlands, same-sex relationships 103
Nettle, Kerry 147
New Zealand 10, 11, 257–9
    common traditions and contemporary differences 24–8
    double jeopardy 38, 39, 41, 42, 48, 60–73, 86, 95–6, 258
        merits of double jeopardy under scrutiny 43, 45–6
    freedom of expression/hate speech restriction 160, 167, 248–9, 259
        history and current form of hate speech laws 208–13
        key features of New Zealand balance 223–5
        legal form of free speech and non-discrimination/equality rights after BORA 1990 213–15
        operation of hate speech laws 216–23
    same-sex relationships 99, 100, 102–3, 103, 104, 110, 123, 129, 154, 155, 156–7, 258
        following through on non-discrimination commitment 136–42
        legal environment and lead-up to Civil Union Bill 2004 129–36
Nicholls, Lord 29–30
non-discrimination principle 7, 101
Norwood, Mark 178, 180

Odysseus Trust (UK) 122, 128
Organ, Michael 147
Outrage! (UK) 127

Pannick, David 52
perjury, double jeopardy and 41, 46–7, 48, 76, 77, 79
Peters, Winston 220
Phillips, Lord 184, 185
Potter, Mark 128
PrideAlliance (NZ) 141
proactivity, legal form and 36
propositional claiming 1
Public Interest Advocacy Centre (Australia), same-sex relationships and 149

Queensland Legal Aid Commission, double jeopardy and 87, 91

Race Relations Office (NZ), freedom of expression/hate speech restriction and 209–10
racial discrimination 101
Rae, Bob 75
Robinson, Svend 103
Ruddock, Philip 150, 151

Safadi, Michael 199
same-sex relationships 5, 99–102, 154–7, 252
    Australia 142–3, 155, 261–2
        impotence of human rights discourse 146–54
        legal environment and lead-up to Marriage Amendment Act 2004 143–6
    Canada 17, 99, 103, 104, 105, 150, 151, 154, 155–6, 157, 253
        Bill C-38 and the Charter imperative 108–19
        legal environment and lead-up to Civil Marriage Act 2005 105–8
    demands for recognition 102–4
    legal responses and impact of human rights discourse 104–5
    New Zealand 99, 100, 102–3, 103, 104, 110, 123, 154, 155, 156–7, 258
        following through on non-discrimination commitment 136–42
        legal environment and lead-up to Civil Union Bill 2004 129–36
    United Kingdom 99, 100, 104, 110, 119–20, 154, 155, 156–7, 256
        Civil Union Bill as anticipating emerging EU imperative 124–8
        legal environment and lead-up to Civil Partnership Act 2004 120–3
Scarman, Lord 169
Smith, Jacqui 126
Smith, Robert 195
Society of Labour Lawyers (UK) 57
South Africa 11
Spain, same-sex relationships 103
Steyn, Lord 176
Stonewall (UK) 122, 127

tainted acquittal, double jeopardy and 38, 60, 61, 63–4, 68, 74, 77, 81, 90
Tanczos, Nandor 62, 138
Taylor, John Ross 195
Thomas, Esther 183–5
Tomlins, Jacqueline 147, 152

United Kingdom 10, 11, 255–7
  common traditions and contemporary differences 28–32
  double jeopardy 38–9, 41, 42, 47–8, 64, 67–8, 70–1, 86, 93, 94–5, 255–6
  merits of double jeopardy under scrutiny 43, 44, 45, 46
  shape and impact of human rights discourse 50–60
  from the Stephen Lawrence Inquiry to the Criminal Justice Act 2003 48–50
  freedom of expression/hate speech restriction 160, 167, 248, 256–7
  history and current form of hate speech laws 167–73
  key features of UK balance 186–7
  legal form of free speech and non-discrimination/equality rights after HRA 1998 173–6
  operation of hate speech laws 176–85
  same-sex relationships 99, 100, 104, 110, 119–20, 154, 155, 156–7, 256
  Civil Union Bill as anticipating emerging EU imperative 124–8
  legal environment and lead-up to Civil Partnership Act 2004 120–3
United Nations 4, 89, 150
  Australian freedom of expression/hate speech restriction and 243–4
  Commission on Human Rights, same-sex relationships and 103–4
  Committee Against Torture 90
  Committee on the Elimination of Racial Discrimination 90, 166
  Human Rights Committee 20
    double jeopardy and 40–1, 55, 68, 87, 90
    same-sex relationships and 133–4, 143
  Human Rights Council 104
United States of America, same-sex relationships 103, 156
universal human rights 1, 4, 17

victim's rights movement 44, 74, 85
vox pop law reform 45

Widdecombe, Ann 126
Wilkinson, Sue 127–8
Williams, Daryl 33
Wilson, Margaret 63–4
Worth, Richard 63